FROM
TAMAKI-MAKAU-RAU
TO AUCKLAND

FROM
TAMAKI-MAKAU-RAU
TO AUCKLAND

R. C. J. STONE

AUCKLAND UNIVERSITY PRESS

Dedicated to Lindo, John M.S. and John R.L.

First published 2001

Auckland University Press
University of Auckland
Private Bag 92019
Auckland
New Zealand
http://www.auckland.ac.nz/aup

ISBN 1 86940 259 6

Publication is assisted by the Ministry for Culture and Heritage

National Library of New Zealand Cataloguing-in-Publication Data
Stone, R. C. J.
From Tāmaki-makau-rau to Auckland / R.C.J. Stone.
Includes bibliographical references and index.
ISBN 1-86940-259-6
1. Maori (New Zealand people)—New Zealand—Auckland—History.
2. Auckland (N.Z.)—History. I. Title.
993.2401—dc 21

Cover design by Christine Hansen
Cover image: John Barr Clark Hoyte, *View of Auckland Harbour from Mt Hobson,
Remuera*, watercolour, 1927. Auckland Art Gallery Toi o Tamaki.

Printed by Astra Print Ltd, Wellington

CONTENTS

LIST OF ABBREVIATIONS

AJHR *Appendices to the Journal of the House of Representatives*

AML Auckland Institute and War Memorial Museum

APL Auckland Public (now City) Libraries

ATL Alexander Turnbull Library

BPP Cols *Parliamentary Papers of Great Britain, Colonies*

CMS Church Missionary Society

DNB *Dictionary of National Biography*

DNZB *Dictionary of New Zealand Biography*

DSC *Daily Southern Cross*

FOJ Fenton's Orakei Judgment

IUP Irish University Press

J. of Ak. His. Soc. *Journal of the Auckland Historical Society*

JPS *Journal of the Polynesian Society*

NLC Native (Maori) Land Court

NZA&BAIG *New Zealand Advertiser and Bay of Islands Gazette*

NZH *New Zealand Herald*

NZJH *New Zealand Journal of History*

OHNZ *Oxford History of New Zealand*

OLC Old Land Claims

OMB Orakei Minutebook

Rec. of Ak. Inst. & Mus. *Records of the Auckland Institute and Museum*

Wai *Waitangi Claim*

ACKNOWLEDGEMENTS

Many people have contributed to this book. Their help has sometimes taken a material form. Certainly the book would not have been written but for the encouragement and financial assistance of the Sir John Logan Campbell Trust. Grants from the Trust enabled me to go to Wellington to study archival records there, to follow on the ground the migrations of the Tamaki tribes during their years of wandering at the time of the Musket Wars, and to tread the battlefields such as Moremonui, Matakitaki, Te Ika-a-ranganui and Taumatawiwi, where the future of the Tamaki tribes was decided. The book owes much to the generosity of the Trust, whose members never doubted that a work dealing with pre-1840 Maori (so admired by Logan Campbell) must go ahead. To the Trust I offer my sincere thanks. I also wish to record my considerable indebtedness to the Historical Branch of the Department of Internal Affairs whose Trustees, at a crucial stage of my work in 1999, awarded a generous grant-in-aid for my research.

I was fortunate once again to have the Auckland University Press as my publishers. The director, Elizabeth Caffin, acted as my copy editor and steered this book through to final publication. Her staff, Annie Irving, Christine O'Brien, Katrina Duncan, in their various ways were particularly helpful. Another University colleague, Louise Cotterall of the Geology Department, converted, at short notice, my crude sketches into outstanding maps.

Once again I am indebted to libraries and repositories, mainly in Auckland, and to the staffs of those institutions who alerted me to resources of which I was initially unaware and when I began to use those resources, patiently answered my enquiries.

I acknowledge the help of the Kinder librarian of St John's Theological College, Judith Bright, and her deputy Helen Greenwood. I spent many fruitful hours in that library, so unexpectedly rich in its resources of early nineteenth-century publications about New Zealand. I also wish to thank the staff of the Auckland War Memorial Museum Library. Readers of this book will soon become aware of how constant has been my use of the papers of George S. Graham, that avid collector of the folklore of the Tamaki tribes, which are housed there. The usefulness of these papers was greatly enhanced by the meticulously annotated inventory of the collection both there and in the Auckland City Library, which was completed by Jenifer Curnow in 1994. Jenifer also answered a number of questions on Maori life and language when I periodically turned to her. Professor Roger Neich, ethnologist of the museum, latterly gave diligent guidance on the museum's artefacts, which I here most gratefully acknowledge.

I am greatly indebted to the staff of the New Zealand and Pacific section of the Auckland University Library. Stephen Innes and his team were ever ready to place at my disposal those items of the so-called Glass Case to which I constantly turned. I particularly wish to thank John Laurie, who frequently brought to my attention Native Land Court cases relevant to Tamaki, and who guided me to their associated minute books, generally preserved on microfilm.

I was fortunate, too, to be able to avail myself also of the unusual riches of the Auckland City Library: its early New Zealand publications and manuscripts, its maps and extensive pictorial material. I should like to pay tribute to the helpfulness of the whole staff on the heritage floor of that library, particularly thanking those with whom I dealt most closely: Donald Kerr, Georgia Prince, Elspeth Orwin and David Verran.

Rather more than the History Department of the University of Auckland may have realised, it too contributed to this publication. Successive departmental heads, Professors Nicholas Tarling, Raewyn Dalziel, and Barry Reay, indulgently provided me with an emeritus professor's room and access to the department's facilities, in the process enabling me to encounter the minds of youthful, up-to-date historians. For these privileges I thank the History Department.

During the writing of this book, I have learned that a warming characteristic of those who have worked in the field of Auckland prehistory is their generosity. In the first year of my research I turned to three knowledgeable people for guidance: David Simmons, Susan Bulmer, and Agnes Sullivan. David patiently shared with me his decades of experience as an ethnologist; all questions, however banal some may have appeared to him, resulted in a courteous, considered answer. And then there was the good advice and instruction of anthropologist Sue Bulmer, who has an enviable reputation (based on field studies) for knowledge of the use to which Maori put the volcanic fields of the region, and of their associated patterns of farming and settlement. It was typical of her helpfulness that, unheralded, she should have turned up at my home one afternoon bearing a boxful of her publications and papers which she gave for my permanent use. Agnes Sullivan of Christchurch is a byword among academics as a researcher into the prehistory of Tamaki. On my first three draft chapters, she gave tactful advice and correction. In the later stages of my research I plied with questions my schoolfellow of years gone by, the late Professor Bruce Biggs, benefiting thereby from his deep understanding of Maori culture and language. Dr Barry Rigby of the Waitangi Tribunal also helped as my investigations approached 1840. I particularly valued his advice and the papers and maps which he proffered dealing with Fairburn's Old Land Claim and the Crown Purchase of Mahurangi. Of course, errors and shortcomings in what I have written cannot in any way be attributed to these people whom I have named above. Mine is the sole responsibility.

Three people have made unusual contributions to this book. The first is Lindo Ferguson. Over many years, while holding high office in the University of Auckland and the City Council and, more recently, while acting as the chairman of the Campbell Trust, Lindo has held an enduring brief for the cause of Auckland history. *From Tamaki-makau-rau to Auckland* is the fruit of his encouragement. Secondly, I wish to express a special word of thanks to John Stacpoole. John has been researching, writing and lecturing on Auckland's history for over forty years, a formidable background indeed. He carefully read, and advised on, the manuscript of this book. His sage advice on content and style I valued highly. John Laurie's contribution to this book (which I mentioned earlier) is incalculable. Over the last three years, I discussed most aspects of my research with him. He, imperceptibly, assumed the role of friendly remembrancer, calling to my mind (as a skilled librarian of anthropological and Maori studies) sources I might otherwise have overlooked, or formulations where he considered I might possibly have given a mistaken emphasis. To these three men I have dedicated this book.

Once again I thank my wife Mary for her cheerful support and assistance at every stage of my work.

FOREWORD

Cesare Beccaria, the late eighteenth-century Italian reformer, famously observed that the happiest nations are those that have no history. Yet this is a questionable dictum. Certainly it does not hold true for smaller communities. A community without knowledge of its past, unable to answer the question that, it is said, poets are forever asking of themselves – 'who am I?' – is essentially disinherited. Cities, above all, are enriched by an awareness of self-identity.

Metropolitan Auckland, the largest and fastest growing of New Zealand cities, oddly enough, is the least well served by recorded histories. Why this neglect? Is it because of central Auckland's commercial character? Founded to be a capital city, Auckland has found its permanent role as a city of capital. Have its leading citizens, as a result, become so preoccupied with getting and spending that they have given little thought to encouraging interpretative accounts of their past? Perhaps it may also be that its inhabitants lack a sense of belonging and just do not care. It has been said – and though I know of no statistical proof of this, intuitively I feel it could be close to the mark – that as many as 40 per cent of those living in Auckland were born elsewhere. Auckland has long been a magnet drawing in and (that done) keeping both migrants from abroad and those New Zealanders moving from south to north or from country to town. Consequently, the emotional roots of many who live there seem embedded in other places.

In 1922, the city librarian John Barr wrote the first historical survey of the city, which he entitled *The City of Auckland New Zealand, 1840–1920*. Sadly, there have been no true successors to Barr's book of eighty years ago. Granted, there have been a few estimable single-topic histories, such as G. W. A. Bush's centennial history of the City Council, and Una Platts's *The Lively Capital*, both published in 1971. But almost all historical

publications on Auckland have tended to be piecemeal in character, with facts faithfully recorded but connections between
those facts not made. They have tended to neglect what the historian, E. J. Hobsbawm, has called the 'iron law of context'.

Four years ago I set out to remedy this deficiency, at least in
part. I believed that given Auckland's size and complexity, only
a multi-volume history such as has been written for comparable,
if much larger, cities like Glasgow and New York would serve in
the twenty-first century. Where I should make my contribution
seemed, at first, obvious enough to me – the early colonial
period. I had already written about various aspects of Auckland's
first fifty years in a doctoral thesis, four books and a number of
articles. And like Barr, I proposed to begin at 1840.

But I ended up by writing a quite different book. My change
of heart occurred when I started to put together the first chapter
in which I tried to explain why the tangata whenua or Maori
inhabitants of the isthmus which we now call Auckland, decided
in 1840 to call on the governor to come and live in their midst.
In seeking an answer to this question I ran into a paradox: the
relatively unpeopled condition of the Tamaki isthmus at that
time was quite at odds with obvious natural wealth of the area,
and the evidence on every hand of heavy Maori settlement in
years gone by. At this point the idea took root in my mind that
the first volume of Auckland's history must concern itself primarily with the period *before* the Europeans established themselves there. I became convinced that my original conception
was flawed. To regard the Maori occupation of the isthmus for
possibly as long as a millennium as being a mere preliminary to
British colonisation seemed academically indefensible and culturally crass. But whether I should be the one to attempt a pre-
1840 study was debatable. For that would mean departing from
a historical field in which I had worked for many years, in order
to work in a new and far different one where I would be a tyro.
But I took the leap. And this book is the result.

My draft manuscript when finished was turned over to an
accomplished Maori scholar who, after some generous comments,
observed that it was not a history that a Maori would have written.
Perhaps. But what I have written was never intended to be the last
word. One hopes that other historians, and Maori most of all, will
work over the sources and produce alternative versions. All trained

historians know that, try as they might to follow Leopold von Ranke's precept to reconstruct the past *wie es eigentlich gewesen* (just as it was), their interpretations will generally differ. Maori nowadays need no convincing of that. Tribal claimants appearing before the Waitangi Tribunal in recent years have learnt, after hearing the conflicting evidence of 'experts', that historical generalisations are never absolute, never permanent. The prolific nineteenth-century English historian, Bishop Stubbs, recognised that his historical judgments were 'justiciable in courts of interminable appeal'. Mine are too.

I should like to comment on sources that I have used. For the period up to about 1760, which marks the Ngati Whatua take-over of Tamaki, roughly the first two chapters, I carried out little fundamental research; what I have written, therefore, can lay little claim to originality. This section is largely a work of synthesis, a putting together of the findings and formulations of others, mainly archaeologists and prehistorians. The second and far greater part of the book, taking in the years 1760 to 1837, represents an attempt to capture the Maori version of that period, a recording in some sections of the hitherto largely unheard voices of the past. I have made intensive use of the Native Land Court minutebooks, especially noting the evidence of aged witnesses, Apihai Te Kawau, Te Keene, Haora Tipa and the like, as they recalled events they knew of at first hand, some dating back to the later decades of the eighteenth century. Particularly in the later part of this section, the work of synthesis continues, but with somewhat greater complexity. I have placed beside these Maori accounts the testimony contained in the journals of missionaries – Samuel Marsden, John Butler, Henry and William Williams, and W. T. Fairburn – and the memoirs of travellers and adventurers, such as Captain Cruise, Dumont d'Urville, William White and Joel Polack. Over the years 1837–41 the book takes on a more conventional aspect. The oral testimony of Maori and the memoirs of Europeans still remain a prominent element. But the close concern of the British government with New Zealand affairs has meant that published official records became much more abundant. The text reflects that.

Although this book has the imprint of a university press, it is aimed at a general readership. It is a traditional, even an old-fashioned history, in the sense that it is chronological rather than thematic in its progression. The aim has been to keep to a firm narrative line, with only limited digressions to take up historiographical debates, though these are not dodged.

Most of the episodes take place within a limited geographical region, roughly within a circle of about seventy kilometres radius, of which the Tamaki isthmus is the centre. But it would be mistaken to look on this book as an exercise in local history. 'The history of this isthmus', observed the Chief Judge of the Native Land Court in 1869, 'is almost an epitome of the history of New Zealand during many years, for this was the highway of the armies of the tribes in the old days; and whether going North or South, all war parties passed through or touched at Tamaki.' In times of peace no less than those of war Tamaki was the node of canoe transport, a frontier of convergence of the tribes. It is my hope that, even if this region does not provide an epitome of the history of all Aotearoa, the story of what happened there will make accessible for readers the mainsprings and values of Maori life and culture over a much wider area than the mere name 'Tamaki-makau-rau' would seem to imply.

MAIN CANOE PORTAGES AND WATERWAYS OF THE TAMAKI REGION

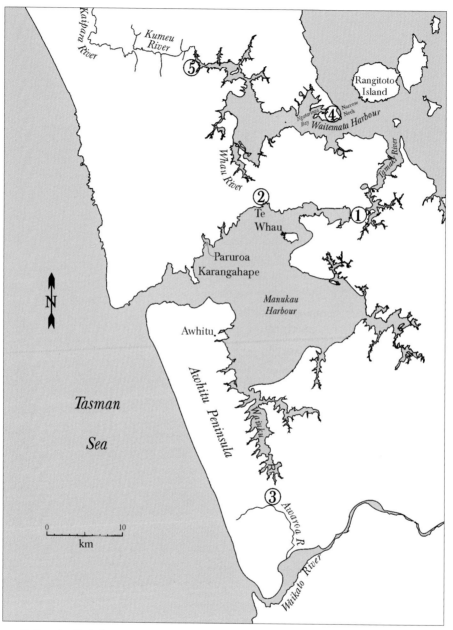

1   Te To-waka: Otahuhu
2   Te Whau: from the headwaters of the Whau to Green Bay on the Manukau
3   Te Pai-o-kaiwaka: from the headwaters of Waiuku estuary to Awaroa Stream
4   Takapuna: from Ngataringa Bay to Narrow Neck
5   Waitemata to Kaipara: from Kumeu River to Kaipara River

CHAPTER I

Tamaki-makau-rau and its Peoples

I

Modern Auckland is a conurbation, which extends almost un-
broken from Albany in the north to Papakura in the south. But
the heart of the region is the Tamaki isthmus. It was in Maori
times; it remains so today.

This small north–south-facing landbridge takes shape
where the Northland peninsula ends, as it shrinks and skews to
give the North Island of New Zealand the narrowest of wasp
waists. The isthmus is approached from the Pacific Ocean by
way of the Hauraki gulf. Maori called this gulf Tikapa moana
(the sea of Tikapa), or more poetically – as one Maori historian
observed – 'Nga Tai Whakarewa Kauri' ('the kauri-bearing
tides of Hauraki'), a name that recalls 'the numerous canoes
which surged up and down . . . the enclosed waters of the gulf'.[1]
The gulf, it has been claimed, provided 'surely the busiest
waterways of pre-European Aotearoa'.[2] All canoe-travellers
moving north or south, as a matter of prudence, hugged the
shelter of the gulf islands, while those wanting to cross the
mainland itself from east to west, used Hauraki waters to take
advantage of the time-saving portages of the isthmus.

Waitemata, the main harbour of the gulf, in geological terms
a drowned river valley, is superbly protected on its seaward
(northern) side by a peninsula which modern Aucklanders refer

to as 'the North Shore', and from there eastwards by a barrier of inner gulf islands.[3] Hence the name of 'Waitemata', which Maori gave to the harbour, generally taken to mean 'waters [as smooth as] obsidian'.

Tamaki is essentially a miniature plateau whose monotony is broken by a series of projecting volcanic cones created by about fifty, now extinct, eruptive outlets. The isthmus itself is small; about twenty kilometres by ten. But that latter figure is only notional; the width varies considerably because the Waitemata coastline is deeply embayed and has extensive tidal reaches; it was more so before 160 years of European reclamation. All parts of Tamaki, therefore, are in easy walking distance of the sea. The narrowest part of the isthmus is the portage at Otahuhu separating tidal inlets of each of the two enclosing harbours, which, at that point, are no more than one kilometre apart. Here was the famed Te To-waka (the dragging place for canoes), already in use, according to Maori tradition, when the Great Fleet arrived from Hawaiiki about the mid-fourteenth century. The *Tainui* canoe, it was said, was dragged across there, on skids made up of logs[4] greased by mud, before sailing on, first oceanwards and then to Kawhia.[5] In what was essentially a canoe age, this portage must be regarded as one of the major features of the Aotearoa coastline. For those wishing to move either way between the Tasman Sea and the Pacific Ocean at this greatly frequented part of the North Island, Te To-waka eliminated a 1000-kilometre journey around the North Cape. The shortness of this portage and its gentle gradient – an early British trader claimed to have dragged a whale across it in forty minutes, whether he used Maori men or draught animals he did not say[6] – made this dragging place the most convenient of the eight portages of the isthmus.

Walter Brodie, who claimed to have dragged a whale across the Otahuhu portage.
AUCKLAND MUSEUM
LIBRARY

Maori travellers, who crossed the isthmus from the Waitemata at Otahuhu, if bound for the heart of the North Island, could make use of yet another portage on the south bank of the Manukau harbour, which enabled them to avoid the treacherous sandbar at the harbour's mouth and the wild west-coast waters beyond. They would paddle their canoes as far as the Waiuku estuary or 'river', and paddle up it to the dragging place called Te Pae-o-kaiwaka, a portage of some four kilometres. This led over a ridge to the headwaters of the Awaroa Creek, a tributary of the

great Waikato river, which virtually opened up the interior of the
North Island. Such was the route taken by the war canoes of
Hongi Hika during the musket wars of the 1820s.

As far as their traditional lore stretches, Maori people prized
Tamaki, its harbours and the islands of the neighbouring gulf.
Abundant good gardening land was there. The sea and forests
were veritable food baskets. Both harbours were rich in seafood
(moana kai) with their good fishing grounds and well-stocked
beds of shellfish. The extensive but shallow Manukau harbour had
ample resources of fish including snapper, stingray, flounder, with
varied shellfish at the fluctuating tidal levels. It also had shark, the
fish which Maori so highly prized. In 1840, when the Scottish
pioneer settler, Logan Campbell, crossed the isthmus in order to
buy land from Te Taou chiefs, he found them at their Mangere
kainga busily curing their catch of shark, almost certainly gummy
shark (dogfish), whose sun-dried flesh and liver Maori considered
most appetising.[7] The Waitemata harbour and its nearby gulf
waters had equally plentiful seafood, and fish of even greater
variety. Bays on the mainland and on the islands of the gulf
acquired many seasonal fishing camps, use of which was regulated
by tangata whenua rights exercised, and sometimes shared, by
different hapu.[8] Freeman's Bay (Wai-kokota), for instance, was a
traditional launching point for shark-fishing expeditions – there
was particularly good shark fishing nearby, in the swift running
tides off Kauri Point (Te Matarae-a-mana), on the farther shore.
George S. Graham has said that the shark fisheries in that particular area were so famous that, 'the canoe fleets came from as far as
Hauraki' to use them.[9] Moreover, before the sweeping transform-
ation brought about by European reclamation, the southern shore
of the Waitemata, between Achilles Point and Cox's Creek, had a
series of bow-shaped, shelly beaches, the foreshores of which were
rich in shellfish such as the local cockle or pipi. And there were
some bays on this same coastline biting deeply inland to become
elongated tidal inlets, which contained mangroves some richly
encrusted with oysters.

In primeval times, Tamaki was covered by a mature, mixed,
subtropical forest. This provided aboriginal settlers with berries,
the ubiquitous fern-root and other tree-foods, together with birds
– though as early as about AD1400 birds and animals were much
depleted and so food from the sea began to provide the bulk of

protein in the local diet.[10] With closer settlement, the isthmus was largely cleared of its larger trees, apart from remnants of bush in steep gullies, such as those running northwards to the Waitemata from Remuera.[11] The moist equable climate soon led to regeneration of bush in the form of bracken fern, tupakihi (tutu) and manuka (tea-tree). Fires, intentional and unintentional, and the timber and fuel requirements of the numerous inhabitants, meant that mature bush, once felled, was rarely able to re-establish itself fully. Outside the garden plantations currently in use, the main bush cover of the isthmus remained relatively stunted therefore, rarely developing beyond a scrubby secondary growth. For forest foods, such as berries and birds, and for heavier timbers, Maori were generally forced to travel further afield, to the stands of bush which clothed the Waitakere ranges in the west, and the Hunua ranges in the south-east.

But this does not mean, as was once thought, that at some time in the prehistoric period, closer settlement and growing pressure on local resources led Tamaki inhabitants to graduate from being fishers/hunters/gatherers to a stage which combined those activities with gardening. Archaeological excavations carried out on gulf islands and on peripheral areas of the isthmus as yet undisturbed by European occupation reveal that Maori, almost a millennium ago, were already combining the cultivation of the kumara with fishing.[12] On the mainland, the incentive to garden was always present, and particularly so on the land surrounding the volcanic cones. Two-fifths or more of the Tamaki region had a rich, friable, volcanic soil – easily tilled by the wooden ko or spade – derived mainly from a cover of air-borne ash (tuff), but sometimes with an admixture of local clay with which it formed a fertile loam, also well suited to kumara growing.[13] Research over years by Susan Bulmer and other archaeologists, into the gardens of Tamaki and of parts of south Auckland beyond the Otahuhu portage, confirms that cultivation of the kumara, and, to a lesser extent, taro, yam and gourd – tropical plants brought in, in the canoes of immigrants – is likely to have been carried on concurrently with fishing and the gathering of shellfish, ever since Tamaki was first settled. This would have been in contrast to primeval Maori settlement in the South Island where an abundance of protein-rich prey such as moa and seals to hunt, made horticulture, at first, much less necessary.

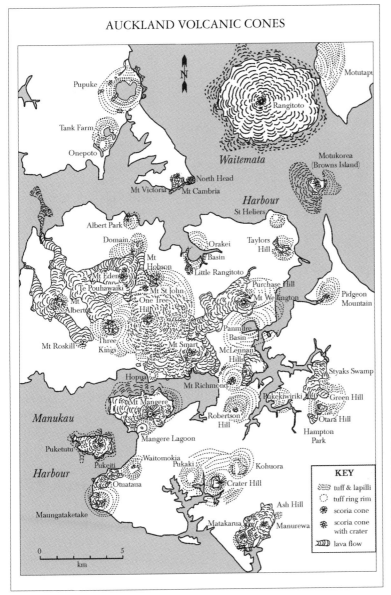

AUCKLAND VOLCANIC CONES

Pupuke

Motutapu

N

Rangitoto

Tank Farm

Onepoto

Waitemata

Motukorea
(Browns Island)

North Head

Mt Victoria — Mt Cambria

Harbour

St Heliers

Albert Park

Domain

Orakei
Basin

Taylors
Hill

Mt
Hobson

Little Rangitoto

Mt Eden

Te Pouhawaiki

Mt St John
One Tree
Hill

Purchase Hill

Mt Wellington

Pidgeon
Mountain

Mt
Albert

Mt Roskill

Three
Kings

Mt Smart

Panmure
Basin

McLennan
Hills

Styaks Swamp

Hopua

Mt Richmond

Pukekiwiriki

Green Hill

Mt Mangere

Robertson
Hill

Otara Hill

Hampton
Park

Manukau

Mangere Lagoon

Puketutu

Pukeiti

Waitomokia

Pukaki

Kohuora

Harbour

Otuataua

Crater Hill

KEY

Ash Hill

Maungataketake

Matakarua

Manurewa

tuff & lapilli	
tuff ring rim	
scoria cone	
scoria cone with crater	
lava flow	

0 ————— 5
km

GEOLOGY DEPARTMENT, UNIVERSITY OF AUCKLAND

As the population of Tamaki grew, gardening expanded in area and intensified in scale, the elaboration of techniques for storage of kumara crops in semi-underground, roofed pits progressively enlarging the yield available.[14] Productivity was high, enabling Tamaki, by about 1700, to support a population of some thousands, though estimates are, of course, conjectural.

5

Maori implements.
AUCKLAND WAR
MEMORIAL MUSEUM

But this was probably the most densely settled region in Aotea-roa.[15] Arable techniques of Maori gardeners were more sophisticated than the mere 'slash and burn' pattern of shifting cultivation practised in some parts of the world. Though there was little obvious use of organic fertilisers, soils had their texture improved by the admixture of shells and gravel, and were enriched by wood ash. On sloping land, there was careful terracing with rock walls, usually constructed of rubble scoria. In all areas, fresh plots were prepared in advance as a matter of course, well before the exhaustion of the old.[16]

Although Tamaki had local supplies of greywacke that could be shaped, ground and honed into adequate chisels and adzes, it lacked self-sufficiency in those rock minerals essential for the high-quality tool-making that developed as part of Aotearoa's stone-age culture. Canoe-borne trade, which emerged in the early period of settlement, particularly that conducted with the Hauraki region, helped to overcome this deficiency. Basalt rock for adzes was brought in from the Tahanga quarry north of Whitianga, while obsidian, a basaltic, glass-like rock useful for cutting, came from other parts of the Coromandel peninsula and from the islands of the Hauraki gulf.[17] Argillite and greenstone were imported from the South Island. The significance of such an exchange economy is not to be underestimated. Canoes carried not only scarce commodities to Tamaki, but innovations in material culture – carving, tattooing, and the making of tools, ornaments, weapons and so forth – as well.[18]

So richly endowed by nature was Tamaki that Maori gave to this highly desirable isthmus a name equating it with earthly passion. Maori came to think of it as a whenua-tamaki (a contested land), most aptly to be likened to a beautiful girl who had a hundred lovers. Hence its name Tamaki-makau-rau, 'Tamaki [the maiden contended for] by a hundred lovers'. Puna Reweti, a Ngati Whatua elder, put it on record four generations ago that he was told how in olden days visitors from other districts would often sing this song of greeting on arrival on Tamaki's shore:

> Tenakoe, e Tamaki!
> Tenakoe, tenakoe:
> Tamaki-makau-rau-e!

This salutation Reweti translated as

> Greetings, oh Tamaki!
> Greetings, greetings to thee,
> Oh! Tamaki of numerous lovers.[19]

Little wonder it had gained that name! George S. Graham, reflecting on the century or so before Captain James Cook's European 'rediscovery' of New Zealand, an era during which 'Tamaki was a land of plenty with a great population',[20] wrote that 'The resources of the district and the extent of the fortifications and cultivation were famous far and near.'[21] Its richness became proverbial. Hence the saying: 'Te pai me te whai-rawa o Tamaki' – 'the luxury and wealth of Tamaki'.

It is appropriate at this point to re-examine the long-held view of Maori Auckland, popularised by Graham and other early prehistorians, that the many terraced hills on and about the isthmus were fortresses, confirming that Tamaki was racked by centuries of 'almost continuous warfare'.[22] Chief Judge of the Native Land Court, Francis Dart Fenton, mindful of the wealth of the isthmus and of its location as the natural access route for canoe transport, also referred to it as 'the highway of armies' and 'war parties'.[23] And certainly Tamaki's inhabitants, soon conscious that they were living, so to speak, on a frontier of convergence, were obliged to develop the arts of defence and war. Further, by about AD1500, population pressures in the Northland region, as in many parts of Aotearoa, had led to growing competition for garden land and for other scarce resources.[24] Not surprisingly, therefore, Tamaki tribes, particularly Waiohua and Ngati Awa (while they were resident on the isthmus), turned to the volcanic cones as natural fortresses and lookout stations. And fortification did not begin and end with mountain pa. They were supplemented by sea-girt, cliff headlands on the harbours, such as Te Wharau (Achilles Point) and Te Rerenga-ora-iti (Bastion Point) on the Waitemata, or Puponga (by Cornwallis) on the Manukau. The islands of the gulf were similarly open to threat, so they too were fortified. At least fifty pa sites, most of them admittedly quite small, have been located on or near Waiheke island.[25]

But the supposition that Tamaki was a constantly embattled region is much open to question. It has relied heavily on the tendency of nineteenth-century Maori folklorists, and more particularly the Europeans who interviewed them, to extrapolate back into the prehistoric era two unique, more recent episodes. The first was the wholesale conquest of the isthmus by Ngati Whatua that took place about AD1750. The second was the chronic warfare and turbulent displacement of tribes eventuating during the 1820s and 1830s, when the advent of the musket gave vent to long dormant blood feuds in northern New Zealand. Nor need the many terraced hillsides be thought of as proof positive that warfare was endemic. Modern prehistorian Janet Davidson

has questioned 'the old view of all the terraces bristling with palisades and manned by huge populations of defending warriors'.[26]
Some terraced hills were fortified only on their upper slopes and
near the crater rims; some were probably not pa at all, but
undefended settlement sites.[27] Susan Bulmer's archaeological digs
at certain Tamaki volcanic sites provide evidence that upper
terraces could often be residential areas, while lower terraces were,
essentially, formed kumara gardens which were coterminous with
cultivations radiating out over a very wide area and tended by
people living in unfortified hamlets.[28] Nor were all pa in continuous or simultaneous use. Many were resorted to only seasonally or
in time of peril. Some were abandoned, others remained in a state
of desuetude for generations. Finally, as we shall later see, the most
cogent proof that there were extended periods of peace in Tamaki
is provided by the socio-economic order that reached its maturity
there about 1700.

Yet even if there were lengthy periods of peace, it is equally
true that a warlike spirit was always present in Tamaki no less
than in Aotearoa as a whole.[29] A warrior mentality came from
Polynesia as part of the cultural cargo of the first canoes. Maori
society was fiercely competitive, had an ethos which placed great
store on mana to which prowess in battle weightily contributed,
on the inviolability of tapu, and on a passionate belief in utu
which fed the hunger for unrelenting revenge to pay back old
scores arising out of alleged past insults, curses, slights, or
kohuru (treacherous murder).[30] These elements, singly or in
combination, were present in the post-AD1600 wars involving
Tamaki tribes, which have been authenticated by cross-tribal
traditions. Tensions building up with neighbouring tribes,
which escalated into blood feuds, and sometimes spiralled into
full-scale war, could arise out of causes, trivial to European eyes,
but perhaps, at bottom, related to competition for gardening
land or to structural changes in the regional balance of power.
But precisely how to make this connection is not easy for historians to work out.

Suffice to say the wealth of the isthmus periodically attracted
outside tribes, and created feuds, some of which could be resolved only by war. But absorption through peaceful assimilation
also took place. Tribal intermarriage was a pacifying principle,
could act as a cement of peace or conversely as a solvent of separ-

atist tribal identity. Proliferating hapu origins gave Tamaki-makau-rau a unique tribal character. It became a melting pot of resident people and incomers alike.

II

Determining precisely when Maori first settled on the Tamaki isthmus is today shrouded in uncertainty. It has not always been thought so. Until the 1950s, conventional wisdom had it that Maori arrived as part of the great migration to Aotearoa from Hawaiiki, in Polynesia. This was an orthodoxy, which was literally graven on bronze and embedded in stone, at the back panel of the obelisk erected on the summit of One Tree Hill in the 1940s. The panel reads:

> The first known Maori to visit these shores was 'Kupe'
> a Polynesian navigator in the year 925.

> The first settlement under Toi took place in 1150.

> The first organised emigration from Hawaiiki took
> place in 1350: when the ancestors of the present Maori
> race arrived at various points on these shores in the
> now historic canoes – Tainui, Arawa, Mata-atua, Aotea,
> Takitimu, Oronta [Horouta?], Tokomaru – and others.

This version of origins grew out of the inquiries made by enthusiastic, amateur, European ethnographers of the late nineteenth and early twentieth centuries, S. Percy Smith, John White, Elsdon Best, George S. Graham and others, who collected whakapapa (genealogical tables) and traditional lore provided by Maori informants. In an attempt to systematise often-conflicting tribal arrival traditions, they concluded that earlier, tentative migrations by Maori had culminated in a mass organised migration (heke) in the form of a Great Fleet of canoes.[31] This thesis is now rejected as myth, however.[32] It has been disproved by the close textual analysis carried out by prehistorians, such as David Simmons, of the oral records somewhat haphazardly collected by Smith and his followers, and by the excavations conducted by a new breed of archaeologists whose findings have been given a measure of additional precision by carbon-dating.[33]

But if the corner stone of the old orthodoxy, the sailing of a Great Fleet whose canoes arrived more or less concurrently has been rejected, no agreed alternative version has as yet been provided for us. 'Neither the date nor the place of the first landing in New Zealand is known', writes Janet Davidson, nor 'whether there was a single colonization, several, or many.'[34] And while the discrediting of the Fleet account has clouded the prehistory of Maori in New Zealand as a whole, it has served to diminish our knowledge of Tamaki even further. Prehistorians reconstructing Auckland's Maori past have already laboured under a double handicap. First, the growth of the metropolis of Auckland has obliterated most of its archaeological sites and all but a remnant of the evidence of local Maori material culture.[35] Second, as Chief Judge Fenton pointed out in his Orakei Judgment of 1869, there is so much 'conflicting evidence' about the tribal origins of Maori Auckland.[36] When George S. Graham, the most influential collector of Maori traditions in Auckland, wrote his 'Maori History of the Auckland Isthmus', he attempted to overcome this problem by tracing all local tribes back to the mythical Great Fleet.[37] This version, written as far back as 1922, is, for want of any other alternative account, still widely read, and is often accepted as gospel in non-academic quarters.

The uncertainty about Auckland's Maori beginnings is further compounded. Because many of the original people of the isthmus, like those of the Northland peninsula, were absorbed by conquering tribes, working out the 'order and sequence' of Maori settlement in the region, as Percy Smith discovered over a century ago, presents great difficulty.[38] In this 'Peopling of the North', as Smith described the process, the story of prehistoric Auckland itself throws up a further particular complication. In the mid-eighteenth century, the Te Taou branch of Ngati Whatua invaded the isthmus, and made a wholesale conquest (raupatu) of the dominant Waiohua iwi whom they then scattered or absorbed. This had the effect of blotting out much of the earlier oral traditions of Waiohua. The loss of significant parts of this traditional lore, while grievous in itself, also deprives the historian of valuable checks on the authenticity and

Maungakiekie and its terraces. GRAHAM DOWNIE

reliability of that remnant of pre-seventeenth-century Tamaki records which has survived.[39] Indeed, so little has been preserved, that there is not a sufficient corpus of knowledge that can be used to provide cross-links with outside genealogies and traditions to establish the authenticity of many of the fragmentary records that do remain.

Has the legend of the Great Fleet, therefore, seemingly disproved, no longer a part to play in the story of Maori Auckland? Historians do not dismiss the legend out of hand. Better, they say, to regard it as a metaphor for an historically authentic group of settlement-canoes that did indeed set out from Hawaiiki, but not as part of an organised mass migration, canoes which often left and arrived singly, and journeyed over a wide period of time.[40] Some would argue, however, that since Maori continue to accept the legend of the 'origin canoes', in some form or other, as historical, this is in itself a reason why we should do so as well. Be that as it may, we must recognise that those canoes remain an integral part of present Maori culture: a source of pride and of self-belief. They have given hapu, iwi and wider tribal confederations, in modern times, a sense of identity and the assurance of a shared heritage. Nor are the canoe stories to be thought of as being devoid of hard factual content. The whakapapa of most tribes, regardless of the supernatural and marvellous elements at those points where reference is made to earliest ancestors, usually meet the test of reliability when the canoe origins of ancestors are recited. Corroboration comes from the consistency of record, in surprising detail, of genealogy of related peoples going back to Great Fleet canoes, even of those tribes who have become geographically remote from one another.[41]

The migration canoes remain, consequently, important in Tamaki's past. Admittedly none of the great canoes made the isthmus its final resting-place. But a number of the most important were reputed to have visited Tamaki, or to have passed over its portages. Some were said to have deposited settlers on or around the isthmus, and four, in time, to have contributed substantially to the mix of people living there. Almost all of the later peoples of Tamaki-makau-rau have been able to trace descent from at least one of the canoes. To that extent the traditional history of the canoes cannot be ignored in the story of Maori Auckland.

Of all the Fleet waka (canoes) which, according to Maori folklore, visited Tamaki, *Tainui* is the most important. After making its landfall near Cape Runaway at the East Cape, this canoe, commanded by the chief Hotu-roa, journeyed northwards up the coast before turning into the Hauraki gulf. Once there, leaders decided to explore the west coast on the farther side of the isthmus. The route chosen was by way of the Tamaki estuary, at the western head of which (modern Glendowie) a small party of migrants chose to stay. These people subsequently intermarried with local inhabitants to found the tribe known as either Ngati Tai, or, more commonly, Ngai Tai.[42]

Taikehu, a chief of great mana on the *Tainui*, was deputed to set off from Wai-Mokoia (Panmure basin) to cross the isthmus with a small exploratory party.[43] He returned to report the exciting news that the Manukau harbour was rich in seafood: his party had encountered great flocks of seabirds, and leaping mullet so plentiful they could almost be grasped by bare hands. Heartened by this intelligence, Hotu-roa decided that the canoe should immediately begin its move to the other side of the isthmus by floating up the estuary on the incoming tide to the Otahuhu portage. But, once there, *Tainui* could proceed no further. Haul as they might on their flaxen ropes, the men could not drag the canoe over the skids. The senior tohunga, Rakataura, who was also a clairvoyant (matakite), soon divined why the hauling spells he had chanted had been ineffective. There had been a breach of tapu. The song of Marama, a secondary wife of Hotu-roa, soon revealed what that breach was; she confessed to committing adultery with a slave. After Marama had been severely rebuked and her slave killed, hauling recommenced. *Tainui*, watched by an assembly of admiring Tamaki tangata whenua, glided on until 'her prow dipped into and drank of the water of Manuka[u]'.[44]

The canoe did not linger in the harbour. Although some of the voyagers had stayed in Tamaki – among them Taikehu, ancestor of important hapu Rakataura, and the disgraced Marama (who founded a tribe that became known as Nga Marama)[45] – the canoe moved on. Probably the presence of numerous, already-established tangata whenua encountered on the east coast of the North Island, and in Tamaki, persuaded *Tainui* leaders that they should press on to a more sparsely settled region. Ultimately the canoe was beached at its last resting-place at Maketu on the Kawhia harbour.[46]

Over the generations, *Tainui* descendants spread far and wide from there, deeply inland and also to the north and the south. Hence the proverb defining the *Tainui* boundaries: 'Mokau ki runga, Tamaki ki raro', 'Mokau [in north Taranaki] above and Tamaki below'. This saying and its implied triumphalist pretensions, when voiced on modern marae, can set on edge the teeth of neighbours of the Tainui iwi – as Waikato tribes now collectively call themselves. But modern Tamaki Maori, mindful of their *Tainui* origins, still seem happy that their isthmus should be known as 'Te kei o te waka Tainui', 'the stern of the Tainui canoe'.[47]

The canoe known as *Arawa* also settled people on Tamaki.[48] Arriving almost simultaneously with *Tainui* at Whangaparaoa by the East Cape,[49] *Arawa*, like its sister canoe, explored the Pacific coast of the North Island as far as the Hauraki gulf. Unlike *Tainui* it decided not to cross the isthmus to the west coast. It established two main settlements: at Maketu in the Bay of Plenty, and in the northern part of the Coromandel range at Moehau, where the tribe became known as Ngati Huarere. A maritime people, Ngati Huarere spread through a number of the islands of the gulf, like Motuihe and Motutapu. Ultimately, Ngati Huarere invaded the isthmus and (according to Graham) established fortified villages in the vicinity of Horotiu, today's Queen Street valley, and at Orakei, Three Kings (Te Tatua-a-riukiuta) and elsewhere.[50] It has also been claimed that this tribe had as occupation sites for some years the volcanic cones of Maungarei, Maungawhau and Maungakiekie – the latter two, presumably, at a time when they were not in the possession of other tribes such as Waiohua or Ngati Awa. Some time after settling in Tamaki, this particular group lost its distinct tribal identity.

This, too, was the experience of another group who claimed descent from members of the crew of *Aotea,* led by Turi, who originally settled at Patea.[51] A descendant of Turi, Turanga-i-mua, at some ill-defined time in prehistory, is said to have led a war-party to Tamaki where he won a great victory at Waitaramoa (Hobson Bay). The victors settled and occupied the pa on the Orakei West headland known as Onepu-whaka-takataka, not far from today's Paratai Drive. Turangi eventually tired of Tamaki and left. But many of his people remained, and in time were absorbed by the local people, just as their Arawa counterparts in the region had been. But their canoe origins, like those of the Tamaki branch of Ngati Huarere just spoken of, were preserved in whakapapa. That is why, before 1750, a number of Tamaki chiefs were proud of being able to claim *Arawa* or *Aotea* origins, or both, as part of their ancestral lineage.

Some Tamaki Maori have claimed descent from the Fleet canoe *Maataatua,* whose emigrants went ashore at Whakatane to found the Ngati Awa tribe.[52] Traditional accounts of how and when a section of this tribe came to Auckland, and how long they resided there in significant numbers, conflict. But a likely version now follows.

Ngati Awa have been regarded within Maoridom as having a 'restless disposition', and as being always on the move.[53] By the fifteenth century, a large group had migrated north and was reputed to occupy a considerable portion of the Northland peninsula. Wearying of conflicts over land arising with their Ngapuhi and Ngati Whatua (Kaipara) neighbours, probably resulting from population growth, this branch of Ngati Awa began a series of migrations to the south. One group carried out its exodus, in stages, by way of the west coast. While in the lower Kaipara it came under the leadership of Titahi. An ariki of great mana, this chief won further renown in this region as an expert builder of pa, most notably his home fortress of Korekore, which he constructed on a ridge some three kilometres inland from Muriwai beach.[54] Titahi and his followers were invited to move to Tamaki where they apparently proceeded to live on friendly terms with the then dominant tribe, Waiohua. While there, Titahi is believed to have constructed or completed the pa defences and terracing of Maungawhau, Maungakiekie (temporarily a centre of Ngati Awa settlement in Tamaki) and a number of other scoria cones including Owairaka – beside which, for a while, he lived with a section of his tribe.[55] In spite of Titahi's reputation as the creator of Tamaki's most spectacular pa, it is likely that he was an improver rather than the originator of their earthworks and fortifications. The old saying that these pa were 'Nga-whaka-iro-a-Titahi', 'the carvings of Titahi', suggests that his main contribution could have been terracing and similar earthworks.

One Tree Hill.
GOTTFRIED BOEHNKE

Prehistorians generally agree that Maungakiekie had the most elaborate fortifications of all pa in Aotearoa. It also has so iconic a place in the folk culture of Auckland's Maori and Pakeha inhabitants alike, that the story of the origin of the tree which gave the hill its English name of One Tree Hill, should be told at this juncture of Ngati Awa residency in Tamaki.[56] Accounts vary in detail, but the essentials are not in doubt. Early in the seventeenth century a first-born son, called in some accounts Koroki, in others Korokino, was born to a Ngati Awa chief Tupaha and his wife Hine-te-ao, then living near Maungakiekie.[57] For Maori, birth was a rite of passage with solemn observances, in the case of those who were bearers of the chiefly bloodline especially so. After Korokino's birth the ancient rite of tohi took place.[58] The umbilical cord was cut on a club (symbol of the warrior status of the child when he had grown up) unusually severed in this case, not by a chip of stone or flake of obsidian, but by a sharpened totara stick. The club showed the dedication of Korokino to Tu, the god of war;

the sprig of totara, a tree that was emblematic of chieftainship, showed his dedication to Tane, who was the god, not only of the forest, but also of growth and fertility. The cord was then buried on the summit of nearby Maungakiekie and, in the soil above it, the totara sprig was planted. This cutting duly took root and, carefully tended in its early years and protected by its tapu, grew during the following decades into a tree of lordly dimensions. George Graham records that this totara became one of the great trees of the land, 'regarded with respect and invested with mana'.[59] Because of this totara's origins, Maori looked on it as very deeply tapu. They called it 'Te-totara-i-ahua', 'the totara which stands alone'. For dwellers in Tamaki-makau-rau, this totara was, continues Graham, 'an emblem of the welfare of the lineal line of the chiefs and their people'. It remained a landmark of the isthmus for perhaps 200 years. However, whether the 'one solitary large tree on [the] crater summit' of Maungakiekie,[60] which led the first settlers to change that hill's name to One Tree Hill, and which, in 1852, an unknown European settler wantonly cut down under cover of night, was still the original sacred totara, is by no means certain.

Logan Campbell, who became owner of One Tree Hill farm in 1853. AUCKLAND MUSEUM LIBRARY

I have discovered only three published sources, admittedly European, which specify what kind of tree was growing in the colonial period. The first is Ernst Dieffenbach's *Travels in New Zealand.* While recording a crossing of the Tamaki isthmus that he made by foot in early 1841, this German scientist observed that 'the extinct crater' of Maungakiekie 'was overgrown with brushwood and trees, and on the top stands an old pohutukawa tree'.[61] An able naturalist, usually distinguishing native trees by their botanical name, Dieffenbach was unlikely to confuse a pohutukawa with a totara. Two decades later, another German scientist spoke of the 'rotted' remains of a 'single lofty' pohutukawa 'on the highest peak'.[62] The final source is the *Daily Southern Cross* for August 1875. It records that: 'In the earliest days of Auckland a majestic pohutukawa crowned the very summit – the very crater-top – until the fell hand of some Goth on Onehunga's shore levelled the grand landmark for firewood's sake.'[63] It is significant that Logan Campbell, owner of the One Tree Hill estate at that time, culled the article from the newspaper, and then pasted it in his handwritten book of 'Reminiscences' which he was at that time compiling for his children. When including such newspaper material, Campbell's practice was to make a marginal note correcting any error that he detected. No such note appears beside this clipping in the 'Reminiscences'. So both Dieffenbach and Campbell, who saw the tree in 1840–41 at first hand, appear to agree that it was a pohutukawa, already dominant enough on the skyline for European colonists to decide to give to Maungakiekie its new name of One Tree Hill. It is conceivable that this pohutukawa had grown close to the totara, and had become a landmark by the time that the old totara had been removed or had died. It is also interesting to note that when Logan Campbell obtained, in 1875, a fourteen-year lease of the Crown Reserve (which took in the volcanic cone), he immediately decided, in the words of the clipping cited above, to attempt 'once again to convert Maungakiekie into One Tree-Hill' by planting a tree on the summit.[64]

Late in the seventeenth century the Ngati Awa exodus recommenced, as this branch of the tribe moved on to its final destination in Taranaki. A remnant of the tribe remained, however, among the medley of people who now made Tamaki-makau-rau their home. But a continuing physical reminder of the Ngati Awa presence, for all to see, were the elegant fortifications of Maungakiekie and the deeply tapu totara.

Even those prehistorians who dismiss the Fleet story as myth, nevertheless generally concede that there was a renewal of Polynesian migration to Aotearoa about the fourteenth century, and that the new wave of settlers encountered, in the northern part of the North Island, an already established Maori population. But determining who the established people were, and what were the tribal affiliations that they had built up with the new immigrants in this part of the country is problematical. Especially is this so for Tamaki.

There is general agreement, however, that Tamaki was settled early. Archaeological investigations indicate that parts of the region had settlements in the so-called Archaic period.[65] Carbon-dating at one excavation site at Maungataketake pa, Ihumatao, indicates that occupation could have been as early as, perhaps, the eleventh century AD.[66] But dates before about AD 1300 usually lack finality, and for the time being must be viewed with some scepticism.

In an attempt to bring out from the shadows these aboriginal people in Tamaki with whom, in the centuries ahead, descendants of later migrations blended, historians have turned to the minutes of a prolonged Native Land Court hearing held in 1868, or more commonly to the judgment which arose out of its sittings, which was delivered in 1869.[67] While presiding over this hearing to determine ownership of a 700-acre estate at Okahu, Orakei, Chief Judge F. D. Fenton considered in detail the pedigrees of rival claimants to this part of Tamaki, especially those of an incumbent subtribe (Te Taou) of Ngati Whatua, and of a rival section of Ngati Paoa. Whakapapa evidence, which he heard, was reputed to stretch back to aboriginal settlement.

His conclusion was that the first settlers of Tamaki, and of a considerable expanse north and south of the isthmus, belonged to 'one great tribe called . . . Ngaoho'. As tribal numbers increased, Ngaoho subdivided themselves territorially into Ngariki 'about and to the south of Papakura', Ngaiwi in 'the interval between Papakura and the waters of Waitemata', and into a further tribe north of the harbour and towards Kaipara, who retained the old name of Ngaoho.[68] Fenton went on to observe that, in time, Ngaiwi on the isthmus divided themselves yet again and threw off a further tribe called Waiohua, though these two names seemed interchangeable among members of these two isthmus tribes.

Chief Judge Francis Dart Fenton (1821–98) of the Native Land Court.
AUCKLAND CITY
LIBRARIES

The limited and (as Fenton admitted)[69] sometimes 'conflicting evidence' which the judge used to support his version of Tamaki's tribal origins, scarcely justified what he so confidently asserted. But there is much to support his view that the constant appearance of what he called 'intruding tribes' in Tamaki and its adjoining lands resulted in the region's inhabitants becoming, as Fenton put it, greatly 'mixed up'.[70] In these circumstances the names that the two main isthmus peoples had adopted for themselves by the seventeenth century, seem peculiarly appropriate: Ngaiwi and Waiohua. The name Ngaiwi, literally 'the tribe of tribes', had developed into a kind of portmanteau word that was likened by a nineteenth-century Ngati Whatua chief to 'this whare [the Provincial Council building] we are in; the roof covers us all'.[71] On the other hand, the Waiohua people took their name from a seventeenth-century chief, Hua, who, mortally ill, is said to have called for a drink from his tapu calabash of water, which as a portent of his imminent death, slipped from the hands of his caregiver and shattered on the ground. There-after, his tribe adopted the name Wai-o-Hua or 'water of Hua'.[72] But what is more pertinent to the present discussion is that, during his lifetime, Hua had acquired the name of Hua-kai-waka 'Hua the eater of canoes', because, as Simmons expresses it, in his person he had gathered together and made into one tribe, people of diverse canoe origins.[73] But it would be mistaken to think of Waiohua as a distinct and united tribe. In this book the name is used to comprehend the loose collec-tion of hapu (of which Waiohua was the most dominant) living on the isthmus, informally linked by intermarriage or by shared rights to resources, or by the imperative of mutual defence.

III

By the seventeenth century, the traditional sources dealing with Tamaki's history begin to be detailed and reliable enough to give a picture of the scale of settlement in the region, and of the nature of its tribal composition. Tamaki-makau-rau was moving to the peak of its fortunes. The 'enormous earthworks' of Maungawhau and Maungakiekie and 'all the volcanic hills of this district', Fenton looked on as proof of how 'thickly peopled' it was.[74] Certainly Maori lore has the people here as 'numerous as sandflies'.[75] What becomes clear is that prosperity continued in this way until the mid-eighteenth century because there were substantial periods of peace between the people of this isthmus and adjoining tribes.[76] The people of Tamaki-makau-rau gener-ally presented a united front to outsiders, actualising the lesson taught by the old Maori proverb, 'A split totara is prey to the axe.' And this unity guaranteeing peace came about because, at least by 1700, and probably for some time before, Waiohua held an undisputed authority (mana whenua) over 'the whole country from the Tamaki River to Te Whau, and stretching from the Manukau to the Waitemata'.[77]

Yet, beyond the two portages, tribal boundaries were more fluid. Since time out of mind, the lands adjoining the isthmus and the extended coastlines of the Manukau and of the Hauraki gulf were a frontier of convergence for intrusive tribes. Boundaries (rohe) ebbed and flowed like the tide.

Immediately north of the isthmus, settlement, though sparser than that to the south, tended to be more stable. The tangata whenua of the Waitakere region were that very ancient people whom Fenton called Nga Oho.[78] Their early boundaries ran north from the Manukau harbour up to south Kaipara and across to Mahurangi. At that locality, the tribe's further claim to east coast land extending as far south as Takapuna (North Head) normally did not survive the arbitrament of war. At some undefined stage in ancient times, this iwi became known as Te Kawerau.[79] The name and composition of the tribe was changed, however, during the seventeenth century. A division of Ngati Awa had migrated north from Taranaki by way of Waikato, settling in Tamaki and establishing its head pa at Rarotonga (Mount Smart). At the instigation of Tamaki tribes, the Ngati Awa chief at Tamaki, Maki, led a war-party against Kawerau destroying many pa as far north as Helensville. For some time Maki settled in South Kaipara and his followers intermarried with the defeated Kawerau, the mixed tribe henceforth bearing the name Te Kawerau-a-Maki, though Maki and some of his followers returned after a period to Taranaki. No longer a large tribe, Te Kawerau continued to be attacked by its more numerous enemies. In the later seventeenth century the tribe was devastated by a fearsome punitive raid, known as 'Te Raupatu-tihore' (the stripping conquest) carried out by a taua from Kaipara led by the giant Ngati Whatua chief, Kawharu.[80] Many Waitakere inhabitants were massacred, and every west-coast pa, extending from Lion Rock at Piha to the northern mouth of the Manukau, is said to have been destroyed. But this was conquest without settlement; Ngati Whatua prevailed, then withdrew. Te Kawerau had the same experience in the east-coast lands beside the north Hauraki gulf, to which it also laid claim. Hostile expeditions of Ngati Marutuahu made sporadic forays there, but usually returned to their Hauraki territories after the campaigns. In spite of these attacks, Te Kawerau seems to have been able to keep its separate identity intact by forging kinship bonds through intermarriage with invaders and potential enemies: above all with Waiohua and Ngati Whatua, its neighbours, respectively, to the south and to the north.[81] In time, it became

He Taua! A War Party!
*Sounding the alarm. (Artist
unknown).* AUCKLAND
CITY LIBRARIES

much 'mixed up' with Waiohua, and by the opening of the eighteenth century had developed into a somewhat dutiful ally of that powerful tribe.

South-east of the Tamaki river the tangata whenua were the Ngai Tai, descendants of immigrants from the *Tainui* canoe. They claimed rohe (boundaries) which ran from the Te Naupata (Musick Point) headland of the Tamaki estuary in an easterly direction to the mouth of the Wairoa river and thence inland to the Hunua ranges.[82] Towards the Otahuhu portage their claim to further land tended to be disputed, as was their claim to further islands of the gulf such as Motuihe, where tribal customary rights were notoriously complex and multiple.[83] But in their heartland – the Maraetai area – they were able to keep a stability of location. This tribe characteristically eased, by intermarriage, tensions with Ngati Paoa, its powerful southern neighbour, and with other powerful intruders. As with Kawerau to the northwest of the isthmus, so with Ngai Tai in the south-east, intermarriage and diplomatic marriages served as an assurance against invasion and as the guarantee of a continuing separate tribal identity.[84]

Although Ngati Paoa were a Hauraki iwi (albeit founded by Tainui chiefs), they had close associations with Tamaki-makau-rau and (after 1840) with colonial Auckland as well. Their traditional lands were on the western and southern coasts of the Firth of Thames and on certain gulf islands.[85] The tribe was part of what became known as the Marutuahu confederation: four Hauraki iwi whose founding chiefs were descendants of the fighting sons of Marutuahu. Hence the tribal names Ngati Maru, Ngati Paoa, Ngati Tama-Te-Ra and Ngati Whanaunga — although it has been complained that the name Ngati Paoa has often been loosely applied as a collective name for the whole Marutuahu group.[86] Hauraki tribal lands covered the littoral of the Firth of Thames, including the entire Coromandel peninsula and on either side of the inland range as far south as Waihi and thence westward to Te Aroha. Hauraki settlement was much muddled. And to further complicate boundaries there was a confused intermingling of tribes and subtribes with overlapping rights of ownership.[87]

With the passage of time, Ngati Paoa became a formidable presence in Tamaki. Taimoana Turoa, the Hauraki historian, characterised Ngati Paoa as a 'prickly, explosive people' who were (he said) in bygone days, as quick to take offence as they were formidable in war.[88] Turoa said that the adopted tribal motto, 'Ngati Paoa taringa-rahi' (which he glosses as 'Ngati Paoa's large ears brook no insult'), exemplifies their pugnacious reaction to 'the merest of slights'.[89] Their seaward movement towards Tamaki-makau-rau, though slow and discontinuous, can be seen with historical hindsight as having been almost irreversible. By the end of the eighteenth century they were established on islands near Tamaki such as Waiheke, on the western bank of the Tamaki river, and on parts of the east coast lying north of the Waitemata between Takapuna and Mahurangi. Their other Hauraki brethren were not far behind. During the same century, on the east bank of the Tamaki river, Ngati Whanaunga and Ngati Tama-Te-Ra had acquired lands. Ngati Tama-Te-Ra also had islands in the gulf; in 1840 its chiefs sold Brown's Island (Motukorea) to Logan Campbell and his partner William Brown.[90] By this time Ngai Tai had fallen so much under the sway of the Marutuahu confederacy that some Maori had begun regarding it as virtually a Hauraki iwi.

Back in the seventeenth century, the hapu occupying the lands of the Otahuhu portage were Ngai Tahuhu, whose founding chief was said to have come on one of the Heke (Great Fleet) canoes.[91] They became much associated with their Tamaki neighbours with whom they intermarried. Indeed, so integrated were they within the Tamaki economy and society, and so close were the bloodlines developed with Waiohua, that they ultimately became a constituent hapu of that iwi.[92] They controlled fertile lands with good kumara soils on either side of the portage, which, like the dragging place itself, exposed them to attack by war parties.[93] They created pa on nearby Mount Richmond (Te pa o Tahuhu), and fortified other, rather more distant, volcanic cones – probably including Rarotonga (Mount Smart) – in the region.

This overview of the bloodlines of the Tamaki peoples and of their customary habitations in the period before 1750 is completed by moving west from Ngai Tahuhu, the tribe of the portage. On either side of the Manukau harbour at Onehunga and Mangere were permanent settlements of the Waiohua hapu. Beyond Mangere, on the southern and western shores of the Manukau, were Ngati Tamaoho, Ngati Te Ata, Ngati Naho and Ngati Pou, each of whom represented a mingling of earlier peoples and hapu with the great Waikato iwi, with whom, consequently, the original south Manukau inhabitants became increasingly associated.[94]

IV

For the whole of the seventeenth century and the opening decades of the eighteenth, the neighbours who most threatened the Tamaki peoples were the Hauraki tribes. They were warlike and ambitious; their closeness to the busiest waterway in Aotearoa, the Tikapa moana (Hauraki gulf), tended to make them so. For most of this time, however, their threat was more potential than real and this for two reasons. First, the Hauraki tribes were very prone to indulge in internecine squabbling. Second, the four dominant Marutuahu tribes busied themselves 'for many generations', writes Monin, 'consolidating their power bases at Hauraki (Thames) and on both sides of the Firth of Thames. Only once these were secured could they consider projecting their power into the wider Hauraki Gulf: to the inner Gulf islands, to Tamaki and eventually to the Mahurangi coast.'[95] And, as we have seen, when expansion began, Ngati Paoa was in the forefront.

The earliest clash of the Hauraki tribes with the Tamaki peoples contains a strong mythical element; but it also confirms how potent a cause of war in Maori culture were suspected treachery and violation of tapu.[96] A widely recorded tradition of Ngati Tama-Te-Ra recounts that a taniwha guardian of their tribe (some versions speak of the animal as a pet seal called Ureia) was lured into the Manukau harbour by the local people who trapped, killed and ate it.[97] Hauraki tribes determined to exact their revenge on the tribes of Tamaki all of whom they held equally responsible. They invaded Tamaki destroying some of the most prominent pa including Maungawhau. Once the utu account had been squared by the spilling of blood, they returned home. The invasion seems to have a factual basis, even though the *casus belli* perhaps has not.

The next Hauraki invasion arose out of a further alleged act of treachery that revived in Hauraki minds memories of the deceitful killing of Ureia.[98] In the later seventeenth century, a Marutuahu chief, Kahurautao, while returning from a visit to Waikato, broke his journey at the Tamaki river where he left his canoes, in order to accept an offer of hospitality from Waiohua people at Maungawhau. On his way back to the Tamaki estuary, Kahurautao, his son Kiwi, and certain other followers, were waylaid by warriors sent by their Maungawhau host who had so recently entertained them, and murdered in the bracken fern on the ridge at Meadowbank where St John's College now stands. Thereafter the site of the ambush was named Patutahi ('killed together'). Once again, Hauraki exacted full blood-payment for this murder. Kiwi's brother, Rautao, led a taua of Ngati Maru and related tribes, which sacked the great pa of the isthmus: Maungarei, Maungakiekie and Maungawhau. Once again they moved on to Takapuna and campaigned as far north as Mahurangi. There is one oral tradition, that Maungawhau was so devastated and the loss of life there so heavy, that the area henceforth became tapu and the pa permanently abandoned.[99] But it has also been suggested that it was not the loss of life but the treachery towards Kahurautao that was the reason for Maungawhau being declared tapu.[100] However that may be, whether Maungawhau was abandoned then, or after a later assault, is likewise not certain. All that can be said is that when Pakeha first came to Auckland they reported that regenerating bush had fully taken over Maungawhau and its terraces were rankly overgrown. In 1841, it took the youthful settler, James Dilworth, a whole day to make the return journey from the waterfront to the summit of the hill.[101] Fourteen years earlier, a small party led by the French explorer Dumont D'Urville had found the bush and brushwood so impenetrable, that they had to give up their attempt to scale the 200-metre hill.[102]

The third episode in what some historians have called the Hauraki wars began about 1700. A Hauraki boy, Kapetaua, temporarily residing at Kohimarama, angered his Waiohua brother-in-law, Taramokomoko,[103] by pilfering kumara from the storehouse.[104] On the pretext of taking the boy on a fishing trip, Taramokomoko marooned him at low water on the reef off Bastion Point that is now known as Bean Rock. Kapetaua would surely have been drowned by the incoming tide had not his sister heard his piteous cries and come out by canoe to rescue him. (Thereafter Maori called that rock 'Te toka a Kapetaua' – 'Kapetaua's rock'.)

Kapetaua, who was of chiefly rank, never forgave the insult. On reaching adult years on Waiheke, he gathered a Ngati Paoa war-party about him and attacked Kohimarama and Orakei, and, according to some accounts, Takapuna as well. By killing his Waiohua brother-in-law and a number of his warriors, Kapetaua considered he had squared the utu account. Kapetaua returned to Waiheke for a time, but on hearing of a famous kumara garden at Waiau (Coromandel), he took another war-party there and seized it, settling himself and some of his hapu there permanently.[105] The small Patukirikiri tribe, which still survives in Coromandel, looks on Kapetaua as its ancestor.

In the 1860s a descendant of Kapetaua laid claim to Tamaki land on the ground (take) of conquest. The judge dismissed the claim on the ground that 'it is abundantly clear that this alleged conquest is nothing but a raid made for revenge'.[106] Kapetaua and his followers, like the earlier Hauraki victors on Tamaki, had shown no intention of 'permanently settling' on the land and thereby establishing their mana whenua over it.

But these three attacks were significant. They were fore-warning of the expansion into the inner gulf islands and into Tamaki itself that Ngati Paoa and other Hauraki iwi were poised to make by the mid-eighteenth century. More ominously they foreshadowed the Ngati Whatua conquest at much the same time.

CHAPTER II

From Waiohua to Ngati Whatua,
c.1600–1800

I

The conquest, in the mid-eighteenth century, of the resident tribes of the isthmus by Ngati Whatua invaders was a great watershed in the history of Maori Auckland. Over the previous century and a half, the many hapu living on the isthmus and in the areas immediately adjacent were loosely grouped under the mana of the chief of the most powerful tribe, latterly called Waiohua. The celebrated chief, Hua, after whom the tribe was named, flourished in the mid-seventeenth century.[1] Maungawhau was his pa; that was where he died. However, his even more powerful descendant, Kiwi Tamaki, made nearby Maungakiekie his pa. Paora Tuhaere, the Ngati Whatua ariki and folklorist, regarded 1720–50 as the period of Kiwi's ascendancy and called it 'The Era of Kiwi'. This was by all accounts the golden age of Tamaki.[2] In those years, wrote George S. Graham, Tamaki people were famed 'far and near' for their wealth, their hillside pa and their cultivations.[3] On the Manukau and Waitemata there were 'large fleets of canoes for fishing and war'. Waiohua leaders were renowned for their 'opulence . . . hospitality and industry'.

Though Graham's claims for Tamaki in its Waiohua heyday are most probably correct, they lack firm documentary confirmation. The reason for this is that, unlike most other significant regions in Aotearoa, Tamaki has few substantial records extant that can tell us in detail what life was like for its inhabitants before 1750. Unfortunately the defeat and displacement of Waiohua and related hapu in the mid-eighteenth century erased most of the existing oral history of the people of the isthmus: their ancestral stories, genealogies, karakia and waiata. Consequently, the version of events that has come down to the present to dominate, by default, all traditional accounts is that of Te Taou, a division of Ngati Whatua, the victors, so to speak, in the historical process.[4] (This particular hapu, originally known as Ngaririki, renamed itself Te Taou – literally 'the spear thrust in the breast' – when a female ancestor called Toutara perished from just such a wound during an old-time tribal war.)[5] The most fully recorded episode of the eighteenth century, for instance, is the background to the quarrel, and the ensuing conflicts that led to the Te Taou takeover of the isthmus. It is a triumphalist account from the Ngati Whatua viewpoint, with a marked warlike flavour. It tells how treacherous murder (kohuru), carried out by Waiohua chiefs, provoked the condign punishment of retaliatory invasions of Tamaki, resulting in much spilling of blood and the destruction of many pa. This bellicose version, coincidentally, also serves to reinforce the long-held conventional view that the highly visible presence of so many terraced hillsides in Tamaki prove that the region was, in Maori times, subject to constant wars.

Not much in fact is known about the day-by-day life of Maori on the isthmus during the many generations that these hillside villages and pa were being constructed and lived in. Unfortunately, these gaps in Tamaki's prehistoric past have become difficult to fill. By the 1960s, to be sure, archaeological expertise in New Zealand had reached the stage where it could have been utilised to uncover much of Auckland's prehistoric past. But by then it was virtually too late. Already New Zealand's largest city had blanketed the isthmus, obliterating almost the entire pre-European surface, and putting all but a small remnant of subterranean records beyond discovery and recall. In order to build up a picture of the material achievement of the people of this isthmus in the pre-1750 period, therefore, we are often obliged to go beyond Auckland and to turn to the lore of outside iwi, to their oral traditions, and to their artefacts.

Long before Pakeha had established some sort of regular presence in Aotearoa, Maori had overcome the double disadvantage

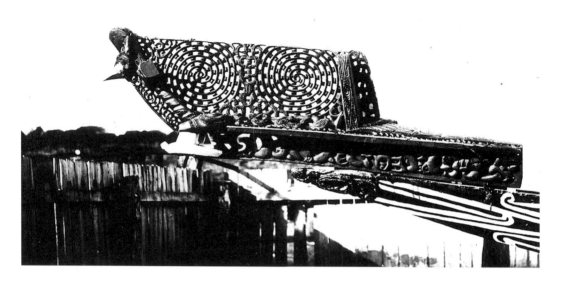

of limited resources and centuries of technological isolation to create what Sir Peter H. Buck describes as a uniquely 'rich and extensive' material culture.[6] The abundance of large trees throughout New Zealand superbly suited to woodworking had stimulated Maori to construct communal houses of hand-dressed timber, elaborately carved to a standard unmatched anywhere in the south Pacific.[7] With stone adzes and chisels, Maori lavished their burgeoning carving skills on wood, bone, stone and greenstone – the last-named being of such 'rarity and beauty' that Buck considered it should be thought of as a separate medium in its own right.[8] Craftsmen took meticulous care over detail, regardless of the size of the object being carved. Canoes over twenty metres in length had their intricately patterned prows and stern-post pieces, showing an almost filigree delicacy no less than that to be found in small items, such as handles for tools and weapons, or the exterior surfaces of miniature treasure boxes. Womanly decorative crafts, more culturally restricted one admits, found expression, nevertheless, in such activities as weaving, plaiting and cloak-making. And there is no doubt that, in the lattice-work reed panels (tukutuku) which women prepared for the interiors of meeting houses, their work imaginatively matched that of the men.

Maori skill in carving raised itself from craftsmanship to the realm of high art. Like most early visitors to New Zealand, Sir

Joseph Banks was taken aback by the beauty of Maori carving, feeling unable in mere words to capture and convey its excellence.[9] The unique and most admired feature of Maori carving was the use of the curvilinear or spiral motif. The natural world could well have suggested to carvers the koru – as this device was usually called – for the unfolding shoot of the forest fern was a constant feature of the New Zealand landscape. (The spiral pattern found in wood was replicated in the tattoo (moko) upon Maori heads and bodies. But on which surface – skin or wood – was it first used? Who can say?)[10] The spiral curve, appearing in both single and double forms, together with stylised wooden figures of man and beast, were the chief features of the richly carved barge boards and door frames of buildings in these years of high artistic achievement.

But can we infer from this broader New Zealand experience that Tamaki people fully shared in the material and cultural advances made elsewhere? Yes, and with some confidence. Tamaki, as a nodal point where canoe transport converged, was unusually placed to take advantage of Aotearoa's dense and wide-ranging exchange network, and so to be able to appropriate for its own use, the innovations of other regions.[11] There was every incentive to do so. It is a commonplace of tribal traditions that Tamaki, in the years of Waiohua ascendancy, was one of the most closely settled and extensively cultivated regions in Aotearoa, and that it was, in Maori terms, extraordinarily wealthy. We may assume that this prosperity spurred Tamaki peoples to emulate the cultural achievements of rival tribes. For Maori fiercely competed in practising the arts of peace no less than the craft of war. In this regard, the main pataka, or storehouse for food – one of the most prized buildings in all villages – provides an instructive parable. Elevated high above the ground to preserve its contents against damp and rats, it was also lavishly carved to draw attention to the

ABOVE: *Tamati Waka Nene.*
SHERRIN AND WALLACE

BOTTOM: *A wakahuia or carved treasure box.*
ETHNOLOGY DEPARTMENT, AUCKLAND WAR MEMORIAL MUSEUM

value of the food inside, and thereby to the wealth of the tribe.[12] Anne Salmond cites the growth in the display of wealth in greenstone ornaments as an instance of 'the competition for prestige' which had emerged in this later period.[13] The spirit of conspicuous consumption, we may conjecture, was an ever-present inducement to emulate the cultural achievements and lavish hospitality of rival tribes. So Graham's surmise that this was a golden age for Tamaki seems well founded enough.

The close settlement and prosperity of Tamaki in these years of Waiohua hegemony were sustained by a stable, mixed economy, based on horticulture, complemented by foods gathered from the sea and the forest. In such an economy, kumara was king. Kumara is a nutritious crop of high yield, but one that demands constant and careful attention.[14] Much of the year's labour, therefore, was devoted to gardening, broken by seasonal (usually summer) migrations to coastal encampments, mainly on the Waitemata harbour, which were used as bases for fishing and for shellfish gathering. George Graham spoke of kumara as the basic crop for Auckland Maori, 'the staff of life' (he wrote), which they supplemented by 'taro, hue (gourd), and uwhi (yam)'.[15] All these introduced crops, save the gourd, did well in the mild, moist climate of Tamaki. That the key activity was cultivating the kumara tends to be confirmed by the excavations of archaeologists and the soil profiles extracted by geologists working in the few (as yet) relatively undisturbed areas such as the Epsom valley, where there are deep deposits of volcanic ash.[16] Kumara is reasonably soil-tolerant and grows well in many locations. But settlement and horticulture in Tamaki were heaviest in volcanic areas with a scoria or basalt underlay, beside hills such as Remuera (Mount Hobson), Maungawhau (Mount Eden), Three Kings (Te Tatua) and Mangere mountain. And, of all the areas cultivated, that on the apron of land about Maungakiekie was the most prominent.

A proverb of the early eighteenth century obliquely refers to the extent of this plantation, the most famous of Tamaki's kumara gardens. It was located near Maungakiekie pa, headquarters of the ariki or paramount chief of the Waiohua tribe.[17] The proverb proclaimed that if you wanted to see an abundance of awheto[18] (a horned, grass caterpillar, generally about the size of a man's little finger, which preyed on kumara foliage, but was

Storehouse for kumara.
SHERRIN AND WALLACE

also collected by Maori as a delicacy), you should visit 'te mara a Te Tahuri' – 'the garden of Te Tahuri'. Te Tahuri was a chieftainess of the dominant Waiohua, like many highborn women traditionally in charge of the tending of tribal gardens.

Large-scale kumara plantations functioned best when there was periodical rotation of gardens to overcome soil depletion. This, in turn, was most likely to occur when there was undisturbed occupation of the same land over some years. Kumara was essentially the staff of life for people at peace just as fernroot (aruhe) – the edible rhizome of bracken – was generally the basic crop of people either at war, or otherwise displaced or socially dislocated, say by migration.[19] That was why the Tamaki kumara gardens of this era, covering hundreds of hectares, some of them remote from fortified settlements, betokened a stable social order with people in peaceful occupation of their cultivations. Here is a picture which calls into question the conventional wisdom of early prehistorians with their image of Tamaki-makau-rau, the maiden (region) contended for by a hundred lovers (warriors),[20] a disputed territory subject to, in Graham's phrase, 'many repeated invasions and incessant warfare'.[21]

As we have seen, Tamaki did have its wars. But it also had prolonged periods of peace. When peace was broken this was

33

rarely because of discord within the region – the Kapetaua episode was an exceptional instance of intra-hapu strife.[22] As the periodic Hauraki wars showed, the main threat came from without. But, even then, invasion had not culminated in the annexation of land.[23] Conflict arose not out of land-hunger but out of what traditional, Maori society considered inimical acts – treachery, insults, curses, slights to mana, inhospitable or disrespectful behaviour, the unacceptable elopement or abduction of women, especially those who were high-born. All such violations of the code called for the shedding of blood as payment. When the aggrieved party felt that it had made the account square (tika), it normally withdrew. This was so in Tamaki. No invasion of the isthmus before the mid-eighteenth century led to the actual takeover of land.

Like most parts of the country Tamaki was subject to sporadic attack. War-parties raided unharvested gardens. There were raids for revenge, or to acquire booty such as canoes (prized tribal assets), or to abduct women. Raids could, of course, lead to a retaliatory counter-attack, even spiral into war. Such conflicts, however, were a feature of Maori life throughout all Aotearoa. What was distinctive to Tamaki, and this in spite of the received wisdom of historians to the contrary, was the fact that tribes enjoyed long periods of relative peace. This was remarkable. The diverse mixture of tribes, with their overlapping rights on this closely settled isthmus, might have been expected to increase the likelihood of war. Why then was regional peace almost the norm? Evidence provided by Maori witnesses at the sitting of the Native Land Court deliberating on Orakei, in the 1860s, suggests a plausible explanation. Tribal leaders, perhaps in a mood of excessively roseate nostalgia, spoke of a tradition of peaceful co-existence in Tamaki during the pre-musket-war era, a tradition that had roots extending deep into the eighteenth century and possibly further.[24] They testified to long-standing, overlapping rights of ownership, to a sharing of fishing grounds with outside hapu, or at least with elements within those hapu bonded with tangata whenua by kinship; they also spoke of uncontested criss-crossing of tribal territories. Hori Tauroa of Ngati Te Ata (Waikato) recalled in court how, in pre-Pakeha times, his tribe used to 'come backwards and forwards to catch sharks in [the] Waitemata. . . . The lands were not divided

in those days.'[25] (Had portages habituated tangata whenua to that freedom of movement, one wonders?) There was also a general recognition of the customary rights of hapu within the region, and even of certain tribes, without the region, especially hapu of lower Waikato on the south shore of the Manukau harbour, to share fishing encampments on the Waitemata – though not necessarily with the further right to establish gardens there.

Self-interest on the part of the tangata whenua of Tamaki could have been at work. In this region, where many peoples converged, the stability of the integrated economy of the isthmus depended on the sharing of rights, and on the practice of 'live and let live'. Nicholas Freeling, the novelist, has observed that 'Nothing propinques like propinquity.' This was so in Tamaki. Tribes are like individuals who live at close quarters. Concession and compromise can sometimes become the only alternative to strife.

Anyway, Maori society had its own safeguards against conflict.[26] Customs and customary law provided ritual prohibitions and retributions – mana, tapu (in the sense of respect for authority), rahui,[27] utu and the like – which exercised a restraining influence on those tempted to disregard law and order and thereby provoke the possibility of retaliatory war.[28] Widespread intermarriage among isthmus peoples themselves, and also with neighbouring tribes, established many kinship bonds that, in the last resort, perhaps provided the best means of sharing customary rights and of resolving conflict.[29]

By the early eighteenth century the linkage of Tamaki peoples in a defensive alliance system under Waiohua showed the emergence of a mentality of 'peace within the pa'. Keen awareness of the danger of disunity when confronted by external enemies seems also to have encouraged harmonious close-quarter relationships among the hapu of Tamaki-makau-rau, most of all when war from outside threatened.

II

By the early eighteenth century Tamaki, as we have seen, was renowned for its power and prosperity. Its numerous people, their widespread cultivations, and the great concentration of pa made it so. Its paramount chief (ariki nui), Kiwi Tamaki, shared in this acclaim. His mother Te Tahuri and his father Te Ika-mau-poho, according to George S. Graham, 'united in their ancestry all that was aristocratic in lineal descent' from the ancient tribes of the isthmus.[30]

Tamaki under Kiwi seemed powerful and secure. Waiohua headed a district confederation of tribes, united in a defensive military alliance. And further, Kiwi Tamaki had behind him a system of defence that could withstand any attack – or so it was believed. Maori tradition holds that there were originally three great pa in the region – Maungakiekie, Mangere and Maunga-taketake (Ihumatao).[31] Yet Percy Smith has listed no fewer than twenty-two major pa in existence in Kiwi's time. Together, they constituted a kind of fortress Tamaki.[32]

The most spectacular pa of all was at Maungakiekie.[33] Lady Fox, an English archaeologist who made a special study of that pa, considered it 'the most impressive of all Auckland pa, daunting in its extent and complexity'.[34] But she urged us not to regard it as a self-contained fortress; rather should we place it in a much broader military context.[35] Maungakiekie was intended, she believed, to act as the pivot of a general defence system using other pa of the isthmus and beyond – one thinks here of Tara-taua at south Manukau head, or Te Pane Matao Pa

(Mangere Mountain) – as outliers to delay an attack, perhaps to blunt its edge completely.[36]

The fortress-builders of Maungakiekie itself exploited the defensive qualities of the volcano's three main craters and their adjacent steep slopes. Where slopes were gentler, the builders had created a succession of terraced scarps, which barred the way to carefully selected strong points, usually defensible high points or spurs.[37] The heart of the Maungakiekie defence system was the citadel (toi) on the summit. Major earthworking had created terraces and banks which guarded it, and a substantial palisade surrounded the flattened summit.[38] There is little hard evidence about how this citadel was used, apart from its being the home of the paramount chief in time of war.[39] According to Maori traditions, the two best-known features of the toi were the sacred totara (Te totara-i-ahua), by Kiwi's time a lofty and noble tree and nearby a huge pahu or gong.[40] One account speaks of the pahu as being entirely of greenstone. This seems fanciful. Another refers to it as a slab of unpolished stone.[41] Most likely it was a great wooden slab slung either vertically from a single wooden post, or horizontally between two, with one side of the slab embellished with greenstone.[42] According to Percy Smith, when the gong was struck to sound the alarm for an invasion, it could be heard across the countryside 'for miles [a]round'.[43]

In Kiwi Tamaki's time, serious invasion was likely to come from two quarters: either from Ngati Paoa in the south-east, or Ngati Whatua in the north-west. In the event, Ngati Whatua proved to be the nemesis. This was the tribe that brought Waiohua hegemony to an end.

Ngati Whatua was an iwi that originated in the far north.[44] Over hundreds of years it made a long move south. This tribal migration almost certainly resulted from the pressure of a growing population upon the limited resources of the upper Northland peninsula. It is recorded that, by the beginning of the seventeenth century, the Ngati Whatua people had established themselves in the Upper Kaipara with settlements in the Kaihu and [Northern] Wairoa river valleys. A century later found them 'numerously' settled and influential on the southern shores of the Kaipara harbour, where they shared, with Kawerau and Waiohua, an unstable frontier that Graham called 'the Waitakerei-Kaipara borderland'. Border clashes multiplied. 'Unacceptable killings'[45] on both sides led to a sequence of revenge raids. One of these was the 'stripping conquest' of the giant Ngati Whatua chief Kawharu, which, as we have seen, escalated from a retaliatory raid into a wholesale invasion, though not one which led to permanent occupation or to annexation of land. Kawerau people under Te Huhunu, it could be noted, subsequently murdered Kawharu and this in turn led to Ngati Whatua's expelling of Kawerau from part of south Kaipara.[46]

Over some generations, a great deal of bad blood built up between Ngati Whatua and tribes of the Waiohua federation, leaving, as a recent Waitangi Tribunal report slyly observed, 'more than a few unsettled scores'.[47] There is a strong case for regarding these frontier clashes and the accumulating ill will that they left as a fundamental cause of the Ngati Whatua revenge raids that culminated in the conquest of Tamaki. It is questionable that the catalogue of Waiohua treachery and of Kiwi Tamaki's arrogance, which was passed on by Ngati Whatua informants to European recorders like Judge Fenton and Percy Smith, can remain the simple explanation of how a new tribe acquired the mana whenua over Auckland by right of annexation.

If the old Maori adage that 'war is a devouring fire kindled by a spark' be true, then the kindling spark which led to the great Tamaki war was an appeal for assistance made to Kiwi Tamaki by Te Raraku. A chief of the Ngati Rongo branch of the Ngati Whatua confederation but bearing in his person ancestral connections with Waiohua and Kawerau, Te Raraku was, according to Percy Smith, 'a noted warrior'.[48] He was also notorious for changing sides in tribal quarrels. This practice resulted in his acquiring (Smith asserts) the 'second name of Taharua, or "two-sided", on account of his assisting equally both sides in their wars'. As leader of an anti-Taou faction within Ngati Whatua, he asked Kiwi to help him in pursuing his feud with that hapu. Why Kiwi should have agreed to act in his cause is not certain. It could have been because of old enmities between Waiohua and Te Taou arising out of their troublesome borderland. Equally, Kiwi may have felt bound to give military assistance, because Te Raraku had a claim on his support brought about by past services, or by kinship links through inter-tribal marriage.[49]

For whatever reason, Kiwi agreed to support Te Raraku's cause. His chance to act came when, in company with a group of his

warriors attending an uhunga, or funeral wake,[50] at Waituoro, near Helensville, he fell upon unsuspecting Te Taou mourners and killed a considerable number of them, some of whom were chiefs.[51] Two Te Taou chiefs, Tuperiri and Te Waha-akiaki, escaped, vowing dire vengeance. According to the nineteenth-century Ngati Whatua chief, Paora Tuhaere, a repository of his tribe's lore, before Kiwi and Waha-akiaki parted, they interchanged threats of a terrible desecration of bones. In Paora's words;

Lamentations over a deceased chief. *Watercolour by G. F. Angus.* AUCKLAND UNIVERSITY LIBRARY

> Kiwi (of Waiohua) then offered a proverb to Waha-akiaki, 'Let it be thus; thy breastbone tomorrow shall be hanging on the pohutukawa tree at Kai-arero!' [Kai-arero is a locality on the northern slope of One Tree Hill where a historic pohutukawa or Christmas tree grew.][52] Waha-akiaki replied thereto, 'Rather thus shall it be, thy breastbone shall be hanging from the *puriri* at Maunga-a-Nu' [a hill close to modern Helensville]. Kiwi retorted, 'When Rehua-i-te-rangi [a god supposed to dwell within Kiwi's body] perhaps decides that Kiwi should die, yes, then shall he die!'[53]

39

On his way back to Tamaki, Kiwi chanced upon Tuperiri's sister, Tahataha. He killed her and a number of her followers, as well. Both Fenton and Smith unite in calling these massacres 'treacherous'.[54] But the two most powerful causes of inter-tribal war had already been established, each of which, alone, was unforgivable: the murderous betrayal of hospitality and the exchange of curses between chiefs.

When the historian takes up his account of the retaliatory raids that flowed from this episode, he enters upon a difficult interpretative terrain. When did they begin? Estimates range from about 1740 to about 1750. Furthermore, the sequence of raid and counter-raid between the Kaipara and Tamaki peoples has usually been presented as an occurrence lasting no more than about eighteen months, probably less. It is possible, however, that this conflict between Kaipara and Tamaki peoples extended, from first to last, over a considerable period of time, perhaps years. And it is also unclear just when Te Taou decided to convert their punitive attack into a takeover involving occupation of the isthmus.

On one point there is no doubt: when Te Taou retaliation came, it was swift and unrelenting. To avenge the Waituoru massacre and the kanga (curse) uttered by Kiwi before he left the Kaipara, Te Waha-akiaki raised a taua of 100 men who advanced through the Waitakere ranges as far as Titirangi. There the taua mauled Kiwi's forces so severely that Kiwi, although not completely defeated, was forced to fall back to the safety of his pa at Maungakiekie. The Te Taou war-party continued their raid. But they by-passed Maungakiekie and other main pa of the isthmus, attacking instead the pa of Taurere (Taylor's Hill), which commanded the entrance to the Tamaki river. This they took by storm, killing the chief Takapunga. (The site of the hill-fort, today somewhat reduced by quarrying, is still to be seen on the reserve adjoining Sacred Heart College and Glendowie College.) After some further skirmishes, the raiding party returned to Kaipara. But, for Ngati Whatua, the utu account was still not tika (correct).

The next invasion was made by a larger war-party, 240 all told, assembled by and under the joint leadership of Tuperiri and Te Waha-akiaki.[55] This taua came from Kaipara to Puponga Point on the northern shore of the Manukau. There the warriors made rafts of raupo, on which overnight they crossed the waters of the Manukau near the harbour heads to lay siege to the powerful Tarataua pa. On the following morning, the expedition made a successful surprise attack on this pa, killing most of its inhabitants. The Te Taou force pursued refugees from this pa and other pa that they stormed on the Awhitu peninsula and on the south shore of the Manukau. Upon reaching Papakura the taua stopped, and moved back to the north side of the harbour, where they encamped and regrouped at Paruroa, better known today as Big Muddy Creek. (People today can view the site of this camp at Paruroa as they pass along the road between Titirangi and Huia; it was located on the estuary just below the massive earthen wall of the Nihotupu reservoir.)

Waiohua determined on a final reckoning with Te Taou's invasion force. 'Then was heard', wrote Percy Smith, the 'great gong on Maunga-kiekie, and the *pukaeas*[56] from the various *pas* in the neighbourhood, notifying the [Waiohua] tribe to assemble for war.'[57] A Waiohua host, many travelling by canoe, advanced on Paruroa.

Because during the ensuing battle of Paruroa, the early death of Kiwi Tamaki had much to do with its final outcome, it is well to recall, at this stage, how crucial was the traditional role of Maori chiefs in battle. George S. Graham explained why in this fashion:

> In war, the personality of the chief played a great part. Frequently, when a leader fell, the ardour of his followers evaporated even when victory was within their grasp. No warrior of common descent could rally the tribe in battle no matter how great his personal valour. Disputes between tribes were often settled by duels between chieftains of the warring tribes.[58]

Traditional accounts all agree that the turning point in this clash between Waiohua and Te Taou was the duel of Kiwi and Waha-akiaki. Paul D'Arcy, who has recently reviewed Maori warfare from a pan-Polynesian perspective, emphasises that it was customary in a number of Polynesian societies, to regard the triumph of one champion over another in battle 'as an indication of the gods' support', and that this 'could have a decisive effect on the morale of both sides'.[59] This proved so at Paruroa.

According to Paora Tuhaere, who has passed on to posterity the Ngati Whatua version of the battle of Paruroa, as Kiwi's warriors approached the shore where Te Taou had been encamped, Waha-akiaki ordered his taua to resort to the strategy of 'hawaiki-pepeke' (a feigned retreat to draw on the enemy). He told his men to fall back and back, upon a rising spur projecting from the range behind, in this way continuing to draw their opponents up the hill. 'Let us go on, let the bird be drawn into the snare', he is reported to have said to his brother.[60] He commanded his men not to 'face about until we see the waters of the Waitemata'.[61] We may surmise that they retreated up a spur beside the steep valley down which the Nihotupu stream flowed, until they reached the main ridge along which today's Scenic Drive runs near the Arataki Centre. When that watershed was reached, Waha-akiaki put a calabash of oil down on the ground, as a pre-arranged signal for his men to turn and fall upon their pursuers. Percy Smith recorded that, early in the ensuing battle, 'Te Waha-akiaki, recognising Kiwi by his plumes, rushed at him; they closed, and both fell to the ground, but Te Waha-akiaki managed to get his stone weapon free, and killed his antagonist.'[62] The tide of battle immediately turned. Waiohua became demoralised, fell back and fled in a rout. Few escaped. The slaughter was great.[63] There is a tradition that so many Waiohua warriors were killed on the seashore or on the sea while trying to escape, that in consequence the local shellfish beds became polluted by corpses and stank.[64] All the important Waihoua chiefs are said to have fallen at this battle; hence its name 'Te Rangi-hinganga-tahi' (the day when all fell together).[65]

After the battle, according to Paora Tuhaere, 'The body of Kiwi was cut up, and his god [Rehua] was found within him in the shape of a reptile. One of Te Taou swallowed the god and fell dead in consequence.[66] The trunk of Kiwi's body was [later] carried to the trees of Maunga-a-Nu and hung up, verifying the proverb of Waha-akiaki.'[67] After sating themselves on the bodies of the slain, Te Taou went on to capture Maungakiekie, the main pa of the central isthmus. This they were able to do with relative ease. Most of the defenders, leaderless and demoralised after hearing of the calamitous defeat at Big Muddy Creek, had fled.[68] Those who failed to escape were either killed or (especially if women or children) enslaved.

The Waiohua remnant regrouped in readiness to make a final stand at the great pa of Mangere.[69] Anticipating a surprise attack, the defenders had strewn pipi shells on the paths leading to the pa, so that the feet of the taua, by crushing the shells, would alert the sentinels within to any secret attack carried out by night. But the Ngati Whatua taua under Tuperiri – who was determined to avenge the death of his sister Tahataha – was in Percy Smith's phrase 'equal to the occasion'. They took off their 'dogskin mats . . . carefully placed them over the shells, and thus formed a silent road to the *pa*. At the break of dawn they delivered their attack, and were very soon in possession.'[70] Because of the method of Mangere's capture, Ngati Whatua gave the pa a new name: Te-ara-pueru, which means 'the garment (or clothing) pathway'.[71] Many defenders were asleep when the pa was stormed. Once again the slaughter was great. According to Percy Smith:

> A few of the Wai-o-Hua escaped the massacre, and fled to the lava rocks near the shore to seek a hiding-place in the holes and corners of that part. Many took refuge in a lava cave, which was discovered by Ngati Whatua, who collected dry scrub and drift-wood, which they piled against the entrance, and then set fire to. The story says, the *taua* had then 'nothing to do but to drag them forth and eat them.' Some few of the Wai-o-Hua were captured alive, and taken back by their captors as slaves, principally women and children.[72]

With the fall of Mangere pa, the Waiohua confederacy was a spent force. The tribal remnants (parahuhare) fled, taking refuge, generally, among various Waikato peoples from Papakura southwards and on the south shore of the Manukau.[73] The Tamaki isthmus lay defenceless before Te Taou. At that point, Tuperiri seemed completely to change the purpose of his campaign. What he had launched as a series of revenge raids now became converted into raupatu (outright annexation). But exactly when he brought down his people to take over Tamaki is a matter of conjecture; and is likely to remain so. There is the further possibility that, contrary to what Percy Smith wrote, Ngati Whatua attacked and wiped out the Waiohua fortresses on the Waitemata shoreline, *before* the decisive battles of Paruroa and Mangere.[74] There are conflicting traditional versions. What is undoubted is that, before Te Taou

finally settled, Waiohua pa remained on the Waitemata shoreline. The main fortified places were a pa on the cliff facing Bastion Rock,[75] Toka-Purewa on the headland on the east of Okahu Bay, and Taurarua pa on the point at the east of Judge's Bay.[76] How long this Waiohua remnant remained unmolested after the fall of Mangere (if that is indeed the sequence) is unclear. Estimates vary widely. Judge Fenton, acting on what the Te Taou chieftain, Warena Hengia, told him in 1868, said these pa were attacked within two months.[77] Paora Tuhaere, the renowned nineteenth-century recorder of Ngati Whatua folklore, recorded a gap of five years.[78] Tuhaere is the more believable. Indeed, he could even have underestimated the delay.

What is not a matter of debate is the nature of the final Waiohua defeat that was the prelude to Te Taou settlement of

Tamaki. Some Ngati Whatua chiefs in Kaipara, believing that there was a further utu account to be settled because of past Waiohua wrongdoings, formed an expedition made up of non-Taou elements. This taua, which came down the harbour by stealth from Riverhead (Rangi-topuni), fell on the remaining Waitemata fortresses at Kohimarama, Orakei and Taurarua. These they overthrew one by one over the next two days, killing many inhabitants, and cooking and eating a number of chiefs.[79] The taua then withdrew, 'leaving the fruits of their victory', declared Fenton, 'to be enjoyed by their friends Te Taou. . . . Te Waiohua were extirpated as a tribe, and individuals only existed in a subject state, or as wives amongst the conquering [Te Taou] tribe.'[80]

III

The conquest of Tamaki was complete. But in maintaining that the defeated Te Waiohua became 'extirpated' and 'extinct', Fenton had repeated a misconception about the fate of conquered tribes all too common among nineteenth-century Native Land Court judges.[81] Paora Te Iwi, a Waikato chieftain, speaking a century later of the fate of the Ngariki hapu, which had been part of the Waiohua alliance defeated by Te Taou, roundly declared: 'The name [Ngariki] is extinct but the blood remains.'[82] Rarely, if ever, did a Maori tribe become 'extinct'.[83] Nor did Waiohua.

Some Waiohua survivors sought refuge in other regions, usually among hapu with a shared ancestry, in the lower Waikato[84] or in Hauraki. What had been eliminated were not the former Tamaki peoples themselves, but their previous hapu structures, and their customary rights to lands based on ancestral descent. Other survivors who remained in Tamaki, as has been noted, were enslaved. In time they became absorbed into a new mixture of people, going under the revived name of Ngaoho. By marrying Waiohua women, whose issue became known as Ngaoho, Te Taou effectively strengthened their claim to the mana whenua of the isthmus. The right which they had established on the ground of annexation (take raupatu) was now reinforced in their children from intermarriage, who could claim descent from tangata whenua, and a title, therefore, based on ancestry (take tupuna).[85] Thereafter, Ngaoho became caught up in the web of kinship obligations and rights with the dominant Te Taou. One nineteenth-century Ngati Whatua chief, Te Keene Tangaroa, enjoyed considerable status and authority simply because of his descent from Te Taou conquerors on the one hand, and, on the other, because he could claim in his pedigree (in Judge Fenton's words) 'the very pure blood' of the conquered.[86] It is significant that, in the early years of the Crown Colony, Maori claimants in a dispute over Tamaki land would sometimes call on Te Keene to indicate where traditional rohe (boundaries) ran in the central isthmus. His rulings were, seemingly, accepted without demur.[87] His strong credentials for land entitlement were also confirmed by the frequency with which his name appeared on deeds of sale made by the Ngati Whatua tribe in the 1840s.[88]

Two groups of remnants who fled the isthmus after the Ngati Whatua invasion were to return in the later decades of the eighteenth century. One group, who became known as Te Uringutu, included a number who had escaped from Mangere pa at the time of its overthrow.[89] A further group of refugees, who had settled temporarily in South Auckland after the Te Taou invasion, flowed back towards the Otahuhu region where they became incorporated in Te Akitai.

As in former days, the isthmus had become, by the early nineteenth century, a frontier of confluence with a mixture of peoples that, by the time of the musket wars, was generally known as 'Ngati Whatua of Tamaki'. To some extent, the people of the isthmus, with the exception of a branch of Ngati Paoa on the west bank of Whangamakau (Tamaki river), were united under the person of the Ngati Whatua chief, Apihai Te Kawau. When pressed at the court hearing over Orakei in October 1868, to declare from which of the constituent tribes Apihai derived his claim to have the mana whenua of Tamaki, he confidently stated 'I claim equally through all'.[90] Judge Fenton did not dispute this. In his judicial report on Orakei, Fenton observed that 'Apihai Te Kawau, by intermarriages of his ancestors on all sides', was the acknowledged chief of the three tribes with the strongest claim to central Tamaki. Likening him to a Highland chief mentioned in a novel by Sir Walter Scott, the judge labelled Apihai 'the man of many cousins'.[91]

A conciliatory policy followed by Te Taou towards those whom they had conquered, leaving some of them in 'undisturbed

Ahipai Te Kawai, t.d c. 1790–1869. Leader of Ngati Whatua o Tamaki. P. Gauci after J. J. Merrett. C. Terry, New Zealand

possession'[92] of certain parts of the isthmus or close to it, was not an unusual outcome of war among Maori. But it did have for Te Taou practical advantages. At the time of the takeover, they were not a large hapu; and they had also suffered significant losses in battle. '[C]onsiderably weakened in fighting strength', Percy Smith wrote, they seemed to have followed the 'ancient custom . . . where tribes decimated by war have quietly determined to avoid giving offence, and thus remain at peace until the young people had grown up and were able to bear arms.'[93]

But over the next eighty years, Tamaki's population remained relatively small, a fraction of what it had been in the heyday of

47

Kiwi Tamaki. Settlement and cultivation no longer covered much of the isthmus. During his lifetime, Tuperiri, leader of Te Taou, maintained and fortified Maungakiekie as his principal pa.[94] Some pa on the central isthmus, however, were allowed to fall into disuse. Tuperiri's chieftains occupied outlying settlements on the two harbours. There were settlements, some fortified some not: on the Waitemata at Freeman's Bay, on either side of Kauri Point and at Paremoremo; and on the Manukau, at Mangere and Ihumatao, whose people became increasingly mixed by marriage with Waikato people living on the southern shore of the harbour.[95] On Tuperiri's death around about 1795, Maungakiekie itself was abandoned. A Te Taou chief recalled in old age how, as a small boy at the end of the eighteenth century, he had seen that once mighty pa rotting away. 'I saw only the stumps of the posts', he said.[96] By that time, the centre of Te Taou occupation was in the area from Onehunga to Ihumatao, with seasonal shifts, for fishing or shellfish gathering, to Paruroa on the Manukau, and (more frequently) to Orakei and Kauri Point on the Waitemata.[97]

But the population never returned to its pre-1750 level. Historians of Maori Auckland have been inclined to attribute this to the impact of European diseases. They have spoken, for instance, of visitations of an epidemic disease Maori called rewharewha (thought to have been influenza) as having devastated inhabitants twice over, in approximately 1790 and 1810.[98] Maori oral traditions for Tamaki do not confirm this either way. There is firm evidence, however, that in the second half of the eighteenth century, settlement was relatively sparse, that hill forts were abandoned and that some former plantations were becoming overrun by fern and scrub. Good fishing and shellfish grounds probably drew Maori to settle by the shore.

A moderate population, possible military weakness, and more probably the need to stabilise relationships within the region, help to explain why Te Taou, like their Waiohua predecessors in days gone by, practised conciliation towards neighbouring tribes. As long as their claim to hold mana over the land from the Tamaki river to the Whau was recognised, Te Taou seemed prepared to readmit former people to occupy surplus land and to exercise rights to resources. This same mood led Te Taou, after its takeover of Tamaki, to seek peaceful diplomatic accommodations with its powerful Waikato and Hauraki neighbours. These links were strengthened by intermarriage between Ngati Whatua and the Waikato peoples of south Manukau.[99] The union in the nineteenth century of Te Hira, son of Te Kawau, and a Te Ata woman was by that time simply the continuation of a long-standing trend.[100]

IV

However, the attempt made by Te Taou to reach a diplomatic settlement with Ngati Paoa, the most powerful of its isthmus neighbours, proved less successful. For more than a generation, the new relationship between the two tribes, which followed upon a gift of land, imperilled rather than consolidated regional peace.

By the mid-eighteenth century, Ngati Paoa had expanded to establish itself on a number of gulf islands, including Waiheke, and on the western shore of the Firth of Thames almost as far as the Tamaki estuary.[101] It had been from this base, writes Taimoana Turoa, that Ngati Paoa had been able to 'launch an assault upon the peaceful Kawerau people', threatening to dislodge them from 'much of the coastal strip and islands commencing at Takapuna and extending north to the Whangaparaoa peninsula and Mahurangi'.[102]

Like its Waiohua predecessor, Te Taou felt it needed to treat this powerful Hauraki neighbour with caution. This conciliatory mood led Te Taou in the mid-1780s[103] to agree to an arrangement that Judge Fenton described as 'fruitful in disturbances'.[104] By this time, Ngati Paoa were securely settled on the eastern shore of the Tamaki estuary, and a smaller group of the tribe, after 'drifting about in the sea without any land', as Hengia poetically described it, 'took a small piece to live on' on the western shore, probably near modern Panmure.[105]

Two high-born women were responsible for moving Te Taou and Ngati Paoa into the new relationship. They were Te Tahuri,[106] a senior Te Taou chieftainess by virtue of marriage, yet of Waiohua descent, and Kehu her cousin, who was half Ngaoho, half Waikato.[107] The new phase began when Kehu came to Te Tahuri at Onehunga, to inform her that her (Kehu's) husband, Te Putu, leader of the small Ngati Hura hapu of Ngati Paoa, no longer wished to live at Whakatiwai among his kin with whom he had recently quarrelled. 'I have come to you', Kehu told Te Tahuri, 'that you may give me a place on which to kindle my fires.'[108] Here was a direct request for 'tuku whenua', a piece of gifted land which Ngati Hura could permanently occupy. Te Tahuri gave a large tract called Tauoma, on the west bank of the Tamaki estuary, running from about today's Point England to West Tamaki head (Glendowie), and extending inland as far as Lake Waiatarua, where the Ngati Hura hapu of Ngati Paoa was given the sole right to catch eels.[109] (It seems that, in anticipation of this particular grant of land being made, some of Ngati Hura had already settled at Tauoma, and planted a crop.) The effect of this grant, called by Ngati Whatua a 'koha' or gift, was also to formalise the existing Ngati Paoa settlement in the Panmure area. Kay Holloway, historian of Mount Wellington, believed the concession of land was astute.

> As the Ngati Whatua were unable to occupy all the pa that had been held by Wai-o-hua, this was undoubtedly a shrewd move to win the friendship of an ambitious neighbour and at the same time to place the new ally in a position to bear the brunt of any attempt by the Wai-o-hua and their relatives in the south to regain what they had lost.[110]

The hindsight provided by history, however, shows the gift to have been far from astute. The Ngati Paoa population grew so quickly that, within a generation, it threatened to outnumber that of Ngati Whatua on the isthmus. But, more seriously, as a result of this concession of land, two dissimilar tribes, both war-like, were now living cheek by jowl in Tamaki. Further, the powerful Northland iwi, Nga Puhi, was the traditional enemy of the Hauraki (Marutuahu) tribes to which Ngati Paoa belonged. A Ngati Paoa presence on the isthmus was, therefore, likely to act as a magnet to draw in Nga Puhi war parties in the years ahead. When Waikato chiefs first heard of the gift, they immediately prophesied trouble, saying, 'Now these two women will be drunken with tutu'.[111] Tauoma, in its unoccupied state, had a profuse growth of tupakihi, whose purple berries, called tutu, are intoxicating when fermented.[112] What these 'Waikato sages'[113]

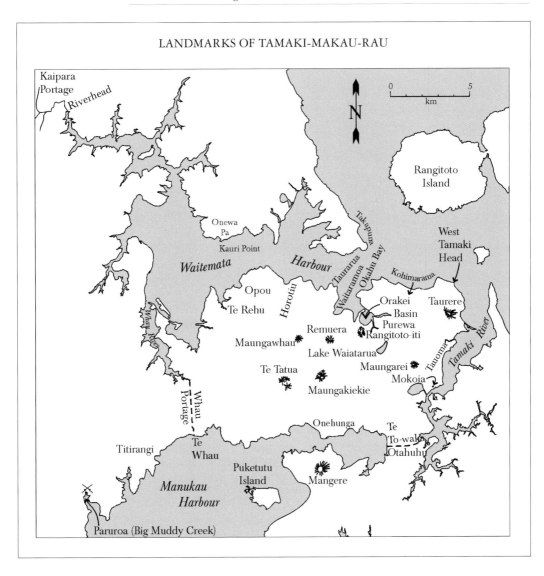

LANDMARKS OF TAMAKI-MAKAU-RAU

were metaphorically saying was that the two women involved in the gift had committed an act of supreme folly. In effect the chiefs were predicting (as Fenton expressed it) 'future quarrels and misfortunes as likely to result from the intrusion of a strange people into the hitherto compact territory, peopled alone by the cognate [Ngati Whatua] tribes'.[114]

The Waikato prophecy was fully borne out. And trouble came quickly. At a shark-fishing expedition, near Saddle Island at Mahurangi, held shortly after, members of the Ngaoho hapu of Ngati Whatua clashed with Ngati Paoa fishermen, albeit not of a hapu from Tamaki.[115] A quarrel broke out when the Ngati Whatua fishing party caught a shark which they laughingly named 'Te Haupo', after a Ngati Paoa chief. (Paora Tuhaere, in later years, considered this to be tantamount to a curse.)[116] At the time it enraged Ngati Paoa; for, likening the tapu head of a chief to a shark – generally regarded by Maori as ugly – was the grossest of insults.[117] During the fighting which followed, a number were killed on both sides, including Tarahawaiiki, son of Tuperiri and father of Apihai Te Kawau, who fell at Mori-oterariki pa. After this initial fighting, each side continued to feel aggrieved. The scene was set for a cycle of revenge attacks. Shortly after (1792), Ngati Paoa, with the assistance of Hauraki allies, clashed again with Ngati Whatua in battles first at Puponga on the northern Manukau coastline, and then at Rangimatarau (near Point Chevalier)[118] on the Waitemata. On both occasions, Ngati Paoa and its allies were defeated, at Rangimatarau heavily so. 'You may see hangis (ovens) to this day', grimly remarked Tamati Tangiteruru of Ngati Paoa, over seventy years later.[119] In 1793, Ngati Whatua of Tamaki called on Waikato allies from south Manukau to help in an attack on Ngati Paoa at Maraetai and on Waiheke island; but the initial engagements were inconclusive. Ngati Paoa warriors pursued Ngati Whatua to the mainland and fought a final pitched battle on the west bank of the Tamaki river at Orohe, near today's Churchill Park, Glendowie. Ngati Whatua were victorious there.

Although, as Fenton expressed it, 'the debtor and creditor account of slain appears to have been finally left unbalanced',[120] war weariness led to a peacemaking which ended the fighting between the two tribes. Ngati Whatua hegemony over Tamaki appeared established, and Ngati Paoa hapu returned to west Tamaki from which they had been temporarily ousted. Years of watchful peace followed. Fenton's last word on the matter is convincing: 'It is probable that both sides were for some time suspicious and in fear of each other, and kept as far apart as possible.'[121]

This forbearance of isthmus tribes towards each other was not unrelated to their shared awareness of the growing threat of Nga Puhi of the Bay of Islands.[122] Nga Puhi and the Hauraki tribes –

of which Ngati Paoa was, for geographical reasons, the most exposed – were enemies of long standing. Bad feeling between the tribes had been usually expressed in a spate of raids and counter-raids during which canoes and prisoners were taken. Feuding came to a head in 1793 when a Nga Puhi war-party appeared in the Hauraki gulf seeking satisfaction from Ngati Paoa for past Marutuahu (Hauraki) raids in Northland. In a pitched battle at Takapuna, Ngati Paoa were put to flight. Nga Puhi pursued fugitives to Waiheke Island and subsequently up the Wairoa valley as far as Clevedon. A reassembled Ngati Paoa war-party was then defeated at Takapuna with great loss of life. A further battle with another Nga Puhi force took place at the mouth of the Tamaki river, but with a different outcome. Nga Puhi fled defeated, leaving behind their canoes as booty.

Ngati Paoa still held a grudge for earlier defeats. Bent on revenge, it recruited from within its own tribe and within Ngati Maru a canoe-borne taua for an attack on Nga Puhi territory. This group landed at Waitangi in the Bay of Islands, and after advancing inland, confronted the Nga Puhi warriors at Waihariki. Nga Puhi were utterly defeated; many were slaughtered during both the battle and the later pursuit of refugees. The Hauraki force considered its past defeats avenged at last, not least because it had recovered Kaahua-mauroa, a great Ngati Paoa canoe that had been stolen in the early 1770s.

The war petered out in a series of lesser raids and counter-raids. At the end of the 1790s, 'a very shaky peace', was arranged between the antagonists.[123] With this peacemaking, Tamaki had freedom from invasion for over twenty years.

V

There is an oral tradition among Tainui Maori that, at some time during this era, Ngati Maniapoto invaded Tamaki and overthrew the two great fortresses of Maungakiekie (One Tree Hill) and Maungarei (Mount Wellington). The main published source for this episode is Leslie G. Kelly's *Tainui*. From calculations that arise mainly out of genealogy, Kelly states that this expedition took place 'at the beginning of the nineteenth century'.[124] However, the attack, according to the Maori sources used by

Kelly, was directed 'against the Waiohua . . . still in possession of Tamaki.'[125] But, as Kelly concedes, 'this can hardly be', since Ngati Whatua had already conquered Waiohua in the middle of the previous century. Kelly overcomes this apparent contradiction by surmising that, at the time of the Maniapoto invasion, a Waiohua remnant (Ngaoho or Uringutu?) were 'living at Maungakiekie' (and presumably at Maungarei) 'under the rule of their Ngati Whatua masters'.[126] What undermines this supposition is the incontrovertible evidence that, by the end of the eighteenth century, the fortifications of both of these great pa had fallen into disuse, and that neither was occupied by Waiohua survivors, or indeed by their Ngati Whatua overlords. By this time, Ngati Whatua of Tamaki had shifted their permanent settlements to the inner Manukau, while Maungarei had become part of the Tauoma territories of Ngati Paoa.

The account that now follows assumes, therefore, that if the invasion did take place (which one has little reason to doubt), it did so at some indeterminate time in the earlier half of the eighteenth century. Moreover, in spite of the uncertainty as to its exact timing, so entrenched is this episode in Maori lore, that it must be part of any account of pre-historic Auckland which aims at completeness from the Maori point of view.

The roots of the Ngati Maniapoto invasion of Auckland stretch as far back as the first quarter of the seventeenth century. At that time, a famous Ngati Maniapoto chief, Te Kawa-iri-rangi, came to live in Tamaki, where he married Maroa and Marei, twin sisters of great beauty and chiefly pedigree belonging to the Waiohua tribe.[127] While residing at Maungawhau, Te Kawa was treacherously murdered by a Waiohua brother-in-law.[128] For generations, this killing remained unavenged by Ngati Maniapoto, although that tribe made two unsuccessful attempts to exact blood payment.[129] Retribution finally came when two brothers, Maungatautari and Wahanui, descendants of Te Kawa, assembled a great war-party in the Ngati Maniapoto lands of the central North Island, and led an expedition north to attack the Tamaki tribes. According to Tainui traditions, these Maniapoto warriors, led by Wahanui, stormed Maungakiekie, subduing the seven separate sections of that formidable pa, one by one, until the defenders were completely defeated. 'Great numbers of the Tamaki people were killed in this attack', records Kelly.[130]

Shortly after, the great hill fort of Maungarei also fell to the Maniapoto expedition, although Kelly was unsure whether Wahanui himself took part in this particular action. But he states that:

> So many were killed on this occasion that the invaders were unable to eat them all, in consequence of which the slain were dragged to an ancient geyser mouth on the west side of the mountain [a lava cave since destroyed by quarrying] and there rolled in, hence the name Te Rua-potaka [the pit or grave for spinning tops] for that spot.

In modern times, a suburban marae and a primary school in the same district, have separately adopted the name Ruapotaka. Kay Holloway has observed that, given its gruesome provenance, Ruapotaka 'seems rather a strange name for a school'.[131] One can only agree.

CHAPTER III

Peace and War, c. 1800–21

I

By the end of the eighteenth century two forces were at work disrupting traditional Maori society. They will provide the backdrop to the present chapter.

First to appear, though the less important in its consequences, was the widening scope of tribal warfare. This trend had emerged during the eighteenth century in an era when traditional weapons (rakau-maori) were exclusively used, and battles were still the age-old, hand-to-hand encounters, virtually duels between warriors, fought mainly with mere (clubs) and taiaha (hardwood spears).[1] Not that there was necessarily an increase in warfare itself. In northern New Zealand, for instance, wars continued between Nga Puhi, Ngati Whatua and Hauraki iwi or between their subtribes, and seemingly on much the same scale as before. But even there a new element in warfare made its appearance. Whereas, in days gone by, tribal conflict tended to be contained within a region with warriors drawn from that region, the new trend was for battles to become enlarged, as combatants formed alliances which drew on tribes from outside regions, and from kinship zones greatly widened by exogamous marriages.[2] The result was large-scale battles, and, increasingly, long-range expeditions made by war-parties, some travelling over hundreds of miles. One of the first historians of the colony,

Dr A. S. Thomson, declared in 1859: 'All the great wars the New Zealanders [Maori people] of the present generation knew much about occurred not more than a hundred years ago.'[3] Until recently, historians had not provided satisfactory explanations for the origins of this phenomenon. Perhaps this increase in the scale of warfare had its genesis in population growth, leading to competition for scarce resources. Be that as it may, there is much to be said for Ballara's suggestion that perhaps 'the long-distance "musket" expeditions of the early 19th century were a continuation of a phenomenon that had become apparent for the first time in the late 18th century. The potential for destruction represented by muskets contributed to it and greatly accelerated it but did not initiate it.'[4] Furthermore, James Belich has provided a convincing connection between the later of these far-travelling taua and 'the agricultural revolution' (as he calls it) which manifested itself in 'the mass production of pigs and potatoes' that had set in by the second decade of the nineteenth century.[5] He goes on to explain that 'Potatoes helped feed long-range expeditions, to an extent limited by carrying capacity, and more importantly helped replace absent warriors in the home economy.' He concludes by suggesting that 'Potato Wars' might well be a more accurate label than 'Musket Wars'.

The reference to muskets, pigs and potatoes brings us to the second great agency of change, one that was ultimately to shake Maori society to its very foundations. This was contact with western society that began with the visit of Captain James Cook in 1769 to end centuries of physical isolation of Maori from the outside world. Explorers (like Cook) in search of knowledge[6] were followed by sealers and whalers in search of prey, and sea captains anxious to exchange western goods for provisions of food, timber and flax. In the process, westerners introduced into the country revolutionary products like the common potato and the pig as well as bringing to a Stone Age people new tools of iron, like axes and spades and nails. When, at the turn of the century, whaling got under way in the northern waters of New Zealand, the Bay of Islands became the part of the country which western visitors most frequently visited. There, and in other districts frequented by white men, a barter economy grew up enabling Maori to trade timber, flax, salted pork and potatoes, for prized iron goods and, increasingly, for muskets, powder

Kororareka beach, Bay of Islands, 1836. SHERRIN AND WALLACE

and shot. According to one early western observer, 'an axe in this country . . . before the introduction of powder and muskets, was the most valuable payment a New Zealander [as a Maori was then invariably called] could obtain.'[7] But when Maori found out how firearms could revolutionise tribal warfare, guns quite supplanted axes in the regard of the native people. 'A double-barrelled gun', remarked that same observer, 'in the opinion of a New Zealander, exceeds in value all other earthly possessions.'[8] The inequality in the number of western weapons possessed by rival tribes was ultimately to work great mischief among Maori. And especially was this so among the tribes of the Tamaki region.

If new commodities were the material expression of the impact of the west, its immaterial expression, so to speak, was the entry of infectious diseases to which Maori had no inherited immunity. As New Zealand's foremost demographer Ian Pool expresses it, confronted by these new 'pathogens', the Maori people were 'immunological virgins'.[9] Unsurprisingly, between 1769 and 1840 (when New Zealand became a Crown Colony) Maori numbers declined. Yet historians no longer speak of Maori people having been devastated by a 'fatal contact' with European diseases.[10] Nevertheless, the fall in population over the seventy-year period, while not so numerically great as was once imagined, was serious enough; and far more serious than mere totals indicate. The portents were ominous. Maori had moved from a trend of rising population in 1769 to one of continuing 'negative growth' by 1840; that is, the adult population had developed an inability to replace itself. Infectious diseases had played an important part in this decline, not only the obvious life-threatening diseases – venereal disease, tuberculosis and typhus – but also those lesser illnesses, such as the common cold, influenza and measles, which the indigenous people had never before encountered. Before 1840, when the European population was very small, the threat to Maori was, for the most part, potential rather than actual. Thereafter, once the settler population grew into the tens of thousands and was spread over a wide area, the Maori population, especially the vulnerable part of it that was made up by children, became dangerously exposed to endemic infection.[11]

There are other objections to the received view that the pre-1840 population decline among Maori arose out of the 'fatal contact' with European diseases. Introduced diseases are now seen as but one factor in causing the Maori population to fall, though arguably remaining a most important one. We should also notice that the extent of population decline varied from district to district, often reflecting the degree of western contact.[12] Nor should we forget the nefarious part in the process played by the musket wars, so devastating when one tribe had an excessive share of western weapons. But the point should be emphasised here that the forced migration of people and the general social turmoil were a more potent source of population decline than death through muskets. (The early muskets were notoriously inaccurate when fired from any distance.)

Because of the limited exposure of the Tamaki peoples to these European influences in the period before 1821, neither western diseases nor western muskets will figure prominently in this chapter. But it is logical that, having considered long-term population trends, we should look beyond the date with which this chapter finishes. The great solvent of traditional life in the region during the 1820s was the changed balance of power in northern Aotearoa brought about by the unequal share of guns possessed by Nga Puhi. This led, for example, to the slaughter of hundreds of Ngati Paoa and their abandonment of populous east Tamaki settlements. Ngati Whatua o Tamaki, on the other hand, were not directly exposed to slaughterous attacks of Nga Puhi. But their numerical decline must also be related to domination of the region by Nga Puhi, the tribe exercising a kind of tyranny of fear that persisted until the mid-1830s and beyond. As we shall see, Ngati Whatua o Tamaki became reduced in numbers, not directly through musket battles, but indirectly through flight from this Nga Puhi threat. This in turn led to the turmoil of constant migration, social dislocation, and recourse to inadequately nutritious food supplies, all with the probable consequence of reduced fertility.[13]

II

We are able to measure the impact of these forces of change on the tribes of Tamaki during the early nineteenth century much better than for the years before. After 1800 new evidence becomes available for the historian to supplement the oral record of the Maori. It comes from two main sources:

- the testimony given by aged Maori witnesses at hearings of the Native Land Court set up in 1865, who were able to recall what life was like in the region in the days of their youth; and
- the detailed accounts of Europeans visiting the region from 1820 onwards, describing at first hand the changes they observed taking place among Maori.

The sharp rise in our knowledge of Tamaki provided by these European visitors is closely related to the spread of Anglican missionary activity in northern New Zealand. Just before Christmas 1814, the Rev. Samuel Marsden, principal chaplain of the colony of New South Wales, arrived on the brig *Active* at the Bay of Islands to inaugurate the first mission in New Zealand.[14] When the time came for him to return to Sydney he left behind him at Rangihoua, a small bay near the northern headlands of the Bay, three lay missionaries, Thomas Kendall, William Hall and John King, whom he had entrusted to carry on the work of conversion. In 1819, Marsden came on a further visit, bringing with him his first ordained missionary, the Rev. John Butler, whom he installed at Kerikeri.[15] But it is because of his third and lengthy visit, which lasted from February to December 1820, that Marsden enters directly into the story of early Auckland.

On this particular occasion, Marsden came to the Bay of Islands on HMS *Dromedary,* after it had completed landing a consignment of 369 convicts at New South Wales. When this task had been completed, Admiralty officials ordered the ship to leave Port Jackson for the Bay of Islands in order to acquire a cargo of spars for the Royal Navy. Marsden was officially included in the ship's party as one who might be able to use his (by then) exceptional influence among Maori in northern New Zealand to secure the desired timber. Marsden is too complex a character to be captured by a thumbnail sketch here. But what is pertinent to this account of his nine-month visit in 1820 are his enthusiasm for investigative travel and his skill as an observer and recorder of the life and conditions of the Maori people in those districts through which he passed. Tamaki he visited twice. The first visit was during July and August 1820. After travelling to the Thames on HMS *Coromandel* – commissioned in that year to return to England with a cargo of kauri spars – Marsden made three separate side-trips to the Tamaki isthmus, and on one occasion proceeded overland, from there, by a further stage to the lower Kaipara.[16]

Samuel Marsden, 1765–1838. First European to cross the Tamaki isthmus.
AUCKLAND CITY
LIBRARIES

In November, he came to Tamaki once again from the Bay of Islands, this time in a whaleboat crewed by three fellow missionaries: James Shepherd, William Puckey and the Rev. John Butler. After completing an excursion to the Hauraki region, he sailed up the Tamaki river (Whangamakau) to make a thorough investigation of Mokoia, the main Ngati Paoa settlement there. After spending some time with his Maori hosts at Mokoia, Marsden, accompanied by Butler, made an overland crossing of the isthmus as far as the Manukau harbour, becoming (it is thought) the first Europeans to do so. Butler, who travelled separately from Marsden for some of the time that he was at Tamaki, included in his own journals a section recording his personal reaction to life on the isthmus. Although Butler's comments are somewhat artless, and much briefer than is Marsden's account, they nevertheless supplement usefully what the senior missionary has to say.[17]

These two missionary accounts are complemented by the journal of R. A. Cruise, who also recorded what life was like in Tamaki in 1820. Captain Cruise of the 84th (Foot) Regiment had been the officer in charge of the armed guard on the convict transport ship the *Dromedary* during its voyage from England to Australia. When the ship was detailed to collect its cargo of kauri spars, Cruise went too. Although he spent the greater part of his enforced stay in New Zealand in the Northland region, he made a visit to Tamaki as one of the party on the *Prince Regent* – a colonial launch[18] from Sydney which attended the *Dromedary* during its New Zealand stay – when it came down on official business to the Thames. While in New Zealand, Cruise apparently had much free time on his hands; and this he chose to use in close observation of the life and customs of the Maori people whom he chanced to meet. What he recorded was published in London three years later as *A Journal of a Ten Months' Residence in New Zealand*. Like Marsden, who had been his fellow passenger on the Tasman crossing, Cruise was a perceptive and sympathetic observer. But he was also a man of the world. This makes his urbane reactions to Maori life in the early nineteenth century a useful corrective to those sections of the missionary record, where Evangelical pieties have sometimes prevented the acceptance of the native people on their own terms.

III

These early European visitors remarked on three distinctive features which they considered were characteristic of the Tamaki region at this time. These were: material evidence of western influence in spite of very limited contact with European traders or missionaries, a low density of population, and a relative harmony among the resident tribes.[19]

Before 1820, Europeans were virtually unknown both in the Tamaki region and the land on the west coast between the Manukau harbour and the lower Kaipara. It astonished Marsden, for instance, when he first entered a Ngati Whatua village (near present-day Helensville) in August 1820, that the children were 'dreadfully terrified. They shrieked aloud and ran in all directions to hide themselves: screaming with all their might.'[20] Some months later, the Rev. John Butler recorded that his small party of Europeans, which visited a Maori settlement called 'Manukau' [Mangere?], had aroused extraordinary interest. 'No Europeans had ever been here before, and everyone, young and old, was eager, if possible, to touch the hem of our garments.'[21]

Yet in spite of the absence of direct contact of Tamaki Maori with Pakeha before 1820, farming in the region had already been transformed by the introduction of the common western potato and the pig.[22] The canoe network had proved an ideal medium for the transmission of these new commodities. One imagines they had come to Tamaki originally from the Hauraki region. (Te Horeta, the elderly Ngati Whanaunga leader, claimed that Captain Cook had introduced the potato into Coromandel, when long ago he 'gave the people a double handful of potatoes'.)[23] Whether canoe transport, which had obviously brought potatoes into Tamaki, had also brought in – as seems possible, though that fact remains unrecorded – contagious European diseases including the dreaded rewharewha, we do not know. But, by 1820, the western potato, a much heavier cropper than the kumara, and easier to cultivate and to store, was well established at Tamaki. As indeed it was, according to Marsden, in almost every district between the Bay of Islands and Tauranga which he visited that year.[24] Reporting on the Ngati Paoa settlement at Mokoia, beside the Tamaki river, in August 1820, Marsden wrote that 'their stores were full of potatoes, containing some thousands of baskets, and they had some very fine hogs'.[25] While walking the land between Mokoia and Maungarei (Mount Wellington) shortly after, John Butler formed an equally favourable impression of the gardens, catching sight of 'a fine tract of land, principally cultivated, and set with potatoes'.[26] Butler went on to ascend Mount Wellington, having first to pass through the overgrown earthworks of the abandoned pa. 'The prospect from the summit', he wrote enthusiastically, 'is grand and nobly pleasing. I observed twenty villages in the valley below, and, with a single glance, beheld the largest portion of cultivated land I had ever met with in one place in New Zealand.'[27] When, towards nightfall, Butler returned to Mokoia to link up with the remainder of the party led by Marsden, he had occasion to comment upon the western goods that the community did *not* have. He reported:

> The next thing to be done was to cook for supper, and the natives were very anxious to see this performed. Our utensils consisted of a frying-pan, an iron pot, and tea kettle. On seeing the flour, they were at a loss to know its utility; we fried pancakes, boiled pork, and made tea; and after supper, we handed the chiefs and their children some pancakes, who appeared very fond of it.[28]

Iron pots, pans, kettles and refined flour were utterly strange to these Maori. As well they might be.

For at that stage, because the inhabitants of Tamaki had virtually no direct trading with Europeans, few of the products of western technology and manufacture were yet to be seen. Marsden noticed 'a couple of muskets, and a few iron hatchets' but little else. This dearth explains why, on this occasion, Tamaki and Hauraki chiefs were particularly anxious for missionaries to come and work among their people: not particularly because missionaries brought the Gospel of Peace, but because it was expected that, as in the Bay of Islands, they would be the forerunners of a trading relationship that would bring in prized western goods.[29] Axes, knives, fishhooks, and above all else muskets (Cruise asserted) were commodities which, once seen by Maori, were forever after coveted. But missionaries were wanted for yet another reason. It was believed that once established, missionaries would also bring security,[30] for by their very presence they would fend off Nga Puhi attack. Cruise recorded that when an inter-racial party took place on board the schooner *Prince Regent*, while it lay off the Tamaki heads, visiting Ngati Paoa men and women sang extempore songs including

> one which they frequently repeated. It commemorated the arrival of the *Coromandel* in their part of the island [the Hauraki Gulf]; their hopes that other ships would come among them; and their wish that the white men would trade with them for muskets and powder, and thus enable their tribe to defend their wives, their children, and their koomeras,[31] from the invasion of their enemies.[32]

What this anecdote prophetically signifies is further illuminated in the reminiscences of F. E. Maning, a trader in the Hokianga in the 1830s:

> Here I must remark that in those days the value of a pakeha to a tribe was enormous. For want of pakehas to trade with, and from whom to procure gunpowder and muskets, many tribes or sections of tribes were about this time exterminated or nearly so by their more fortunate neighbours who got pakehas before them, and who subsequently became armed with muskets first. A pakeha trader was therefore of a value say about twenty times his own weight in muskets.[33]

F. E. Maning, 1811–83, Trader, Judge and Author.
SHERRIN AND WALLACE

Furthermore, Maori believed that a Pakeha of mana – be he trader or missionary – would help deflect the hostile attentions of neighbouring tribes.

The second feature of Tamaki that these first Europeans visitors found remarkable was the relatively small population, given the fertility of the land, in the setting of abundant evidence of past close settlement.[34] Much of the central isthmus which Marsden and Cruise observed lay uncultivated. Apart from isolated trees such as cabbage trees and nikau, and clumps of bush in steeper gullies, secondary growth had generally taken over. In many places, bracken fern, manuka and tupakihi were established where gardens had once been. Most of the hill forts had been abandoned. Settlement, no longer concentrated on the pa, had become more open, and tended to be located on those fertile areas of both harbours which were close to fishing grounds.[35]

As evidence heard during the Orakei hearing of the Native Land Court in 1868 made clear, this had become the distinctive pattern of settlement of Ngati Whatua of Tamaki who, in the early nineteenth century, held the mana whenua over the greater part of the isthmus.[36] Testifying of this era, Apihai Te Kawau, ariki of the Tamaki branch of Ngati Whatua (which took in Te Taou, Uringutu and Ngaoho), recalled that his tribe had its main gardens and permanent settlement on the upper Manukau at Onehunga and Ihumatao – where he himself was born.[37] In those days, said Te Kawau, Te Taou spent the greater part of the year at these Manukau settlements. Few of his people dwelt permanently in kainga (villages) on the Waitemata, where there were, however, important summer fishing and shellfish-gathering stations, with associated gardens, at locations such as Okahu and Orakei on the south shore of the harbour, and Onewa on its north. There were similar summer encampments at either end of the Whau portage, in the vicinity of today's Avondale and Green Bay where, for convenience, Ngati Whatua permanently left canoes. Te Taou, the dominant hapu, also had fishing stations on the northern shore of the Manukau, lying (roughly) between modern Laingholm and Huia. Te Taou witnesses testifying at the Orakei court reiterated that their tribe had made a point of following the age-old custom of regularly kindling fires on those fishing-station lands where they did not have permanent residents. In that way they demonstrated continuing occupancy of the sites and thereby preserved their traditional rights of possession.[38]

Numerically greater than Ngati Whatua of Tamaki, but much more confined in the land that they occupied, was a large branch of Ngati Paoa (mainly Ngati Hura) then living beside the Tamaki river. Marsden thought highly of these people. After his visit in August 1820 to the main settlement of Mokoia, he spoke of it as 'a very populous settlement, [which] contains the finest race of people I had seen in New Zealand, and very healthy. The houses are superior to most I have met with.'[39] Butler also spoke of the density of settlement of this group. At Mokoia (he wrote)

> The natives are very numerous. Enackee [Te Hinaki, the Ngati Paoa chief] informed me that there were as many as seven thousand men, women and children, but, judging it impossible for him to tell accurately, I put down four thousand, which I think, from observation, is near the mark.[40]

Captain Cruise, who had visited Mokoia some weeks before Butler, also remarked on the 'immense number of people [who] received us upon landing'[41] and this community (he noted) extended up and down the Tamaki river far beyond the main settlement of Mokoia. After leaving Mokoia on one occasion, he reported that his party 'pulled up the river for about three miles; the banks continued to be thickly inhabited, the ground flat, arable, and well cultivated, producing potatoes, koomeras, and in the more swampy places a great quantity of flax'.[42] Ngati Paoa appear to have spread their settlement as far as the Otahuhu portage, perhaps to the point where they were beginning to encroach on Te Akitai territory. In the opposite direction, their cultivations stretched north of Mokoia as far as Te Wharau (Achilles Point).

Any estimate today of Ngati Paoa numbers in Tamaki at that time would be sheer conjecture. But there is no doubt that, by 1820, the Ngati Paoa community occupied the most closely settled and intensively cultivated district in the region. Yet no attempt was made by Te Hinaki's tribe to challenge its Ngati Whatua neighbours. Taimoana Turoa, the Hauraki historian, believed that the strength of Ngati Whatua in their Kaipara homelands and the rising threat of Nga Puhi would have deterred the Tauoma people from adopting so provocative a course. At this time, hapu of Ngati Paoa, both on the gulf islands and on the mainland, avoided conflict with neighbours, intermarrying and often forming diplomatic alliances with them.

At the Otahuhu portage, the tangata whenua were the much smaller tribe of Te Akitai.[43] Their lands extended southwards from Otahuhu, with its rich, light volcanic soils, through Puhinui and Wiri, and on towards Papakura. Te Akitai lived, apparently, on good terms with their larger neighbours, and in 1821 were militarily allied to Te Taou.[44]

Te Taou also enjoyed harmonious relations with the people to the west of Te Akitai, the Waikato tribes on the southern shores of the Manukau harbour, such as Ngati Tamaoho, and Ngati Te Ata of the Waiuku region, whose territories extended as far as the Awhitu peninsula.[45] Te Kawau recalled in old age that, early in the century, Tamaoho and Te Ata used 'to come and catch sharks' on the Waitemata, and 'then return to their own settlements', although (as he emphasised) 'they did [not] make any cultivations or build houses during the time they came to fish for sharks'.[46]

This peaceful relationship between the tribes of Tamaki seemed, to the visiting Europeans in 1820, to be in so great a contrast to the sense of impending war elsewhere in north New Zealand, that they marked it out as a distinct regional characteristic. This was no new development. Free from external attack and internal conflict since the beginning of the century, Tamaki had enjoyed an interlude of two decades of relative stability that for those who lived through them must have appeared, in roseate hindsight, to be utterly unlike the unsettled half-century which went before them and the nightmarish years of the musket wars which followed. After hearing, in the 1860s, the recollections of elderly chiefs whose lives began in the eighteenth century, and who had also experienced, at first hand, life in Tamaki during the first decades of the nineteenth, Chief Judge Fenton was in no doubt that the tribes of this region 'were in a state of perfect amity at this time'.[47] The witnesses had told him of unfortified settlements and extensive kumara and potato gardens, tokens of a stable society; they spoke of shared seasonal encampments for shark fishing and pipi collection, and of criss-crossing of tribal boundaries.[48]

Good tribal relationships in the first decades of the century were not just a continuation of the tradition of co-existence that seemed to have appeared in the later years of the Waiohua hegemony.[49] The most significant factor in this situation was, surely, that the population continued to remain low after the Te Taou takeover. Whether this was a consequence of the contagion of European disease, such as rewharewha, as George Graham once suggested,[50] is open to serious doubt. If there were epidemics, that fact has remained unrecorded. What is not in dispute, however, is that there was a continuing, low density of population. Here we have the two economic preconditions for tribal harmony: an abundance of garden land, and no great pressure on sea resources. Ngati Whatua of Tamaki could afford, therefore, to be conciliatory. Provided neighbouring tribes acknowledged their mana whenua, they were ready to concede a share of the resources of the land and its adjacent seas.

Politically, the Tamaki peoples were doubly blessed. For not only was there little friction between them but, for about two decades, the isthmus was also spared all threat of armed incursion by outside tribes. That was the fortunate lot of the Tamaki people over these years.

The Tamaki economy in this period was a mixed one. It was 'mixed' in the traditional sense that gardening was combined with fishing and food gathering. But it was also mixed inasmuch as new modes of farming were now blending with old: the European potato was joining the kumara as the staple root crop, and pork was now supplementing fish as a main source of protein.

The kumara (which with taro, yam and the gourd had come from Hawaiiki) remained, as it had been since time out of mind, a food of fabulous origins. Serious religious rituals surrounded all aspects of its cultivation, from the planting of the first tubers to the lifting of the final crop. Cultivating the kumara was also labour-intensive and time-consuming. An early Auckland settler described it as a crop which required 'very great pains, care and attention: in cleansing the ground for the seed root, then protecting by fences and hedges the young plants from the winds, and during their growth, continually clearing the field from all weeds, and keeping the plants free from the large caterpillar [awhato], which is so destructive to them'.[51] But with the introduction of the potato, gardening in Tamaki was revolutionised. The potato had distinct advantages. A heavier cropper than kumara though less drought resistant, it tolerated a greater variety of soils, and was slower in exhausting them.[52] However, if agricultural productivity grew, so also did the demand for additional labour in the gardens, needed, moreover, for a greater part of the year. Kumara gardens traditionally delivered, at most, two crops a year. But in the mild Tamaki climate, potatoes could (and can) be planted in the late winter, and skilful Maori gardeners, with careful planning and staggered planting, could stretch production under optimum conditions to up to four crops a year.

Supplementary crops in these early years of cultural interaction became a combination of the traditional and the introduced. Marsden put it on record that 'sweet and common potatoes, with turnips and cabbages, constitute [the] principal food' of the Ngati Paoa people of Tamaki.[53] Celery was also established on their plantations by 1820.[54] By the time of the first permanent European settlers, the staple crops of the Maori gardens of Tamaki were: kumara, maize, taro, watermelon, pumpkin and potato.[55] Terry spoke of the cultivation of maize as having a dual purpose. He wrote:

> The natives cultivate maize for winter stock of food for themselves, and in many districts also for trade with the Europeans. For their own food, they steep the grains of ripe dry corn in fresh water for some days, until it becomes almost putrescent, then draw off the water and steam it over hot stones.[56]

Anticipating somewhat, we can note that, as the century went by, the potato, which initially took the place of traditional foods like fern-root and taro, later displaced the kumara itself from its pre-eminent position.[57] Richard Taylor, the missionary, recorded that, by 1855, the potato had become the 'staple article of food' for Maori,[58] adding that, 'it is now more universally cultivated than the kumara'. In this instance, Taylor was speaking of New Zealand in general. But there is abundant anecdotal evidence that, in colonial times, this development was equally true for Maori in the Auckland region.

The introduction of the pig, while less disruptive of traditional Maori farming practices, had become, by 1820, a significant aspect of the Tamaki economy. In contrast to the Bay of Islands, where pigs were often kept by local tribes as a commodity for bartering with visiting ships, the tribes of Tamaki obviously farmed pigs for their own consumption. Pigs, though highly valued, were not usually penned. In north New Zealand as a whole, they were allowed by their owners, according to one observer, to 'run wild in the woods',[59] or to range about in the bracken until the time came for them to be rounded up. Then, wrote Captain Cruise, they were 'caught with much difficulty and with the assistance of [native] dogs'. Marsden thought this practice of allowing pigs to range freely was much the best way of rearing them. 'Hogs in New Zealand', he wrote, 'get very fat on fern-root alone. They require no grass to feed them, and their meat is of the best quality.'[60] (Fern-root had the additional merit of being a food resource of 'inexhaustible abundance'.)[61] Although only relatively recently introduced into the Hauraki gulf area, pigs multiplied with great rapidity. During the late 1830s, Bully Webster, the famous Pakeha-Maori on the Coromandel coast, consigned to the Australian colonies cargoes of casked, salted pork made up from the hogs which he had bought from local Maori.[62] Pigs were to be plentiful in colonial Auckland, too. In the winter of 1840, the pioneer merchant, Logan Campbell, bought with little difficulty or delay, from Apihai Te Kawau (probably acting on behalf of Te Uringutu, who at the time worked Puketutu Island as a large pig farm) a herd of sixty hogs to run on the island of Motukorea.[63] (Campbell was furious when these pigs were later stolen by, he suspected, a couple of impudent, ex-convict rustlers.)[64] Pork and

potatoes supplied by local Maori, according to Campbell's reminiscences in old age, were the staple diet and 'the oft-told menu'
of Auckland's pioneer Pakeha colonists in 1841.[65]

Back in the early years of the nineteenth century, however,
pork was no rival to fish in the Maori diet. Speaking of the
northern part of New Zealand in general, Cruise observed that
Maori consumed fish 'in great abundance',[66] and he included
under that heading, 'an immense quantity of cockles [pipi]'. The
practice of preserving fish by sun drying (without salt) ensured
that it was available for eating, together with shellfish (also preserved), far beyond the fishing season and well into the winter
months. Marine resources were especially important for the
people of Tamaki. Tamaki's isthmus location and its enclosing
harbours with their rich harvest of moana kai made them so.
Records of the early nineteenth century speak of a close network
of fishing stations some of which, as we have seen, Ngati
Whatua were prepared to share with their Ngati Paoa[67] and
Waikato neighbours. Whether this custom had grown out of
invitations made in the distant past, or out of kinship links
through marriage, or both, is not known. But it stands as further
proof of the friendly relations of the tribes of the isthmus and of
neighbouring lands.

IV

In these years before the musket wars, the annual round for those
members of the local tribes directly involved in the production
of food[68] began with the planting of the first potato tubers about
late June or early July. From this point, the demands upon
labour in the main gardens, whose aggregated size must be calculated in hundreds of hectares, would have been constant and
unremitting. Garden duties which, after the initial digging,
were mainly borne by women and slaves (men, women and older
children), consisted of work such as fine tilling, heaping up of
mounds, weeding, removing pests, preparation of brushwood
fences as windbreaks, and the like. Women of rank continued to
supervise gardens. Te Kawau once spoke of leaving women in
charge of his Mangere gardens after the initial planting when,
late in the winter of 1821, he set out with Te Taou warriors on a

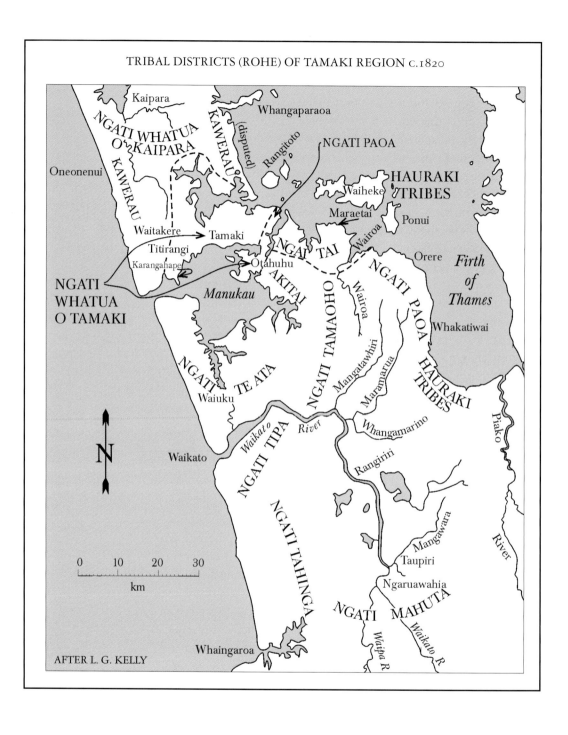

TRIBAL DISTRICTS (ROHE) OF TAMAKI REGION C.1820

Kaipara

NGATI WHATUA O KAIPARA

KAWERAU

(disputed)

Whangaparaoa

Rangitoto

NGATI PAOA

Oneonenui

KAWERAU

HAURAKI TRIBES

Waiheke

Maraetai

Ponui

Waitakere

Tamaki

Titirangi

Karangahape

Otahuhu

NGAI TAI

AKITAI

Manukau

Wairoa

Orere

Firth of Thames

NGATI WHATUA O TAMAKI

NGATI PAOA

Whakatiwai

NGATI TE ATA

NGATI TAMAOHO

Mangatawhiri

Maramarua

HAURAKI TRIBES

Waiuku

Piako

NGATI TIPA

Waikato River

Whangamarino

Rangiriri

Waikato

NGATI TAHINGA

Mangawara

Taupiri

Ngaruawahia

River

NGATI MAHUTA

Whaingaroa

Waipa R.

Waikato R.

N

0   10   20   30
km

AFTER L. G. KELLY

prolonged campaign of war.[69] Normally, after the first planting of main gardens had been completed, working parties would go to fishing or food-gathering stations, located on both harbours, to prepare ground and plant tubers in subsidiary gardens there, so that an early crop would be ready for lifting at the beginning of the fishing season in late November. But specifying actual times when such things happened can be tricky, because movement about encampments, which could extend over a period of three months, often depended on the peak of migration of schools of fish, such as snapper, shark and kahawai, which fluctuated from year to year.[70] Fishing by line, usually from canoes, was, for reasons of tapu, a male preserve, although women could be members of teams involved in netting from beaches. But the main marine occupation of the women at these summer encampments was shellfish gathering.

Autumn activity meant for some a return to the permanent gardens, and for others a movement to the bush[71] for berry picking (hinau, karaka, tawa, and tutu) and food gathering (kiekie, cabbage-tree, nikau). This was also the season for rounding-up the free-range pigs. Other kinds of food gathering were not seasonal but could continue over much of the year – eeling,[72] catching birds, collecting fern-root, and gathering wild vegetables such as wild swede, cress and sow thistle (puha). The climax of the yearly round was the lifting of the final root crop in late April or May. This was celebrated by a special feast or hakari, in this case a kind of lavish harvest home, but one with great spiritual significance.[73]

Winding down the productive year saw a rechannelling rather than a reduction of labour. There was much to do. Food and crops must be gathered together in order that they could be moved into storehouses, to be available over the lean months of winter and early spring. Kumara would be shifted into roofed pits – these were frequently re-located and re-dug to guard against fungus infection.[74] Potatoes were buried for storage; seed tubers separately stored, just as they had been separately grown in their own gardens; dried shark, shellfish and eels, together with preserves of flesh, such as birds, cooked in their own fat and stored in gourds; all were moved into their appropriate store-places. This was the time, too, for laying up stocks of fern-root, both as a staple food and as a hedge against famine. Autumn's end also gave the opportunity for bush and scrub to be cleared, usually at least a year in advance, in preparation for new gardens, say, for kumara – three successive years of cropping were usually enough to exhaust existing sites.[75]

V

This then was the annual round of the people of Tamaki, during the first two decades of the nineteenth century, at a time when the region was at peace. But it was a relative peace rather than an absolute one. Sir Peter Buck has equated the most enduring kind of peace enjoyed by prehistoric Maori to a greenstone door, a tatau pounamu. Greenstone could play a special role in peace-making. The exchange of mere pounamu (greenstone hand-clubs) – often prized, mana-filled, tribal heirlooms – was thought to impart solemnity and sincerity to the peace-making.[76] Since greenstone is imperishable (Buck explains), it can, metaphorically speaking, provide a door that can be permanently shut against war and so furnish in the space behind, a sanctuary where women, children and the unprotected could shelter.[77]

There was no greenstone door at Tamaki, in spite of the tribes of the isthmus having been in apparent concord, and free from external attack, for two decades or more. There was not the intimacy of relationship between, say Ngati Whatua and Ngati Paoa – each part of wider, potentially hostile confederations – that had existed between the resident tribes of the Waiohua confederation a century before. Indeed, by 1820, the threat from without, which had never quite gone away since the mid-1790s, was menacing once again. And the two main hapu of Tamaki, Te Taou of Ngati Whatua and Ngati Hura of Ngati Paoa had, long since, been drawn into conflict with outsiders, either through enduring vendetta, or through the enlarging scale of tribal war (the powerful impersonal agent of change mentioned earlier in this chapter). Further, there is the paradox that, in spite of the prevailing internal peace in Tamaki in 1820, there could be no doubt as to the warlike propensities of either the two dominant chiefs of the region, or the tribes which they led.

Consider what Marsden had to say about Ngati Paoa during his first visit to their settlement at Mokoia in August 1820:

'[M]ost of the fighting men were gone on a war expedition to the southward.'[78] Or his description of Te Hinaki, on first meeting that senior chief at Mokoia:

> Enakee is a great warrior, a very fine, tall, handsome man, apparently
> about thirty-six years of age, and has been in many actions.
> Mr. Anderson [first mate of HMS *Coromandel*] and I had the curiosity
> to count the scars on his body, which he had received from spear
> wounds, and found them to amount to fifty. One of his front teeth
> had been knocked out with a patoo-patoo [club] and another
> broken.[79]

Marsden did not report how these injuries came about. Some, undoubtedly, had resulted from the internecine feuds of the Marutuahu tribes of Hauraki which had long been their undoing. (During this particular visit to the Hauraki gulf, Marsden had offered to act as peacemaker between two such tribes on either side of the Firth of Thames, Ngati Whanaunga and a branch of Ngati Paoa.)[80] Equally likely, wounds could have been suffered, because the Ngati Paoa hapu of Tamaki – Ngati Hura and Matikiwhao – had been drawn into conflicts that were the response of the Hauraki tribes to the growing Nga Puhi threat. As Taimoana Turoa observed, for the first time in generations, the Marutuahu tribes had become, by the end of the eighteenth century, 'the defenders and not the aggressors in their [Hauraki] realms'.[81]

Apihai Te Kawau, the paramount chief (ariki) of Tamaki, was even more renowned as a warrior than was Te Hinaki.[82] In or about 1807, while still in his early twenties, he had been the brilliant second in command to Te Murupaenga ('considered one of the greatest warriors in New Zealand', remarked Marsden),[83] when that chief had led a northern war-party to assist the chiefs of the Waikato iwi who had appealed to them for help. At that time, Waikato were confronted, and outnumbered, by a huge combined force which Ngati Toa – a traditional enemy then resident in the Kawhia region – had drawn together from many parts of the North Island. In what has been considered as the greatest battle fought in Aotearoa before the advent of muskets, these two great armies clashed at Lake Ngaroto, close to today's Highway 3, and some five kilometres north of Te Awamutu.[84] The Waikato tribes and their northern allies, under the great warrior chief Te Rau-anga-anga, won a mighty victory over their more numerous invaders, who proved to be in the field an unwieldy and uncoordinated host. During the battle and the subsequent rout, large numbers of the invading warriors were slaughtered, their means of escape being cut off by swamp and lake. Among the dead who lay thickly on the battlefield, writes Phillips, were 'scores of high chiefs from distant tribes, distinguished by the fine parrot-feather cloaks they wore'.[85] That is why this epic action has come down to the present day, in Maori lore, as Hingakaka, 'the fall of the [bright-plumaged] parrots'. (There are, however, other possible explanations for the name given to this epic battle.)[86]

Shortly after Hingakaka, Te Kawau and his Tamaki warriors are said to have joined with Te Murupaenga's men once again, in a famous action against a Nga Puhi expedition at Moremonui, on the west coast, north of the Kaipara harbour heads, where Ngati Whatua inflicted a heavy defeat on Nga Puhi.[87] It is also likely that Te Kawau and the Tamaki branch of Ngati Whatua were drawn into some of the affrays arising out of the continuing feud between Nga Puhi and Ngati Whatua of Kaipara, which smouldered on for a number of years after this battle.

Te Kawau's reputation as a warrior chief was unassailably established when, during 1820–21, he became a joint leader of the taua which embarked on a long-range campaign, called by Maori, Te Amiowhenua, 'the circling of the land'.[88] The cause of this prolonged expedition, which was brought together by Tukorehu of Ngati Maniapoto, is obscure. The most northerly recruits, Ngati Whatua warriors from Kaipara, who were ultimately to travel over 1500 kilometres, on passing through Tamaki picked up a further contingent of 100 under Te Kawau's command, mainly Te Taou, but with other elements such as Te Akitai.[89] As the expedition went up the Waikato, and travelled overland towards Rotorua – thus far by canoe – braves from other tribes joined. By the time all elements in the war-party had made their rendezvous in Heretaunga, in Hawkes Bay, the taua had a complement of 600. It had become a truly inter-tribal group, drawing upon many hapu and iwi, including Ngati Raukawa, Ngati Maru and Ngati Tuwharetoa. Tukorehu, a renowned warrior, and Te Kawau were the acknowledged leaders. In speaking of Te Kawau's credentials as a warrior chief, we can note that, during this prolonged campaign, he is said to have habitually used a basket of human flesh for a pillow.[90] It should be recalled, however, that the source of this oft-repeated grisly story is the not-always-reliable Percy Smith who, after attributing the information to a Maori folklorist, qualified it with an unconvincing disclaimer: 'Probably this was a mere façon de parler' (manner of speaking).[91]

The group was equipped with only a few muskets, enough, however, to spread dismay and alarm among those who were initially attacked. But most battles were fought with, and decided by, traditional weapons. The taua first ravaged Hawkes Bay. But with that region subdued, the expedition did not stop. Whatever its original cause – one suggestion is that it would have been originally undertaken to avenge past deaths – it soon acquired a dynamism of its own, almost becoming transformed into a war-party of mercenaries. It broke through the Manawatu Gorge, and overran the country as far as Wairarapa.[92] Whole communities deserted their villages, retreating into remote areas and the bush. Those who failed to escape were usually massacred.

After eventually reaching Te Whanga-nui-a-tara (Wellington harbour), the raiders began to work their way homewards up the west coast of the lower North Island, fighting a number of actions, not all successful – especially was this so after the taua moved northwards from modern Wanganui. In Taranaki, the invaders suffered their first major setback. Those who had massacred others had now to fight desperately for their own lives, as resolute Ati Awa warriors, drawn from Waitara and thereabouts, finally penned them in, in Pukerangiora pa. This besieged pa has come down in Maori history as raihe-poaka (the pigsty), a name of derision which tells its own story. With provisions running short, Tukorehu appealed to the Waikato iwi for help. Te Wherowhero (Potatau),[93] the great Waikato warlord, came with a relieving force of Ngati Mahuta, Ngati Haua and Ngati Maniapoto. But he was checked en route when the famous Ngati Toa general, Te Rauparaha, at the battle Okoki, not far from the besieged pa, defeated him.[94] But for reasons that Maori tribal historians still dispute, Te Rauparaha decided not press home his advantage, and allowed Potatau to carry on to Waitara and lift the siege.

Thus extricated, elements of the weary taua made their separate ways home. On passing through the Waikato lands, Te Kawau learned from a remnant of Ngati Paoa, who had taken refuge there, the alarming news that, while the war-party had been away, Nga Puhi had destroyed the two great fortresses of Mokoia and Mauinaina, and had annihilated the Ngati Paoa settlements beside the Tamaki river. Te Kawau also learned that the members of his own tribe, Ngati Whatua of Tamaki, though as yet unmolested by Nga Puhi, were in fear that their turn was at hand. With their only pa, at Mangere, still under construction and incomplete, Ngati Whatua felt particularly vulnerable.[95] Once Mokoia had fallen, the Ngati Whatua inhabitants of Tamaki had evacuated the isthmus completely. Te Kawau and his followers joined them at their refuge at the south Manukau heads. Recalling this time, one of the Tamaki chiefs, who had returned with Te Kawau after the Amiowhenua campaign, remarked: 'Who would [now] live in Orakei in fear of Ngapuhi?'[96] This explains why Te Kawau and his followers vacated the Tamaki isthmus and sought refuge among the tribes on the south Manukau heads.

The era of peace had ended in Tamaki.

CHAPTER IV

War from the North, 1821–26

I

War was at the centre of traditional Maori life.[1] 'The study of war', wrote an early observer of pre-1840 Maori, was 'the primary instruction' of every boy.[2] 'From the earliest years of infancy', each male child (wrote George Graham) 'imbibed the warrior spirit' and was 'trained in the art of war'.[3] And yet it has also been persuasively argued that while pre-contact Maori were 'not slow in seeing causes for strife', especially when the issue had been 'brooded over' for some time, they 'shuddered at striking the first blow, and in every dispute mediators were gladly accepted until blood was actually shed'.[4] Even after war had actually broken out, the path to reconciliation was often kept open, so that should the combatants weary of strife, peacemaking could be conducted by emissaries, who would enjoy safe conduct even in the most hostile of territories. And if those emissaries were related by blood to one or both of the quarrelling tribes, then the prospects for peace would be all the more assured. Traditionally, the most enduring peace was one where there was a 'binding' through an arranged marriage between a man and a woman of chiefly rank drawn from each of the contending tribes. A chieftainess who took part in just such an irenic union in 1823, confirmed, while giving evidence in court, that there was a 'Maori saying that a peacemaking made by giving a woman is never to be broken'.[5]

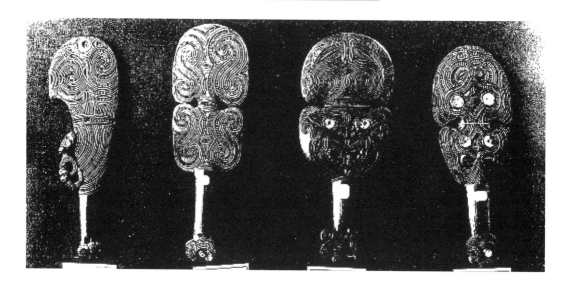

If, before the advent of the musket, a willingness to negotiate had been a curb on warfare, similarly effective had been the emergence of a rough parity of strength between tribes or between groups of tribes in alliance. To attack even a small tribe could involve risks if that tribe had powerful allies.[6] In brief, a resort to war usually carried the real danger of ultimate defeat. This 'precarious balance of power' meant that, not infrequently, in spite of the provocation of insults or treachery, tribes would either decide against war to 'equalise an utu account', or delay a retaliatory expedition to do so, perhaps for decades. It is mistaken, therefore, to regard the age-old custom of utu simply as a crude incitement to war. Reinforced by tapu, rahui and other prohibitive conventions, it could work in the opposite direction and stabilise relationships by preventing, in A. W. Reed's phrase, 'wanton contempt for law and order in the community' and, through its threat of retribution, prevent a hasty resort to armed conflict.

However, the rules (so to speak) of the game of war had changed entirely by the 1820s. By then, tribes from the Bay of Islands, and their neighbours, had acquired the lion's share of the firearms in Maori hands in Aotearoa. As a result, the deterrent effect of the former parity of power quite disappeared. Having 'cornered the firearms market',[7] northern tribes could now travel south, armed with muskets, to pay back old scores, with the added bonus of 'easy plunder'.[8] For a generation, New Zealand became one great battlefield. Warfare intensified, became widespread; tribes were destroyed, or put to flight; mass migrations were set in motion.[9] Nor was Tamaki spared. For over fifteen years, a region of over a hundred miles around the isthmus was in turmoil.

Let us go forward here two decades to 1840, to the beginning of British rule of New Zealand. Two circumstances at that time particularly encouraged Captain Hobson, the first governor, to choose Tamaki as his site for the permanent capital of the colony. First, although Tamaki was still the epicentre of a wide region of heavy Maori settlement, the isthmus itself had few native inhabitants. Second, Ngati Whatua of Tamaki, the tribe holding the customary title to Tamaki, was particularly anxious that the governor should set up the seat of government within their district (rohe). This state of affairs is directly attributable to the musket wars which, for a number of years, had uprooted the inhabitants of Tamaki and propelled them into a life of constant migration, converting the isthmus into a virtual population void. These musket wars give us the key, therefore, to an understanding of how Tamaki-makau-rau of the Maori came to be Auckland of the Pakeha. And here we come to a paradox: in none of the three bloody battles which were decisive in shaping this situation – Mauinaina, Matakitaki and Te Ika-a-ranganui – were the warriors of Ngati Whatua of Tamaki, customary owners of Tamaki, directly involved. The impact of these battles upon the people of Tamaki was enormous just the same.

Hongi Hika, 1772–1828.
AUCKLAND CITY
LIBRARIES

II

No person did more to destroy the peace of Tamaki than the Nga Puhi chief, Hongi Hika (1772–1828).[10] A squat but physically powerful man of commanding presence, Hongi comes down in history as both a famous and an infamous leader. He was famous for his bravery, intelligence and guile. He became infamous because his vaulting ambition and vengeful nature combined to make him extraordinarily treacherous and cruel. Much of Tamaki's travail during the 1820s can be seen through the career of this ardent musket-warrior.

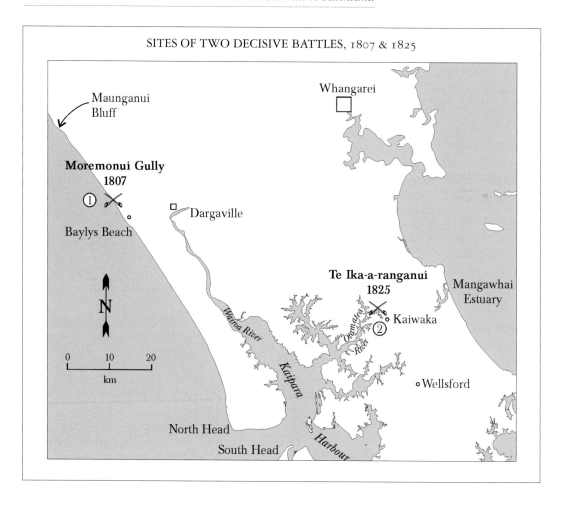

SITES OF TWO DECISIVE BATTLES, 1807 & 1825

Scion of Nga Puhi's senior chiefly line, Hongi unexpectedly rose to the paramountcy of his iwi in the Bay of Islands in 1807, when his predecessor, the famous war leader, Pokaia, was killed at the battle of Moremonui, which was touched on in a previous chapter. Although this particular action took place over 200 kilometres north-west of Tamaki, the consequences for the isthmus were so far-reaching that more must now be said about this engagement. Perhaps the best known of all Maori proverbial sayings is 'By women and land are men lost'. So it could well have been in this particular case. A credible source attributes the vendetta that led to this bloody battle to 'the misconduct' of a daughter-in-law of Pokaia, the Nga Puhi chief, with a Ngati Whatua man living in Kaipara.[11] A cycle of revenge raids is said to have followed which culminated in a full-scale war once Pokaia had assembled a great taua to attack the Kaipara people.[12] But Ngati Whatua scouts alerted their chiefs to the warpath of the invaders, who had decided to make their final approach to the Northern Wairoa river, not by the usual Kaihu valley route, but along the sands of the west coast beach.[13] The track they used to reach this beach ran along the gully of the Moremonui stream, the mouth of which lies some twenty kilometres south of Maunganui Bluff. There, in that part of the gully where the stream makes its last meanders towards the beach, Ngati Whatua executed an ambush. Thus began the Maori battle in which muskets, some say, were used for the first time,[14] although they were so few in number that they had no significant influence on the outcome of the action. At a pre-arranged signal, Ngati Whatua warriors, who had hidden in the tall scrub, flax and toi-toi shrouding the lower part of the gully, fell upon the unsuspecting Nga Puhi taua. After killing many warriors in the initial ambuscade, Ngati Whatua drove the remainder of the invaders onto the beach. In the pitched battle that then took place, Pokaia was killed. Nga Puhi fled in panic. But many were trapped. Escape was difficult, with the sea on one side and, on the other, a steep crumbling cliff-face. It was a crushing defeat. So numerous were the corpses of the invading force, that the Ngati Whatua victors were unable to eat them all, and had to leave many carcasses as carrion for scavenging black-backed gulls to devour. Hence the name given to this battle 'Te Kai-a-karoro' (the seagulls' feast).[15]

In March 1999 I walked the six kilometres south from Omamari along the sandy west coast beach that took me to Moremonui Gully. There was not a soul in sight. An Historic Places Trust plaque at the foot of the steep valley near the stream's mouth marked the site of the battle, now in the midst of quiet farmland. Yet it eerily recalled the violent episode that took place almost two centuries before. Flax and concealing scrub still shrouded the stream, whilst on the beach, beside the stream as it seeped through the sand to the sea, gulls stood motionless waiting patiently for food as they have done, one imagines, for time out of mind.

Among those who fell with Pokaia were a number of Hongi's relatives, including two of his brothers. Hongi himself was forced to flee to save his skin. Moremonui became the turning point in his life. As Pokaia's successor, he brooded over that Nga Puhi defeat, burning to avenge it. But he bided his time; for years.

Minor campaigns, which Hongi conducted against certain neighbouring tribes in the north over the next decade, convinced him that the muskets of the Pakeha had become crucial to victory in war. He set about acquiring guns by encouraging trade with Europeans and Americans, especially with the crews of whaling ships which, with increasing frequency, began visiting that part of the Bay of Islands where he lived. He encouraged missionaries to come there, too. And when they were installed, he acted as their protector. It was his belief, justified in the event, that when the Bay of Islands became known as a stable centre of trade, sea captains and traders from the metropolitan world would come in even greater numbers. With these people he built up a huge barter trade. He exchanged timber, flax and pigs and, above all, great stocks of potatoes (grown on large plantations around Taiamai and Pouerua,[16] often tended by slaves who had been captured in war) for guns and powder, and also for iron tools such as spades which, in turn, he could use to expand his agricultural production and so provide the means of buying yet more guns.

By 1817, Hongi and certain other northern chiefs began a series of raids to the south with war parties armed with muskets. They ravaged tribes in the Bay of Plenty, the East Coast, the Coromandel peninsula and the Firth which that peninsula enclosed (then called 'The Thames'). Forays were also made, nearer to hand, into the Kaipara region. But for the time being, Tamaki tribes were spared. This was soon to change. In March 1820, Hongi and his Nga Puhi relative, Waikato, sailed with the missionary Thomas Kendall to England, where they had been invited to assist an eminent Cambridge philologist, Professor Samuel Lee, in the compilation of a Maori dictionary. While in England, Hongi played the part of the devout Christian deceptively well. He also became a social lion. Prominent people, from King George IV downward, generally made a great fuss of him. He was given many gifts, including a set of regimentals (a scarlet military uniform) and a suit of medieval armour, which he was later to wear in battle in New Zealand. At a stopover in

Sydney on his way home (May–June 1821), he added significantly to his armoury of guns. He sold many of the gifts he had acquired in England and reconverted the money thus gained into further muskets.

While in Sydney, Hongi met two visiting Hauraki chiefs, Te Horeta of Ngati Whanaunga (a man sufficiently elderly that he could remember having met Captain Cook)[17] and Te Hinaki of Ngati Paoa. Among Hauraki Maori, there is a tradition that when Te Hinaki asked Hongi, 'Mo hea engei ou pu?' (Where are your guns for?),[18] Hongi gave a 'vengeful reply', making no attempt to conceal his 'smouldering malice'.[19] He answered: 'Mou aku pu!' (For you are my guns!) This was no 'veiled threat'.[20] Hongi was bent on revenge for what he considered had been the humiliating defeats which Ngati Paoa and Ngati Maru, and their allies, had inflicted on Nga Puhi in years gone by. In his account of this incident, Percy Smith (repeating the information passed on to him by Hoani Nahe, the eminent nineteenth-century Ngati Maru folklorist) says that Hongi then went on to exhibit to the two Hauraki chiefs

> all his guns and powder brought from England, arranging the former in rows, and giving each its name, saying: – '*E mara ma!* O friends! O Te Horeta! and Te Hinaki! Behold! this gun is "Te Wai-whariki",[21] this is "Kaikai-a-te-karoro",[22] this is "Wai-kohu", this is "Te Ringa-huru-huru", this is "Mahurangi"' thus naming all the battles in which Nga-Puhi had been defeated.[23]

Hongi called his own private musket 'Patu-iwi' (killer of iwi). It was aptly and prophetically named. On his return to New Zealand, Hongi turned immediately to planning his campaigns of revenge and conquest. Nga Puhi had already begun to ravage Te Horeta's lands. But it was against Te Hinaki's tribe in Tamaki that Hongi prepared to make his first great strike.

III

Mindful of Hongi's threats, it was with well-justified alarm that, in July 1821, Te Horeta and Te Hinaki had returned to New Zealand.[24] Te Hinaki warned his Tauoma branch of the Ngati

Paoa people that Nga Puhi attack was now inevitable. The tribe began to lay in great stocks of food in readiness for a siege, and strengthened its recently built twin pa of Mauinaina and Mokoia, by throwing up about them additional great earth-works.[25] As for Hongi, on his return to the Bay of Islands, he was provided with fresh intelligence that gave him an added incentive to attack the Ngati Paoa settlements on the west bank of the Tamaki river.

In the early winter of 1821, whilst Hongi had been still abroad, the Nga Puhi chief, Te Koperu, had been killed at, or near, Mauinaina pa (versions differ on this point), while leading an expedition to Tamaki from the Bay of Islands. Surviving oral accounts also conflict as to whether the chief was on a friendly visit, or whether he was, in fact, leading a raiding party. The accounts stressing Te Koperu's peaceful intentions usually go on to relate his 'treacherous murder' by a Ngati Paoa chief, Te Paraoa-rahi.[26] A different version of this episode has been provided by other sources, usually coming from those who were living in the Tamaki district at that time. Apihai Te Kawau who, on this matter, could be regarded as an impartial witness, testified in the Native Land Court many years later that the Nga Puhi chief had been killed, 'while destroying a plantation'.[27] Shortly after the killing, Te Koperu's brother, Te Morenga, made a night-time attack on Mauinaina, in order to exact revenge. Te Kawau had himself taken part in this action, having responded to a plea for assistance, which had been sent to him at his pa in Onehunga by his sister Roherohe, who was then living at Mauinaina.[28] Te Kawau is said to have arrived at the pa the day before it was about to be attacked, bringing with him a hundred Ngati Whatua warriors drawn from three local hapu.[29] But whether Apihai's claim that 'I saved the pa' is justified, is not now known.[30] Anyway, the assault on the pa was not a full-scale battle. In the opinion of Apihai's lieutenant, Warena Hengia, who was also there, it was not much more than 'a sortie'.[31] Only four of Apihai's men were killed,[32] though rather more of the Ngati Paoa warriors whom he was helping. Nevertheless, when Te Morenga arrived back in the Bay of Islands on 29 July 1821, two days before Hongi returned from England, he still did not consider that his somewhat abortive attack on Mauinaina had given adequate utu (recompense) for the death of Te Koperu. Nor did Hongi.

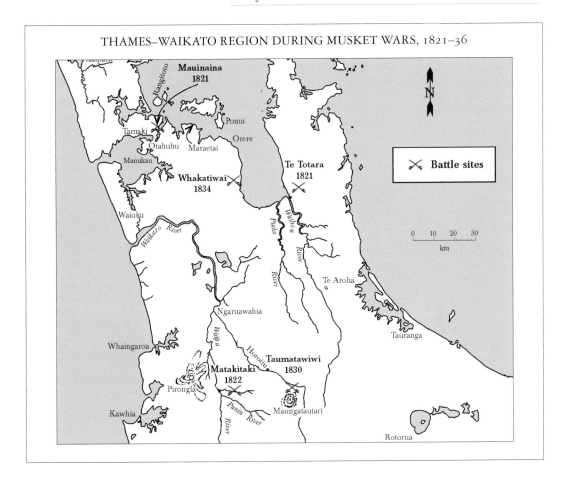

THAMES–WAIKATO REGION DURING MUSKET WARS, 1821–36

Once back in the Bay of Islands, Hongi had begun immediate preparations for an attack on Ngati Paoa of Tamaki, an action he looked on as the first step in his great campaign to avenge past defeats at the hands of Hauraki. By September 1821, he was ready. He assembled a great war party of 2000 men, drawn not only from the Bay but from a wide surrounding area. Between them the warriors were said to have at least a thousand muskets.[33] Travelling in a fleet of more than fifty waka, the expedition came south to Whangarei, the final place of assembly of the war-party. There this huge taua picked up further recruits. 'There has never been anything like such an armament in New Zealand before',[34] reported the missionary, the Rev. Butler, in alarm. As the invasion force moved further south, it attacked various villages which it passed, at Mahurangi, Orewa, Whangaparaoa and Takapuna; also

87

some of the Ngati Paoa settlements on the nearby, inner gulf islands.[35] When the expedition reached the Tamaki isthmus, it found the Waitemata villages virtually deserted. The Ngati Whatua people normally living there, mainly women, children and slaves – for many men were away under Te Kawau on the Amiowhenua expedition – forewarned of the attack, had moved to a refuge near the north Manukau heads.[36]

After having plundered the abandoned isthmus gardens for food, the Nga Puhi invaders laid siege to the two Ngati Paoa pa beside the Tamaki river. Te Hinaki, who commanded the force within Mauinaina, feeling that the contest between the two armies was hopelessly unequal – for the defenders had only five muskets to match the attackers' 1000 – attempted to make terms. In soliciting peace, he followed the age-old convention of a tribe not wishing to fight because it felt that the disparity in strength between the two sides made defeat a foregone conclusion. A deputation was sent outside the pa, offering tribal treasures: greenstone mere and similar heirlooms. These Hongi kept; but (defying convention) not as a prelude to peace.[37] He refused to treat, and resumed the siege. As a sign that the battle had begun, he discarded his scarlet regimentals for his chain-mail armour and metal helmet. In the following engagement he was struck twice by musket shots which failed to penetrate his armour, incidents that afterwards gave rise to the unjustified belief that this armour gave him full immunity from gunfire in battle.[38]

The full weight of Nga Puhi attack initially fell on Mauinaina. The first stage of the battle was a hand-to-hand struggle outside the pa, mainly with old-style Maori weapons. When the attackers began to win the upper hand, Ngati Paoa warriors retreated within the pa. Hongi was then able to exploit his monopoly of firearms by erecting an elevated wooden platform on the summit of a nearby ridge which he had seized, enabling his best marksmen to shoot down upon and pick off the defenders guarding the entrance to the pa, who had hitherto been protected by a thick wall of earth.[39] Once these guardians of the entrance had been eliminated, the three-day battle turned decisively Hongi's way. A compact group of his warriors, adopting a wedge formation with Hongi in the van, successfully stormed the pa.[40] Smith (quoting a French source) reported that with the fall of the pa, 'a fearful slaughter took place, men, women and children all shared the same fate'.[41]

No one was spared. 'The wounded warriors were all killed.' During the battle Te Hinaki was shot and killed – most traditional sources say by Hongi himself;[42] but this has been disputed.[43] Te Hinaki was decapitated on the spot, and his head sent back as a trophy to the Bay of Islands, where it was publicly exhibited.

There is a tradition that, during the night following the fall of Mauinaina, Rewa, a senior Nga Puhi chief, sent words of warning to his former comrade in war, Te Rauroha, a Ngati Paoa chief in the Mokoia pa which stood beside the river: 'Oh friend Rauroha! I advise thee to depart home, for tomorrow at dawn thou wilt be attacked.'[44] As a Ngati Tai source reports the episode, Te Rauroha acted on this advice, 'and that night most of his people departed, and had reached as far as Tuakau by daylight'.[45] A majority of the refugees who fled to the south ultimately migrated to the Waikato, where they sought the protection of friendly tribes at Maungatautari, Patetere and elsewhere.[46] Others escaped without actually crossing the river, by hiding in the lava caves on the flanks of Mount Wellington (Maungarei). There they remained concealed until, under cover of night, they were able to resume their flight to the western side of the isthmus (Te Whau) whence they moved on to the Waitakere bush, there to take refuge. However, a resolute group of warriors determined that they would stay at Mokoia. They died to a man, apart from a few who swam the Tamaki river when the pa was about to fall.

A Ngati Paoa chief, Rangi-whenua (also known as Kaea), who had succeeded in swimming the river once his tribe's cause had become hopeless, is honoured in Maori oral history for his outstanding bravery.[47] Kaea is said to have fought with great skill in the defence of the pa, using as his weapon a cooper's adze (kapu-kapu), which he had obtained the year before from one of the European visitors who had travelled with Captain Cruise on the Royal Navy schooner, *The Prince Regent*. As Kaea was about to land safely on the eastern shore of the river which he had swum after the pa had fallen, Rewa and two other Nga Puhi chiefs, who knew Kaea of old, having been fellow warriors on a past expedition, challenged him to return and duel with them. This he did, fighting each in turn with his steel adze. The first two he wounded; they were forced to retire. However, the chief who was his third opponent, Te Ihi, succeeded in killing Kaea with a left-handed blow from his tomahawk, a stratagem which, in the opinion of disapproving Nga Puhi onlookers, was executed in a discreditable manner that broke the long-honoured etiquette of the Maori duel.

Those who were not killed after capture, mainly women and children, were enslaved; that was the lot of Te Hinaki's sister, who was taken back to the Bay as the wife of a Nga Puhi chief.[48] The number of Ngati Paoa killed in the battle for these two pa is a matter of debate among Maori historians. Kelly speaks of a death toll of a thousand;[49] John Waititi's estimate is 1000–1300 at Mauinaina, and 300 at Mokoia.[50] And hundreds of Nga Puhi fell as well. Percy Smith wrote that 'a traveller who visited the battle-field in 1844 records that the bones of 2,000 men still lay whitening on the plain', and that the ovens used for the 'horrible repasts' of the victorious party still remained.[51] Hyperbole perhaps, but this conquest was a sad fate for that branch of the Ngati Paoa that Cruise had described as being 'in appearance . . . far superior to any of the New Zealanders we had hitherto seen: they were fairer, taller, and more athletic; their canoes were larger, and more richly carved and ornamented'.[52] With this battle, their glory days were over. In later years, a small remnant of the two main Tauoma hapu returned to the region, and lived on the banks towards the mouth of the Tamaki estuary. But most settled on gulf islands such as Waiheke and Motutapu, or on the western coast of the Firth of Thames from Orere Point southwards.[53] They never went back to Mokoia and Mauinaina. Charles Terry, one of Auckland's earliest settlers, who visited the 'quite deserted' settlements beside the Tamaki river about twenty years later, wrote that the 'remains of a most extensive Pa, with their former cultivated grounds' were 'now growing wild, in luxuriant vegetation, tares, cabbages, turnips, celery, and grass'.[54] He spoke of the spring tares as being 'in full blossom, four feet high, and there were some acres completely covered with them'. It had become a deserted land, very deeply 'tapu from blood'.[55] Among Ngati Paoa descendants sensitive to old ways it still remains tapu. After the carnage of 1821, one can understand why.

After having feasted for some days on the bodies of the Ngati Paoa slain, Nga Puhi moved on to Te Totara, the great strong-hold of Ngati Maru.[56] Te Totara, a fortress on a low but steep hill, with commanding views of all the sea and land approaches to the southern Firth of Thames, was the greatest of eight pa, extending southwards from Tararu, that had been erected to protect the Ngati Maru people.[57] (A modern traveller is still able to see the remaining earthworks of this once mighty pa just the south of the township of Thames, on the Paeroa road.) The fortress had been weakened at the time by the absence of many Maru warriors on a southern expedition. But Hongi contrived to take the pa, not by a direct frontal assault as at Mauinaina, but through a strategy of deceit.[58] The Ngati Maru people were willing to appease Nga Puhi by offering gifts, which included the famous greenstone mere, Te Kahotea, and certain other tribal heirlooms.[59] Hongi pretended to be bought off in this way, and departed with his canoes. But once beyond Tararu, Nga Puhi concealed themselves, and returned overnight by cover of darkness, to make a surprise dawn attack on the unsuspecting Totara people. The pa was quickly taken. The presence of some Waikato warriors in the pa did not alter the outcome of the battle, though it did give Hongi a pretext for his intended attack on Waikato the following year – if such were needed.

Reverend Henry Williams, 1782–1867. Pioneer CMS missionary. SHERRIN AND WALLACE

As at Mauinaina, so at Te Totara, with the fall of the pa, there was great slaughter. The missionary Henry Williams, who was shown over the deserted Te Totara pa thirteen years later by some of the Ngati Maru survivors, recorded that 'Human bones lay scattered up and down, and the spot was pointed out where their relatives had been killed and eaten.'[60] Shortly after, his brother William Williams, en route to Kauaeranga, called in at Te Totara where he saw 'human bones still lying by the side of the ovens, the remains of the horrid feast of Ngapuhi'.[61] As at Mauinaina, so here, where so many had been killed, the site was declared tapu and permanently abandoned. (It is not unfitting that the pa has provided the main burial ground for the people of today's Thames.) Unsurprisingly, the act of kohuru – treachery leading to murder – perpetrated by Hongi at Te Totara has never been completely forgotten by the Marutuahu people. It was a turning point in their history. With the annihilation of the Ngati Maru defence system and the persistence of the annual raids from the north, the Hauraki people, albeit (as Maning put it) 'powerful, numerous, and warlike', decided that they could no longer confront 'the scourge of New Zealand' (the Nga Puhi).[62] They decided therefore, that they should not hesitate to abandon for a time their own country and to remove to a position inland, where, if they could not escape the attacks of their most dreaded enemies, they would at least have a better chance of having notice of their approach, and be less likely to be taken by surprise.[63]

IV

As a result of these two great battles of Mauinaina and Te Totara, Hongi's war party came back to the Bay with 2000 prisoners and many heads. A number of the prisoners were executed on the beach (some by distraught new widows) to avenge the death of Nga Puhi warriors.[64] But Hongi quickly set about preparing for his next expedition, against Waikato. He reconstituted his forces, recruiting fighting men far and wide from the Bay, Hokianga, and the far north, to join his followers in their next expedition. On 2 March 1822, the day that a large contingent of Hongi's party left, the missionary the Rev. John Butler wrote a worried letter to his superiors:

> The natives . . . departed from Te Kiddie Kiddie [Kerikeri] this morning, (I should think a thousand strong),[65] to be reinforced at every village as they pass, until the numbers will become very formidable indeed, and with a full determination to sweep the whole of the River Thames, and all the country round for some hundred miles, with the besom of destruction.[66]

Butler was mistaken in marking out the Thames region as the next objective in Hongi's campaign. But he was correct in his forecast that the broom of 'destruction' in the hands of Hongi, Pomare, Rewa and other northern chiefs would bring, in the long run, great grief to the Marutuahu peoples of the Hauraki gulf and its hinterland. Tai Turoa, a modern Hauraki kaumatua and historian, using the rhetoric of the marae, dramatically described the tribulations of his people during the 1820s.

> Commencing at Tamaki, the armies of the great warlord, Hongi-Hika attacked every bastion of Marutuahu, which stood in his way, leaving a trail of bloody devastation in his wake. The tribes of Paoa,

Whanaunga,[67] Maru, Tamatera[68] and Hei[69] felt the foreign might of
the musket for the first time. Most retreated inland to seek refuge
with their Ngati Raukawa relatives at Maungatautari and Horotiu
(Cambridge) in order to escape the fury unleashed upon them. They
dwelt among these people for ten years until 1831 when the danger
had long abated. During this period of time Hauraki became almost a
deserted land.[70]

Tamaki was in a like state during these troubled years. In or
about January 1822, shortly after the Amiowhenua expedition
had disbanded in the Waikato, Te Kawau and his followers
slipped back into Tamaki. It was just as the Ngati Paoa refugees,
whom Te Kawau had encountered sheltering in the middle
Waikato valley, had reported. Mokoia and the other settlements
beside the Tamaki river (Whangamakau) had been annihilated;
Te Kawau's three main hapu, Te Taou, Ngaoho and Te Uringutu
had fled the isthmus.[71] In later years, Judge Fenton spoke in
these terms of the new Tamaki which confronted Te Kawau in
early 1822:

> Mauinaina, which he left a flourishing settlement, was desolated and
> vacant, and the survivors of the slaughter, who fled from Mauinaina,
> were dispersed among their friends up the Horotiu [in the middle
> Waikato][72] or had been killed at Matakitaki. It appears probable, also,
> that those of his own tribe whom he had left behind him at Mangere,
> and scattered about the country across to the Waitemata, had fled
> away to the broken country known as the Manukau Ranges, where
> they at all times of great danger appear to have found certain refuge.[73]

Te Kawau himself had every reason quickly to vacate the
isthmus. He and one of his brothers, together with Te Hinaki
(now dead), had been designated as three of the eight chiefs
whom Nga Puhi had personally marked out to be killed when
in 1821 that tribe had embarked under Hongi on its campaign
of revenge.[74] Te Kawau rejoined his people where they were in
hiding in the bush close to the northern heads of the Manukau
harbour. But he took them further from the reach of danger. By
the time that Hongi's huge, canoe-borne war-party passed over
the isthmus in March 1822 to attack Waikato, Te Kawau and
his Te Taou followers had shifted into Hikurangi,[75] the name

Maori gave to the rugged, forested portion of the Waitakere ranges lying between the Waitakere river valley and the northern shore of the Manukau.[76] 'I left the portage of Manukau [Otahuhu] for Ngapuhi to pass over', remarked Te Kawau dryly in retrospect.[77] For some time he continued to move away from the dangerous Tamaki isthmus; his tribe was reported shortly after as staying at Oneonenui, a pa a short way back from Muriwai beach in the lower Kaipara.[78]

The invasion of the Waikato by Nga Puhi was to have such far-reaching consequences for the Tamaki peoples that more must now be said about it.[79] After Hongi's forces had moved from the Otahuhu dragging-place to the Waiuku arm of the Manukau harbour, progress became very slow. Negotiating Te-pae-o-kai-waka, the famous portage which lay between the Waiuku estuary and the Awaroa stream – the tributary giving access to the Waikato river – was full of difficulties. Retreating Waikato warriors had felled logs to block the stream. And not only had these obstacles to be removed, but channels had also to be cut by the invaders across loops in the stream so that the larger canoes could pass through to the Waikato river.

A delay of two months in crossing this portage meant that great numbers of people in flight had time to seek refuge in Matakitaki, the extensive triple pa where Waikato had chosen to make their stand, under their great war leader Te Wherowhero (later known as Potatau), of the Ngati Mahuta tribe, and his second-in-command, Te Kanawa. For today's practising historian, visiting the site of the Matakitaki battleground has a double advantage. It is easy to reach, for it lies three kilometres north of Pirongia, beside the main road; and it is easy to identify as its main physical features have been changed little by the passage of over 170 years. Many people sought refuge there.[80] Together with the Waikato hapu, which had been drawn from a wide area, there were Ngati Maniapoto and some Ngati Whatua people as well. While the figure of 10,000 inhabitants that is sometimes given seems exaggerated, a large number was undoubtedly concentrated on the six-hectare plateau that lay within the defences of the pa.

Matakitaki would have been almost impregnable in the pre-musket era.[81] The great pa was enclosed on three sides by the Waipa river and its tributary the Mangapiko stream, both of which had scoured deep and steep-sided valleys to provide nat-

Te Hiahia, drawn by H. G. Robley. The gun and cartouche were of the type used in the later stages of the Musket Wars. ALEXANDER TURNBULL LIBRARY

ural ramparts for the fortress. Numerous defenders comple-mented these. But in the post-musket age, these warriors and the people whom they protected were, in effect, trapped in an indefensible fortress. Waikato scouts who had escaped the fire of the advancing Nga Puhi are said, on entering the pa, to have given an ominous warning to its defenders: 'Koia ano he tika te atua e haria mai nei!' (It is true what is said of the god (gun) which is being brought!)[82]

On his arrival at the pa, Hongi, aware that it was futile for those without guns to try to resist him, called on the defenders to surrender. His appeal was disregarded. But when the first con-certed roar of his muskets was heard and its bloody consequences were seen, there was panic among the non-combatants within the pa. Well-drilled volleys across the Mangapiko stream denied Te Wherowhero's men any opportunity of getting into that close-quarter combat with traditional weapons, which alone (as an early sally from the eastern end of the pa had shown) could have given them any chance of victory.[83] Once they had established ascend-

Te Wherowhero, 1844.
Lithograph after original
in G. F. *Angus,*
The New Zealanders
Illustrated, *1847.*

ancy by virtue of their firepower, Hongi's men stormed the pa. Only in that section of the pa where Te Wherowhero was in charge, was resistance prolonged. As in past battles, Te Wherowhero fought with exemplary courage, subduing a number of his opponents single-handed.[84] But despite acts of individual bravery on the part of this great warrior-chief and of Te Kanawa, and of those who followed them, the defenders were powerless against the weaponry of the modern industrial world. The pa quickly fell, its inhabitants put to flight. Both within the pa, and through a wide area of the surrounding lands, there was either widespread slaughter or enslavement of the defeated people. John Cowell, ex-missionary turned trader,[85] who lived among Waikato Maori during the 1820s, maintained that about 2000 were killed as a result of the fall of Matakitaki.[86] Hongi himself put the figure at 1500.[87] Whatever the final figure, no one disputes either that the slaughter was very great, or that many people were carried off as slaves.[88]

After the return of the Nga Puhi expedition along the route by which it had originally come, the Waikato people who had scattered 'to the fastnesses of the forests' regathered under Te Wherowhero in the upper Mokau.[89] Henceforth, the Tainui people set about buying guns as quickly as they could, so that, by the early 1830s, they had achieved more or less parity of muskets with the Northland tribes. Nor had Matakitaki been, even at the time, an unrelieved disaster for them. In the irregular warfare that had followed on the battle for the pa, groups of Waikato warriors had successfully harried their marauding Nga Puhi pursuers, isolating and killing a considerable number of them. This rear-guard action chastened Hongi, causing him to call off any thought of attempting to subjugate Tainui, and persuading him that it might be wiser after all to seek peace. The reverses suffered by Nga Puhi explain why (writes Kelly) they were forced to 'cut short their stay', and why, before leaving Matakitaki, 'they released several captive women, one being Parekohu, sister to Te Kanawa [trusted counsellor of Te Wherowhero], another being his wife Te Rahuruake, this action being a move to open up peace negotiations should Waikato wish it'.[90]

Waikato leaders responded positively to the overture. The result was an exchange of meetings that led, in February 1823, to a great peace gathering at the Bay of Islands attended by 100 chiefs.[91] The participants were Nga Puhi, Waikato (led by Te Kanawa, and Kati, a younger brother of Te Wherowhero), and some Ngati Paoa, who played, however, a minor role in the negotiations. Nga Puhi returned a few slaves as a peace offering. But the true business of reconciliation was carried out at the main meeting where, according to Judge Fenton's account:

> After the usual speeches, peace was made, and one of the chief women of Ngapuhi, Matire Toha, was betrothed to Te Kati, who was Potatau's brother, as a pledge of peace and permanent friendship. The Waikato party, accompanied by the bride and sixty Ngapuhi chiefs under Rewa and others, started away from the Bay by the direction of Hongi to

return the visit of the Waikato chiefs, and to complete the peace by formally reinstating the tribes of Waikato in their usual residences. When the party arrived at Takapuna [North Head?], they were met by Apihai at the head of all Te Taou, Ngaoho and Te Uringutu, who treated them courteously and supplied them with food from Okahu, where at that time they were sojourning. The Taou took the Ngapuhi up the [Waitemata] river to Ongarahu [near Kumeu], where they entertained them for three days. The Ngapuhi party then went to Te Whau dragged their canoes over the neck of land into the Manukau, and thence, pursuing the route formerly traversed by Hongi, they passed up the Waikato.[92]

This extract has two unusual points of interest. First, it makes no reference at all to a traditional Maori story that Kati, on his way home from the Bay of Islands, called in at Whakatiwai, on the west shore of the Hauraki gulf, the chief settlement of Ngati Paoa.[93] There, so one traditional account runs, he was plundered of Matire Toha's dowry of ammunition and dresses – valued (so Polack asserts) at £200. This 'Native account', in Percy Smith's opinion, 'seems rather improbable, for, so far as we know, Ngati-Paoa were at peace at this time with Waikato.'[94] As we shall see in the next chapter, this story mistakenly anticipates a later episode, an act of muru or retaliatory retribution, which was actually carried out by Ngati Paoa against Kati some ten years after his marriage to Matire. There is no reason to doubt, however, the extent of the peace binding, valued at the (then) very considerable sum of £200 sterling.

Second, Fenton's account of the Bay of Islands peace mission has a further usefulness. It tells us what is not explained anywhere else, namely why it was that Apihai Te Kawau and his followers, some time either just before or during the early summer of 1822–23, felt sufficiently secure to come out of hiding in the lower Kaipara and return to Tamaki. One can assume that, through the oral communications network so well developed in Maori society, they had learnt of the peace negotiations under way between Waikato and Nga Puhi, and concluded that it would now be safe to go back to Tamaki. Fenton speaks of their returning there by way of Waikumete (Little Muddy Creek), before settling down at Te Rehu, the small district between Western Springs and the Waitemata harbour that lies just to the west of modern Westmere.[95] Te Rehu, a small valley called after a stream of that name (known today, however, as Motions Creek) which drains the Western Springs, provided Ngati Whatua with a settlement that was conveniently handy to traditional Waitemata fishing grounds and to the old Orakei cultivations, without being perilously close to the Otahuhu portage, that notorious path of war-parties. Fenton stated that, for nearly two years, Te Rehu, a traditional habitation,[96] 'appears to have been the principal domicile' of Te Kawau's people, though they still retained some gardens in south Kaipara, and had small cultivations at Orakei and Horotiu (modern Queen Street).[97]

V

If 1823–25 was a period of peace for Te Kawau and his followers, that peace was an ambiguous and transitory one. Over these years, Tamaki was virtually an island of calm, so to speak, in a sea of war. The North Island remained in a state of great turbulence. Te Rauparaha of Ngati Toa, for instance, who in 1822 had vacated his traditional lands in the Kawhia region, in order to migrate with a substantial section of his tribe to the Cook Strait area, illustrates two great pressures at work in this period: the need to escape the attentions of nearby powerful tribes, and the desire to live in a district where there was easy access to white traders and therefore to firearms. By 1824 he had realised his intention. He had established himself securely in the south-west of the North Island, and had begun purchasing large stocks of muskets and powder that were later used in his own wars of conquest.[98] Furthermore, with the overthrow of Matakitaki, Hongi's campaigns were by no means at an end. In 1823 he made his attack upon the tribes of Rotorua.

Hongi's example worked a great mischief; for other chiefs sought to emulate him. As attacks multiplied, new utu accounts opened up, and conflicts, driven by the entrenched, tikanga principle of retaliation, started to spin out of control. Old certainties disappeared; allies became enemies, and alliances were rapidly formed and dissolved for reasons often now impossible to discern. The result was the depopulation of once closely settled

regions and the displacement and enforced migration of so many
tribes that it seemed that 'almost the whole of the North Island
[was] on the move'.[99] Over the resulting two decades of strife,
directly or indirectly, something of the order of 20,000 lives
were lost and, for many of those who survived, there was incalculable misery and suffering.[100]

The battle of Te Ika-a-ranganui, fought in 1825, inextricably
entangled the Tamaki tribes under Te Kawau in the great social
dislocation that these wars brought in their wake. This battle
resulted from the decision of Hongi to expunge from the record,
once and for all, those past defeats that Nga Puhi had suffered at
the hands of Ngati Whatua o Kaipara – and especially the humiliating defeat at Moremonui.[101] He assembled a war-party of well-
armed warriors led by himself, his son Hare, and a number of
redoubtable chiefs such as Te Whare-umu, Te Morenga, Patuone,
and Tamati Waka Nene. When Ngati Whatua of Kaipara learned
of the impending invasion, they appealed to the Tamaki branch
of their iwi for assistance. The summons came during the fishing
season while Te Kawau was at Okahu. There he assembled a
contingent of Te Taou and Ngaoho warriors, who set out for
Kaipara by way of the Manukau harbour and the west coast.
Meanwhile, the Nga Puhi war-party had arrived at Mangawhai
and was encamped there. Ngati Whatua o Kaipara closed in, in
order to select as their battlefield a downlands area of stunted fern
and manuka, twelve kilometres inland from Mangawhai and just
north-west of the small present-day settlement of Kaiwaka. Here
they awaited their foes at the head of canoe navigation of the
Kaiwaka river – although that name has now been subsumed in
the more general term, the Otamatea river – at the point where
its freshwater tributary, the Waimako, joins it.

When the two armies clashed, it soon became apparent that
they were unequally matched. For though Ngati Whatua had
mustered over 1000 warriors, they had virtually no firearms, in
contrast to the 500 warriors of the invasion taua, who had an
abundance of muskets. That the battle proved to be a long drawn-
out affair says much for the reckless valour of Ngati Whatua.[102]
In spite of the massed musket fire against them, they continued
to charge, leaving, 'among the hills and valleys of Kaiwaka', wrote
George Graham, a 'corpse strewn field of strife'. Graham went on
to record that 'the dead lay in serried lines, from which incident

the clash was named "the great array of fish laid out"'.[103] The battle was described years later by a Nga Puhi warrior who was there, as 'one of the most sanguinary battles ever fought in this country'.[104] Certainly, Ngati Whatua losses were crippling, although Percy Smith believed the figure of 1000 to be 'an over-estimate'.[105] Nevertheless, the number of Ngati Whatua chiefs who fell was a disaster for that tribe. When years later, Te Kawau was asked to make an estimate of the Ngati Whatua chiefs killed, he replied 'they are so numerous I cannot count them'.[106]

Once it became clear that the battle was irretrievably lost, Ngati Whatua fled pell-mell in all directions. Nga Puhi relent-lessly pursued the fugitives, slaughtering great numbers. Some survivors made a frantic but largely successful escape by canoe down the Kaiwaka river, which flows into the great, salt-water, estuarine reach of the Kaipara harbour known as the Otamatea river. It was here that they met Te Kawau and his band of warriors, who were arriving too late to take any part in the battle.[107] Apihai and his men turned about, joining this major group of fugitives, who gathered in their families where they could, and fled south by way of Muriwai as far as Waikumete. At this strategic location near the Whau portage, the Kaipara people paused to await stragglers before moving on to the Waikato heads. And it was at Waikumete that Te Kawau left Ngati Whatua o Kaipara to rejoin his own people at Tamaki.

Ngati Whatua was broken as a tribe. Its people were no longer concentrated within their traditional rohe, the coastal valleys of the Kaipara harbour. In the early 1860s, Percy Smith, while acting as interpreter and surveyor in this region, spoke to elderly Ngati Whatua survivors of Te Ika-a-ranganui. They told him that those who did not go with the main party of refugees to the Waikato, or who had sought the protection of relatives – as did some of the Ngati Rongo hapu who went to live with their kin at Whangarei – found shelter of sorts 'in the fastnesses of [interior] mountains' and 'in the wilds of the forests'. They further explained:

The fear of Nga-Puhi prevented them from occupying their old homes for many years afterwards, indeed not until Auckland was founded [in 1840] did they feel safe. It is a well-known fact that those who went to Waikato were nearly all exterminated at the taking of Nohoawatea in 1825 or 1826. The old men have often described to me the state of

fear and alarm they lived in during their wild life in the mountains . . .
they rarely approached the rivers or the paths, but confined themselves
to the wild bush, living on eels, birds, and the produce of a few hidden
cultivations.[108]

In the long run, the main branch of the tribe that had sought
refuge in the Waikato suffered most of all. After the women and
children had been resettled temporarily at the Waikato heads,
warriors from this group came north once again to avenge those
who had been killed at Te Ika-a-ranganui. At Otamatea they fell
upon a party of eighty Te Parawhau from the Whangarei region,
which as the southernmost of the Nga Puhi tribes was so often
the target for retaliation.[109] This group of Te Parawhau was annihilated. The Ngati Whatua war-party then returned to the
Waikato heads. Certain that Hongi would pursue them – for he
had declared his intention of avenging the death of his son Hare
who had fallen at Te Ika-a-ranganui – they gathered up the
remainder of their tribe and retreated into the interior, finding
their final refuge in a pa on a tributary of the Waipa river. While
some accounts say this was on the Mangapiko, Phillips says (as
seems more likely) that the pa, which he precisely names 'Haere
Awatea', was beside the Puniu river. What is not in dispute is
that the pa was shared with Ngati Paoa fugitives under Te
Rauroha who, it will be recalled, had been in charge of the
defence of Mokoia before it fell to Nga Puhi some years earlier.[110]
Shortly after the Ngati Whatua refugees were admitted within
the palisades, Hongi arrived with his taua. He then called on
Ngati Paoa to leave the pa, stating that he had no quarrel with
them, but with Ngati Whatua alone. Once Ngati Paoa did what
Hongi demanded, he immediately stormed the pa and slaughtered the Ngati Whatua inhabitants. Among historians it has
now become the conventional wisdom that, first, Hongi's invitation to Ngati Paoa to leave the pa unharmed was tantamount to
his declaration of peace to them, and second, that it was this
invitation which persuaded Ngati Paoa to return to and occupy
(albeit hesitantly) parts of the Hauraki islands and the coastline
of the Firth of Thames. As for Ngati Whatua, from this time
forward they were destroyed as an iwi of power.

The scattering and destruction of Ngati Whatua o Kaipara
immediately endangered Te Kawau and his tribe. Although the

Tamaki people had not directly taken part in the battle of Te Ika-a-ranganui, they were the close kin of the Kaipara tribe, of whom they had also been traditional allies. The Tamaki branch of Ngati Whatua feared, therefore, that they, too, would now become the targets of Nga Puhi wrath and muskets. Not surprisingly, in the summer of 1825–26, Te Taou decided to evacuate the isthmus. After assembling at Waikumete, the tribe fled up the Waikato to the region of Cambridge[111] and, according to Fenton, also to Pukewhau on the Waipa.[112] In the winter of 1826 they decided to shift once again. Te Kawau's followers (excluding Te Uringutu, whose own wanderings had ended for the time being at Pokeno) now took temporary refuge in a variety of places. They made a short-lived return to the Tamaki region initially residing at their old fishing-camp at Karangahape on the north shore of the Manukau. During their next move, as they made their way to the Otahuhu portage, they had an amicable meeting with the Nga Puhi warrior chief, Pomare, who was leading a war-party to the Waikato on that expedition in which he met his death.[113] After crossing to the waters of the Hauraki gulf, they sojourned briefly at Takapuna before moving on to Mahurangi, in the neighbourhood of which there was said to be a branch of Nga Puhi, who, we are told, 'were friendly to Apihai',[114] and well disposed towards his Tamaki followers because they were related to them.[115] Apihai's followers settled on an outer eastern arm of the Mahurangi headland, at Waiaro (since colonial times renamed as Dairy Bay). Physically, though perhaps not politically, it was a suitable location. It was reasonably isolated, yet close to shark-fishing grounds, with the further advantage that adjoining the kainga was raised land which they could fortify. At Waiaro, Te Kawau constructed what one might describe as a pa for fugitives. For there, 'hiding away from Hongi',[116] together with Te Kawau's Te Taou and Ngaoho, were remnants of Ngati Rongo, and of Ngati Whatua o Kaipara.[117]

VI

Although the impact of the musket wars upon the Tamaki tribes by the close of 1826 was far from complete, we have now reached a point where we can provisionally assess the effect of those wars on the population of that region. The key question that arises is how many died as a result of the wars. Unfortunately, data on the Maori population of Aotearoa as a whole is at best uncertain. There are three main obstacles to our moving beyond conjecture on this issue. First, the estimates of the size of Maori population in 1769 when Cook first came,[118] and of demographic trends between that date and 1840, vary widely. Professor Ian Pool has presented a credible case for a figure of (possibly) just on 100,000 for 1769 and for a diminished figure of 70,000 to 90,000 for 1840.[119] But there can be no finality in these figures; they can be looked on as no more than informed demographic estimates for a pre-census age. Moreover, the severity of the wars and the magnitude of the migrations that they set in train varied from region to region. (Historians have recognised this for some years by teasing out their conclusions about the demographic effects of the wars from regional and discrete tribal studies; a justification indeed for the case study embodied in this present chapter.)[120] The final impediment to a more accurate understanding of the musket wars has been our too ready acceptance in the past of an overstatement of numbers killed in military engagements – usually originating with nineteenth- and early twentieth-century European chroniclers of the wars. And in estimating our tally of deaths we have failed to take fully into account the harmful effects of the enforced migrations that flowed from the wars, particularly with regard to lowered standards of health and fertility. This last issue is one to which I shall return in a later chapter.

However, there are three conclusions about the impact of the musket wars upon Tamaki-makau-rau that can be made with some degree of confidence. First, of the three main theatres of war among the tribes of Aotearoa in the 1820s,[121] that region centred upon the Tamaki isthmus appears to have suffered the greatest devastation.[122] Second, a revisionist tendency to lower the death toll ensuing from musket battles seems less applicable to the major engagements of this region. To be sure, much has been rightly made of the crudity of the weapons in Maori hands: of their inaccuracy except at the closest of ranges, of their slowness in reloading, and of their occasional threat to the lives of the musketeers firing them no less than to the enemy at whom they were aimed.[123] And it is well known that at the later, close-quarter stages of a battle, the warriors about to become victors would often resort to traditional weapons to drive home their advantage or to complete the slaughter of the defeated. Yet it must not be forgotten that in battles of the 1820s involving Nga Puhi, Ngati Whatua, Waikato and Marutuahu iwi, it was often the dreaded muskets of the side with the greater firepower that (as at Matakitaki) had demoralised the vanquished in the first place. Kerry Howe has also stressed that it was 'the abnormally large . . . number of warriors' that 'caused unprecedented killing' by Nga Puhi war-parties in the years immediately after Hongi's return from England.[124]

> The Ngapuhi chiefs' possession of firearms and their association with Europeans generally was an exciting inducement for large numbers of young men to join campaigns against longstanding enemies who enjoyed no such advantages. Nothing inspires fighting men like the expectation of easy victories.[125]

And it must also be borne in mind that it was on the tribes of 'the Thames' and of the Waikato that the great weight of the large Nga Puhi war-parties with their superiority of firepower was to fall.[126]

A third conclusion can be drawn, once we distinguish between the loss of life from battles fought in the field such as Hingakaka and Te Ika-a-ranganui, and those fights which terminated in the overthrow and laying waste of a pa, as at Mauinaina and Te Totara. Battles fought in the field were usually less slaughterous for the army against whom the tide of battle had turned because of the possibility open to them of a *sauve qui peut* flight. (Such a flight, incidentally, often indicated not cowardice but a desire to escape in order to resume the struggle under more favourable circumstances.) On the other hand, where a pa was besieged and overthrown, the loss of life and social devastation were generally much greater. Limited opportunities for escape meant that whole communities could be destroyed, with women and children as well as men being killed or enslaved. It was the misfortune of the region made up of Tamaki, Thames and Waikato to have an unusual number of large pa overthrown in the early stages of the wars while Nga Puhi still enjoyed a monopoly of firearms. The death toll from the overthrow of

Mauinaina, Mokoia, Te Totara and Matakitaki alone could well have approached 5000.[127] That explains why the loss of life among Maori living north of a line connecting western Bay of Plenty to Kawhia harbour must be calculated in terms of thousands rather than hundreds.

But the indirect consequences of the musket wars were also a cause of much tribulation in the region. As we shall find in the next chapter, although Apihai Te Kawau lost few of his people in pitched battles, their enforced wanderings greatly enfeebled the tribe.

Dumont d'Urville, 1790–1842, captain of L'Astrolabe, *and renowned French explorer.* AUCKLAND CITY LIBRARIES

In February 1827, during the course of his second visit to New Zealand, the renowned French explorer, Dumont d'Urville, captain of the frigate *L'Astrolabe*, entered the Hauraki gulf and sailed by way of the Rangitoto channel towards the Tamaki isthmus. He recorded that an air of desolation hung over the isthmus and its surrounding lands: 'We did not notice any trace of inhabitants, nothing but one or two fires a very long way off in the interior. There can be no doubt that this extreme depopulation is due to the ravages of war.'[128] He was able to confirm this surmise over the next few days, after he had observed a further sequence of 'deserted villages',[129] and had spoken to Ngati Paoa and Waikato chiefs living in small communities on the fringe of the isthmus. They gave accounts of how, year after year, they had had to endure annual attacks from the north.[130]

Years later, Judge Fenton was to characterise Tamaki of this era as an 'isthmus without an inhabitant'.[131] No tribe was 'in its own place'. Ngati Paoa had been driven away. Te Taou and Ngaoho were 'in refuge near Mahurangi, subject to constant attacks and dangers'. The Manukau tribes were far away, sheltering in the Waikato and Waipa valleys, while Te Uringutu had moved from Pokeno to be the guests of the Whakatiwai branch of the Ngati Paoa.[132] When the Fenton Judgment, generally so workaday in its prose, reaches these years of diaspora, called by the judge 'this dreadful interval' in the story of Tamaki, it sloughs off its legal language, and captures in cadences reminiscent of the King James Bible, the poignant lot of a people alienated from their ancestral land.

For many years there is, in truth, a blank in the history of Tamaki. About 1832, Mr Cowell, sailing from Waihopuhopu [near

Whakatiwai], at the head of the Hauraki Gulf, opposite Shortland, to Mahurangi, did not see a single inhabitant nor observe a single fire.[133] From Whakatiwai to Mahurangi the country was quite empty. The dread of Ngapuhi was so great that the people thought of nothing but securing their personal safety, and the mountain ranges and inaccessible or little-frequented places were then more sought for than fertile lands. 'All the tribes were being driven backwards and forwards,' said Mr. Cowell. 'Everything was in confusion, and no one settled anywhere,' was Mr. Marshall's recollection of this period.[134] 'All the men were wandering about the face of the earth,' was Warena Hengia's evidence. Hori Tauroa said that all people thought of was to save their lives and get guns. And Apihai asked, 'How could a man settle anywhere with the fear of Ngapuhi?' Ngati Paoa seem to have gradually formed a large settlement at Waihopuhopu [north of Whakatiwai], but they never returned to their old place Mauinaina, because, as they alleged, the land was tapu from blood; most likely because, although they had made peace with Ngapuhi, they had a natural feeling that this isthmus – the highway of all war parties – was not a desirable place for a tribe to live in such evil days as those.[135]

The years ahead were to confirm that for the people of Tamaki these were indeed evil days.

CHAPTER V

'Wandering about the Face of the Earth', 1826–31

I

The pa known as 'Whatua Taou Rongo' which Apihai Te Kawau set up at Waiaro on the Mahurangi headlands for his Te Taou and Nga Oho followers (often referred to in these years of wandering as 'Apihai's people')[1] proved an imperfect refuge.[2] The pa was too close to hostile northern tribes, whose feuds with Ngati Whatua blighted any prospect of a lasting friendly relationship. Predictably, the refugees were subject (as Fenton put it) to 'constant attacks and dangers'.[3] 'We had not been long there', recalled one Nga Oho chief, before the Whangarei tribe of Te Parawhau, under Tirarau, mounted a decisive attack, capturing the pa and killing many within.[4] The survivors scattered to the mountains and the bush. Te Kawau gathered them together again at Orewa. Thence they returned overland to Tamaki in two separate groups. One party made the coastal journey by way of Takapuna. The other took the more rugged but less perilous inland route.[5] After camping briefly at Te Whau (Avondale), where they regrouped once again, these Te Taou and Nga Oho survivors moved well up-harbour with their chiefs – Apihai, Tinana, Uruamo and Watarangi. There they established a somewhat more permanent if still insecure settlement at Kopupaka, in the vicinity of modern Whenuapai.[6]

Understandably, Te Kawau made no attempt to resettle the isthmus itself. When, as already noted, the French explorer d'Urville visited Tamaki in his ship *L'Astrolabe* about this time (February 1827), he took it to be a region made desolate by endemic warfare. With the portages of the isthmus acting as a constant highway for war-parties during these disturbed years, this situation was unlikely to change. Some months before, Pomare, the Nga Puhi warrior chief,[7] had led a war-party up the Waipa valley to Te Rore. There Pomare and his party encountered a combined force made up of Ngati Tipa of Waikato, and Ngati Paoa and Ngati Maru from the Thames, who surrounded, killed and ate them. No one imagined that Nga Puhi (and Hongi least of all) would leave that humiliation unavenged. While visiting Whangarei just before coming on to Tamaki, d'Urville had noticed that Nga Puhi were already forming an expedition to square the account created by Pomare's death.[8] That aside, Nga Puhi were still contemplating other and more distant districts to raid. Missionaries reported shortly after d'Urville's visit that yet another Nga Puhi expedition, under Te Koki, had left the Bay of Islands to raid the Hauraki region.[9] With war-parties continuing to pass over its portages, Tamaki would obviously have been a dangerous place for Apihai's people to be.

Even as these Tamaki refugees sheltered uncertainly in the upper harbour, relief came from an unexpected quarter. Early in 1827, ten Ngati Paoa canoes arrived at Kopupaka, each with two Te Uringutu paddlers. These canoes had been sent by two chiefs, Hakopa Te Paerimu of Te Uringutu, and Kohirangatira of Ngati Paoa, under whose protection Te Uringutu were living at that time in a pa just north of Whakatiwai, on the western shore of the Firth of Thames.[10] The canoes carried all of Apihai's fol-lowers – that is, most of the members of the Te Taou and Nga Oho hapu – to Whakatiwai. Like Te Uringutu they too remained briefly there under Ngati Paoa protection.

However, the threat of continued and unpredictable raids by Nga Puhi convinced Apihai Te Kawau and his people that they must move on yet again from the Firth of Thames and seek the greater safety of the interior of the island. During the summer of 1827–28, therefore, they migrated up the Piako river and crossed to that part of Horotiu (as the middle Waikato valley was then called) which lay a few kilometres to the east and

Flotte de Guerre à la
Nouvelle Zélande.
*A fleet of war canoes sets
out from the Bay of
Islands.* AUCKLAND
CITY LIBRARIES

south-east of today's Cambridge. There they settled, once again
under the protection of Ngati Paoa and of other Hauraki tribes
living in the region, all refugees from the Nga Puhi onslaught.
Te Kawau's people established a pa near Tauwhare called Te
Kopai.[11] After many months 'wandering about the face of the
earth', migration for Apihai's followers seemed to be at an end.

II

But since such security as these Tamaki people now enjoyed
depended on the ability of the Hauraki tribes to protect them
effectively, more must now be said about Marutuahu, as the
Hauraki people then were more generally known. From 1822
on, after the shattering defeats of Mauinaina and Te Totara, large
elements of Hauraki tribes dwelling on either side of the Firth
of Thames and in the Waihou valley evacuated their homelands
and settled in the Horotiu. As Judge Maning later observed,
once the tribes were away from the Firth, they felt that, even 'if
they could not escape the attacks of their most dreaded enemies,
they would at least have a better chance of having notice of their
approach, and be less likely to be taken by surprise'.[12] Over a
period of about four years these Marutuahu people settled in the
middle Waikato valley on a largish area of land stretching from
Maungakawa in the north, to the foothills of that famous moun-

tain which Maori called Maungatautari in the south. On parts of this land they simply 'squatted', with the apparent acquiescence of the traditional owners. In like manner, a hapu of Ngati Paoa settled on Ngati Haua territory near Maungakawa.[13] Most of the land which these outsiders occupied seems to have been taken over by the 'permission or invitation' of the powerful Waikato tribes.[14] But not entirely so. The Hauraki people had begun to lay highly questionable claim to certain lands, south of the Waikato river, on the grounds (*take*) of continued occupation, even of conquest. On such grounds they justified their right to occupy the desirable downlands, which fell away northwards, from Maungatautari to the Waikato river. In truth, they had simply taken over these territories from their original hosts, Ngati Raukawa,[15] after that tribe, wearying of constant battles with their Waikato neighbours, had evacuated their ancestral lands. (Ngati Raukawa had migrated to the Otaki region, at the invitation of Te Rauparaha's Ngati Toa tribe, with whom they had a number of kinship ties.)[16]

Judges Maning and Monro stated in their Te Aroha Judgment that at first the Waikato tribes, because of 'their own fear of the restless and warlike Ngapuhi', were apparently happy to have the powerful Marutuahu peoples 'enter and establish themselves in their [Waikato] country'.[17] They originally imagined that the Hauraki incomers, in the face of 'the common danger', would 'act as faithful allies', enabling the Waikato tribes 'to defend their country against all comers'.[18] But Hauraki and Waikato were soon to prove uneasy bedfellows. They shared no common interest beyond the short-term necessity of presenting a united front against dreaded Nga Puhi attack. And this solitary bond disappeared when, in the mid-1820s, Nga Puhi, perhaps deterred by the formidable joint forces now guarding this part of the Waikato territories, left that region largely unmolested as they turned to carry out raids elsewhere. As a result, Marutuahu and Waikato, fundamentally incompatible allies with much to divide them, soon found themselves, as Maning expressed it, 'accidentally living in peace'.[19]

By the time that Te Kawau's people entered the Horotiu in late 1827, relations between Waikato and Marutuahu had deteriorated badly. The Hauraki people no longer gave any indication that they were prepared to return to their Thames homelands. Indeed they

*Paora Tuhaere,
1825(?)–1892, nephew of
Te Kawau, passed his early
years in exile. Lithograph by
P. Gauci after J. J. Merrett,
in Terry's* New Zealand.

behaved, in the words of the Te Aroha Judgment, as though they
were 'taking permanent possession, not only of the lands of the
expelled Ngatiraukawa tribe, but also those of the Waikato people
at Horotiu and the surrounding districts, to which they had only
been permitted to come to reside in the character of friends and
allies while absent from their own proper district'.[20] The
Marutuahu chiefs began to show their determination to stay in
their newly adopted lands in two ways. First, they attached a
'stockaded and rifle-pitted pa' to each of their twenty or so settlements (and this included Te Kawau's); and second, they began to
behave more and more aggressively towards their Waikato
neighbours.[21]

These Hauraki pretensions were resented most of all by the
small but famously warlike tribe, Ngati Haua, who, under their
redoubtable leader Te Waharoa – whose principal pa was
Matamata – considered themselves as holding the mana whenua
over the lands which Ngati Raukawa had recently abandoned,
some of which the Hauraki tribes now occupied. In 1827, in a
violent attempt to coerce these Hauraki interlopers to return to
their homelands, Te Waharoa made a surprise night-time raid on
the pa of the Marutuahu chief Takurua, at Kaipaka, located at
the foot of the Maungakawa hills.[22] Two hundred unsuspecting
inhabitants were said to have been slaughtered.[23]

However, the massacre which was usually referred to in contemporary accounts as 'the Takurua murder', far from intimi-
dating the Maru tribes, infuriated them and strengthened their
resolve to stay. They regarded the attack as 'kohuru' (treachery),
calling for blood vengeance. Over the next two years, they resorted
to guerrilla war against their Ngati Haua neighbours: 'isolated
murders, night attacks, open battles and skirmishes'.[24] With full-
scale war seemingly in the offing, all tribes in the region hastened
to buy guns. The great Waikato iwi, under Te Wherowhero,
continued to import guns from Port Jackson (Sydney) through
John Cowell and other traders, with Kawhia and the Waikato
heads acting as the main places of entry.[25] Ngati Haua bought
guns from James Farrow, a musket trader operating out of
Tauranga. Farrow exchanged guns for flax, which Ngati Haua had
cut, scraped and prepared in the Matamata district.[26] (It took a
two-day journey for groups of about forty carriers, men, women
and slaves, to lug this processed flax to the agent in Tauranga.

After crossing the Matamata plain, the carriers ascended the rugged, bush-clad Kaimai range by way of the Wairere falls, and once over the watershed they completed the rest of their journey by way of a difficult native track.)[27] Some years later Farrow recalled that 'Maori saw great value in guns in former times. They would work day and night to get them.'[28] To some effect, it would seem. It has been claimed that, by 1830, nine out of ten Ngati Haua warriors had a firearm of some kind.[29] Marutuahu, similarly, bought guns from Pakeha traders. But their stock of firearms they supplemented in a novel way. Using logs drawn from a nearby forest, they set up a canoe-making industry inside their main pa, where specialist builders recruited from other tribes rapidly turned out waka for sale to Marutuahu which they could barter for 'guns from Nga Puhi'.[30] Work was apparently carried out by these craftsmen at so feverish a pace, that little time was left for ornamentation or carving. Warena Hengia, the Nga Oho chief, who saw the canoe-makers (drawn from Ngati Pukenga, Patuwai and Tawera hapu) at work, admitted that 'some [canoes] were negligently done. The great thing was to get guns.'[31]

As a result of the regional turmoil provoked by the Takurua massacre, the Marutuahu chiefs decided to abandon their scattered pa, and gather all their people (including Apihai's followers) within one great fortress. The place chosen was an existing pa on the Maungatautari foothills, standing about two kilometres back from where the Waikato river was to be dammed over a century later to form Lake Karapiro. The site was that of an ancient pa known by its previous owners as Te-Puru-o-Raukawa, 'the mainstay of Ngati Raukawa'. But when, in the mid-1820s, Ngati Raukawa withdrew from the area north of Maungatautari, Ngati Maru and Ngati Pukenga (a Bay of Plenty tribe which, not long since, had settled on the Coromandel peninsula under Ngati Maru protection)[32] jointly took over this pa.[33] It was to this powerful pa, which dominated the surrounding territory, that the Marutuahu and Tamaki tribes living throughout the Horotiu now shifted. To accommodate the thousands that congregated there, the pa was greatly enlarged, with each tribe occupying a designated section – the living quarters occupied by Te Kawau's followers, for instance, were by the main entrance (waharoa). A chief who had lived in this capacious new pa, later estimated its dimensions to have been about one kilometre by half a kilometre.[34]

The pa was the strategic key to the possession of the Maunga-tautari lands.[35] George S. Graham emphasised another great advantage of this fortress:

> This pa was selected as eminently suitable for adaptation and re-fortification to meet the new methods of warfare due to the introduction of guns. Many thousands of people laboured for a year or more completing and altering the old scheme of earth-works. They then made a practically impregnable stronghold.[36]

It was Graham's further belief that the new name which Maru-tuahu gave to the pa, Hao Whenua ('the land enclosed as in a net'), was 'intended as a taunt and a challenge' to other claimants to the district. By giving this particular name to the fortress (Graham concluded), Marutuahu 'indicated that they had come to stay and had by means of this fortified position netted in [and] claimed permanent possession of the Maungatautari district'.[37]

Regardless of whether Marutuahu were, in fact, acting provocatively in so naming the pa, the Waikato tribes, and Ngati Haua most of all, had come to believe that the visitors had out-stayed their welcome, and must now be expelled. All parties, wrote Maning, 'at the same time and, as it were, by common consent, made up their minds to end the contest in one great and final battle'.[38] Te Waharoa of Ngati Haua acted first and put together an alliance of tribes strong enough, he believed, to force the intruders to return to their homelands. Aware that the Waikato iwi had lost all patience with Marutuahu, he deliberately involved that great tribe from the outset, in order to forestall any independent action on its part. He was determined, however, that the mana extracted from victory must go primarily to Ngati Haua in order that his tribe could lay sole claim to the Maungatautari lands.[39] He also recruited a thousand warriors from Ngai Te Rangi of Tauranga, relying on that tribe's enduring and murderous feud with Ngati Pukenga, who were currently sheltering with Ngati Maru in Hao Whenua pa.[40]

In December 1830,[41] Te Waharoa, the acknowledged commander of the tribal coalition which he had put together, encamped with his army at Te Tiki o Te Ihi, a raised area close to Hao Whenua.[42] In arranging the disposition of his forces, Te Waharoa allotted the right wing to Waikato; Ngai Te Rangi he asked to hold the centre, where they were to act largely as a reserve force; while his own Ngati Haua warriors, 600 in number, he placed on the left wing. It was his deliberate intention that his own men should bear the brunt of the assault. Victory, he knew, would not come easily. Nor, of course, would the battlefield be one of his choosing. On the day of the battle, Marutuahu decided to make their stand, not at their pa, but on a terrace just south of the river known as Taumatawiwi ('the lookout among the rushes'). This promontory would have been a formidable place to storm. The Taumatawiwi terrace was protected on one side by a steep gully carved out by the Hauoira, a tributary of the Waikato river, and on its extensive northern side by a natural *glacis* made up of precipitous shingle banks.[43]

Fighting began in early morning, after a Ngati Paoa reconnoitring party (hurahura) stood on the Taumatawiwi terrace opposite the allied encampment and fired challenging musket volleys at Te Waharoa's expedition.[44] Ngati Haua quickly took up the challenge. In the ensuing battle, Marutuahu initially held their own against their attackers, exploiting their advantage of the higher ground, in order to fire down upon members of the exposed Ngati Haua assault group, who (said one onlooker) 'fell in heaps'.[45] That Te Waharoa's taua ultimately succeeded in overcoming the advantages that a great natural fortress like Taumatawiwi provided for its defenders, can only be attributed to the display, in this encounter, of military prowess of a high order. During the battle, two skills were in evidence. First was Te Waharoa's mastery of the novel tactics of musket warfare. Second was the ingenuity and reckless courage of the Ngati Haua left wing, crucially supported by Ngai Te Rangi, who were called on to join in the final storming of the approaches to Taumatawiwi. Upon the terrace itself, Ngati Haua and Ngai Te Rangi pressed home their advantage by close-range musket fire and hand-to-hand combat. The Marutuahu defenders, fearing the battle lost, and with their powder and shot now almost exhausted, turned tail and fled to the pa 'in bad order'.[46]

The disorderly retreat of these men for the safety of Hao Whenua caused consternation there among those onlookers who, stationed on high ground by the outer defences of the pa, had been watching the battle from afar. Their alarm spread to the women and children sheltering inside the pa, some of whom panicked, and made to flee for the safety of the bush and hills, disregarding the appeals of the elderly Ngati Whanaunga chief, Te Horeta (Te Taniwha), who called on his people 'to rally'.[47] But other rangatira of mana soon succeeded in restoring order. Kohirangatira of Ngati Paoa and two other chiefs planted themselves at the mouth of the main entrance, where they 'prevented egress' (it was said) to the faint-hearted.[48] Apihai Te Kawau also helped to quell the panic, by moving to the head of his 100 Ngati Whatua warriors,[49] who had been held in reserve in the pa, and by commanding them to 'Belt up {or 'Gird yourselves'} and attack Ngati Haua!'[50] He and the Hauraki chief, Te Rauroha, then led fresh fighting-men outside the pa, where they made one or two sorties, which forced the foremost Ngati Haua attackers to fall back to a less exposed position. But the threat of attack remained. Until darkness fell, Ngati Haua bullets continued to howl over Hao Whenua.

There is little doubt that Ngati Haua had won the battle of Taumatawiwi. Admittedly their losses were heavier than those of Marutuahu were. The Te Aroha Judgment put the ratio of Ngati Haua to Marutuahu deaths at, 'probably', four to one, a figure that tallies closely with the evidence of the minutebooks.[51] Figures given for the total casualties are inconclusive, but provide no justification for the oft-repeated wildly extravagant estimates of warriors killed that have appeared in twentieth-century accounts. One historian wrote in the 1920s that, at the battle of Taumatawiwi, 'many thousands of the flower of Maori manhood lost their lives'.[52] Another writer, some years later, spoke of the expanse between the Hao Whenua pa and the Waikato river as having been 'strewn with the bodies of four hundred and forty Ngati Marutuahu, including those of eighteen chiefs'. He continued: 'among them also lay the bodies of seventy of Te Waharoa's little army. Ninety more would carry marks of the fight to the grave.'[53] But if the sworn evidence of those who took part in the battle is to be our guide, then the reality is that the numbers killed on both sides must surely be calculated, not in terms of thousands or even hundreds but rather as multiples of ten.[54] A Ngati Whatua chief, who fought at the battle, later testified in the Native Land Court that Ngati Haua 'lost sixty in all' and 'Marutuahu lost ten', the latter figure probably an underestimate, but not grossly so.[55] Interestingly, the same chief maintained that not one of the hundred Tamaki warriors under Apihai Te Kawau, who were 'in the fight', was killed or wounded.[56]

At nightfall, the outcome of the engagement had still remained unclear. For although the Marutuahu forces had retreated to the pa in confusion, they had not been routed.[57] Indeed, the pattern of inter-tribal fighting of this era gives grounds for perhaps regarding Taumatawiwi as a preliminary skirmish (though admittedly a large-scale one) which, had events followed their customary course, would have been followed by a drawn-out siege culminating in the decisive battle.[58] And yet Judge Maning was surely right in declaring that Te Waharoa's forces 'won the battle of Taumatawiwi'.[59] While Ngati Haua's casualties may have been considerably heavier – after the battle, even Te Waharoa himself carried two severe flesh wounds, one from a musket ball, the other a gash from a tomahawk – they were the moral victors on the first day of fighting. After all, they gained possession of the field of battle, and they held all save one of the bodies of the Marutuahu warriors who fell on the battlefield or during the flight back to the pa. From these two circumstances they could derive considerable prestige. But the fact also remains that the military strength of the Maru tribes had been left intact. And if the battle had been resumed on the following day between those two evenly matched sides, who with confidence could have predicted the outcome? Those within the pa who had lost relatives at Taumatawiwi and had revenge in their hearts were certainly anxious for fighting to recommence.[60]

Apihai Te Kawau. Detail of a handcoloured lithograph after G. F. Angus.
AUCKLAND CITY
LIBRARIES

There was little sleep in the two opposing camps in the night that followed the battle. The warriors in Hao Whenua manned the rifle pits and trenches.[61] In the Waikato encampment at Teiroa, a prominence midway between Hao Whenua and Taumatawiwi,[62] Ngati Haua acted in a way that was as exceptional as it was revealing. Te Waharoa ordered his men to gather wood for funeral pyres on which the bodies of his dead were to be burnt lest on the following day they should end up in Marutuahu ovens.[63] Here is convincing evidence that Te Waharoa recognised that victory on the first day gave no assured outcome on the second.

However, fighting did not resume. On the second day an unexpected peace was made. There are contrasting versions of how this came about. According to Marutuahu, Te Waharoa made the first overture. They maintained that, at daybreak on the day after the battle of Taumatawiwi,[64] three women – two of Ngati Haua extraction and one Ngai Te Rangi, a kinship connection with the enemy which, through ancient custom, guaranteed immunity to hostile treatment should they encounter them – set out from Hao Whenua. Their purpose was to go to, to identify, and to weep over, the Marutuahu slain who were laid out in line on the Taumata-wiwi battlefield. After the women had finished their wailing over the bodies, Te Waharoa (according to this account) approached them, to request that on their return to Hao Whenua they should tell Taharoku, the Ngati Paoa chief, to come for a korero. (Taharoku would have been the obvious man to ask for because, as the younger brother of Takurua, whose tribe had been massacred in 1827, he was, according to Maori tradition, the chief who would have been the most aggrieved by Ngati Haua's kohuru.) According to this account, Taharoku returned, as asked, with a small, unarmed party. The two sides then negotiated a peace, made the more binding by the exchange of ten muskets by each side.[65]

The contrary version maintains that the first move to parley peace came, however, from the Marutuahu-Tamaki camp. According to this account, in the early morning of the day after the battle, the people in Hao Whenua pa held a mass meeting on the large flattish space in front of the pa, called Taumatapuhipuhi, where all war dances and meetings took place. That meeting unanimously decided to send a deputation, headed by Taharoku, to negotiate a peace with Te Waharoa.[66] When these two chiefs met, the Ngati Haua leader was said to have adopted the stance of a victor, and to have demanded that the Hauraki and Tamaki tribes go back to their homelands.

However, in spite of these conflicting renditions of the past, which owed much to the need of rival land claimants to make a strong case before the Native Land Court later in the nineteenth century, it is clear that an understanding of what happened depends on three key facts, on which Maori oral traditions substantially agree. These are that:

- both parties wanted peace;
- negotiators on both sides quickly agreed on the terms of peace; and

- the tribes who took part in the mass migration which resulted from the peace, though vulnerable, were guaranteed immunity from attack by Ngati Haua.

This common ground of agreement revealed itself in the evidence of witnesses at the Native Land Court hearing on the Te Aroha block in 1871, a case where the nature of the peace settlement after Taumatawiwi was crucial to the decision of the judges as to ownership of disputed land. Disinterested witnesses were of one mind on the following pieces of evidence. At the meeting between the peace negotiators, regardless of whether that had taken place on the first or the second afternoon following the battle, or whether the initiative came from Ngai Haua or Marutuahu, Te Waharoa had used few words in stating, in effect, 'You must leave these [Maungatautari] lands and go back to Hauraki and Tamaki.'[67] Taharoku, who had left his warriors putting trenches in order and, like his followers (including Ngati Whatua),[68] had not lost all stomach for battle, astutely countered Te Waharoa's demand by asking, 'How am I to get away?' Marutuahu were indeed in no mood to be cowed. Te Tuhua – a fellow chief, who accompanied Taharoku – on observing the smouldering bodies of Ngati Haua on funeral pyres, remarked to Te Waharoa, according to the Aroha Judgment:

> 'Why are you spoiling my provisions?' or words to that effect. The burning of their own dead on the battle-field is a very unusual practice, and never had recourse to by natives, especially near their own country or district, except under very desperate circumstances, when hope is lost of saving the bodies from the enemy's ovens in any other way. The laconic speech of Te Tuhua contained a volume of acuteness, and showed him to be keenly alive to the position of both parties. It was as much to say to Te Waharoa, 'You are putting the best face you can on matters, and trying to dictate terms to us, and are nevertheless ready to run yourself at a moment's notice.'[69]

Moreover, Taharoku's question 'How am I to get away?' was shrewdly practical. To shift this collection of tribes and their provisions and baggage would pose enormous problems – both logistical and pertaining to security. Relocating all these people and their impedimenta, with the tribes going either their separate ways or if to the same destination, in a succession of relays, would involve splitting them up in such a way as to expose them to Ngati Haua attack. Te Waharoa's laconic answer, 'You will be led out', implied such enormous safeguards that the negotiators were perfectly assured. Essentially the Ngati Haua chieftain was saying: 'I promise to place in your keeping people of rank from my tribe, who will be your hostages, acting as a guarantee of my good faith and as a pledge against all threat of molestation.'[70]

The evidence of those onetime inhabitants of Hao Whenua, who lived on more than forty years afterwards to give sworn testimony in court as to the nature of the peace settlement after Taumatawiwi, is remarkably consistent. Those witnesses maintained that Taharoku, on his return to the Taumatapuhipuhi meeting-ground, where the mass of the Hao Whenua inhabitants waited expectantly, simply repeated without embellishment what Te Waharoa had said to him. The first to rise and comment was Kohirangatira, a leader of such mana that a chief, not incidentally one of his tribe, called him 'our shelter'.[71] Kohirangatira was emphatically brief. He simply shouted, 'Whakarongo e Marutuahu! Whakatika! Whakatika!' ('Listen O Marutuahu! Let us go! Let us go!') Other influential chiefs, seemingly reassured by Te Waharoa's promise of safe conduct, supported Kohirangatira, and urged the tribes to accept the terms offered. The people of the pa did not hesitate. In old age a Ngati Whatua chief recalled the mood of those who were at that meeting: 'All our minds were made up to return to Tamaki and Hauraki,' he said.[72]

III

Over the next few weeks,[73] the inhabitants of Hao Whenua set out for their homelands. They travelled by three main routes. Those destined for Tamaki (Ngati Whatua and a branch of Ngati Paoa) went down the Waikato with the intention of crossing into the Manukau harbour by way of the Waiuku portage. The main Ngati Paoa contingent bound for the western shore of the Firth of Thames and the neighbouring gulf islands used the Piako river route. The largest group, made up of various hapu of Ngati Maru, Ngati Whanaunga and Ngati Tama-Te-Ra, returned to their homelands by crossing overland to the

Waihou river, down which some travelled by canoe.[74] There was
no firm evidence given in court that the guides (or hostages, if
you will) whom Te Waharoa had promised were in fact provided.
But Maning and Monro do suggest in their Te Aroha Judgment
that Marutuahu 'very probably were accompanied on their
return to the Thames by a chief of the Ngati Haua called
Pakerahake and two chief women of the same tribe'.[75] We do
know, however, that the party that went down the Waikato with
Te Kawau was unattended. 'None of the Waikato came to escort
us,' testified Warena Hengia; 'we were not led.'[76] It seems that
the promise given by Te Waharoa at the peacemaking, which his
followers subsequently honoured, was to prove safeguard
enough. A chief, who was asked whether Ngati Haua had inter-
fered with the canoes which Ngati Whatua had placed in the
Waikato river before evacuation, remarked: 'Ngati Haua were
too rangatira (honourable?) to meddle with our canoes.'[77] The
fact remains that, in the wording of the Te Aroha Judgment, all
three parties having been granted 'a secure and unmolested
retreat . . . arrived in due time, and without molestation or mis-
adventure, in their own district'.[78]

*Taraia, chief of Ngati
Tama-Te-Ra: 'a warrior of
dread renown'.* AUCKLAND
CITY LIBRARIES

In the years ahead, Taraia, chief of Ngati Tama-Te-Ra, scorn-
fully remarked that the Maru tribes had been led out of Horotiu
like pigs on a string,[79] while Pakeha traders (usually echoing a
Ngati Haua boast) asserted that Waikato tribes drove Hauraki
back to the sea.[80] So often were these opinions repeated that, as
Maning put it, in time 'the truth became obscure and falsehood
established as truth'.[81] Maning was right. What happened was
otherwise.

For the historian, this is not an issue of tribal mana concerned
with a battle (won or lost), or with subsequent peace negotiations, important though each of these was at the time. What
must be grasped is that the decision not to resume fighting after
the one-day battle of Taumatawiwi, and the readiness of the
Hauraki and Tamaki peoples to agree to a return to their homelands, reflected a changed military situation. By 1830, there had
been two influential developments, not unconnected, in both
Maori warfare and the distribution of tribal power in northern
New Zealand. Guns had become more evenly spread among the
tribes. And no longer were they a Nga Puhi monopoly. The
approximate equality of power between tribes, which in the pre-

musket era had acted as a restraint on war, had reappeared once more in those regions where there was more or less musket parity. Further, Maori, inventive and adaptive in their ideas of armed conflict – as in much else – had developed new tactics to cope with musket warfare. Pa-builders placed less reliance on palisades and concentrated more on earthworks, most notably constructing carefully placed rifle pits and trenches, with inter-connecting saps. Moreover, the military advantage was tipping towards the defenders. Taking a pa by frontal assault was becoming correspondingly more difficult and sieges less pre-dictable in their outcome.

With these considerations in mind, one turns to the opinion expressed in the Te Aroha Judgment that Marutuahu had not 'been expelled from Waikato under circumstances of marked defeat and humiliation'.[82] Certainly the one-day battle of Tau-matawiwi was less decisive in its result than has been commonly held. Nor was either side demoralised. As has been noted, after the first day of fighting, Ngati Haua were in possession of the battlefield chosen by Marutuahu, and they had in their hands all but one of the enemy dead; proof, according to Maori custom, that they had prevailed. Yet Ngati Haua had suffered the heavier losses including some of their most courageous warriors, while Marutuahu could claim to be heartened by having killed the first and last man to fall,[83] episodes of considerable consequence in the Maori culture of war. Most importantly, after the first day, both sides were essentially intact. If the struggle had continued beyond the first day its character would have changed. For the forces of Waikato would have had to switch from a contest on a battlefield to mounting a (possibly drawn-out) siege, in which success would turn on their untested ability to storm Hao Whenua, a pa well prepared for musket warfare. And should the siege have dragged on in an attempt to starve out the defenders, those in the pa would have been able to appeal for assistance to two powerful Marutuahu warlords who had missed the original action, Te Hira of Ngati Maru and Taraia of Ngati Tama-Te-Ra, the latter rightly described as a 'warrior of dread renown'.[84] The reality was that, in 1830, Hauraki iwi were anything but a spent force. That was evident over the next five years when, under Taraia, Te Taniwha, Te Rohu and other chiefs, they mounted four major attacks on Ngati Haua and other Waikato tribes, in quarrels over disputed borderlands.[85] In these circumstances, talk of 'victors' and 'vanquished' at Taumatawiwi is ill considered. Immediately after the battle of Taumatawiwi, both sides were anxious for peace.

Equally is it mistaken to speak of Marutuahu as having been *driven* to the coast. On this question of returning home, the Hauraki tribes (but as we shall see, not those from Tamaki) had undergone, by this time, a change of heart. Nga Puhi raids in the Hauraki region had fallen away significantly. Furthermore, the tribes there had acquired the means of protecting themselves at last. It was generally known that trading vessels and Pakeha traders had made arms and ammunition freely available in the area.[86] Angela Ballara has recounted that Taraia set out diligently in the 1820s to procure arms and ammunition, to such effect that, by 1830, he and his people had built up a surplus which 'they were able to trade' with other tribes 'for pigs, flax fibre or slaves'.[87] The availability of muskets, and the security they offered, gave all that was needed to induce the Hauraki people to return to that accustomed environment where streams, rocks, hills, forests, eel-rich swamps and tides gave life for them its rhythms and deeper meanings.

IV

No sooner had the inhabitants of Hao Whenua confirmed the terms of peace, than all prepared to leave the large pa. Since each of the main groups was travelling by a different route and with separate arrangements, this account of the evacuation will confine itself to the recollections of members of Apihai Te Kawau's group, who originally set out on the long journey home to Tamaki.[88]

Shifting Apihai's people by river, portage and inland sea (the Manukau) to a new location almost 200 kilometres away entailed transport problems of great complexity. Nowhere are we told how many Te Taou and Nga Oho were with Apihai Te Kawau at Hao Whenua, apart from a number of references to the fact that he had 100 adult braves under his command.[89] An estimate of the total figure, which took in women, children and, possibly, slaves,[90] would certainly be of the order of 300 or so.[91]

Since this tribal group would have had to wait for about eight months before harvesting their next (spring) crop, one assumes that its members would be obliged to carry in their canoes scores of tonnes of stored food.[92]

Doubtless Ngati Whatua chiefs, and those Ngati Paoa chiefs who were travelling with Te Kawau, had to make calculations such as these when, on the day following the peacemaking, they set about buying canoes which Ngati Pukenga and Patuwai craftsmen had constructed in the pa. Ngati Whatua bought ten large canoes, paying for them with guns. Three only were complete at the time of purchase. The rest were almost finished; requiring only stern pieces or strakes (upper planks) 'to be sewn', that is, lashed on with flax cords. Over the next six days Apihai's own workmen completed this task.[93] On the following two days, 'all hands' (as one of Apihai's fellow chiefs put it) were called on to drag these large canoes down to the bank of the Waikato river.[94] This was immediately followed by a further three days of labour, during which 'all hands', once again, 'joined in carrying down the potatoes'. No crops were left unharvested. Pumpkins, maize (though still soft and unripened) and available calabash were all taken.[95] At midnight, when those about to depart had finally placed all provisions in the canoes, they took a seemly and solemn leavetaking of the dead. The bodies and skeletons of all who had died during the occupation of Hao Whenua were collected and burned to guard against discovery and desecration.[96] Before Ngati Whatua and Ngati Paoa left the pa the following day, they put to the torch all the buildings (whare) they had occupied.

It was generally understood among members of the joint party of Ngati Whatua and Ngati Paoa that set out from Pukekura – as the area around Cambridge was then commonly called – that the destination of both tribes was to be somewhere in the Tamaki district. When the two tribes arrived at Ngaruawahia a month later, however, they separated. During the slow journey down the river, moving (one assumes) in relays and using bankside encampments, Te Kawau had prevailed on his followers to change the original arrangement of returning to Tamaki, and to paddle up the Waipa river and seek refuge there instead. Ngati Paoa, on the other hand, kept to its initial intention, and continued down the Waikato river, crossed the Awaroa and Otahuhu portages, and settled in, or beside, the inner Hauraki gulf.

Why did Ngati Whatua of Tamaki not accompany them? Concern for the safety of his tribe had induced Te Kawau to postpone his return to Tamaki-makau-rau. Information he had picked up after the peace arrangements had convinced him that the continuing threat of Nga Puhi invasion still made life hazardous beside both the Waitemata and Manukau harbours. There was a readymade alternative. It will be recalled that when the Nga Puhi victory at the battle of Te Ika-a-ranganui had placed the whole of the lower Kaipara and Tamaki districts in jeopardy, the inhabitants had scattered far and wide. Not all Ngati Whatua of Tamaki had stayed with Apihai Te Kawau. Some had fled south with the Kaipara branch of the tribe and established themselves in a pa called Te Horo on the banks of the Waipa river, just north of Mount Pirongia and near Kaniwhaniwha. 'Along with them', wrote Fenton, were 'Ngatiteata, Ngatitamaoho, Te Akitai, and most of the Manukau tribes.'[97] These people Apihai decided to join. His followers, he believed, would be safer among old allies, not least because they would then come under the benign protection of the great Waikato chief, Te Wherowhero, who was at that time at the height of his military powers.

Thus it came about that, in 1831, the followers of Apihai settled at Te Horo beside the Waipa. And there they remained for four years, their folk-wandering temporarily at an end.

CHAPTER VI

Years of Exile, 1831–35

I

Apihai Te Kawau acted wisely in persuading his followers to go into indefinite refuge in the upper Waipa valley rather than follow the original plan of returning to Tamaki. In 1831, Tamaki continued to be a dangerous place to visit, let alone be one in which to live. And it remained so. In the years ahead small Ngati Whatua fishing groups who made surreptitious excursions to the Manukau to fish for sharks,[1] confirmed this when they reported back to their chiefs (Apihai, Tinana, Tamaki, and others) at Te Horo. The reality was that for much of the 1830s, the three dominant iwi in the region, Nga Puhi, Hauraki and Waikato, were either at war with each other or, at best, in a state of armed truce. So Tamaki, as the regional node of canoe transport, remained on the likely itinerary of war-parties that would live off the land as they travelled, would ransack gardens and villages, and generally terrorise those in their path. One missionary visiting a Hauraki kainga in 1832 reported how 'all [had] fled' when they heard that a Nga Puhi war-party was coming south, 'such terror does the name of Nga Puhi convey'.[2]

This explains why, over the next four years, Apihai's followers continued to live in the pa at Te Horo, on the west bank of the Waipa river.[3] There they became part of a heterogeneous community of hapu, many of whom had little in common other than

126

Tuakau on the Waikato.

some kinship link and the need for protection that isolation and the might and mana of Te Wherowhero could provide.[4] At the time of the arrival of Ngati Whatua of Tamaki, there were already upwards of 600 people living in the pa. But these numbers swelled further in August 1832 when Nga Puhi invaders drove a branch of Ngati Paoa, who had been living in the area now known as Port Waikato, up the Waipa to seek refuge at Te Horo. When William Williams visited the pa two years later, numbers had built up even more. He spoke of its 'numerous population' that, in his opinion, made it 'as large as Ngaruawahia',[5] now, under Te Wherowhero, the headquarters of the Waikato people.

Because the Nga Puhi invasion of August 1832, which took place when many of Te Wherowhero's warriors were tied down campaigning in Taranaki, was the last incursion that the northern tribes made into Waikato territory, more must be said about it here. This particular war-party, drawn mainly from the

Tuakau on the Waikato by John Johnson MD, Johnson Album. AUCKLAND MUSEUM LIBRARY

Whangarei region, breached the uneasily held peace that Hongi had constructed nine years before. The expedition was actually an embarrassment to the Bay of Islands tribes, who were anxious not to provoke Te Wherowhero. But the northern taua under the leadership of Motutara, Pukerangi and Te Tirarau[6] was punished for its temerity.[7] After fighting its way up the lower Waikato valley as far as today's Mercer, the expedition was repulsed by Ngati Te Ata, and driven back towards the Waiuku portage. Lower Waikato tribes – Ngati Tipa, Ngati Mahanga, and Ngati Tamaoho – joined Ngati Te Ata in vengeful pursuit of the retreating invaders. They harried them even to their Whangarei homelands where they inflicted heavy damage as a final retribution.

But war remained an ever-present threat, not least in the Hauraki gulf region, where, as late as 1837, a resident missionary lamented 'the uncertainty of peace in <u>an ungoverned savage land</u>'.[8] Cultural myopia perhaps. But it is well documented that Tamaki, in the early 1830s, was a population void, a region of desolation. A Pakeha trader who, in 1831, crossed the isthmus with a group of Ngati Paoa by way of the Otahuhu dragging-place, saw 'no native residences on the northern banks of Tamaki', and 'no signs of clearings'.[9] Only at Pukaki-tapu, beside an inlet of the upper Manukau harbour near Papatoetoe, did he observe 'a few natives of Akitai' who 'had come from Waikato to fish'. Shortly after, John Cowell, another trader, who went up the Waitemata harbour by canoe with the Ngati Whanaunga chief, Te Taniwha (Te Horeta), reported that when he passed the old pa sites at Orakei he 'saw no fires there. If we had, I should have gone on shore and put on the kettle. I did not see any cultivations of any kind.'[10]

Missionary reports of these years speak of Tamaki and its approaches as a region laid waste by war. The CMS catechist, W. T. Fairburn, who went up the Tamaki river in 1832 in order to assess the potential of Mokoia (Panmure) as a future site for a mission station, lauded what he saw. 'Certainly a beautiful place', he remarked, 'and I think without exaggeration [it] may be termed the garden of New Zealand, containing a large tract of first-rate land for cultivation, well watered and plenty of timber accessible by water about 8 miles distant.'[11] Among the site's further recommendations, he noted its 'central situation', and the nearby Manukau harbour, which was 'navigable for small vessels nearly as far as Waikato'.[12] But, he concluded, what was the point of setting up a mission station in a region where there were virtually no people to convert? Late in 1833, Fairburn revisited Mokoia, this time as a member of a small party which included the Rev. Henry Williams, superintendent of CMS work in New Zealand.[13] Once again, the Tamaki isthmus presented itself to the group as a man-made desert. Williams wrote:

> The land was now overgrown with firn [*sic*] and *tupakihi* bushes. No signs of an inhabitant could be observed in any direction. Part of a human skull lay on the ground close to us, which was more than half an inch thick; there were three deep cuts on it from a hatchet, most probably inflicted at the time of the general massacre [of 1821].[14]

William Thomas Fairburn, CMS missionary.

During that visit, three of the missionary party scrambled up Mount Wellington to gaze upon (in Fairburn's words) 'one of the finest views I have ever beheld'.[15] He went on to speak of 'majestic beautiful rivers [harbours]', and of a great 'extent of level country' still bearing

> the marks of having been very thickly inhabited. . . . And yet notwithstanding the beauty of the scenery, the fertile appearance of the country, the rivers and bays abounding with fish, the land producing spontaneously the best of fern root (a very nutritious food), yet not a Native to be seen, the mind could not but revert to that period when the blessing of the Gospel should convert the swords into ploughshares, and the spears into pruning hooks.

But there was little prospect of peace. For some time after this visit, the region remained blighted by warfare or the threat of it. Early in 1835, the Rev. Henry Williams, travelling on the mission schooner *Columbine*, touched briefly on Tamaki's shore. Apart from evidence of fern having been recently burnt off, probably by transient fishermen, he was unable to 'discover any signs of natives. All was quietness around, no appearance of smoke. . . .'[16]

The approaches to Tamaki and the gulf islands as well told the same story of the ravages of war. During a reconnoitring trip which Williams made with his assistant Thomas Chapman on the mission's cutter *Karere* in 1831, to mark out places in the upper North Island into which the Church Missionary Society could begin expanding, he stopped briefly at the northern end of Great Barrier Island. In his journal he noted that they had made a '[r]un in shore for the purpose of replenishing our wood and water. . . . No appearance of natives on the island all killed or dispersed.' What struck him, as it had others, was that the dearth of people seemed quite at odds with the many 'small rivers and bays, and timber in every part of the island, and fish in greatest abundance. . . . How blessed might hundreds of families be here!' he concluded.[17] The inner islands of the gulf and the littoral were equally ravaged and desolate. During a subsequent journey to the Thames region, Williams was detained at Pakihi island by the late arrival of the *Karere.* He filled in his waiting time by crossing to a nearby 'large island', which he did not name, but which was either Ponui or (less likely) Waiheke,

> in order to give the boys opportunity to dig firn [*sic*] root as our stock of provision is getting low and no appearance of the *Karere.* We ascended one of the hills from which we had a commanding view. The Island on which we were was large and [had an] abundance of ground for many families; the rocks were covered with oysters and *pipis* on the mud banks which run out for a long distance, and the sea was full of fish of all kinds. It was melancholy to look around; all was perfect stillness, except here and there a bird, no bustle of civil life. No vessels, boats or canoes moving on either hand over the surfaces of these waters which spread like magnificent rivers among the numerous islands. The hills in the rear are clothed with timber without rendering service to any. Traces of former Towns and settlements were visible as we came along and where'er we turned, but all were either destroyed, taken captive or fled.[18]

In parts of the Firth of Thames rather more distant from Tamaki, pockets of substantial Marutuahu settlement were still to be found. But learning how missionaries reacted in the 1830s to the depopulated state of Tamaki and the gulf islands is useful to the historian, quite apart from the intrinsic vividness of what they wrote. Their accounts help to explain why, with so few Maori to convert, both Anglican and Wesleyan mission societies then saw little point in establishing mission stations in the district which today is easily the most densely settled urban area in

New Zealand. When Hobson came as governor to Tamaki in 1840, the nearest mission station was one at Maraetai, which, in fact, had only recently been set up and was a good twenty kilometres away by sea from the heart of Tamaki. Against this reluctance of the missionaries to proselytise in a deserted district must be set, however, the high opinion that they formed of Tamaki in the 1830s. Their journals and correspondence are full of praise of this large fertile district, bounded by waterways endowed with superb anchorages for ships of all sizes, yet (most conveniently) lacking a large Maori population, which European settlers could otherwise have found it troublesome to displace should they decide to settle there. This favourable opinion of the missionaries, and that of Henry Williams above all, was to prove influential when New Zealand became a British possession in 1840. The enthusiasm of Williams for Tamaki's great natural advantages counted for much when Hobson sought his opinion on where the site of the capital of the new colony should be.

II

As today's historians enter upon a new millennium, they cannot fail to be aware that at the hub of the debate on race relations in New Zealand is the Treaty of Waitangi and the alleged failure of the Crown in past years to honour its principles. Claims, now numbering many hundreds, which have been laid year after year before the permanent commission of inquiry known as the Waitangi Tribunal, have ensured that the 1840 treaty remains an enduring centre of attention in New Zealand's political life. As a result, we have been tempted to look on 1840 as *the* great disjunction in early New Zealand history, with the implication that not until the Crown government began, did Maori society become 'marginalised' or experience the full consequences of 'colonisation'. Advocates of this viewpoint often seem to fear that any admission that Maori society was being drastically undermined before 1840 will either blunt the edge of claims against the Crown yet to be heard before the Waitangi Tribunal, or (much more defensibly) will somehow depreciate the early achievement in adaptation made by the Maori people. It is undeniable that this indigenous people responded to western penetration in a dynamic and creative way, grafting western innovation and technology on to traditional life so that (so to speak) they were able successfully to play the white man's game into the 1850s and beyond, and to play it very well indeed. But I here emphasise that, even though the Treaty of Waitangi made Aotearoa a British colony in 1840, the colonisation of Maori minds had set in well before that date.

By the 1830s, in those parts of northern New Zealand of which Tamaki was the geographical centre, three aspects of the western world had begun to impact seriously on Maori culture and society. They were economic penetration, the introduction of firearms, and the spread of Christianity.

Timber draggers on Waiheke island. Pen and ink drawing by C. H. Kennett Watkins. AUCKLAND MUSEUM LIBRARY

The west took the initiative, in the first instance, in establishing the economic relationship, by pursuing prized raw materials such as flax and timber, and by attempting to satisfy the need of ships' masters and crews for food for revictualling, and for women as sexual partners.[19] Maori in those regions which had access to shipping quickly responded. They took advantage of the opportunity to barter, building up an insistent demand for convenient, and (to them) attractive goods like guns, tools, new exotic foods and textiles. Some of these commodities, such as iron tools, clearly made Maori more productive; others seemed to make life more enjoyable. But by entering into the exchange economy of the metropolitan world, Maori people became, in time, captives to that distinctive phenomenon of modern industrial capitalism known as consumerism.

We have seen how harsh experience of the early musket wars demonstrated to Maori that guns were essential to survival.[20] 'Old weapons', wrote a historian of these early days, 'were no match against the new. . . . A small body of cowards with firearms were stronger than numerous bands of brave warriors wielding meris [*sic*] and tomahawks.'[21] The race to procure guns diverted many tribes in northern New Zealand from their traditional economy of subsistence farming, fishing and food gathering to the preparation of flax, a cash crop of high commercial value.[22] 'In 1830', according to Thomson, 'vessels amounting to 5888 tons cleared out of Sydney for New Zealand; and twenty-six vessels, having an average burden of one hundred tons, arrived there from the latter country laden with flax.'[23] This activity spread. 'Nearly every tribe round the Bay [of Islands]',

A thunderous war dance.
From Thomson's Story of
New Zealand.
AUCKLAND CITY
LIBRARIES

noted William Williams in his 1831 Journal, 'is at present collecting this material. . . . They have been stirred up by the
activity of the people to the southward who have exported very
many tons during the last two years.'[24] Three years later, while
travelling through a remote part of the upper Waipa valley close
to the pa where Apihai's people then lived, William Williams
observed how many of the Maori there were also engrossed in the
activity of scraping flax.[25]

And when the demand for flax fell away, Maori in northern
New Zealand turned to the milling of kauri timber, the extractive
industry that progressively began to supersede flax fibre as the
region's main export. Maori workmen provided the great labour
force for the two main tasks involved in this activity: felling trees,
and then dragging the logs from the bush. As timber draggers,
they turned to account the age-old skill acquired from lugging
huge canoes across portages. Now, working in teams of up to
'eighty or more',[26] they 'pulled and hauled and sweated like
Horses' to bring logs and spars to the water's edge.[27] Nor had the
enthusiasm of Maori to work for the export market died away
when their demand for munitions of war had been satisfied.
Thomson calculated that, between 1825 and 1839, £30,000
worth of goods was on average imported annually into New

Zealand, a figure that does not take into account the large amount of informal trade conducted between Maori and South Sea whalers for which there are no statistical returns.[28] There were new consumer hungers to be satisfied as the decade neared its end: 'for tobacco, blankets, pipes, shirts, cooking-pots, trowsers, gowns, cottons, hoes and spades'.[29] And much else. Thus did consumerism begin insidiously to strike at the roots of the traditional socio-economic order of the Maori people, among whom, since time out of mind, all large-scale productive activity had been conducted along co-operative, communal lines, with labour arising out of kinship obligations within the whanau or hapu and regulated by chiefs. But these changes to the social and economic order were gradual, extended over decades. Individualism, that concomitant of consumer acquisitiveness, did not come fully into its destructive own within Maori society until the settler government individualised tribal land titles through the 1862 and 1865 Native Land Acts.

The impact which western firearms made on Maori life, was, however, more immediate. In northern Aotearoa, the musket wars passed through two main phases. As we have seen, the most destructive tribal battles were those where one side only, usually the Nga Puhi, had a monopoly of firearms. These battles – Mauinaina and Mokoia, Te Totara, Matakitaki, and Te Ika-a-ranganui come to mind – were particularly slaughterous. The usual upshot, after battle had been joined, was for the muskets to induce such panic among those who did not have them, that the attackers could fall upon the demoralised defenders, using axe and tomahawk to deadly effect. But when, by the 1830s, both sides possessed firearms, as at the battle of Taumatawiwi, casualties diminished. Some missionaries of the time believed that this emerging equality of firepower (reinforced, of course, by the gospel working in 'its silent way') would ultimately end tribal wars.[30] 'The distribution of firearms, which is now become general', wrote William Williams in 1834, 'deprives in a great measure the strong of their ability to oppress the weak.' His expectation was premature. Although slaughter tended to fall away once both sides had guns, the engrained urge to resort to war, when there were past wrongs to be avenged, did not.

Long-standing quarrels among the powerful northern iwi remained: between Nga Puhi and Hauraki; between each of them

and the people of Tauranga; and between Waikato and Te Ati Awa of Taranaki. Gudgeon has pointed out that it was characteristic of that era that, after Taumatawiwi, the Marutuahu tribes did not quickly forget that 'Ngati Haua were their deadly enemy, whom it was their duty to attack and worry on every possible occasion'.[31] And harass Ngati Haua they did. On four separate occasions in the early 1830s, war-parties under Taraia, Te Taniwha, Te Rohu and other warrior chiefs made incursions into the Ngati Haua borderlands in the upper Waihou.[32] The most unusual expedition of revenge was that undertaken in 1832 by a joint force drawn from Marutuahu people and a contingent of Nga Puhi led by Rewharewha (who was related by marriage to Ngati Paoa). After some hundreds of warriors performed a thunderous war dance at Tararu, near Thames, the combined taua, led by Te Hira of Ngati Maru, went up the Waihou and inflicted a heavy defeat on Ngati Haua at Matamata.[33] (After this excursion, Rewharewha's party of 260 men rejoined the large Nga Puhi taua, of which it had

Village on Waiheke by Charles Heaphy, Heaphy Album. AUCKLAND MUSEUM LIBRARY

135

formerly been part, which was going to Tauranga to punish Ngai Te Rangi). It should also be noted that, in addition to the old incitements to war, such as the search for revenge or the pursuit of mana, were new incentives (albeit at times concealed by talk of utu) that had been generated by western contact. One gathers under this head the struggle to possess harbours through which tribes could trade with Pakeha, or the resort to war to seize slaves whose labour as growers of crops and scrapers of flax, or whose services as prostitutes for ships' crews, would provide the means of securing western goods.[34]

During the 1830s, changes in the relative strength of iwi encouraged some ambitious chiefs to go to war to extend their tribal rohe. War gave the means by which Te Rauparaha tightened his control over neighbouring tribes in the south-west region of the North Island to which his Ngati Toa people had recently migrated, and that achieved, war then enabled him to compete successfully for land and resources in the upper half of the South Island.[35] These years also saw the Waikato ariki, Te Wherowhero, who at about this time acquired the nickname 'Potatau', extend his domination over a wider area of the upper North Island.[36] More importantly, in view of the concern of this book, his new hegemonic position made him, by the end of the decade, the virtual arbiter of peace and war in Tamaki and the lands adjoining.

Observe how markedly the military situation had moved in his favour by 1831. Ngati Raukawa and the Marutuahu federation, his former troublesome neighbours on his eastern boundaries, had been harried into removing themselves. This development freed Te Wherowhero to attack Te Ati Awa, his Taranaki neighbours in the south-west, and thus avenge past defeats which they had inflicted on Waikato.[37] In November 1831 he led a large war-party into Ati Awa lands. After laying waste much of north Taranaki, he besieged and overthrew the giant pa Pukerangiora, at Waitara, killing many of its numerous inhabitants. The story is told how on the day following the final battle, Potatau sat at a gateway of the pa, 'and as the prisoners were brought in he struck them down with his greenstone *mere* "Whakarewa" killing a hundred and fifty. He only stopped when he said his arm was tired.'[38] The expedition continued its assault on the Taranaki peoples until the late summer of 1832, but with diminishing success and Waikato were forced to withdraw.

After a further and indecisive attack on Te Ati Awa in 1833,[39] the Waikato tribes resumed their vendetta against the Taranaki peoples in the following year. A large war-party led by Te Wherowhero, Te Kanawa, Te Waharoa and other brave chiefs besieged the south Taranaki pa, Te Ruaki, near Hawera, finally starving its Ngati Ruanui inhabitants into surrender.[40] But the siege of the nearby coastal pa, Orangituapeka, which took place later in the same year, was unsuccessful, a number of Waikato chiefs falling in battle. At that point, Te Wherowhero decided to make peace and promised to end Waikato raids against Taranaki forever.[41]

We can only speculate as to why Potatau Te Wherowhero and his fellow Waikato chiefs decided to end their wars with the Taranaki peoples. Perhaps the obvious answer of war-weariness is the most convincing. But the habit of exacting blood retribution died hard. Kelly wrote that certain Ngati Maniapoto chiefs did not recognise the general peace just concluded and, shortly after the peacemaking, organised a small war-party to fight against Ngati Ruanui hapu in south Taranaki, in order to avenge the death of relatives.[42] Yet, generally speaking, the peace held in that part of the North Island. But only just. In August 1834, the missionary William Williams had a discussion at Ngaruawahia with Potatau, in which the chief spoke of some of his followers as still spoiling for war.

> I learnt from [Te] Wherowhero today that the various tribes of Waikato are still bent on war in various directions. One numerous party which has nearly cut off the inhabitants of Mt Egmont is talking of going this summer to complete the work of extermination, and then take up their abode there, while others are intending to assert their claims to their old possessions further to the northward which step is likely to involve them again in war with the Thames natives.[43]

Those planning to go to the south claimed that they still needed to go 'to Taranaki to obtain revenge for relatives'. The 'others' whose ambitions 'to the northward' were likely to provoke war were the lower Waikato tribes such as Ngati Te Ata and Ngati Tamaoho, who were determined to repossess land in the south-ern Manukau, from which they had earlier been driven by Nga

Puhi. To do this, they would have to contend with Ngati Paoa, whose further claim to disputed borderlands east and south of Otahuhu would also be strenuously opposed by a number of Tamaki tribes, when the time came for them to return. There was no guarantee that the ending of conflict in the regions contiguous to the Tamaki region would bring peace to the isthmus itself.

III

But all this lay in the future. In the earlier 1830s, the eastern coast of northern New Zealand was as much plagued by war, as was its western counterpart. After journeying home by boat from Tauranga to the Bay of Islands in 1833, a missionary party reported that the whole coastline was 'desolate and without inhabitants'.[44] In fact, both north and south of this particular stretch of coastline, there were similar signs of the ravages of war. Even Ngati Porou settlements at the East Cape and beyond had been blighted. In his report on a missionary journey that he made in 1834, William Williams recorded that kainga on the lower Waiapu river were still suffering from raids that Nga Puhi had made some years before, 'solely for the purpose of making slaves'.[45] Even settlements on the Mahia peninsula, 420 miles from the Bay of Islands, which Williams contended was the furthest extent of Nga Puhi expeditions, had yet to recover from the raids.

The two great iwi of the east coast north of Tauranga in this period were Nga Puhi and Hauraki (Marutuahu). Past wars had left between them a residue of grievance and festering mistrust. But because, by 1830, both were equally well armed with muskets, they were reluctant to go to war with each other. As early as 1828 missionaries in the Bay of Islands reported that local tribes were loath to attack tribes in the Thames because they were now able to carry out reprisal raids with firearms.[46] Not that iwi were homogeneous entities. Tribal elements within Nga Puhi acted quite independently. Indeed some, on occasion, fought each other. (CMS missionaries in the Bay of Islands served their apprenticeship as peacemakers, in the 1820s, by mediating between quarrelling groups in the Bay, Hokianga and Whangaroa.)[47] So, at the time of the enforced Marutuahu return to the Thames in 1830, the threat of war from assertively minded northern hapu still remained. The Thames flax trader Chapman reported, in 1832, that

> For these five years past, the natives of that beautiful part had not been allowed to cultivate except here and there in secluded valleys – those of Whangarei, a stronger party making a continual attack on them, and they had been so driven about that with few exceptions, they had left all their seed and food, and were therefore living almost exclusively on fern-root and fish, and live in a dreadful state of continuous alarm.[48]

William Williams, 1800–78. Missionary, linguist and educator.
AUCKLAND CITY LIBRARIES

But after 1832, the year when the Whangarei branch of Nga Puhi was defeated consequent on its attempted invasion of the Waikato,[49] the northern iwi acted more cautiously towards its neighbours immediately south of Tamaki.

Nevertheless, Nga Puhi and Marutuahu continued to fight other tribes. Mention has already been made of the vendetta, which persisted in the 1830s, between Marutuahu and its southern neighbour, Ngati Haua. Nga Puhi expeditions in this period tended to bypass the Firth of Thames. For them the main theatre of war was the Bay of Plenty. A prolonged war was set in train with tribes there when a taua left the Bay of Islands in 1831[50] to procure payment (utu) by the shedding of blood, to avenge the death of chiefs killed in tribal quarrels. The quarrels had taken place, incidentally, entirely in Northland itself. But Maori custom allowed for retribution to be exacted from another tribe. In this case the people chosen lived 230 miles from the Bay of Islands, on the Mercury islands, east of the Coromandel range.[51] The taua killed many inhabitants there, but then was itself virtually wiped out when Tauranga Maori came by canoe and counter-attacked.

Full-scale war resulted.[52] In January 1832 a war-party of 800 left the Bay of Islands under Titore to attack Ngai Te Rangi of Tauranga to obtain utu for the loss of mana brought about by the annihilation, in the previous year, of the Nga Puhi war-party. This expedition failed in its purpose. Cheap victories for Nga Puhi were no longer to be had for the asking. Tauranga natives were now, it was reported, 'exceedingly well armed', having for some time exchanged flax for guns with a Pakeha agent working for a Sydney merchant.[53] Nga Puhi, having been repulsed in their early attacks on the Tauranga pa, were 'less disposed to be saucy', according to European witnesses, than they once had been.[54] The Tauranga warriors refused to fight the decisive pitched battle that Nga Puhi wanted. They stayed put behind their fortifications, well aware that it would be a most difficult task for Nga Puhi warriors to take a prepared pa whose defenders were equipped with firearms. As the siege dragged on, the northern invaders, who admitted that they were running 'very short of food',[55] would gladly have gone home had it not been that they 'were afraid of their countrymen's "tawai" (jeering)',[56] should they reappear in their homeland, their mana diminished by failure.[57] But denied the pitched battle by which they hoped to humble Ngai Te Rangi, Nga Puhi ultimately returned to the Bay of Islands.[58]

Titore led a further expedition against Tauranga early the following year. This time he recruited warriors from northern hapu in Mangonui, Kaitaia and elsewhere to assist his warriors from the Bay. And as he moved south he enlisted still more. When Fairburn the missionary visited Te Kari pa in the Firth of Thames during April 1833, he discovered that 'the greater number [of men] ha[d] been pressed into the service of Titori [*sic*] to assist him against Tauranga. They are so situated that they dare not refuse to assist when called upon by Ngapuhi.'[59] With so large a war-party under his command, and with rivalries and divisions having appeared among the Bay of Plenty tribes, Titore could well have expected success on this second occasion. But the northern invading force was denied its victory once again. The lesson of the second phase of the musket era was plain to read. When all had guns, an entrenched and stockaded pa was extremely difficult for attackers to storm. The northerners were sufficiently discouraged not to resume hostilities against the Tauranga tribes after this further failure.

IV

An unusual feature of the Nga Puhi expeditions to the Bay of Plenty was the presence of missionaries, who tagged along in order to act as peacemakers while at the very seat of war. The

brutal slaughter of so many of their people during the earlier
years of the musket wars had produced among many Maori a
mood of revulsion towards the continual spilling of blood.
Judith Binney has convincingly argued that the efforts of missionaries to promote peace among quarrelling tribes occurred at
the very time in the 1830s that war weariness had already begun
to set in among Maori. This, she considers, gave the missionaries
what had previously eluded them – success as conciliators and a
decisive influence on Maori society.[60] Before the first war-party
set out in early 1832, the Anglican missionaries in the Bay of
Islands made strenuous efforts to dissuade them from going.[61]
When that failed, the missionaries extracted some sort of
promise from the leaders of the expedition, that the bodies of the
enemy slain would not be eaten.[62] Furthermore, after each war-
party set out for Tauranga in this and subsequent years, missionaries accompanied them, but entirely as neutrals, moving
between the warring encampments seeking to negotiate peace.

Missionaries were convinced that utu, inspiring the spirit of
retaliation that led to chronic warfare, was the very 'heart of
darkness', as it were, within the Maori belief system. So long as
'every man's hand is against his brother', said Henry Williams,
the land would remain 'polluted with blood'.[63] It was the conviction of the missionaries that not merely was war abhorrent to
God, making vengeful Maori people 'tenfold more servants of
Satan than before', but continuing warfare was also the great
stumbling block preventing the spread of the gospel of Christ.
The expeditions mounted in the early 1830s by Nga Puhi
against Tauranga, the tribal wars that broke out in the Firth of
Thames, the Waipa, and at Matamata, Rotorua and elsewhere,
reduced the Anglican and Methodist missionaries to despair. For
at last they had acquired the resources to respond to the pleas of
chiefs to establish new mission stations in their midst. Yet all
too often in the past the missionary response to these requests
had to be: we cannot come unless you are at peace with your
neighbours; only then will our stations and schools be safe and
missionaries able to do their work. But the situation had
changed. For their part, most of the chiefs by this time were anxious for peace. They also knew that having a missionary living
among one's tribe could bring many benefits. As in the Bay of
Islands, the missionary's presence added to the mana of the

chiefs, attracted trade, and gave access to the increasingly coveted skills of reading and writing. Some Maori were ripe for conversion to the Christian religion, perhaps because they equated it with the western technology and learning that they were so anxious to embrace. Finally on a political level, it was hoped that having a resident missionary could serve to deflect the onslaught of enemy tribes.

Rev. Robert Maunsell, 1810–84. Missionary and linguist. SHERRIN AND WALLACE

Since the story of the coming of peace to northern New Zealand is inseparable from the work of the missionaries, more must be said about that group.[64] They had an influence in this period quite disproportionate to their actual numbers. After uncertain beginnings in the Bay of Islands, the Anglican mission under the forceful leadership of the Rev. Henry Williams developed, in the mid-1820s, a more fruitful strategy. Williams placed the main emphasis on conversion, took steps to mediate the gospel to Maori in their own tongue, and to establish schools which could offer sustained instruction. With such a policy, the printed word became the great tool of conversion. Historians divide over the efficacy of the evangelising work of the Anglican and Wesleyan missionaries.[65] But all agree that through their work as teachers the missionaries offered to the native people an essential ready-made bridge to western learning. As in Africa and the Pacific, so in New Zealand, missionaries were the first purveyors of western education to the indigenous people.

It is paradoxical that although the mission societies, during their great period of expansion in the 1830s, established no mission stations in Tamaki itself, they helped greatly to restore stability to the tribes of Tamaki-makau-rau by the end of the decade. Mission activity took place not on the isthmus itself but in the areas adjacent. By the later 1830s, for instance, the catechist Fairburn had begun to minister to members of Ngai Tai and of tribes of the inner Hauraki gulf. A little later, the Rev. Robert Maunsell began working among lower Waikato tribes residing in the region of the Waikato heads, and on the southern coast of the Manukau. Nor should it be forgotten that Tamaki tribes, while sheltering in the Waipa, encountered and fell under the influence of itinerant missionaries of both the Anglican and Wesleyan denominations. At Te Horo, Ngati Whatua of Tamaki and Ngati Tamaoho of the south Manukau were actually caught up as opponents in a tribal war, which ended only when Henry Williams successfully mediated between the two parties, who then joined in a 'tangi of reconciliation' followed by a religious service.[66] It is significant, too, that two lay missionaries, W. T. Fairburn and James Hamlin, were large purchasers of south Tamaki land. Finally, we should note that CMS missionaries are credited, perhaps excessively, with contributing so much to the stability of the region by their success in reconciling estranged tribes, that tangata whenua were encouraged to return to the isthmus. Clearly it is not possible to ignore missionaries in the story of Tamaki in the 1830s.

V

It was the threat from the Nga Puhi and Marutuahu iwi during the mid-1830s that made the Tamaki tribes hesitant about returning to Tamaki. By 1835, however, the chiefs of the Tamaki and lower Waikato tribes in exile had sufficiently overcome their fears to decide, regardless of remaining dangers, to move back to their former lands. But they did so only after a lengthy discussion with Potatau seeking his assistance.[67] Knowing that Potatau had 'six thousand fighting men' at his disposal,[68] Tamaki chiefs believed that he alone would be able to lead them back in safety and that, once they were there, only he would be strong enough to guard them from molestation. Potatau was reassuringly supportive. He agreed to reinstate the tribes and, as an additional safeguard, to live in their midst for some time.[69] But his scheme to do so was unexpectedly delayed when a blood feud, which broke out in 1834, put the Waikato and Marutuahu peoples at one another's throats.[70]

The rupture between these major tribes and their allies in exile had its beginnings in an episode which has come down in Maori oral history as the 'Whakatiwai murders'. The trouble began when, in May 1834, a ferocious Ngati Paoa chief called Koinake set about to square an utu account which most of his kinsmen had long since forgotten. After a treacherous pretence of hospitality, he suddenly fell upon a Waikato chief Kapa and his wife Matakara, while accompanying them on their way back from a Thames mission station, and killed both with his hatchet. Koinake then took their bodies to his own settlement to be eaten by his tribe.[71] The people of Waikato were outraged. One group retaliated quickly by coming into Hauraki territory where, in order to provoke Ngati Paoa,[72] they plundered the funeral site of one of that tribe's chiefs, Rauroha, who had recently died.[73] In the meantime two Waikato chiefs, Te Ironui[74] and Te Kauae, without reference to Potatau, put together a large expedition.[75] This was made up of 200 or more Waikato – including Manukau tribes such as Ngati Tamaoho and Ngati Te Ata – 60 Ngati Haua, and 1000 Ngati Whatua whom Te Kauae recruited from his home pa of Te Horo.[76]

In the third week of July 1834 this war-party came from Waikato to the Firth of Thames. On a moonlit night which was so cold (one of the warriors recalled) that 'our hands were numbed with frost while carrying guns',[77] they stole up to Whakatiwai, the chief pa of Ngati Paoa, and made a dawn attack. During this assault (or 'huaki', as it was called in the Court records), most of the fighting took place in the vicinity of the pa rather than at the pa itself. The defenders were taken by surprise; they were further handicapped by the absence of a considerable number of their warriors. So for Ngati Paoa it proved a close-run thing. '[We] narrowly escaped being cut up', one of the tribe later admitted. But they were not defeated. When asked years later what the true outcome of the engagement was, a Ngati Whatua chief who had been with the war-party conceded that both sides 'were equal'.[78] In spite of their great advantage of surprise, the Waikato-led party had been unable to take the pa. Unaware that the pa was still under construction, they unwittingly attacked that portion of it where fortifications had been completed.[79] Upon failing to take the pa by storm, the attackers decided to close the engagement, and go home. They were apparently satisfied with what they had already achieved. They had lost no men; and they had killed a number of the enemy – estimates of the Ngati Paoa slain range from five to fifty.[80] But what was considered significant at the time was that of the Ngati Paoa who were slain, three were chiefs. From the viewpoint of the attackers (as Fenton later put it), that number 'wound up the [utu] account; and the whole proceeding was "tika" [correct]'.[81] On the other hand, Marutuahu tribes considered the killings treacherous and unjustified, calling therefore for future blood payment. Thereafter, Marutuahu referred to the attack as 'the Whakatiwai murders'. Unfortunately for Apihai's followers, Ngati Paoa, in the years ahead, decided that utu should be exacted from them, even though they had been minor players in the attack on the pa. Ngati Paoa made Ngati Whatua o Tamaki the target for retribution because, whereas the Waikato tribes were formidable, Apihai Te Kawau's tribe was relatively weak.

The war-party under Te Kauae withdrew from Whakatiwai on the day of the attack. '[We] retired in good order', recalled one chief, the warriors carrying their own powder and shot, and some booty. They also took with them thirty-six prisoners, mainly women and children, who had been captured by Ngati Tamaoho and Te Kohuriki; these prisoners were later enslaved.[82] That Ngati Paoa warriors from Whakatiwai were able to pursue and fire at the taua for some kilometres along the trail to Maramarua shows that they were far from defeated.

On a visit to Ngaruawahia about three weeks after the raid, William Williams found the paramount Waikato chief, Potatau Te Wherowhero, 'exceedingly angry' about this attack made by some of his chiefs without his knowledge.[83] The raid had cut through Potatau's policy which, by this time, was to stabilise the whole Waikato region as far north as Tamaki. He was further exasperated by the rumour that certain firebrand Waikato chiefs were planning to resume the engagement with Ngati Paoa by making 'a second visit' to the Thames. At Whakatiwai itself a fresh invasion was expected daily. But this time the defenders were determined to be better prepared. Within days of the first attack, 800 Marutuahu warriors had gathered at Whakatiwai, many coming by canoe from far parts of the Firth. According to a missionary source, these men set to work completing the pa, which they 'strongly enclosed' by two fences (specially designed to cope with musket fire, offensive and defensive) between which they dug a large ditch that acted 'as a general shelter for the inhabitants'.[84] When, after two months, the expected Waikato attack failed to eventuate, most of the Hauraki reinforcements decided to return home.[85] But the whole region remained on the alert, the prevailing mood of distrust towards Waikato being shown by the speed with which settlements in various parts of the Thames proceeded to strengthen their fortifications.[86] Indeed, had influential chiefs not exercised great restraint, hot-headed chiefs within Marutuahu ranks could well have provoked Potatau to the point where Waikato and Hauraki became embroiled in a full-scale war. This restraint was nowhere better demonstrated than in the historical drama which was known in the years ahead as the 'stripping of Kati'.[87]

In early 1834, the younger brother of Potatau, Kati Te Whero-whero, spent some weeks with his wife Matire visiting her kin at Waimate in the Bay of Islands.[88] (It will be recalled that, some ten years before, Kati had married Matire Toha, daughter of the powerful Nga Puhi chief Rewa, in order to consolidate a peace-making between Nga Puhi and Waikato after the battle of Matakitaki.) The time having come for their return to the Waikato, the couple and their entourage left the Bay of Islands, on 19 July, on the barque *Bolina,* under its master Captain Ranulph Dacre. With them on the *Bolina* was a missionary group composed of William Williams, A. N. Browne and Henry Pilley. Both sets of passengers were bound for the Thames. The chiefly couple intended to go to Whakatiwai, whence they were to take one of the two well-known native trails to Ngaruawahia, to rejoin Potatau.[89] The missionary group, on the other hand, was to accompany them as far as Ngaruawahia before continuing up the Waipa valley, to the new mission station at Mangapouri. When, four days out from the Bay of Islands, the *Bolina* lay at anchor at Mahurangi, members of a branch of the Ngati Paoa living there came out by canoe to inform those on board of the attack on Whakatiwai, which had taken place the week before. These particular Ngati Paoa people at Mahurangi were so incensed by the attack on their kinsmen that it was feared, at first, that they would attempt to board the ship and kill Kati and his group. But they calmed down, some even deciding to travel on the same ship to Whakatiwai. Kati had determined, rashly it would seem, to keep to his original intention of landing at Whakatiwai in order to travel by foot and canoe to Ngaruawahia. But he had seriously misjudged the mood of Ngati Paoa. On landing at Whakatiwai, he and his party were immediately taken prisoner. Only the intervention of a prestigious chief, Kupenga, protected Kati and his wife Matire from personal attack on that first day. The anger of Ngati Paoa overflowed when the canoe containing the party's entire luggage, including muskets and powder, was beached. William Williams recorded that 'the people of the place were helping themselves to . . . the property of Kati . . . and in a few minutes not a vestige of it was left'.[90] This act of muru was the famous 'stripping of Kati'.

Te Kawau and his nephew, Tamahiki or Te Reweti. *Handcoloured lithograph by J. W. Giles, after watercolour by G. F. Angus, in* The New Zealanders Illustrated, 1847. AUCKLAND CITY LIBRARIES

Haora Tipa Te Koinaki of Ngati Paoa. *Oil on canvas, by Gottfried Lindauer.*

AUCKLAND CITY ART GALLERY

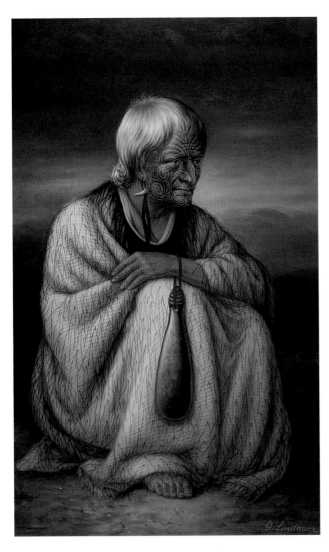

LEFT: Te Horeta (Te Taniwha) of Ngati Whanaunga. *Oil on canvas, by Gottfried Lindauer.*
AUCKLAND CITY ART GALLERY

BELOW LEFT: *A wakahuia, or treasure box, containing items (tiki, pendants, huia feathers) customarily stored in such boxes.* ETHNOLOGY DEPARTMENT, AUCKLAND WAR MEMORIAL MUSEUM

BELOW RIGHT: *A wakahuia from Sir George Grey Collection.*
AUCKLAND WAR MEMORIAL MUSEUM

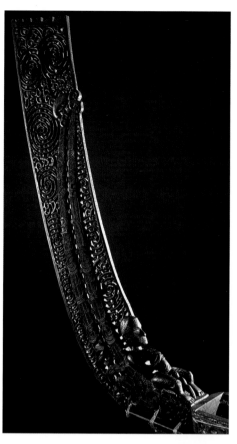

ABOVE: *Hei-tiki, collected by the Rev. Wade, CMS at the Bay of Islands 1834–40.* ETHNOLOGY DEPARTMENT, AUCKLAND WAR MEMORIAL MUSEUM

RIGHT: *Stern-post (taurapa) of war canoe, Te Tokia Tapiri.* ETHNOLOGY DEPARTMENT, AUCKLAND WAR MEMORIAL MUSEUM

BELOW: *Tauihu, war canoe prow carved by Wiremu Kingi of Te Ati Awa.* ETHNOLOGY DEPARTMENT, AUCKLAND WAR MEMORIAL MUSEUM

ABOVE: War speech previous to a Naval Expedition, *by Augustus Earle. Tinted lithograph with contemporary handcolouring.* AUCKLAND CITY LIBRARIES

BELOW: The meeting of the Artist and the Wounded Chief Honghi, at the Bay of Islands, November 1827. *Oil on canvas, by Augustus Earle.* AUCKLAND CITY LIBRARIES

ABOVE: Auckland in December 1840.
Sepia wash, by WY (monogram).
AUCKLAND CITY ART GALLERIES

LEFT: Pataka, and Maori figures
with blankets, *by J. J. Merrett.*
Heaphy Album, Print No. 2.
AUCKLAND WAR MEMORIAL MUSEUM

OPPOSITE (TOP): *New Zealand's first*
Capital, Russell. Kororareka (Russell)
with a fleet of American whalers in
harbour. *Undated watercolour by*
J. B. C. Hoyte. AUCKLAND CITY LIBRARIES

OPPOSITE (BOTTOM): *New Zealand's*
second Capital, Auckland.
First government settlement on the
Waitemata River, 1st October 1840.
Watercolour by John Johnson MD.
ALEXANDER TURNBULL LIBRARY

The British flag first hoisted on the shores of the Waitemata, 18 September 1840. *Watercolour by John Johnson MD. Sarah Mathew described the scene in her journal: 'Then the flag was run up, and the whole assembly gave three cheers, the ship's colours were also instantly hoisted and a Salute of 21 guns fired. Her Majesty's health was then most rapturously drunk with cheers long and loud repeated from the ships; to the very evident delight of the Natives of whom nearly 100 had assembled round us. A few of the Rangatiras or chiefs were given wine to drink the Queen's health, and afterwards the Governor's was proposed and saluted with 7 guns.' (Sarah Mathew's Journal, 18 September 1840).* HOCKEN LIBRARY, UNIVERSITY OF OTAGO

Williams went on to conclude that 'as long as the people are safe, the property is of little consequence'. He, like Kati, greatly underestimated the danger to that chief, his wife and party. Among the assembled Ngati Paoa there were chiefs like Koinake, who thought that plundering was insufficient retribution and that the visiting group should be killed forthwith. After all, it was generally expected that any day a war-party of Kati's iwi, led by Te Kauae, would return to resume the attack on the pa. For some time the fate of the captive group hung in the balance. However, after the party had been held prisoner for fourteen days, moderate chiefs of mana like Kupenga and Te Horeta prevailed over the militants and Kati's group and the missionary party were allowed to move on in safety to Ngaruawahia. Testifying many years later as to the forbearing state of mind of his fellow Ngati Paoa chiefs, Haora Tipa said: 'my rangatiratanga [chiefly magnanimity] was then exhibited by saving the life of that great chief [Kati]. We contented ourselves by taking his guns and powder.'[91] The diplomacy of prudent self-interest was no less an influence on chiefs than their sense of rangatiratanga. The killing of Kati would have brought down on Marutuahu the whole wrath of Tainui, as terrible in its consequences as those that later flowed (in December 1835) from the murder by an Arawa chief of Hunga of Ngati Haua.[92] It is also most probable, had Matire been killed, Nga Puhi would have been unrelentingly vengeful.

Thus war was averted. But the Thames and lower Waikato region remained unstable. In early March 1835, after 'much consultation' with members of a party of missionaries which he led, Henry Williams 'determined to proceed by way of W[h]akatiwai to Waikato and see what can be done by way of establishing peace amongst these uncertain and turbulent people'.[93] After visiting the Thames, where he everywhere found fear of a renewed Waikato attack, he was encouraged, nevertheless, by the general will to peace. Crossing to Te Horo on the Waipa, he discovered that Te Kauae, leader of the previous year's attack on Whakatiwai, was quite prepared to bring his feud with Ngati Paoa to an end. As an earnest of his goodwill, Kauae entrusted his personal hatchet to the missionaries, urging them to take it to Ngati Paoa leaders as a preliminary step towards a general peacemaking.[94] At Ngaruawahia, Potatau – who had disapproved of the Whakatiwai expedition in the first place – was equally content that the missionaries, on their return to Thames, should act as his emissaries in negotiating a peace.[95] Accompanied by some Waikato chiefs headed by Wharepu, the missionaries journeyed back to Whakatiwai to deliver, as directed, the hatchet to Herua, a senior chief. However, suspicion of Waikato died hard. Herua and Te Kupenga, acting on behalf of Ngati Paoa, were very chary in their reception of these overtures for peace.[96]

The continuing animosity of Hauraki Maori, combined with abiding fear of Nga Puhi, served to delay the long-discussed return of the peoples of Tamaki-makau-rau in the mid-1830s.[97] But by 1835 Potatau was ready to bring the impasse to an end. He assured missionaries who had visited him in March of that year that 'in four months' time' (the beginning of the planting season) he was going to lead back the exiled tribes, Ngati Whatua, Ngati Tamaoho, Ngati Te Ata and Ngati Mahuta, to the shores of the outer Manukau harbour. He also voiced a hope that the CMS would establish a mission station there to help secure the position of the resettled people.

The ending of the diaspora of Ngati Whatua is recorded in considerable detail in the Minutebooks of the Orakei Native Land Court (1866, 1868). Because of the evidence recorded at that court, rather more is known about the return of Apihai's people to Tamaki than about the return of other tribes in the region. It appears that after Ngati Whatua planted their 'new-year' crop at Te Horo in the early spring of 1835, they migrated to the Waikato heads. There, on land granted by the tangata whenua (the Waikato tribe called Ngati Tipa), they established kainga at Waihakura and Kaitangata, where they cleared nearby land and cultivated fresh gardens.[98] In early summer, members of the tribe went back to Te Horo for the last time to lift their crops. They then returned once more to the mouth of the Waikato to their new habitations.[99] Over the summer of 1835–36, parties of Ngati Whatua also made clandestine trips to their old shark-fishing grounds in the Manukau and the Waitemata and even went as far north as their traditional fishing grounds off the Mahurangi peninsula. They were careful, however, not to disclose to any possible enemies their intention to fish by planting temporary potato plots in advance.[100] Asked by Chief Judge Fenton what they had lived on, witnesses simply replied 'Fernroot'.[101] But they had been encouraged by the fact that they had not encountered enemies. Fishermen and other scouts were able to persuade Ngati Whatua leaders that the omens were propitious, and that the time had at last come to cross the Awaroa portage and to return home.

CHAPTER VII

The Search for Peace, 1836–38

I

The next two chapters, which trace the coming of peace to the Tamaki region and the return there of its former inhabitants, rely heavily on the minutebooks of evidence recorded during the 1866 and 1868 sittings of the Native Land Court which deliberated upon the ownership of the Orakei block. The verbatim account contained in the minutes, made initially as a record for the use of the presiding judge, Francis Dart Fenton, is uniquely valuable for those who seek to put together the story of Maori in Auckland in the years before 1840. I acknowledge my own great indebtedness to those manuscript records. Most readers will be aware that evidence drawn from the Orakei case has figured in almost every chapter of this book so far.

But there is a note of warning to be sounded about the kind of oral evidence used in this and other land court hearings. Attention must be drawn to the unreliability of the testimony, either of eyewitnesses seeking to recall events which took place, in this case forty or more years before, or where witnesses drew on hearsay information which others had passed on to them concerning episodes long past. What is particularly relevant to the present chapters is the conflict of evidence recorded in the Orakei minutes with regard to critical events of the 1830s. Witnesses often confused the sequence of key events; and mistook the year when parts of the region were resettled or when estranged tribes finally made peace. And even though the final ruling of Chief Judge Fenton as to who held the mana whenua over the disputed block, was regarded at the time as a landmark decision and subsequently published, yet it must be said that even this long and weighty judgment in some measure repeats the confused evidence of witnesses who testified in court. Regrettably, alternative sources, which could have acted as a corrective to such misinformation, are few. Since missionaries in these years were no closer to Tamaki than its periphery, their records for the isthmus, already distorted by their Evangelical worldview, tend to be meagre, and are therefore of limited use in acting as a check on court testimony. Consequently, the Orakei minutebooks, for all their usefulness, are to be treated with caution. We must remember the limitations of oral 'history'; that what has become accepted as 'true' may have become corrupted over time, that hearsay may have been misheard, memories played false, imaginations embellished, and that self-interest may have led some who testified to misrepresent reality. European witnesses, with no apparent vested interest, were just as prone to error in their recall as were Maori claimants. Nevertheless, when the dross of the Orakei minutebooks is discarded, rich nuggets remain to reward the careful researcher.[1] They were vital in the compilation of this chapter.

II

The movement in 1835 of Apihai's people – who were among the estimated 600 members of the Ngati Whatua tribe who had sheltered in Te Horo[2] – from the Waikato heads to the Manukau harbour, must be seen as part of a much wider migration. The first group of Ngati Whatua had gone as an advance party to the mouth of the Waikato, to plant crops in preparation for the greater migration which was destined for the Manukau.[3] By the time the crops were 'beginning to grow', said one Ngati Whatua chief, the returning tribes 'came down in a body' over the Awaroa portage and moved down the Waiuku estuary into the Manukau.[4] Te Wherowhero not only escorted the Tamaki tribes and their former neighbours on the south Manukau shore – Te Akitai,

Ngati Te Ata, and Ngati Tamaoho – he also brought down members of (in Fenton's phraseology) 'his own personal tribes, Ngatimahuta, Ngatiapakura &c.'[5] The traditional Manukau tribes returned cautiously and hesitantly. Te Akitai edged towards their lands on the south-west side of the Otahuhu portage and Ngati Tamaoho began infiltrating the inner southern shore of the harbour to the west of Papakura. Ngati Te Ata were rather more assured in taking up their old lands about Waiuku and on the Awhitu peninsula.[6] There, protection was close to hand. Kaihau, the Te Ata chief, had given to Te Wherowhero and his followers land adjoining his own at Awhitu near the south Manukau heads.[7] This gift was no coincidence. Te Wherowhero had made it known that he wished to shift temporarily from Ngaruawahia and re-locate himself on just such a strategic pa site on the Manukau. He calculated that this commanding position would enable him to safeguard the resettled tribes against Nga Puhi and Ngati Paoa attack, and thereby guarantee them in the possession of their old lands.[8]

Apihai Te Kawau's people were the only tribe to settle on the north side of the harbour. But they too remained under the pro-tective cloak of Te Wherowhero, since the site which they chose was but a brief canoe journey from that mighty chief's pa at Awhitu. In the later part of 1835 – for Ngati Whatua were obviously well established when missionaries visited them in January of the following year – Apihai's followers took up resi-dence at their old fishing station at Karangahape, known nowa-days as Cornwallis. Once there, they lost no time in erecting fortifications,[9] building a pa on the inner (northern) side of Puponga Point, and clearing bush and planting gardens on the nearby flat land beside the beach.[10] The Ngati Whatua chiefs decided, however, that for the time being a return to the former Te Taou and Nga Oho settlements on the Tamaki isthmus was quite out of the question. In view of their enduring vendettas with the Parawhau branch of Nga Puhi to the north and with the Ngati Paoa of Whakatiwai to the south-east, Apihai's fol-lowers thought it prudent to avoid the isthmus. Consequently, the once-populous lands bordering the Waitemata remained deserted; as Te Kawau later recalled, 'there were no people living in this land at that time'.[11] However, while at Karangahape, Ngati Whatua gathered sufficient confidence to break out from their headquarters there and establish gardens elsewhere, especially on accessible volcanic lands. Paora Tuhaere testified before the Land Court that, during the tribe's first year at Karangahape, Ngati Whatua ventured out to plant, and later to harvest crops, at Ihumatao and at Mangere. But once these tasks were complete, they withdrew to the safety of the Karangahape pa.[12] They also began to run a herd of pigs on Puketutu island where there was no need, of course, for either fences or continuing supervision.

Paora Tuhaere in 1864, leader of Ngati Whatua-o-Tamaki after the death of Te Kawau in 1869.
AUCKLAND CITY
LIBRARIES

In spite of the presence of Te Wherowhero, the returning tribes took a considerable time to settle down beside the Manukau. Henry Williams, who in January 1836 visited the harbour – this 'scene of former desolation' he called it – observed that the returning tribes still did 'not feel themselves secure'.[13] Another CMS missionary, the Rev. Robert Maunsell, who on 2 August 1836 came from the Thames to Orua Bay near the south Manukau heads to set up the first Anglican mission station for the region,[14] reported on the state of flux among the tribes who made up his new cure of souls. 'As the tide of emigration has only flowed lately into this district, our people are characterised by more restlessness than ordinary. Roaming up and down the coast, they are engaged in establishing their claims to their various possessions.'[15]

The progressive resettlement by the tribes, first on the Manukau and later on the Tamaki isthmus itself, is often associated with the efforts of the missionaries to reconcile those tribes most likely to disturb the stability of the region. Historians have often spoken, therefore, of the establishment of 'the missionary peace'. Less frequently, however, have they convincingly demonstrated whether that term was well founded.

By the late 1830s, the west coast of the North Island south of the Manukau harbour had become a designated Anglican mission field. This was a recent development. Before 1833, the respective fields for evangelisation marked out by the Anglican and Wesleyan mission societies had not overlapped. Operating out of its established headquarters in the Bay of Islands, the CMS had confined its mission work to the east coast, whereas the Wesleyans, working out of their Hokianga harbour base at Mangungu, had concentrated their efforts among tribes living on the west coast of upper Northland. By 1834 the situation had changed. Tribes living in the Thames, the Bay of Plenty and the

Waikato were clamouring for mission stations to be set up in their midst. Both mission societies were anxious to respond. In December 1833, the CMS took the first decisive step in its expansion to the south, by establishing a station at Puriri in the lower Waihou valley, not far from the site of the modern town of Thames.[16] Once there among the Hauraki people, it seemed to the Rev. Henry Williams and his fellow missionaries no more than common sense to establish mission stations in the lower Waikato and Waipa valleys as well. In that way missionaries would be able not only to spread the gospel, but also to build a bridge of reconciliation between the Nga Puhi, Hauraki and Waikato tribes, who were still divided by blood feuds. In early 1835, the Anglicans established further stations: at Matamata, headquarters pa of the Ngati Haua warrior chief Te Waharoa, and, more significantly, at Mangapouri, where there was a large settlement of Waikato people led by Awarahi, on the confluence of the Puniu and Waipa rivers.[17]

William White,
1794–1875. Wesleyan
missionary. AUCKLAND
CITY LIBRARIES

More significantly, because the move to Mangapouri brought the CMS towards the west coast, taking its missionaries into the very region that William White, superintendent of the Wesleyan mission, had marked out as his denomination's exclusive field for expansion.[18] For the first time, sectarian competition threatened the state of friendly co-operation that had hitherto existed between the two societies. White, a resourceful, determined, though disputatious leader,[19] considered that the west-coast harbours from the Kaipara to the Kawhia and their hinterlands were the logical sphere of activity for the Wesleyan mission now that it was ready to expand from the Hokianga. He was aware that the Wesleyans could not rival the Anglicans in resources of either men or money. But he had already demonstrated at Mangungu, in a quite ingenious way, how he believed this deficiency could be offset. There, he expected his missionaries to combine pastoral work with trading and timber-milling activity – which also meant the buying of forestland. (This alleged preoccupation with trading, to the neglect of proclaiming the gospel, ultimately led, in 1838, to the dismissal of White by his British superiors.)[20] White was prepared to improvise further. Because ordained Wesleyan missionaries were not available in sufficient numbers, he hit upon the device of using the services of laymen who would act as preacher-merchants. These Methodist laymen would be self-

154

supporting Pakeha who, as they worked at selling goods or milling timber, would also minister to the spiritual needs of the Maori people among whom they would work and live.[21] At first their activities were confined to Mangungu, but White believed these people could be equally effective if used further afield.

During 1835 White placed accredited missionaries, the Revs John Whiteley and William Woon, at Kawhia and the Rev. James Wallis at Whaingaroa (Raglan).[22] Furthermore, aware that plans were afoot for the migration of Waikato and Ngati Whatua tribes back to the Manukau, he planned to carry out, as it were, a pre-emptive strike there in a way that would prevent the CMS from establishing a monopoly in the area. In April 1835, he confided to his colleagues that, with the migration from the Waipa in the near future, the Manukau was an 'important place likely soon to be thickly populated'.[23] Here was a field for evangelism, which, in biblical terms, was 'white unto harvest'. White obviously believed that he had a moral obligation to establish a Wesleyan presence in the region. While visiting Te Wherowhero in May 1834, he had promised that if peace were restored between the Waikato and Ngati Paoa tribes, and if Waikato tribes resettled on the shores of the Manukau, he would set up a mission station for them there.[24] While visiting Te Horo (on the Waipa) at about the same time, he had made a similar promise to the Ngati Whatua chiefs, assuring them that, once they had removed themselves to the Manukau, he would 'get a Pakeha to live with them'.[25] An historian of the Wesleyan mission considers that, in his enthusiasm for the Manukau, White could well have had 'an eye for business'. For did he not also confide in his colleagues that 'the harbour was one of the best on the Western Coast and abounded with good timber and land'?[26] Much of the land that surrounded the harbour was heavily bushed with stands of valuable totara, and on both the northern shore and the Awhitu peninsula there was said to be 'a great quantity of kauri'.[27] Under these circumstances, it is not surprising that the Pakeha whom White brought to Ngati Whatua, once they settled on the northern shore of the harbour, was an experienced sawyer. His name was Thomas Mitchell.

Mitchell, the son of a Sydney merchant, had arrived in New Zealand in 1831 while still in his mid-twenties, accompanied by his wife and young family. After working for four years as a

sawyer and timber agent at Mangamuka and elsewhere in the
Hokianga district, he shifted to the Wesleyan station at
Mangungu. There he became one of White's four lay allies
engaged in the mission's timber-sawing operations.[28] While at
Mangungu he served the Methodist cause as a lay preacher.[29]
White selected him as the God-fearing European whom he
handpicked to live among Apihai's tribe. On 10 January 1835,
the small sailing vessel *Fanny* (master, Thomas Wing)[30] entered
the Manukau harbour with White and Mitchell on board. It
went immediately to the new Ngati Whatua settlement beside
Puponga Point.[31] There, White introduced Mitchell to the
Ngati Whatua chiefs as the Pakeha whom he had promised,
months before, to bring to live in their midst.[32] Later that day,
Ngati Whatua took White's party by canoe to Awhitu on the
opposite side of the harbour, to camp overnight with the CMS
group led by Henry Williams, which had been in the region for
the past ten days. During their brief stay, White learned that
Williams and his missionary colleagues, Fairburn and Hamlin,
had been investigating possible Anglican mission sites in the
Manukau.[33] What White seemed not to appreciate, however,
was that these explorations were of minor consequence to Henry
Williams, who was primarily concerned, at this juncture, with
trying to broker a tricky peace deal between the Waikato and
Hauraki tribes.[34] But as White saw it, the race was on; he must
act swiftly if he was to forestall the Anglicans.

The following day (11 January), he went back to Karangahape with Mitchell and negotiated, on his behalf, the 'purchase' of – in the words of a later claimant to whom the land had been subsequently conveyed – an 'immense' block of land, of about 400 square miles.[35] The deed of agreement, signed by Apihai Te Kawau, Kawae, Tinana Te Tamaki and other Ngati Whatua chiefs, seemed to transfer an area whose boundaries may be summarised thus:

- the northern shoreline of the Manukau as far as the Otahuhu portage, thence along the western bank of the Tamaki river as far as the Waitemata harbour;
- the boundary then to follow the southern bank of the harbour as far as today's Hobsonville, that is, almost to the head of the Waitemata;
- from the estuary there to the headwaters of Waiteputa (Brigham's creek); thence across the North Island to the Tasman Sea;
- south-west down the west coast to the north Manukau heads.

In sum, this block which White and Mitchell claimed to have bought took in virtually the whole of the Tamaki isthmus and the heavily bush-clad southern portion of the Waitakere ranges.[36]

The negotiations that led to this agreement were carried out almost by stealth. On the day that the deed was signed, Henry Williams and his party left Awhitu for Otahuhu. But on his way Williams made a special detour to Karangahape to afford 'an opportunity', he explained, for the peace delegation of chiefs who accompanied him, 'to pay their respect to Ngatiwhatua'.[37] Apihai's people received the visitors in an unexpectedly offhand way. But almost certainly Ngati Whatua acted in what appeared a disrespectful fashion (as Williams characterised it) out of embarrassment at the secret 'sale' of Tamaki land which they were that very day negotiating. On the following day, Williams was informed through native sources, albeit in a rather mangled form, of White's land-buying coup. He recorded in his journal that he had been told that White had purchased 'a tract of land, about twenty miles square, for four casks of leaf tobacco, value £8, whereby he had bought up all the sitting place of the natives'.[38] He added, in a mood of understandable pique, that as a consequence White had 'hindered our Mission movement'.

Having negotiated this purchase, White left Mitchell at Puponga Point to build a house for himself. White then recrossed the harbour to purchase from Ngati Te Ata a mission site at Orua bay, close to the south Manukau heads. This done, he delegated to Edward Meurant, a Wesleyan lay-worker, the task of building a dwelling for William Woon, presently at Kawhia, but now designated to be the first Wesleyan missionary in the Manukau. On 12 January, White left for Kawhia on the *Fanny* to pick up Woon, returning eleven days later to install him at Orua.[39]

Woon was not destined to stay long at this new mission station. During 1836, the Wesleyan mission society in London, alarmed at the unaccustomed rivalry that had sprung up between Methodist and Anglican missionaries in New Zealand, decided to conciliate its CMS counterpart. Henceforth, it undertook to concede to the Anglicans as their exclusive sphere of missionary activity, the entire west coast region between the Manukau and Taranaki. This meant that the Wesleyans in New Zealand had not only to give up their newly acquired Manukau station but also, much to their chagrin, to withdraw James Wallis (at Raglan) and John Whiteley (at Kawhia) from their well-established stations.[40] This expulsion – as the Wesleyans understandably thought of it – aroused sore feelings between the two sets of missionaries labouring in north New Zealand for some considerable time.[41]

Because the so-called sale of land to Mitchell (later to have an important influence on the European settlement of Auckland) was a private transaction, it was not affected by the compromise that was subsequently arrived at between the two parent missionary societies. Yet Mitchell played virtually no part in the development of the area which, in a manner of speaking, seemed to have gratuitously fallen into his lap. It appears that he resided at Karangahape only nineteen days in all, because it is recorded that he departed with White and Captain Wing on the *Fanny* on 30 January, to rejoin his wife and children then living at Hokianga.[42] During this brief time, he had hastily erected, presumably with some Ngati Whatua help, part of the house which he later intended to occupy as a Wesleyan lay missionary and part-time timber-merchant. Long after, White said that his impression was that at this stage only 'the shell of a house had been put up'.[43] In the week before the *Fanny* left, Wing made a rough chart of that part of the harbour in the vicinity of the heads, which showed 'Mr Mitchell's house, as then standing at Karangahape'.[44] There is no record that Mitchell ever returned from Hokianga to Karangahape, either to cut timber or to finish and occupy his house.[45] Perhaps his purpose was simply to forestall the CMS and, that done, to return to the Hokianga where his services were still urgently required.[46] What is firm fact is that he died on 6 November 1836,[47] whether from sickness or an accident is not known. His widow then left the Hokianga, returning with her children to Sydney.[48]

More must be said about the deed by which, so it was later claimed, Ngati Whatua had conveyed to Mitchell a mammoth area of land. At the Orakei hearing many years later, William White, choosing to act out, one suspects, at the age of seventy-four the joint role of old colonial-hand-cum-court-jester, testified that he had secured the block, which included the site of the future town of Auckland, for 'some tobacco and old biscuits'.[49] The price paid, though ridiculously low, was in fact more substantial than that. White's biographer, Murray Gittos, puts the consideration listed on the deed of conveyance as '1,000lb of tobacco, 100 dozen pipes, and six muskets, a total value of 160 pounds'.[50] Nor is this transaction to be looked on as a genuine *sale* of the land, at least in any European sense of the word. Apihai Te Kawau was too intelligent a chief, and too experienced and adroit a politician, to let slip for a paltry sum those lands which were the birthright of his tribe. He was simply buying a Pakeha to live at Karangahape. Mitchell at Karangahape, it was imagined, would bring mana to the chief, help ward off hostile attack, attract trade, provide an interpreter, and above all would become one of those Pakeha who (it has been aptly said) 'fulfilled a critical role as mediators of meaning between Maori and the mysterious world beyond New Zealand'.[51] In payment for these prospective services, Te Kawau was simply adapting an age-old Maori practice to a novel situation by provisionally gifting to Mitchell the right to use designated land for a particular purpose, in this case the milling of timber. This transaction was a world apart from any European notion of the absolute transfer of virtually all the land owned by Ngati Whatua in Tamaki and in the north Manukau hinterland.

The truth of the matter is surely contained in an attested statement with regard to the original deed of conveyance, which Te Kawau's nephew, Te Reweti (Davis Tamaki), made in October 1840 to the Protector of the Aborigines, George Clarke. The tribe had entrusted the hereditary chief, Te Reweti – extolled by one European observer as 'very acute and intelligent, particularly as to the interests of his tribe, in all his transactions with Europeans'[52] – to negotiate in January 1836 with White on their behalf.[53] As one of the original vendors named on the deed, Te Reweti testified that

Te Reweti Tamaki,
nephew of Te Kawau.
Lithograph by P. Gauci
after J. J. Merrett, in
C. Terry, New Zealand.

> When we spoke to Mitchell and White, when we pointed out to them the extent of country belonging to us, they had said to us, 'Have you a large country in your possession?' We then said, 'Our boundary line is at Otahuhu, and runs along the district belonging to Ngati Paoa until it reaches the Waitemata.' This is what we said when we pointed out to them the extent of our territory. From thence their hearts avariciously conjectured that the whole was for them, we having only intended to point out the extent of our land.
>
> The exact spot that was pointed out to them was Karangahape. The boundary lines of that place are these: – The boundary on the outside, that is, looking towards Orua [south Manukau heads] is Kakamatua; proceed inwards along the coast to Puponga, on to Karangahape, till you arrive at Nihotupu.
>
> Our names, that were attached to that deed, were intended for that portion of the land only.[54]

This explanation given by Te Reweti convinced the Land Commissioners who later investigated the land claim that arose of this highly dubious original transaction. They awarded only a small area of land on the northern shore of the Manukau to the claimants who had bought their interest in it from the Mitchell estate.

III

Missionaries, both Anglican and Wesleyan alike, had long believed that chronic warfare was the greatest obstacle to the conversion of Maori.[55] Had not these wars, wrote the Rev. William Williams, made the Maori people 'tenfold more servants of Satan than before'?[56] According to Carleton, by the 1830s it had become the fixed conviction of Henry Williams (William's brother, and superintendent of CMS endeavours in New Zealand) that 'no real impression could be made on the country at large until [the] state of chronic warfare in which the natives were plunged should be brought to an end'.[57] To achieve his objective, he had tried (as we have seen) to act as peacemaker in the Bay of Plenty wars of the early 1830s, and to reconcile the tribes caught up in the Whakatiwai murders of 1834. In December 1835, this policy of pacification had developed a particular urgency for Williams. At that date, Hunga, a Ngati Haua chief and Te Waharoa's cousin, was killed and eaten, unleashing a particularly murderous war between tribes of the upper Waikato and of those of the Rotorua region,[58] which forced the abandonment of mission stations that Williams had recently established in those inland areas.

It is in this wider context that the missionary efforts of 1835 and 1836 to promote peace and stability in the Tamaki region are to be seen. In mid-December 1835, Henry Williams, accompanied by the recently recruited Rev. Robert Maunsell, sailed from the Bay of Islands to the Thames to bring about a reconciliation between the tribes of that region and their Waikato neighbours, who were currently at war.[59] With him on the missionary schooner *Columbine* was a group of Nga Puhi chiefs led by Rewa, in bygone days one of Hongi's most fearsome generals, but now a Christian,[60] and ready at last, according to Fairburn, 'to make peace with Ngati Paoa of the Thames'.[61] Thus escorted, Williams visited Hauraki settlements at Puriri, Kopu, Kauaeranga (modern Thames) and Whakatiwai, at each place pressing the Marutuahu leaders to end their quarrel with the Waikato tribes, while assuring them, in the person of Rewa, of Nga Puhi goodwill in this pursuit of regional peace.[62]

The meeting at Whakatiwai, headquarters of Ngati Paoa — the tribe still seriously estranged from Waikato and Ngati Whatua o Tamaki — was the decisive one. After some hesitation on Ngati Paoa's part, for initially they found the mere presence of Rewa of Nga Puhi in the Williams party threatening, their senior chiefs Kahukoti and Kupenga agreed to receive peace overtures from Waikato. The missionaries then outlined their strategy for peace.[63] First, Ngati Paoa and Waikato tribes were

Panoramic view from Remuera (Mount Hobson) of the mouth of the Waitemata and the inner gulf. Sketch by Kennett Watkins. CAMPBELL PAPERS, AUCKLAND MUSEUM LIBRARY

to meet at Otahuhu, which had the advantage of being currently deserted and therefore neutral ground. Second, the basis for reconciliation was to be agreement over the disputed borderland south of Otahuhu that lay between the two iwi. Williams suggested that this disputed land, mistakenly referred to at the time as 'Tamaki', be transferred to the Anglican missionaries, who would then hold it in trust as a kind of buffer zone between these two formidable tribes.[64] Two years later, Fairburn, the missionary to whom the land was ultimately transferred, maintained that the initiative came from the 'Thames Natives'. He explained that they wished 'to sell at once their portion of the land joining on to that of Waikato, declaring that peace could not exist for any length of time unless they did so, as there would be perpetual infringement on each others' territories'.[65] What Fairburn contended is not repeated in any other source; it is likely that the original idea came from Henry Williams rather than from the Hauraki people. Regardless of who initiated the proposals, the Ngati Paoa leaders accepted them without demur. They also agreed that a missionary party should go to Awhitu and place the proposals before the Waikato chiefs stationed there in an 'endeavour to establish a general peace between that people and the whole of the Thames tribes'.[66] This was the assignment to which a missionary group made up of the Revs Williams and Maunsell and the catechists Fairburn and Hamlin devoted themselves during the first weeks of 1836.[67]

At this point one must turn aside to write of another peace meeting which took place between Ngati Paoa and Waikato in the later part of 1835, almost certainly before Henry Williams came to the Thames. Leaders of those two tribes met at Puneke, a location near the eastern headland of the Tamaki river, and probably somewhere in that general area nowadays known as Buckland's Beach. Fenton's Orakei Judgment, which is the main nineteenth-century printed source for this meeting, has this to say about it:

> In December, 1835, Kahukoti, chief of Ngatipaoa, and Taraia, chief of Ngatitamatera, arrived at Tamaki with Dr. Maunsell; and Te Wherowhero and Kaihau, on behalf of Waikato, went over to Puneke, on the Tamaki River, to meet them. Here peace was finally concluded. Uruamo and Watarangi, of Te Taou, accompanied Te Wherowhero; but Apihai and Ngaoho, and the bulk of the people, remained on the Manukau side, and did not join in the peace-making.[68]

Evidence from manuscript sources calls into question certain details contained in this excerpt that Fenton had accepted as fact. That the Puneke meeting did indeed take place is not in doubt, but the date which Fenton provided for it almost certainly is. There is evidence that the Puneke peacemaking may have occurred weeks before the date that Fenton suggested, and even before Apihai's people actually settled at Karangahape.[69] Nor could Maunsell have been individually involved; he did not arrive in New Zealand until 26 November 1835 and did not separate from the Rev. Henry Williams until seven weeks later.[70] Further, it is possible that the Puneke peacemaking owed little to the inspiration of missionary mediators and that it was initiated and conducted along traditional lines by the chiefs themselves. (However, Maori present at Puneke and at the later CMS-sponsored meeting some weeks later at Otahuhu, recognised that both had an unusual feature that marked them off from similar occasions in the past. As Paora Te Iwi of Ngati Tamaoho put it: here was peace being made 'not because there had been a battle but because they were in fear'.)[71]

Yet in spite of this 'fear', and in spite of the heightened alarm of the missionaries at the news of fighting of great virulence which had broken out at Rotorua, they found bringing the hostile Waikato and Hauraki tribes together to negotiate at Otahuhu was to prove a drawn-out business.[72] Fairburn later wrote that there had been 'nearly three weeks' of 'the most tedious' negotiation between the two parties before 'a reconciliation and peace was made'.[73] Te Wherowhero had pushed along proceedings as best he could when he promptly fell in with the plan of the missionaries by which they would 'occupy the land between the tribes', entrusting the adjustment of details to them as well,[74] and, later, when he received the Ngati Paoa emissaries in a marked spirit of conciliation. The presence of Nga Puhi chiefs in the missionary party seems to have reassured Te Wherowhero, because the tribes whom he had escorted back to the Manukau were in fear of Nga Puhi no less than of Ngati Paoa.[75] By 18 January 1836, a deputation of Ngati Paoa chiefs led by Kahukoti, and supported by Patuone,[76] who had been waiting cautiously at Puneke, came across to Otahuhu to negotiate face to face with Waikato chiefs.[77] Within three days agreement had been reached.

The precise nature of the Otahuhu peace was not spelt out in the Orakei Judgment, mainly because of the failure of Judge Fenton to unravel the sometimes-confusing evidence that witnesses gave at the court hearings. Uncertainty seems to have arisen out of three circumstances:

- an underestimation of the achievement of the earlier informal meeting at Puneke;
- a failure to make clear that there were two missionary-inspired peace meetings at Otahuhu, one in January 1836, the other in March 1838; and
- the limited nature of the first Otahuhu negotiations.

Dr Robert Maunsell, the only surviving missionary who could testify directly to the court in 1868 as to the nature of the 1836 meeting at Otahuhu, thought it was not a general peacemaking. 'I think they [the chiefs who attended] simply came to point out the boundaries of Mr Fairburn's land';[78] that is, the land which was to be assigned to the missionaries to be held in trust as the means of (as Fairburn himself expressed it) 'keeping unpleasant neighbours at a distance'.[79] This problematic transfer of land, which has come down in history as Fairburn's Old Land Claim, is of such importance in the story of early Auckland that it will shortly be discussed in more detail.

In the meantime, one can say that, independently of what was formally settled at the 1836 peacemaking at Otahuhu, the meeting there built on and reinforced the general will to peace shown by the chiefs at their earlier gathering at Puneke. Paora Te Iwi recaptured the spirit of the occasion when he said that 'after peace was made, they [the exiled tribes] were not afraid'.[80] It appeared that they could now begin to go back in some confidence to their old lands. Ngati Whatua as we have already seen, were sufficiently emboldened after the 1836 meeting to venture out from Karangahape to plant gardens on the more fertile lands of Mangere.[81] And then after a year at Karangahape, they picked up enough confidence to go a step further and actually establish Mangere as their permanent settlement. Waikato tribes on the south bank of the Manukau similarly moved closer to their old habitations on the borders of Tamaki-makau-rau.

IV

It is paradoxical that the Otahuhu peacemaking came about because the missionaries misunderstood the underlying reason for the instability of the Tamaki region. Henry Williams held the sincere, if mistaken, view that the chief bone of contention between the Waikato and Thames tribes was the large slab of borderland – at that time relatively unpeopled – south of Otahuhu and extending as far south as today's Clevedon. Williams argued that if this disputed land lying 'between the contending parties' were ceded to missionaries, they could hold it in trust as a buffer territory so that the main 'stumbling block' to peace would be 'cleared away'.[82] The reality was that this land was sparsely settled not because these two tribes were ferociously competing for it, but because of the general regional instability arising out of almost two decades of murderous musket wars. And if there were rival claimants for the territory, Ngati Paoa and Waikato were but two among many. Te Akitai, Ngai Tai, and other Hauraki tribes had strong claims to various parts of this land that was ultimately sold to the missionaries. (This was recognised by Fairburn who, in later payments to Maori, included chiefs from a variety of tribes including Ngati Whatua.)[83] What further added to the confusion was the decision made at the time to call this disputed territory 'Tamaki', the name customarily and properly given to the isthmus land lying between the Otahuhu and Whau portages, and (sometimes) to the land immediately adjacent.

All this Ngati Paoa and Waikato knew well enough at the time of the 'sale'. But the missionary plan, if misconceived, had a positive advantage for the negotiating chiefs. By making this particular block of land the pretext for reconciliation, the two powerful but war-weary tribes could make concessions on territory of less than vital interest to themselves, and thereby give way without loss of mana. It suited the book, so to speak, of the Maori chiefs to maintain the fiction that in negotiating over this block they were actually dealing with Tamaki-makau-rau, which had been fought over from time immemorial. Fairburn records that, at a gathering held at Otahuhu two years later, the famous old Waikato warrior chief, Te Kanawa, stood up and addressed himself to the land thus: "'So thou art Tamaki the Adulteress, the woman of ten husbands, nay of a hundred husbands, and now thou art gone to seek still another husband and a stranger, too; begone, thou adulteress, begone!" at the same time kicking out his foot as though he would spurn the adulteress from his presence.'[84] One wonders whether Te Kanawa was inwardly smiling wryly whilst he uttered his malediction on this so-called Tamaki.

Originally Henry Williams had intended that the land be ceded to himself. But once negotiations for the transfer were under way he appears to have decided that William Fairburn should more appropriately take his place as the putative purchaser. The view has been expressed that 'Henry Williams, fearing the wrath of his parent body the CMS [in London], backed off leaving William [Fairburn] to complete the detail'.[85] Certainly the parent committee in London had made it clear that it strongly disapproved of the scale of land purchases from Maori that had recently been made by New Zealand missionaries including Henry Williams, usually on behalf of their children.[86] Carleton, son-in-law of Henry Williams and a notorious apologist for the large land claims of the missionaries, as ever, put an altruistic interpretation on the motives of Williams in asking Fairburn to take his place. But it does seem that in this instance Williams, without calculation, simply decided that, as Fairburn had become the CMS missionary with the closest association with that part of the Thames currently under negotiation, it would be more fitting if he acted as the purchaser. Who actually provided the goods which Fairburn used as consideration, we are not told.

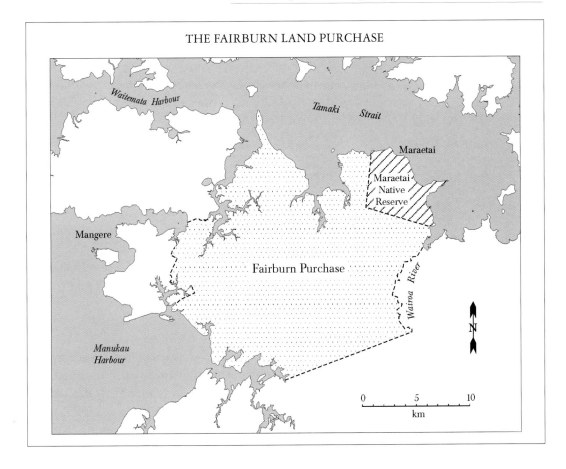

THE FAIRBURN LAND PURCHASE

The deed of sale for the huge block of land called 'Tamaki', but more commonly spoken of nowadays as 'the Fairburn Purchase', was signed by thirty-two chiefs (and witnessed by Henry Williams, two other Pakeha and one Maori) at Puneke, beside the Tamaki river, on 22 January 1836.[87] The boundaries of the block, the nearest part of which was eight miles from what was later to be central Auckland, were spelt out in great detail in the deed.[88] They are best recounted here, however, in general terms. Beginning at 'the Dragging Place at Otahuhu', the boundary line ran south-east to Papakura, then towards modern Clevedon, thence down the Wairoa river to Umupuia, up the western shore of the Hauraki gulf to the Tamaki river and 'thence to Otahuhu, where it ends'.[89] This was a huge block, originally calculated as being 40,000 acres, but found on later survey to be far greater than that. The surveyor-'general, in

This map is an adaptation of the map in Old Land Claims, *a* Rangahaua Whanui *report to the* Waitangi Tribunal, *1997.*

1851, estimated that the purchase contained nearly 75,000 acres; a scientific estimate almost a century later increased the figure to 83,947 acres.[90]

The initial payment was '90 blankets, 24 axes, 24 adzes, 20 hoes, 14 spades, 900 lbs of tobacco, 24 combs and 80$ [*sic*]'. Fairburn made four subsequent payments between December 1836 and December 1839. The last payment, exclusively in goods, while revealing the enduring popularity of blankets and tobacco for Maori, shows that an interesting diversity of consumer goods was becoming increasingly used as 'trade' (hoko): '20 blankets, 6 iron pots, 12 tinder boxes, 6 spades, 6 hatchets, 6 bars soap, 6 Plane irons, 6 fancy pipes, 5 scissors, 2 boxes, 6 shirts, 6 Trowsers, 1 gown, 90 lbs tobacco, 6 adzes, 12 hoes, and 12 axes'.[91] In estimating the value of goods supplied, the Sydney prices were multiplied by three, which was then the usual mark-up for goods imported from Port Jackson to be sold to Maori in New Zealand.

Governor Robert FitzRoy who made a generous allowance for Fairburn's claim, believing it to be a 'special case'. AUCKLAND MUSEUM LIBRARY

The full Fairburn Purchase, because disallowed, was to lock up in government hands so much south Auckland land during the Crown Colony years (1840–52), that it is fitting, at this point, to break out of the time frame of this present chapter, in order to show its impact on the future economic wellbeing of the original Maori owners. In September 1841, Fairburn, who was, at that time, about to quit the CMS and become a private settler, submitted to the Land Commissioners investigating the circumstances of his purchase that he had paid in total £923 17s 6d, of which £16 was in cash, and £907 17s 6d in goods. The commissioners, after deciding under the criteria which they had been instructed to apply, that the purchase had been a bona fide one, and after taking into account the capital improvements which Fairburn claimed to have made to his land as a farmer – by his own very generous estimate totalling £3,357 18s 6d. – recommended that he be awarded 2560 acres, the maximum Crown Grant permissible under regulations. The next governor, FitzRoy, believing Fairburn's claim to be a special case, extended the allocation to 5500 acres, to be held in nine different grants, mainly in Manurewa, Pakuranga and Otahuhu.[92] In 1847, Governor Grey, no lover of land-owning missionaries, issued a new grant to Fairburn, reducing his allocation to 2560 acres. But this entailed no great sacrifice for the claimant. As the Crown required almost immediately some of

Fairburn's Otahuhu land for a new garrison township to be manned by Imperial Army pensioners (the Royal New Zealand Fencibles), it bought this part of his grant on terms that left Fairburn with a tidy profit. He also did well financially from a private subdivision of land, adjoining the new Otahuhu township, which he later carried out.[93]

Fairburn never laid claim to the whole block which he 'purchased'. On 12 July 1837 he had 'made over', in his words, 'one-third of the whole of this purchase' to Maori who had been once resident on the territory purchased.[94] He promised that after boundaries had been surveyed, each of the tribes, which he then listed by name – Ngati Paoa, Ngati Tama-Te-Ra, Ngati Terau, Te Akitai, and Ngati Whanaunga – 'shall have returned to them for their personal use forever, land in proportion to the number of persons of whom their tribes may consist, residing in any part of the north of the Thames and Manukau'.[95] On 5 April 1840 he also 'made over one-third of the whole of the [original] purchase to the Church Missionary Society for the benefit of the New Zealand Mission'.[96] In 1847 Governor Grey declared this conveyance of land to the CMS illegal, having been made after the British Crown assumed authority over the new colony of New Zealand. However, the governor awarded a special Crown Grant of 300 acres to Fairburn, contingent upon its being retransferred as a gift to the CMS 'with the view of making it part of [the CMS] endowment for the Bishopric of New Zealand'.[97] This was duly done and the London committee of the society declared itself quite happy with the revised arrangement.

Governor George Grey. Conté drawing by George Richmond. AUCKLAND CITY ART GALLERY

Local Maori, on the other hand, had every reason to be dissatisfied with the long-term consequences of the sale they had made to Fairburn in 1836. Here it must be understood that, upon New Zealand's becoming a Crown Colony in January 1840, sales of land between Maori and European made before that date (of which the Fairburn Purchase was a most notable instance in Auckland) had to be investigated by Crown Commissioners to determine whether they had been bona fide in transaction and equitable in law.[98] It is also most significant that land disallowed to Fairburn did not revert to the original native sellers but became 'Surplus Land' at the disposal of the Crown. The drastic reduction of the third of the original purchase claimed by Fairburn, and the even more sweeping reduction of the third he had attempted to convey to the CMS, were in all conscience of no great consequence to him or to the colonial church for that matter. The failure to return to Maori their third-share (at least) of the land was, however, of great consequence to *them*. This had been a problem from almost the very beginning of the transaction. Many Maori had not been made fully aware that Fairburn promised in the deed of 1837 to return one-third of the land to the original owners, and this problem was compounded by the failure of the Crown to settle on defining exactly the location(s) of the one-third to be returned.[99]

With the growth of Auckland after its proclamation as a government settlement in September 1840, the Disallowed Surplus of the Fairburn Purchase was transformed into very valuable land held by the Crown. The transaction emerged as a focus of discontent among Maori – and remains so today – aware that what they had sold for a pittance in a very confused transaction had become, even in part, denied them. The early governors seemed to have accepted the justice of the right of Maori to reclaim at least the third, which Fairburn had conveyed back to them in 1837. But they dilly-dallied over the complicated business of surveying and allocating the portions to be returned to the various tribes. What had been dilatory behaviour on the part of the first governors became calculated policy, however, under Governor Grey. Yet he was not solely or even mainly to blame. By holding on to surplus land which the Crown could later sell, he was simply implementing the policy of the early-Victorian Colonial Office, and the parsimonious governments who were its masters, of developing the settlement empire 'on the cheap'.[100] As Matthew Russell has shown in a Waitangi Tribunal research paper, the local administrators, by retaining as much land as possible for sale and settlement, 'offered at least a partial solution to the colony's serious financial problems'.[101] The upshot – nothing was done about returning the Maori third.

Once Auckland became the capital in 1841, settlement in the region intensified. The value of land within the Fairburn Claim skyrocketed. Professor Alan Ward has long maintained that with the rapid appreciation of land values in the south Auckland region, Maori tribes who had been the original occupiers could have enjoyed great financial benefits had they remained effective landowners. But to have done so (Ward continues) they needed to have retained a substantial pool of land there 'which was not only of reasonable quality, but also in reasonable proximity to the areas of European settlement'.[102] And this they no longer had.

By 1850 Maori resentment, which had been steadily building up for some years, came to a head. In that year, licences to cut timber were given to Pakeha millers in parts of the Maraetai-Orere region. According to colonial law this was Crown surplus land. But it was also the traditional domain of certain Hauraki hapu who, considering it rightfully theirs, had begun to resume occupation there. On 1 July 1851, William Gisborne, Commissioner for Crown Lands in New Ulster (Northern New Zealand), alerted the Colonial Secretary to the purchase.

> And now, owing to the immensely enhanced value of their claims, to their great desire of location in the vicinity of Auckland and to their regret at having received so very little from the original sale, (about £300 for 75,000 acres) they [the Maori tribes] have commenced seizing upon some of the most valuable spots they can find.[103]

In the long run the only substantial portion of land returned to Maori – and that to designated tribes only – was a Native Reserve of 5000 acres to the south and east of Maraetai. Not surprisingly, quarrels continued.[104] Between 1851 and 1854, the government made payments to buy out the interests of claimant groups[105] in an ineffectual attempt to settle, in the words of the surveyor-general, 'the various and complicated claims of the natives on the Block of land known as Mr. Fairburn's Purchase'.[106] But the wrong was not righted. Tribes on either coast (Te Akitai, Ngati Terau, Ngati Paoa and others) retained a heavy sense of grievance, which did not go away.

It is ironical that the Fairburn Purchase, originally transacted by missionaries to promote peace, had become a root cause of the inter-racial conflict that was ultimately to express itself in the New Zealand Wars of the 1860s.

V

The peace-meetings held at Puneke and Otahuhu over the summer of 1835–36 lowered tensions among some at least of the tribes living in the inner Hauraki gulf and the Manukau. But this change fell far short of full pacification. Speaking years later of the consequences of the 1836 peacemaking, a Ngati Te Ata elder retrospectively claimed that 'the result was that all malice was at an end' and that the people were placed 'in quiet occupation of this land at Tamaki'.[107] His memory deceived him. A complete peace between Hauraki and Waikato was still far away. Nor was a 'quiet occupation' of Tamaki about to begin. Te Kawau's branch of Ngati Whatua, who held the mana whenua over the bulk of the isthmus, had taken little part in the 1836 negotiations. Further-more, that tribe was still at odds with Ngati Paoa, and greatly in fear of the Te Parawhau section of Nga Puhi living at Whangarei. To the south there was great insecurity among the people of the Firth of Thames. As we have seen, the murder of Hunga at Rotorua had put Tainui and Arawa at one another's throats, throwing the whole of the Thames as well (wrote Fairburn in 1836) 'into a state of alarm'.[108] He continued: 'All [the tribes] around us are repairing and removing to their several fortifications, all communication is now cut off with our different [mission] stations owing to the number of armed scouts prowling about the bush hunting for human prey.' Later in the year he wrote about continuing acts of 'revenge and retaliation on both sides . . . carried on to an alarming extent with the greatest virulence'.[109] In the following year, Fairburn reported from Puriri that, while many of the older Hauraki chiefs had been able to exercise a generally restraining influence on their communities, there were, never-theless, 'many young hot-headed Chiefs in our neighbourhood who were, and still are, desirous of trying their new guns to see if they will carry [shoot] straight'.[110] Some Hauraki warriors were drawn into this violent struggle. In his history of the Tainui tribes, Kelly has registered the presence of 'certain of Ngati Paoa under Puhatu, and some of Ngati Tamatera under Taraia' in the Waikato expedition that attacked Rotorua in August 1836.[111] For two years these wars, even if indirectly, added to the general insecurity of the Tamaki region.

Moreover, being at best merely on the fringes of the 1836 peace negotiations at Otahuhu, Te Kawau's followers had gained least from that accord. They began their own search for security by attempting to mollify potential enemies. Fenton records that Te Taou and Nga Oho chiefs, aware that Ngati Paoa still held them accountable for the Whakatiwai murders, attempted to appease that tribe by a visit made in April 1836. (Both the date which Fenton gave for the visit, and whether there were two, or even possibly three separate visits of reconciliation extending over as much as four years, are issues which Fenton fudges in his report. But witnesses in the Orakei land court hearing certainly attested to this visit of 1836.) As Fenton reported it in his judgment, on that particular occasion, a party of peace made up of two Te Taou chiefs, Uruamo and Watarangi, and sixty followers went from Karangahape to Orere. The purpose of their mission was to meet the Ngati Paoa chief Kahukoti, and to try to end the blood feud by making redress for the Whakatiwai killings.[112] After the deputation had offered a gift of twenty guns and ten cartouche boxes to make amends for the deaths and had performed the requisite ceremonies,[113] Uruamo approached Kahukoti to ask whether the Tamaki tribes could now resume 'undisturbed possession' of their lands on the Waitemata. The reply of the Ngati Paoa chief, while without overt threat, was sufficiently enigmatic as to give little reassurance to the deputation. They departed believing, in Fenton's words,

> that the Thames tribes still nourished feelings of revenge on account
> of the killing of their friends Rewa, Hauruia, and Kapatahi, at
> Whakatiwai; and that they [Te Taou and Ngaoho] were perfectly
> correct in this belief is shown by the fact that even six years later
> [1840] Ngatiwhanaunga[114] gave Haora Tipa [a senior Ngati Paoa
> chief] a paddle and two tomahawks, called after their dead men, as a
> sign that he should go and avenge their deaths. And it is quite natural
> that so long as this feeling was known to exist Te Taou and Ngaoho
> should be unwilling to locate themselves permanently, with their
> women and children, on the shores of the Waitemata, where they
> would be peculiarly open to the attacks and surprises from Ngati
> Paoa, who, although they had suffered greatly, were still a powerful
> tribe.[115]

It is hard to understand why, after having emphasised the extent to which potential enemies still threatened the Tamaki branch of Ngati Whatua, Fenton should then have gone on in his judgment to make the categorical statement that Te Taou returned to cultivate at Okahu bay (Orakei) in 1836, and to build a pa there in the next year.[116] By so doing the judge apparently accepted the evidence of that minority of Ngati Whatua witnesses who, through forgetfulness, or out of anxiety to make their customary title to Orakei unassailable, had predated their return to the shores of the Waitemata.[117] In this particular section of his judgment Fenton, in effect, 'wrote against' the evidence of many of his witnesses, Maori and Pakeha, who spoke of the timing of the return of Ngati Whatua to Tamaki. Captain Wing, who visited both the Waitemata and the Manukau in what he called 'the summer' of 1837 – presumably early in 1837 – recalled that Te Kawau's people were living permanently at only two places at that time, both of them on the Manukau.[118] The great bulk of the people, he said, were with 'Te Kawau at Karangahape' in a pa that was still very much lived in and 'in a good state of repair';[119] but he also encountered some of that chief's people in a small pa at the Karaka end (Green Bay) of Te Whau portage. Wing also remarked on the fact that on two occasions during this visit there was clear evidence of continuing hostility between Ngati Whatua and Nga Puhi.

When Wing's large sailing boat had first rounded North Head to enter the Waitemata, canoes were observed moving offshore to inspect them – an alarmed Nga Puhi chief who was accompanying Wing persuaded him to avoid this group. Almost certainly these canoes contained fishermen from the Manukau, Ngati Whatua or possibly Ngati Te Ata.[120] (After the 1836 peacemaking, Ngati Te Ata had resumed fishing in the Waitemata, coming across as one chief expressed it, to 'steal sharks', an expression he admitted using to express his tribe's fear of attack by Nga Puhi.)[121] The threat to Ngati Whatua was even greater. They were doubly exposed to the attack, not only (as were Ngati Te Ata) from Nga Puhi, but also from Ngati Paoa who, stationed on Waiheke island or in settlements of the inner gulf like Orere and Whakatiwai, fished in waters close to customary Ngati Whatua fishing grounds. It made sense, therefore, that on those occasions when Ngati Whatua fishermen crossed the isthmus from Karangahape, for reasons of safety they 'came in large bodies'.[122] In the spring of 1837, Ngati Whatua were sufficiently emboldened to establish gardens on the Waitemata side.[123] But they did so with great caution. Small 'parties of about ten' cleared and planted at Horotiu (the valley in modern Auckland through which Queen Street now runs – probably on the volcanic soils to the west of Albert Park); and at Rangitoto-iti in the lower Upland Road area in Remuera.[124] 'We were afraid to come here to reside permanently', observed Paoa Tuhaere, 'but not afraid to cultivate.'[125] Consequently, when planting and harvesting had been completed on the Waitemata side, the gardeners always retreated to the safety of the Manukau.[126]

But by the spring of 1837, the time had come for Apihai's people to wind down their occupation of Karangahape. By now they had gardens planted in the fertile volcanic soils of Mangere, Ihumatao, Onehunga, Horotiu and Rangitoto.[127] Was it not logical, therefore, to re-establish themselves in Tamaki? As a first step, they were anxious to shift to Mangere. But to do this would move them from the protective cloak of Potatau Te Wherowhero. The Rev. Robert Maunsell reminded the Orakei Land Court that, militarily speaking, Ngati Whatua had been reduced by this time to 'a very small body', who needed Potatau close by to deflect any threatening attack.[128] Apihai extricated his tribe from its dilemma by renewing an offer of a gift of Tamaki land (originally made by Awanui) to Potatau. This, the Waikato chief accepted. The land which he and his Mahuta retinue took over was described by a Ngati Whatua elder as being 'near Onehunga not far from Te Tatua' [Three Kings].[129] (This description suggests a Hillsborough location not far from the old pa site on which, in 1879, the nineteenth-century notable, James Williamson, built his splendid Italianate residence, 'The Pah'.) From the summer of 1837–38 until the coming of Governor Hobson, Potatau is said to have alternated his residence between Onehunga and Awhitu.[130] This was assurance enough for Te Kawau. He moved his people to Mangere, where he built a new pa on the remains of the old and named it Whakarongo. But it was said that even while this new Mangere pa was being built, both sides of the Tamaki isthmus proper remained deserted.[131]

VI

Shortly after Potatau and Te Kawau had relocated themselves at Onehunga and Mangere, the missionaries sponsored a second meeting at Otahuhu, which had the effect of speeding up the return of Ngati Whatua to the southern seaboard of the Waitemata. This informal gathering, in which (in contrast to the peacemaking of 1836) Ngati Whatua participated, enabled the assembled tribes to talk peace. How this came about is best understood in the setting of the educational work inaugurated by the Anglican missionaries in the Bay of Islands in the 1820s.

In December 1828, the CMS mission schools in the Bay set up a system of combined annual examinations.[132] Students, some of whom were adult, were gathered together for two or three days from the schools at a prearranged central point, to be examined by a panel of mission teachers. The students were generally tested in their knowledge of the catechism, in reading, writing, either 'accounts' or arithmetic, and in perhaps a craft such as carpentry. Maori regarded these 'schools' examinations' as enjoyable rather than inquisitorial, as social occasions providing opportunities for competition and emulation to which Maori culture was certainly no stranger. A few modest prizes, printed sections of the liturgy, slates, looking glasses and the like, were generally awarded to the 'most deserving' candidates in the different classes.[133] These examination schools were extraordinarily well attended. Families of the students undergoing examination generally came too. The missionaries also made a point of inviting chiefs among whose hitherto unevangelised tribes the gospel was likely to prosper. In the 1830s Wesleyan mission schools often took part in these examinations. And there were always many self-invited 'strangers'. At least 1000 people of various kinds attended the 1830 gathering.[134] Apart from the students, twelve missionaries attended, nine of them married and generally philoprogenitive, bringing with them their wives and their forty-five children.

The enthusiasm of Maori for these inter-tribal 'schools' gatherings shows the growing interest in literacy. But schools had a further appeal to the local population. They represented that blend of cultures, an incorporation of western learning with Maori social norms, which many Maori leaders saw as the future path that their people should take. Characteristically, as the tribes gathered, there would be an interchange of haka; yet it is reported that on free afternoons the boys might compete at cricket, in which they had developed an interest.[135] Of course it was the hope of the missionaries that the western new would oust the indigenous old. Reporting on the second schools meeting at Kerikeri in 1829, William Williams observed happily that, as the groups arrived, 'the native mode of salutation at such times is with a rush on both sides and a sham fight but this was exchanged for the more sober welcome of three British cheers'.[136] To celebrate the end of examinations, missionaries provided the students with 'an abundant repast' of pork, potatoes and rolls of bread, followed by tea and a gingercake (or alternatively flour sweetened by sugar).[137] Chiefs as a general rule, and increasingly all who attended, were invited to share in this feasting, which Maori seemed to have valued as happily harmonising with their own conception of hospitality.

Missionaries learned that sometimes an unexpected but (for them) welcome adjunct to these examination hui, was the burying of differences between members of estranged tribes who attended. Henry Williams claimed to be 'much astonished'[138] during the 1830 Paihia examinations, at the co-operation of students from Kororareka, who eight months before had been on opposing sides in the 'Girls' War'.[139] 'Nothing can exceed their desire', he wrote, 'to perfect themselves for the examination.'[140] Williams wrote in his journal that on the day of the break-up feast, when numbers swelled to over 1000, many of these 'strangers . . . were the same people who had fought at Kororarika, every one was armed, yet perfect order was observed. A more gratifying sight had never been witnessed in this land.'[141]

The Bay of Islands experience was to repeat itself when CMS missionaries set up the schools examination system in Tamaki. For, as in the Bay, so in Tamaki, these schools indirectly promoted the cause of peace. No sooner had the catechist Fairburn shifted from Puriri to Maraetai in July 1837,[142] than he became aware of how persistent, in spite of the 1836 agreement, was the antagonism brought about by the Whakatiwai killings. Waikato tribes, moving into the Hauraki gulf on fishing excursions, made Fairburn's new mission station a place of refuge lest they be attacked by what Fairburn called 'the Thames party'.[143] By 1838 the Rev. Robert Maunsell and the catechist James Hamlin had established schools in a substantial mission field on the west coast, extending from the south Manukau heads to the lands at the mouth of the Waikato river. On the western shore of the Firth of Thames, Fairburn also ministered to a large group. He soon drew in a number of students from Waiheke island as well.

These three missionaries were anxious to transplant the traditional annual examination of schools from the Bay of Islands to their region. But they feared that the persistent suspicion between tribes on the two coasts would make that impossible, as 'neither would go into the other's district'.[144] This difficulty they decided to overcome by making the incontestably neutral ground of Otahuhu the examination centre. To their surprise they found that all tribes were amenable to the suggestion. In March 1838 missionaries, their wives (who often shouldered much responsibility for teaching in the mission schools) and their families came as an advance party to Otahuhu. There they erected a tented encampment. On 21 March, an eight-day meeting began, later described by the Ngati Whatua chief, Paora Tuhaere, as a 'a pakeha peacemaking, it was an assemblage of schools, a Missionary meeting'.[145] The examinations on this occasion were a great success.

But the gathering was to have a much wider significance than that. Running parallel to the testing of the students was a series of informal meetings conducted by elders of the tribes. Leading Ngati Paoa was Herua from Whakatiwai, the influential chief to whom, three years before, Henry Williams had proffered Te Kauae's hatchet as a symbol of reconciliation.[146] South Waikato tribes, Ngati Tamaoho, Ngati Te Ata and Ngati Mahuta, also attended in good numbers. Te Kawau arrived with his chiefs from Mangere. More significantly, Potatau came from Onehunga as a kind of presiding presence. Tuhaere said that Te Taou chiefs (Te Kawau's kinsmen) took the opportunity at Otahuhu to meet the Ngati Paoa leaders informally and to 'talk friendly'; 'peace was made with Ngati Paoa by the elders then'.[147] Fairburn reported that the leaders gave 'several speeches' before the final feast. The feast itself was not described. But the Rev. Maunsell depicted a similar missionary feast held in the Manukau district two years later which is worth citing as an illustration of how the celebration had acquired a distinctively Maori character.

> Then came the feast usual on such occasions – not, indeed so neat or varied as you may see in England, but attended with no less ceremony, and highly interesting to the Europeans we had invited to be present. Twelve whole pigs cooked in one hangi and borne on sticks were laid in the middle of the company; on either side were piled a hundred

baskets of potatoes, corn and kumara. A blessing was asked and the
attendants with the master of ceremonies hastened with hatchets and
knives to cut up the pigs into halves and quarters, and having shared
out the baskets of kumara, etc., into parcels proportioned to the
respective tribes, crowned them with a quarter, or a half, or a whole
pig, as either the number or rank of the parties required. All being
ready, the distributor came forward with his blanket wound tightly
around his waist, and another bearing a slate read over the names of
the chief men of the several families, while the distributor, with a large
stick, struck the respective heaps, and in a few minutes the whole
vanished as if by magic. About 1500 had assembled.[148]

The missionaries were gratified at the political arrangements
reached at Otahuhu between hitherto estranged tribes, above all
heartened by the readiness of tribal heads to talk peace. Fairburn
wrote in his journal: 'Much good feeling seemed to prevail
during the whole of the time we were there.'[149] In a new spirit
of amity the tribes went their separate ways, Te Taou to
Mangere, Ngati Te Ata to Awhitu, Ngati Tamaoho to the inner
Manukau, and Ngati Paoa to Waiheke, Maraetai and points
south.[150]

Apihai Te Kawau and his followers were reassured by their new
accord with Ngati Paoa. Though less than a complete peace, it
was encouraging enough to persuade them that, after years of
exile, they could now make ready to take up their ancestral lands
on the Waitemata.

CHAPTER VIII

Return to Tamaki

I

When New Zealand's first lieutenant-governor, William Hobson, decided, in 1840, to shift the capital of the new colony to the Waitemata harbour, missionary advisers told him that it was with members of the Tamaki branch of Ngati Whatua, led by Apihai Te Kawau, that he must deal if he wanted to buy Tamaki land. This information had a certain convenience for the governor because, earlier in the year, Te Kawau had sent an embassy of chiefs inviting him to live at Tamaki. According to native custom, Ngati Whatua were the undisputed owners of the isthmus, save for an area on the western bank of the Tamaki river later called in the old lands deeds 'the Kohimarama Block'.[1] The mana whenua which Apihai's people held over Tamaki was based, in the first instance, on the Te Taou conquest (raupatu) of Waiohua, the previous occupants of the isthmus. This *take* (right) of possession the victors had reinforced by intermarriage with women of the vanquished iwi; consequently, they could also claim through the resulting progeny an ancestral right to Tamaki lands. The constituent tribes of Ngati Whatua of Tamaki (Te Taou, Nga Oho and Te Uringutu) had further cemented their claim to Tamaki by permanent and undisturbed occupation of the isthmus for three generations. Granted, the musket wars had driven Apihai's people into exile for much of the following period (1821–36). But during the later 1830s, Ngati Whatua set about reasserting their rights of ownership over the Tamaki lands once more. The steps by which they resumed occupation of their old gardens and habitations beside the Waitemata become the first concern of this chapter.

It is difficult to give precise dates for the progressive resettlement of the Ngati Whatua people on the Waitemata side of the isthmus. Maori witnesses at the Orakei Land Court sittings of 1866 and 1868 rarely provided exact years when speaking of the tribe's return. They could hardly have been expected to. Elsdon Best reminded us that pre-European Maori lacked 'any dependable system of chronology. No man knew how old he was.'[2] Nor had any Pakeha been permanently resident on the isthmus in the years before 1840 to provide us with the check that European-style chronology can sometimes provide. One is tempted, therefore, to fall back upon the guarded retrospective view of the Rev. Robert Maunsell, who said that, over the later 1830s, Ngati Whatua 'gradually found their way over here'[3] – that is, to the Waitemata shore. Nevertheless, by weighing the testimony of Orakei witnesses who made reference to seasons for gardening and even to lunar months, a sequence of migration can be built up that at least answers up to the test of strong probability. And once 1840 is reached – the year 'when Captain Symonds first came'[4] – and then 1841 – the year 'Hobson came' (a real benchmark for inhabitants of Tamaki) – Maori evidence can usually be attached to the European time scale.

Captain William Hobson, RN, portrait about 1835. From G. H. Scholefield, Captain William Hobson. AUCKLAND CITY LIBRARIES

What becomes obvious is that a full-scale return by Ngati Whatua was delayed by a persistent residual fear of Ngati Paoa of the Thames, and of Te Parawhau of Whangarei. Particularly of Te Parawhau. As the southernmost branch of Nga Puhi, they had borne the brunt of retributive (utu) attacks by those tribes (which included Ngati Whatua) who had been ravaged by Nga Puhi during the musket wars. It will be recalled that in 1825, after having been routed at Te Ika-a-ranganui, Ngati Whatua put together a force, joined by some of Apihai's followers, that had made a revenge raid on Whangarei in which sixty Te Parawhau people were killed.[5] This attack Te Parawhau had not forgotten. As late as 1840, they considered they had an utu debit account with Apihai's people that had yet to be balanced.[6] With threats such as these hanging over the region, it was not until Tamaki became the site of the capital, with the concomitant prospect of

181

the governor's peace and of enriching trade, that Ngati Whatua felt they could safely resettle many of their people back at Orakei.

Before 1838, Ngati Whatua had confined their excursions over to the Waitemata side of the isthmus to small groups whose main concern was to catch fish and establish temporary gardens rather than to assert rights of occupation. Mangere remained the tribe's centre of settlement. Emphatically so when, during the winter of 1838, that part of the tribe which was still living at Karangahape, according to the testimony of Te Waka Tuae, 'gave up the cultivations and pa and came to Mangere'.[7] This group indicated that they were shifting from Karangahape for good by 'destroying the pa' which they had occupied for over three years[8] – probably by burning their houses there, just as Apihai's followers had done when abandoning their pa at Te Horo on the Waipa some years before. Concentrated henceforth in the upper Manukau and close to the Otahuhu portage, the tribe built up extensive gardens at Mangere, Onehunga, and surrounding lands. 'The whole place was covered with our cultivations', Te Waka Tuaea of Ngati Whatua recalled.[9]

Conflicting evidence does not enable us to say confidently whether the first permanent gardens were re-established on the Waitemata side of the isthmus in 1837 or in 1838. But witnesses at the Orakei Land Court hearing seemed to agree that the first two areas cleared for that purpose were, in order, at Takapourewa (on the volcanic soils near the Purewa estuary) and at Horotiu (the Queen Street valley).[10] Those who were members of the first parties to clear the land remembered encountering a desolate landscape covered by scrub, tupakihi and other secondary growth. The aged Nga Oho rangatira, Warena Hengia, testified in 1868 that 'when we came to cut down the timber, we could not see where the old [pre-1821] cultivations, . . . of [Nga Oho and Uringutu] had been. The signs were the newly grown timber. The old plantations were covered with timber. Not quite so tall as the roof of the houses, but as tall as myself and above.'[11] Paora Tuhaere, a senior Ngati Whatua chief, informed the Orakei Court that, at a time which he did not precisely specify (but which was almost certainly shortly after the March 1838 missionary 'peace' meeting at Otahuhu), 'the whole of the Te Taou, Nga Oho and Uringutu came here [the Waitemata side] to make clearings. When they were made, [we] returned to

Mangere.'[12] But before the visitors left, they are said to have built large houses, indicating the intention of Apihai's people to resettle on the Waitemata lands in the near future. Their determination to return is further confirmed by Te Taou's planting of a potato crop at Horotiu – whether in 1837 or 1838 the records do not make clear.[13] The last of the three crops taken, said Paora, 'was intended for seed, as we contemplated settling here [at Orakei]'.[14]

The process of resettlement continued through 1839. An early Pakeha settler, Charles Marshall, recalled that on his arrival at Tamaki in September 1839, the chief habitations of 'Ngati Whatua and Te Taou' were still in the Mangere district with those of Te Akitai nearby.[15] But, by this time, preparations for the return to the Waitemata were well under way. Apihai's followers were cultivating 'at Orakei, Okahu, Whakatakataka [the point between Okahu and Hobson Bay] and Pourewa'.[16] After lifting the crop planted in the spring of 1839, Te Taou abandoned their Horotiu gardens 'because the lands had been worn out'. Nga Oho replaced these exhausted gardens by planting beds of potatoes on freshly cleared land at Waiariki, on the eastern side of the (Princes Street) ridge, a sunny fertile area which became better known in early colonial times as Official Bay.[17] A novel touch here was the planting of peach trees beside these gardens, at the very spot (according to Fenton) which later became the site of the Auckland Provincial Council Chambers and, coincidentally, the site of the Orakei Land Court hearings.[18]

By 1839, there were kainga at Orakei, Okahu and Rangitotoiti. During this year or early in the next, Te Taou protected its Okahu settlement by building a palisaded pa on the flat land beside the stream just before it flowed onto the beach. (It is noteworthy that, even after Auckland became the Pakeha capital, Apihai's small tribe still did not feel entirely secure against enemy attack. During Hobson's governorship a second pa was built at the western end of Okahu bay.)

John Logan Campbell, who with a fellow Scot, William Brown, founded Auckland's first merchant firm, visited the Tamaki isthmus briefly between 29 April and 3 May 1840. He arrived at Tamaki about four months before Captain W. C. Symonds, on the governor's instructions, set in train the purchase of the 3000-acre block needed as the site of the new capital of New Zealand.

John Logan Campbell at the time (1881) of the publication of Poenamo.
CAMPBELL PAPERS, AUCKLAND MUSEUM LIBRARY

Throughout his very long life Campbell was a meticulous keeper of journals. His account of this excursion which he made with Brown, originally written when he was a twenty-two-year-old, he re-presented forty years later in romantically embellished form as the major part of the book, *Poenamo*,[19] now universally regarded as a colonial classic. Campbell and Brown had come to Tamaki for speculative purposes, hoping to buy a substantial area of land from the Ngati Whatua chiefs.[20] They were unsuccessful. But Campbell's report on the state of Tamaki in early 1840 was a complete success; at least from the standpoint of the modern historian for whom it is a unique and objective record, describing what Auckland was like just before Pakeha settled there. Campbell wrote that Apihai's tribe at this particular time was still living on both sides of the isthmus. The two kainga on the Waitemata (he noted) were at Okahu and on the lower slopes of Little Rangitoto, seemingly on or near the narrow neck of land between the western shore of Waitaramoa (Hobson Bay) and the drowned tidal crater known today as the Orakei basin.[21] Those members of the tribe still living on the Manukau were located at Onehunga and Mangere. On the morning that Campbell sailed up the Waitemata as far as Waitaramoa, he saw 'no sign of human life' and found both Orakei kainga deserted.[22] 'In vast fields of fern', he wrote, 'Nature reigned supreme.'[23] We may infer from Campbell's impressions of settlement on the isthmus, which his party also traversed on foot, that Apihai's people were now migrating seasonally between Mangere and Orakei, and that Mangere was at least where they dwelt in winter and was still probably their main habitation.[24]

II

The negotiations between the governor and Ngati Whatua, which resulted in the new capital being set up on the Waitemata, were to revolutionise where Ngati Whatua chose to settle the bulk of their tribe. But the Orakei Court transcripts confirm that, some time before the foundation of Auckland in September 1840, Te Kawau had anticipated that event by shifting his headquarters there. 'I left my other places, namely Mangere and Onehunga', he said, 'to reside permanently here, where I was found by the Europeans.'[25]

However, this shift, in spite of obvious future advantages, laid him more open meanwhile to attack by old enemies. In an attempt to make the new headquarters of his small tribe more secure, Apihai made a point of gifting land beside the Waitemata to Potatau – as he had earlier given him land near Onehunga beside the Manukau – in the hope that that mighty Waikato chief might live on both sides of the Tamaki isthmus and protect it by his mana and power.[26]

Yet in those uncertain times, as Percy Smith wrote, 'fear of neighbours at the north and others to the south' was characteristic not just of Ngati Whatua. Other returning tribes feared attack, particularly those going back to lands to the north of Tamaki. According to Smith, such was the 'state of unrest' in the region at the time that shortly after the news of Hobson's arrival at the Bay of Islands reached the Waitemata, 'a meeting was called of the *morehu*, or remnants of the tribes at Okahu, near the future City of Auckland to determine on what course they should pursue to ensure their safety'.[27] This conference was widely attended.[28] Its convenor, Te Whatarangi (Apihai's cousin), was able to draw in (said one account) 'all the great chiefs of the Tamaki, Waitemata, Kaipara, and other surrounding districts'.[29]

The prolonged discussion at this gathering as to how the tribes could best secure 'peace and order and a cessation of war and strife' was inconclusive. Many years later, Puna Reweti, a Ngati Whatua elder, recalled that at a crucial stage of proceedings, however, Titai, a much-respected matakite or seer, rose and spoke. He told the gathering how the night before, he had fallen into a trance during which his god (atua) had sung a prophetic song to him. Titai then intoned the words of this song to the assembled gathering.

He aha te hau e wawara mai?
He tiu! He raki!
Nana i a mai te pupu tarakihi ki uta
E tikina atu e au te kotiu,
Koia te pou whakairo
Ka tu ki Waitemata
I aku wai te rangi e!

George Graham's translation in English runs thus:

What is the breeze which gently hither blows?
It is a wind of the north-west and north
Which drifts hither the shell of the nautilus.
Were I to bring hitherward from the north-west
The ornamental post
To stand here in Waitemata
Fulfilled would be my vision, e![30]

As Puna Reweti pointed out, the language of this visionary song was figurative. 'The nautilus [pupu tarakihi]' (he explained) 'is the ship of the pakeha, and the carved pole (an emblem of firm peace erected in olden times) is the English law and power, of which the flag of England is the emblem.' To the listeners at the meeting, the meaning of the message, though expressed in metaphor, was clear enough – enduring peace would only come to the Waitemata if the newly arrived governor were invited to establish his power there. The suggestion was acted on. An embassy of chiefs headed by Te Reweti Tamaki (Te Kawau's nephew) – described by Terry as 'very acute and intelligent, particularly as to the interests of his tribe, in all his transactions with Europeans'[31] – travelled north to persuade Hobson to shift his seat of government to Tamaki.[32] Yet whether the governor would act on this advice lay in the uncertain future. In the meantime, Ngati Whatua of Tamaki fortified Okahu and sought to establish friendly relations with their neighbours.

Over the next three years, the tribe was able to restore peaceful relations with its two remaining potential foes, Ngati Paoa and Te Parawhau. At last the times were propitious for reconciliation all round. The conversion of many Maori to Christianity, a growing distaste for war among the tribes, and the establishment of the governor's settlement at Tamaki in September 1840, were all to play a part. But no factor was more significant in reconciling the tribes than the founding of the capital of Auckland.

To illustrate this let us go forward about three years. Following hard upon the first Crown sale of town allotments in April 1841 (about which more will be said later), the Thames tribes, including Ngati Paoa, began trading in large numbers at the new settlement. They developed the practice of locating themselves on arrival not only on the reserve beside the canoe landing-place in Mechanics' Bay, but also on land at adjoining

St George's Bay. There, to the great irritation of George Cooper, the colonial treasurer, they set up encampments on what was his vacant allotment.[33] This particular problem was solved when the colonial secretary, Willoughby Shortland, presented an unsold allotment (No. 89) in the bay for the exclusive use of the 'natives of Thames . . . when they visit the town'. Nor were the Hauraki people alone in their rush to trade with Auckland. Tribes over a wide area scrambled to buy and sell goods at the new settlement. They, like Ngati Paoa, now had every reason to remain on good terms with Ngati Whatua o Tamaki, on whose lands they might require temporarily to reside from time to time, and from whom they might also need to buy food while on their trading visits to Auckland.[34]

But Ngati Whatua took the initiative in restoring good relations as well, especially with regard to their close neighbours, Ngati Paoa. Aware that the mission of reconciliation to Orere in 1836 had achieved no more than 'a partial peacemaking',[35] Ngati Whatua sent a further deputation there in 1840 to make fresh peace overtures.[36] Ngati Paoa responded positively, and this in spite of a recent sharp reminder from their Ngati Whanaunga neighbours at Waihopuhopu that the Whakatiwai murders still remained unavenged.[37] Over the next two years this corrosive feud between Ngati Whatua and Ngati Paoa was brought to an end. Leaders of Ngati Paoa, and of other iwi in the Marutuahu confederation, to which Ngati Paoa belonged, made two trips to Orakei to make peace. Regrettably, while the sequence of these peace visits is unquestioned, their timing (among other lesser detail) is not clearly shown in surviving records, oral or written. What follows, however, is a very likely course of events.

Kahukoti, a chief of great mana and the leader of the Ngati Paoa settlement at Whakatiwai, the community with the strongest sense of grievance towards Ngati Whatua, led the first visit to Okahu. His arrival in a large flotilla of canoes, in June 1841, was an impressive occasion. Kahukoti headed a group of 600 people who were representative of each of the four great iwi of the Marutuahu confederation – Ngati Paoa, Ngati Maru, Ngati Whanaunga and Ngati Tama-Te-Ra. The primary purpose of this visit to Tamaki by 'the united tribes of the Thames' (as they are called in the deeds records) was to see Governor Hobson 'on land sales business'. But they were also anxious to settle their

Lieutenant Willoughby Shortland, RN (1804–69). AUCKLAND CITY LIBRARIES

187

differences for good and all with Ngati Whatua o Tamaki. In a significant gesture of goodwill, the Hauraki tribes made a point of calling in first of all to the people of Orakei. It so happened that Apihai and his influential nephew Tinana were themselves absent from Orakei; they were, just at that very time, meeting Hobson at Official Bay. But other senior rangatira acted on behalf of the absent Apihai. Uruamo, Hotorene and Te Reweti came out of the pa and warmly greeted Kahukoti and his Marutuahu people.[38] Te Reweti and Tautari, close relatives of Apihai, are said to have 'got up' a team of men who put on a war dance.[39] It was also reported that Ngati Whatua chiefs sang waiata of respectful welcome to which visiting chiefs responded. Seven years of tension were apparently at an end.

The 'land sales business' that drew the Thames tribes to Auckland was concerned with two blocks that they had recently sold to the Crown. The first of these was 'Kohimarama', 6000 acres of land beside the west bank of the Tamaki river, a block to which, according to native customary rights, Ngati Paoa had an indisputable title.[40] The second block was called 'Mahurangi'.[41] Much more comprehensive in area than its name seems to suggest,[42] 'Mahurangi' was a huge block of land of about 100,000 acres running southwards from Cape Rodney in the north, to the north shore of the Waitemata in the south. The consideration that the Crown initially paid for the block was: '400 blankets, 60 cloaks, £200 (in cash), 60 gowns, two horses, 2 head of cattle, 200 pairs trousers, 30 coats, 100 caps, 4 casks tobacco, 6 bags flour, 2 bags rice, 1 bag sugar'.[43] Kahukoti's chief purpose in coming to Auckland in 1841 was to collect part payment for Mahurangi in the form of goods[44] and £200 in specie.[45] It must be said here that the claim to exclusive ownership of this block made by the four Thames tribes, Ngati Paoa, Ngati Maru, Ngati Tama-Te-Ra and Ngati Whanaunga, was highly questionable.[46] Te Hemara of Ngati Rangi of Kaipara, a witness at the Orakei hearing in the 1860s and a resident of Mahurangi at the time, derided the Ngati Paoa claim. He contended that in 1841 the Thames tribes had taken advantage of the temporary absence of the chiefs of the tangata whenua as a consequence of the musket wars. They had simply sold the block to the government land purchase officer, George Clarke, (he continued) on the very dubious ground that, because the Hauraki people exercised a traditional right to fish in the district, they could also claim the land. 'They supposed that the owners of the land were out of the way or killed and [so] assumed the ownership of the land', said Te Hemara dryly.[47] Such criticism was well justified. Indeed, so inept were the initial negotiations, that it took the Crown decades to rectify, as best it could, the irregularities of the 1841 purchase, and this never with adequate justice to Maori owners.[48] H. H. Turton, the nineteenth-century civil servant who chronicled early Native Land transactions, listed sixteen separate deeds of sale signed by the Crown between 1841 and 1873, as it attempted to buy out those tribes (amongst whom Te Kawerau, Ngati Rangi and Ngati Whatua were the most prominent) whose interests had been overlooked in the original untidy transaction.[49]

However, what is pertinent to this present account of the pacification of Tamaki, is not just that the original land sales provided an occasion for a meeting of reconciliation at Okahu between Ngati Whatua and Ngati Paoa. In order to clinch its purchase of the Kohimarama block, the government had given a special undertaking to Ngati Paoa that unintentionally re-inforced that reconciliation. Tamati Tangiteruru, a rangatira of the Ngati Hura hapu, testified that 'I remember Mr Clarke giving Ngati Paoa St George's Bay [Wai-a-Takehu] in payment for lands at Mauinaina and Mokoia'.[50] In other words, to induce Ngati Paoa to sell the large Kohimarama block, George Clarke had promised to grant, as an offset against the tribe's loss of its land on the left bank of the Tamaki river, a landed base, close to the new township of Auckland, from which the tribe could conveniently trade with the Pakeha settlement. This explains why, shortly after the sale of the Kohimarama block, Ngati Paoa squatted on unoccupied St George's Bay land that had been sold at a Crown auction to a government official (George Cooper, the colonial treasurer), and why that official pressed the colonial secretary to award the tribe a vacant allotment in the same bay to bring this 'trespass' to an end. We can also understand why it was that Ngati Paoa, having become very near neighbours of Ngati Whatua at Orakei, had now the strongest of incentives to maintain their accord with Apihai's people.

The second and final meeting which put the seal on this reconciliation took place in February 1842, just before the trial of

Maketu, the first Maori to be tried, convicted and hanged for murder under British law in New Zealand.[51] Haora Tipa, chief of the Ngati Paoa of Whakatiwai, who for some years previously had nourished feelings of revenge, came with Harata Patene to Okahu to end the long-standing feud for good and all. Included in his party were members of Ngati Paoa, Ngati Whanaunga and Ngati Tama-Te-Ra. The Ngati Whatua chiefs, Tautari, Te Reweti and Tamaki, formally received the deputation. Chiefs from either side then sang songs to the other, Tipa for Hauraki, and Te Kawau, Tinana and Patene for Ngati Whatua. The reception ended ceremonially when Tipa and Harata laid on the ground the paddle and two tomahawks, respectively called Haramia, Kapotahi and Rewa, after the three chiefs killed at Whakatiwai, whose deaths (Ngati Paoa had been previously told by Ngati Whanaunga) they must never forget to avenge. By ritually presenting these articles to Apihai, Ngati Paoa intimated that enmity between the two tribes had ended at last. Apihai then accompanied the Ngati Paoa people to St George's Bay, where the Crown had awarded land to the Hauraki tribe. As a further gesture of goodwill Apihai made a gift (tuku) to the Ngati Hura hapu of Ngati Paoa of a small area at Orakei to use for gardening purposes.

The peacemaking of 1841–42 had two unusual features. First was the name Maori gave to the occasion – 'the blotting out of the transgressions of the people'.[52] The obvious Old Testament language and imagery[53] indicate the extent to which members of the Tamaki tribes, at last, had become mihinare (missionary), or converts to the Christian faith; until the late 1830s those tribes had had little to do with missionaries. Second was the tendency of witnesses testifying before the Orakei court twenty-five years after, to confuse, often to conflate into a single occasion, the separate visits of Kahukoti and Tipa. That their memory should have played them false is understandable. It was logical for them to regard the great Kahukoti visit of reconciliation as having settled all differences. According to Hengia, this provided an opportunity 'to clear up arrangements . . . to make things straight'.[54] He maintained that it was *then* [that] the peacemaking was put on a solid basis'.[55] However, the later meeting, although smaller in scope, had its own special significance. This time Te Kawau, head chief of Ngati Whatua, was present, as was

Tipa, who, as leader of the Whakatiwai people for whom the murders had to be made right (tika), was able to give finality to the whole process of reconciliation.

There remained only one group with whom Ngati Whatua needed to reach an understanding, and that was Te Parawhau of Whangarei.[56] Shortly after Haora Tipa's visit, Paora Tuhaere, son of Atareta, Apihai's sister, a young Christian chief of great mana who was ultimately to be Apihai's successor, led a Ngati Whatua peace mission to Whangarei.[57] All differences were settled then between these tribes of Tamaki and Whangarei, and a peace made that ended a blood feud of almost twenty years' standing.

III

Thus far we have looked at Maori as the prime movers in the story of Tamaki. But by the later 1830s such a perspective is no longer adequate. European people and influences in places remote from Tamaki, some located on the far side of the world, became increasingly decisive in the country's affairs. A measure of the growing European presence in northern New Zealand lay in the increasing number of Pakeha and ships appearing in the Bay of Islands.[58] In 1838, according to one estimate, 131 ships anchored in that bay, most of them at its chief port of Kororareka, to which they had come either for trade, or for revictualling and repairs, or for the recreation of their crews.[59] The debauchery of the sailors, the rascality of ne'er-do-wells such as escaped convicts and runaway sailors – 'abandoned ruffians', Captain Hobson called them[60] – the binge drinking of spirits, and the prostitution of Maori women, had given Kororareka the reputation of being a hellhole, 'the Cyprus' of the south Pacific.[61] A visiting Presbyterian minister denounced the European population of northern New Zealand as being 'with a few honourable exceptions . . . the veriest refuse of civilized society'.[62] The honourable exceptions whom he had in mind were those 'sober citizens' whom Keith Sinclair denominated as merchants, tradesmen, professional people and missionaries.[63]

As scandalous stories multiplied and spread beyond these shores, Sydney and London began to look on New Zealand as a land not only where the native people were at risk of degradation, but also one lacking the most basic essentials of effective law and order. Nor had the situation significantly improved after 1833, despite the appointment by the Colonial Office of James Busby as its resident magistrate in the Bay of Islands; for he proved powerless either to influence chiefs or to check Pakeha disorder and crime. Missionaries and respectable settlers feared a descent into anarchy. In 1837, 200 Europeans resident in New Zealand petitioned William IV to step in and protect them.[64] At this stage the missionaries, who exercised great influence on the Colonial Office, had become appalled by the sexual promiscuity, drunkenness and Sabbath-breaking of the more licentious of the Pakeha settlers. They were now advocates of what they had previously opposed – outright annexation of the country by the British Crown. The alternative, wrote the catechist Fairburn, and of this 'there can be no question', was a descent into 'Lynch law and everything else that was vile, unjust and abominable'.[65]

In 1837, General Richard Bourke, governor of New South Wales, already alarmed at stories of a deteriorating situation, sent Captain William Hobson, whom he described as 'an experienced and judicious officer',[66] with his ship, the frigate HMS *Rattlesnake,* to New Zealand. Hobson's immediate task was to ensure the safety of white settlers in the Bay of Islands during a tribal war that was thought to threaten them. While at the Bay, Hobson made a point of discussing New Zealand's affairs 'with the Missionaries, and all other classes of British subjects'.[67] Then, after having satisfied himself that the behaviour of the tribes at the Bay gave no cause for alarm, he embarked on an exploratory cruise to the south in order to ascertain how stable was the situation elsewhere.[68] On the strength of what he observed both while in the Bay of Islands and during his southern cruise, which took in parts of the eastern coast of the North Island and the 'Cook's Straits', Hobson, on his return to Sydney, tendered a report to Bourke. He recommended that, while the sovereign independence of the Maori tribes was best left intact, British authorities should now begin a modest, almost minimalist, supervision – but a supervision, nevertheless – of those parts of the country where Europeans had settled in significant numbers. Drawing on old practices pragmatically developed over many years by British administrators in India, he recommended that, in selected places, small blocks of land be bought and enclosed

as enclaves or 'factories', which could then be 'placed within the influence of British jurisdiction, as dependencies of [New South Wales]'.[69] Senior officials of the Colonial Office in London, by now reconciled (however reluctantly) to some degree of supervision of New Zealand affairs, gave serious attention to this report. Not the least of the reasons why they should have done so was that it came into their hands close on the heels of the formation in London of the New Zealand Association, which proposed establishing settlements in New Zealand. Modern historians dismiss the once traditional view that the New Zealand Company, which grew out of the Association, forced the hand of the British government into taking over New Zealand. But the contrary revisionist case, initially presented some fifty years ago, was somewhat overstated. More recently James Belich has written that it was the impending arrival of New Zealand Company immigrants and 'the new, real French threat' to take over New Zealand (which those same mid-century revisionist historians also tended to underestimate) 'that triggered the shift' of the Crown's plans 'from partial to full sovereignty'.[70] This more measured view sums up current historiographical thinking.

HMS Rattlesnake.
Lithograph. In
G. H. Scholefield,
Captain William Hobson.

Over the years, New Zealand historians have written volumin-ously about the New Zealand Company's first organised settle-ments at Port Nicholson, New Plymouth, Nelson, and elsewhere. Auckland's first organised settlement at Cornwallis beside the Manukau, on the other hand, has never been much more than a mere unregarded footnote attached to our nation's story. Under-standably so, perhaps. It never amounted to much. This small community of Scots perched on the rugged, heavily bushed shoreline near Puponga Point, which juts out from the north shore of the Manukau harbour, seemed doomed from the outset, cer-tainly from the moment that Governor Hobson decided some time during 1840 to place his capital on the northern side of the isthmus. The new capital which he created quickly became *the* port of entry to northern New Zealand. It was unthinkable that the shallow Manukau harbour with its treacherous sandbars could ever have been a serious rival to the Waitemata. But that was far less obvious in the later 1830s than it is to us today. We have to remember that, at that time, most of the Maori people in the region that we now call Auckland lived beside the Manukau. It seemed feasible, therefore, that the shore of the Manukau harbour could also provide the site of an organised white township. This was the hope, anyway, of the New Zealand and Manukau Land Company sponsored in Edinburgh in 1838 by a group of Scottish landed gentry.[71]

The Manukau Company developed as an offshoot of the much better known New Zealand Company. Even when it had a completely separate existence, the Manukau Company showed residual signs of the shared origin of these two colonising bodies. Each aimed to build up a substantial emigration fund from the sale of shares or land; each sold land orders whose 'sections' com-prised a holding in the country and one town lot; each required, from those who were to be provided with free or assisted pas-sages, evidence of good character and industrious habits.[72]

The unusual origins of the Manukau scheme are to be found in a book generally regarded as the first historical survey of early New Zealand, A. S. Thomson's *The Story of New Zealand*.[73] Pub-lished in 1859, this book provided what Thomson claimed to be 'the secret history of this abortive Manukau settlement'. He main-tained that his version was based on information provided by an unnamed settler, a 'gentleman' who (according to the author) testified before the House of Commons in 1844. There is little doubt that this anonymous informant was the gentleman-adventurer Walter Brodie.[74] When Thomson's book first appeared, this version of the origins of the Manukau Company was not contradicted by contemporaries who had taken part in the enterprise and who surely would have done so had the truth been other than what Brodie maintained. That this account was repeated without correction in a number of later nineteenth-century publications would appear to confirm its authenticity. According to Thomson:

> At a dinner given by Lord Durham to the New Zealand Association [formed in 1837], when most of the arrangements for sending out emigrants were complete, his Lordship proposed the health of Major Campbell as the Governor of their first settlement.
>
> Mr. Edward Gibbon Wakefield, who was present, and secretly anxious to obtain this office, objected to Major Campbell's appointment, not directly, but in that cunning way so peculiarly characteristic of himself. A meeting of the influential members was in a few days convened, at which circumstances occurred which led to the breaking up of the Association. Mr. Wakefield's party then formed the New Zealand Company, and Mr Campbell's attempted to form a settlement in the Manukau.[75]

The choice of Manukau as the site of the new settlement owed much to the presence in London of the suspended superintendent of the Wesleyan mission in New Zealand, the Rev. William White. For a period of about twelve months over 1837–38, White lived in England, where he had gone to defend himself against charges, first, of misapplying mission funds to promote his own private trading activities, and second, of committing adultery with Maori women.[76] The hearing and final decision by the Wesleyan metropolitan authorities were much delayed. However, when the missionary committee finally made up its mind, its decision was emphatic enough. White was dismissed from the mission, despite the second charge lapsing through want of firm evidence. Yet the resilient White was far from crushed. (In the years ahead he retained both his clerical garb, and his great influence among northern Maori, playing out the contradictory roles – according to Jerningham Wakefield, admittedly a most prejudiced witness – of 'missionary and land-shark'.)[77] Nor had he let the grass grow under his feet during the prolonged inquiry in England. He continued to foster his timber interests, while making himself available as speaker on, and promoter of, New Zealand as an ideal field for colonisation, a topic on which, because of his extensive firsthand experience, his biographer has said he 'enjoyed a considerable reputation'.[78] A long-standing advocate of the colonisation of the Hokianga by 'respectable' European immigrants, he quickly involved himself in the affairs of the New Zealand Association. This organisation initially proposed to take over Hokianga harbour land on the Rawene peninsula where, in the mid-1820s, a certain Captain Herd, agent of an even earlier New Zealand Association, had unsuccessfully attempted to set up a British settlement.[79] When the rupture took place within the New Zealand Association in late 1837, White sided with the faction led by W. F. Campbell, MP, and his formidable ally Captain Sir William Symonds, RN. Always a whole-hearted partisan, White turned on the supporters of Edward Gibbon Wakefield, and 'threatened', according to Wakefield's son, 'to oppose us by means of his influence with the natives'.[80] On the other hand, it must have seemed to the breakaway group that in William White they had stumbled upon a godsend. For not only was he an expert on the Tamaki area, but he was also able to reveal to the breakaway faction that the executors of the Mitchell estate in Sydney, with whom he was on the best of terms, were at that very moment anxious to dispose of their land on and about the Tamaki isthmus to British buyers.[81]

We may surmise that when White arrived back in Sydney in October 1838 on the bounty ship *Coromandel*, he had been commissioned to use his influence with the Mitchell brothers, to secure the sale of the estate, which they now held on behalf of their widowed sister-in-law. What is documented is that on 3 November 1838, Mary Mitchell 'conveyed in fee simple, as a lawful and pure inheritance . . . for the sum of £500' the property, which Thomas Mitchell was recorded as having bought from Ngati Whatua in January 1836.[82] The same source states that the property was conveyed to Robert Roy 'through his agent and attorney', W. C. Symonds. This Robert Roy, Writer to the Signet, was a senior partner in the legal practice of Roy and Wood, 16 Northumberland Street, Edinburgh, a firm that was

W. C. Symonds (right) and Ernst Dieffenbach (left) hear a Maori chief accuse his daughter of murder. Sketch by J. J. Merrett lithographed as the frontispiece of Dieffenbach's Travels in New Zealand, *Vol. 1, 1843.*

later to become the registered office of the Manukau Company. The Symonds who was referred to in this transaction as the company's 'agent' was Lieutenant William Cornwallis Symonds (1810–41) of the 38th Regiment, son of Captain Sir William Symonds, RN (1782–1856),[83] who, as we have seen, was a member of the group which had hived off from the New Zealand Association. When and under what circumstances his son had arrived in Sydney are questions to which existing documents provide no certain answers. There is the possibility that he happened to be in Sydney after an earlier commission recorded by Scholefield, who speaks of his having been responsible for taking back to New Zealand two Maori seamen who had arrived at Le Havre in a French whaler.[84] We do not know whether he stayed on in Sydney over the next year, but almost certainly he remained in the Antipodes. In spite of these ambiguities, there is no question that W. C. Symonds was to become a significant figure in the early days of the colony.

The promoters of the new company back in Edinburgh decided to move cautiously with their scheme of planned colonisation. Much had yet to be done. A knowledgeable agent on the spot was required both to appraise the land that had been acquired and to look into the validity of Mitchell's original purchase. It was also prudent to wait upon action on the part of the British government, which had not, as yet, made known what it intended to do about New Zealand. These considerations explain why the New Zealand Manukau and Waitemata Company did not hurry over issuing a prospectus advertising land orders and why its first 220 sections were not available for application until September 1840.

IV

After his return from England in 1838, William White, never one to dawdle over matters of business, had set himself up as a booster for New Zealand, and particularly for the lands that the Manukau Company had acquired from the Mitchell estate. Before he returned to New Zealand, he placed in the hands of a Sydney publisher copy that became an eighty-page booklet entitled *Important information relative to New Zealand, by a gentleman who has been resident fourteen years at Hokianga*.[85] Published in 1839, this booklet extravagantly praised New Zealand and (most of all) the Manukau region, as the ideal destination for colonists. Depicting the sandbar at the entrance of the harbour, not as a peril to be negotiated (as it surely was) but as a protective shield for the two entrance channels, he assured his readers that 'ships may enter this splendid harbour with perfect safety... the depth of water in the Northern Channel is five fathoms and in the Southern seven'.[86] (On the contrary, the Manukau bar was notoriously treacherous. In 1863, it was responsible for New Zealand's worst sea disaster when the steam corvette HMS *Orpheus* foundered with the loss of 189 lives.)

Back to White's booster's report. There had recently been, he wrote, a return of the tribes to this 'highly valued and very interesting district'. In this encouraging vein, he praised the resources of the Manukau:

> There are nine rivers, which empty themselves into [the harbour]. On the banks of these rivers, with their numerous tributary streams are beautiful and extensive valleys of the richest soil, capable of the

production of every description of European fruits and vegetables. The
natives cultivate small patches here and there, with very little
preparation of the soil, merely burning away the brush and underwood
and putting in the seed in small holes made with the point of a stick,
and it is really astonishing to see the splendid crops of maize, potatoes
and other vegetables produced from so simple a culture, affording the
best possible proof of the surprising fertility of the soil. Near the
source of some of these rivers, the Cowdy [kauri] timber is found in
the greatest perfection, and in this delightful district are to be met
with some of the most sublime and romantic scenery the eye of the
admirer of the picturesque beauties of nature need desire, mountains
with snow clad summits [*sic*] whose sides are covered with gigantic
trees, rivers with their innumerable cataracts and lakes, and rich and
beautiful valleys which may, ere long, be the peaceful and happy abode
of a thriving peasantry, composed of Europeans and natives.[87]

The promoters of the Scottish land company did not try to
match White's urgent and highly imaginative propaganda efforts.
It suited them not to do so. Upon the incorporation of the 'New
Zealand Waitemata and Manakou Company' in September 1840,
the directors explained why, for almost two years, they had deliberately followed a policy of making haste slowly. 'The Company',
they said, 'considered it proper to refrain from incurring the responsibility of selling land to intending emigrants, or inducing
them to go out until Her Majesty's Government had determined
on the course to be adopted with respect to New Zealand, and also
until they should be in possession of Reports from an Officer who
had undertaken to proceed to that country for the purpose of
ensuring authentic information as to the extent and capabilities
of the Company's property.'[88] Unspoken (though obvious) was an
additional reason for the caution of the company – an awareness
of the time required to solicit subscribers for the company, to set
up an emigration fund, and to recruit suitable colonists. The most
important reason why the promoters put off the final incorporation of their company, however, was their decision not to act until
the governor confirmed that he had chosen Tamaki as the site of
his capital.

For the company promoters, postponing action had been a
sensible course. During the first half of 1839 it had become
increasingly likely that New Zealand would be taken over as a

British colony, although whether sovereignty was to be acquired through an attempted annexation, or through negotiation with the native chiefs, still remained unclear. But the haphazard tide of colonisation having set in, unstoppably it seemed, made it ever more likely that the British government would be obliged to act. Speculators in New South Wales were in full cry, negotiating extravagant purchases of land from imagined Maori owners. According to W. C. Symonds, the company's representative in New Zealand, shiploads of passengers from Sydney, and a number of settlers from Adelaide disillusioned with the colony there, were 'thronging' to the new land.[89] The despatch of the *Tory* from England in May 1839, carrying an advance party to set up a New Zealand Company settlement in the Cook Strait region, forced the British government to reconsider the kind of intervention that was best suited to safeguarding Maori society while, at the same time, regulating British settlement. But, as Peter Adams has demonstrated, to say that the New Zealand Company galvanised the government into further action is a far cry from resurrecting the old legend that the company 'forced the Government's hand'.[90]

These circumstances persuaded the Scottish company that the time had come to push on with its emigration scheme. Once again William White had a part to play. After his return to Hokianga in December 1838 White, now stripped of his official missionary responsibilities, had involved himself much more heavily in the milling of kauri timber. During the first half of 1839 he shifted the main sphere of his operations to the Kaipara region, accumulating in the Northern Wairoa river and in its tributaries what was reported to be a 'splendid' cargo of spars.[91] Requiring the means of shipping this cargo to England, White went over to Sydney and chartered the *Navarino*, a vessel that had just brought out a consignment of convicts to New South Wales.[92] One of the three cabin passengers of the *Navarino* when it returned on 15 October 1839 from Port Jackson to the Kaipara was Lieutenant W. C. Symonds. As superintendent of the Manukau Company's affairs in New Zealand, he intended on arrival to make a prompt inspection of the property at Tamaki he had acquired from the Mitchells.[93]

This proved not possible. So for the next few months he lived beside the Kaipara harbour. In a short time, like White before him, he acquired much influence among Ngati Whatua-o-

Kaipara, a tribe much weakened by the recent musket wars. Two decades later, a local chief, Ihikiera Te Tinana, when speaking of the coming of the Europeans to the Kaipara in 1839, recalled Symonds as a significant figure. 'Do not suppose', he said, that 'the pakehas crept in stealthily, no. Mr White was the first pakeha that attached himself to me; after him Captain Symonds arrived. We addressed him thus: "Will you not consent to become our friend?" He answered "yes".'[94] Tinana wound up his reminiscence by remarking that he looked on Symonds as a fore-runner of the governors.

More should now be said about this William Cornwallis Symonds and his connections. His father, Sir William Symonds, who had served during the French wars as a ship-of-the-line officer, later made his real mark in the Royal Navy in the peace-time post of surveyor-general. The appointment was accompa-nied by a knighthood aimed at securing his retention. Over a fifteen-year period (1832–47) Sir William turned to account his well-developed flair for naval construction by bringing into service over 200 ships, which have been praised as 'remarkably fine vessels of their class – fast, weatherly and roomy'.[95] A navy man through and through (he retired with the rank of Rear-Admiral), he named his first-born son Cornwallis, not through any shared pedigree with the aristocratic Cornwallis family but out of admiration for the popular admiral of that name under whom he served during the French wars. Sir William Symonds, as we have seen, was a founder of the Manukau Land Company. It would be tempting but quite mistaken, however, to regard the appointment of his son as custodian of the company's affairs in New Zealand as inspired by nepotism or some such family favouritism. Objectively speaking, W. C. Symonds was a sound choice. The son had considerable qualities of leadership and ini-tiative in his own right.

At the time that Lieutenant W. C. Symonds came to New Zealand on the *Navarino*, he was an unattached, half-pay army officer, though at the end of that year he was gazetted as captain on the strength of the 96th Regiment, then on service in New South Wales.[96] But he never exercised his captaincy there. In spite of his relative youthfulness he quickly rose to prominence in New Zealand, initially in the service of the Manukau Land Company but later in that of the governor as well. He proved to be a natural leader, inspiring confidence on first meeting; 'every inch a gentleman', wrote Logan Campbell, the severest of critics.[97] Felton and Sarah Mathew, among others, praised his ability to temper his firm leadership with a genial manner.[98] He was vigorous and tactful, too, attributes he needed as the person of authority he was to become in the two brief years of his life yet to run.[99] And as the man on the spot for the Manukau Company, he was the pivot on which the success or failure of that organisation was to turn.

On his arrival in the Kaipara in late October 1839, Symonds set himself up in temporary quarters at a riverside spot he spoke of as being 'thirty miles up the [Northern] Wairoa [river]', almost certainly in the Mangawhare–Dargaville area.[100] For undisclosed reasons he found that he was unable to carry out his original plan of going immediately to Tamaki to carry out his inspection of the Mitchell land and to check on the validity of its purchase. But, as he later reported to his fellow directors, who were just as anxious as he to possess this information, his first three months in the country were 'vexed by miserable delays and annoyances beyond my control during nearly the whole time'. As a result he had been prevented 'from devoting more than one week to the survey of the harbour, and examination of this most extensive property'.[101]

Some of these vexations he elaborated on while talking on 4 January 1840 with members of the New Zealand Company advance party, when they became temporarily marooned in northern Wairoa after the *Tory* had been severely damaged on striking a sandbar at the entrance to the Kaipara.[102] He had just returned, Symonds told these newcomers, from his inspection of what he called the 'Scotch Company's land at Manukau'. Accompanied by an unnamed white servant, he had crossed overland from south Kaipara (presumably setting out somewhere in the vicinity of today's Helensville) to reach the Tamaki isthmus, moving on thence to Puponga Point, the least disputed part of the Mitchell claim. His brief inspection of the northern shoreline of the Manukau and parts of Tamaki having been completed, he returned to 'his station up the Kaipara river [the Northern Wairoa] some days after, having provided himself with some necessaries'.[103] Symonds complained that during this journey 'he had endured considerable hardships and privations . . . and described the natives as having been exceedingly dishonest and troublesome in all their transactions with him'.[104] Walter Brodie told a select committee of the British Parliament in 1844 of one such transaction when, on the last stage of Symonds's journey home, a chief tried to extract a large sum of money from Symonds to ferry him, his servant, and stores across the Northern Wairoa river.[105]

> When [Captain Symonds] came to the river . . . the native chief who was with him, a man by the name of Dairs [Davis][106] demanded as much from him for taking the goods across as all the goods were worth. Captain Symonds refused to give it to him, and pitched his tent for the night and cooked his dinner on the bank. The chief came into the tent; Captain Symonds told him to go out; he said he would not. 'This land', he said, 'is mine, I believe.' Captain Symonds said, 'Yes, but you have let me put my tent upon it, and this', he said, 'is my house, and I require you to get out of it.' He would not and Captain Symonds kicked him out. There were four or five hundred natives present while Captain Symonds had but one European servant, and both himself and the servant supposed they were going to be murdered. The next morning, however, the thing was cleared up and the chief offered to take the goods over for nothing.[107]

One suspects that at the bottom of Symonds's irritation with the Maori chief was frustration over his recent inspection visit to Tamaki. After he had 'personally communicated' with the members of the tangata whenua who 'are still resident there or in the vicinity',[108] the Ngati Whatua chiefs had refused to countenance the extravagant land claim which was embodied in the Mitchell 'purchase'.

Early in February 1840, the *Navarino* made its return voyage to England from the Kaipara carrying its cargo of spars. It also bore to the promoters of the land company in Edinburgh, Symonds's report on the lands which Ngati Whatua were supposed to have conveyed to Mitchell in 1836. This highly optimistic report gave no indication – as Symonds must have surely known – that Ngati Whatua no longer regarded the original deed as valid. On the contrary. 'The purchase far exceeds what we believed to be its extent', wrote Symonds, 'and encloses an immense district.'[109]

> That part of the lands on which the hills of Manugari [Maungarei?,
> Mangere?], Mangakiki [Maungakiekie] and Mangawha
> [Maungawhau] are situated, is most excellent soil, fertile to a
> proverb, and contains thousands of acres fit for the plough, and
> having two harbours for the export of its produce. Between the fertile
> land and the forest, there is a great extent of country which will
> become excellent pasture land, besides affording large locations for
> settlers. . . . The forest land . . . is covered with [kauri] timber.

While Symonds never directly admitted that should the
company lay claim to the much more valuable Waitemata land
it would be pursuing a lost cause, his report implied it. He
informed the board in Edinburgh that he had arranged for the
Scottish immigrants enlisted by the company to settle not on
the Waitemata, but in the much more rugged Puponga
Point–Karangahape region. Symonds was well aware (though he
did not state this openly in his report), that the company's claim
for land at Karangahape was more likely to be upheld by virtue
of Mitchell's brief, undisputed occupancy of this site beside the
Manukau and because he had constructed some sort of house
there. Symonds attempted to soften the blow for his Scottish
masters by claiming that this location had much to commend it.
The property was 'well supplied with water', he continued, and
had 'patches of very excellent land', which though 'of small
extent' would be 'sufficient to supply a settlement with garden
stuffs etc. in abundance'.

For Symonds the particular merit of this site lay in its great
resources of kauri timber. 'The high hill Puponga will afford
materials for building, and at its base a wharf and docks may
readily be constructed. . . . The leading trade at the starting of the
colony will be the timber trade. There is abundant work for a
multitude of hands in felling, squaring and sawing of the timber.'
Symonds forecast that strong markets for kauri timber would soon
be opening up in Europe, India and South America as well as
in other parts of New Zealand once they became colonised. Nor
need the full burden of pioneering fall on the first settlers at
Karangahape. Symonds's report indicated that the company could
confidently count on the Maori inhabitants of Manukau, with
their newly acquired hunger for western goods, to provide labour
needed to develop this new settlement. They would play a double

role as skilled assistants in the milling of timber, and as suppliers of food. He informed the directors that for such services Maori preferred to be paid in 'stores'. The company would be well advised, therefore, to send out 'the most marketable description of goods: blankets, slops [cheap ready-made clothing] of all sorts, shirts, trousers, both duck and fustian[110] – fustian jackets, cotton kerchiefs, cloth caps, gown pieces of the commonest chintz, but thick – shoes and calicos, – tobacco, and pipes of all sizes'.[111]

Symonds left his fellow directors in no doubt that New Zealand had a great future as a settlement colony. The recent 'throng' of immigrants from Australia (he wrote) had seen 'land rising in value daily'. He was shrewd enough to see, however, that the success of the Manukau settlement would depend ultimately on the development of the Tamaki isthmus where, before long, 'a colony of many hundreds may be planted. . . . If a good harbour and fertile land, well supplied with water will do the thing, it cannot fail to flourish.' In the meantime he advised the directors to continue their policy of watchful inaction. 'Wait for my next letters before you make sales to any extent.' He also undertook to return, as soon as he could, to Karangahape (which the company decided to rename Cornwallis in honour of their agent). As soon as he had taken up residence in Mitchell's half-finished house, he intended to 'proceed with my survey', and to prepare Cornwallis to receive the first batch of colonists.

No sooner had this letter been written in early February 1840, however, than Symonds decided to scrap these plans. News came through to Kaipara that a large number of northern chiefs had recently met Captain Hobson, the newly appointed British consul, and agreed to cede the sovereignty over their lands to the British Crown. Just when and how Symonds came to know of these things is not recorded. It is possible he was told shortly after the initial treaty meeting at Waitangi in the Bay of Islands. But much more likely, given the speedy information network between the Hokianga and the Kaipara, he heard of Hobson's intended visit to the Hokianga harbour, to persuade chiefs of the region to affix their signatures to the Treaty of Waitangi.[112] Symonds thus prepared to go to the Bay of Islands, which had now become the place of decision in the country's affairs.

CHAPTER IX

Hobson, the Treaty, and Tamaki

I

It has become traditional to call the long-lived Auckland pioneer, John Logan Campbell (1817–1912), the 'Father of Auckland'. Yet there are those who consider Captain William Hobson has a stronger claim to that title.[1] After all it was he who, in the teeth of strong protests from the New Zealand Company, chose land beside the Waitemata as the site of the colony's capital; and it was he who called that infant settlement Auckland. Significantly, the anniversary day (29 January) which is celebrated in Auckland, both city and province, commemorates the day when Hobson, as the lieutenant-governor-to-be, first anchored offshore at the Bay of Islands. And the story of Tamaki-Auckland, in the early 1840s, is inextricably bound up with the last years of his career.

Born in 1793 the third son of an Anglo-Irish barrister, William Hobson was obliged to make his own way in the world.[2] Enlisting in the Royal Navy at the age of ten, he had risen, by the time that the Napoleonic Wars ended in 1815, to the rank of lieutenant. Though his education during his years of naval service was entirely shipboard, he developed into a literate man who, in the opinion of a later associate, was 'fluent of speech and wrote a good despatch'.[3] Between 1816 and 1828 Hobson's naval service continued, mainly in the West Indies. There he contracted yellow fever three times, the source perhaps of the debilitating headaches from which he suffered for the rest of his life. He was also dogged by other medical complaints, such as high blood pressure, which in combination were to bring him to a relatively early grave.

Shortly after his promotion to his captaincy in 1828, Hobson was paid off. Unhappy in his enforced retirement, he pressed for a fresh command. But his appeals were fruitless until 1834, when a new First Lord of the Admiralty, Lord Auckland,[4] responded to his pleas, posting him to the East India fleet, where he was given the command of a sturdy Royal Navy work-horse, the 28-gun frigate HMS *Rattlesnake*. Hobson never forgot the First Lord's sympathetic response and henceforward regarded him, and the aristocratic Eden family to which he belonged, as patrons to be honoured whenever opportunity offered. (We shall see later how place names in Auckland were to reflect the depths of Hobson's gratitude.)

In 1836 the *Rattlesnake* was posted to the headquarters of the Australia station at Port Jackson, Sydney. There, Hobson was to embark on responsibilities that were later to bear on the story of Tamaki-Auckland. Officers on naval ships in that era were frequently called on to survey uncharted coastal waters and harbours.[5] Hobson was no exception. While carrying out a survey of the Port Phillip region in Victoria during 1837, he became much impressed by the abilities of two of his assisting officers, Lieutenants T. M. C. Symonds and P. F. Shortland.[6] This encounter gave him a favourable impression of the families from which these two men came and, in the years ahead, he appointed a brother of each officer – W. C. Symonds and Willoughby Shortland – to a responsible role in the founding of New Zealand. His confidence in the first was well justified; in the second much less so. G. H. Scholefield commented on Hobson's 'family friendship' with the Shortlands in this fashion: 'Three brothers of that talented family [P.F., Willoughby, and Edward]', he wrote, 'served under him at different times. It was unfortunate indeed that the least talented of the three [Willoughby] should have occupied the most responsible position',[7] first as colonial secretary and later as acting governor of New Zealand.

A further consequence of Hobson's service in the Australian arm of the East India fleet was his 1837 encounter with New Zealand, which was spoken of in a previous chapter. It will be

Lord Auckland, First Lord of the Admiralty, 1834.
AUCKLAND CITY
LIBRARIES

recalled that this came about when Governor Richard Bourke of New South Wales commissioned Hobson to go to New Zealand in the *Rattlesnake* to protect British citizens at a time of tribal war, and also to report on that country's reputedly lawless state. Hobson's highly regarded report, which advocated limited yet apparently affordable British intervention in New Zealand's affairs, was to change the course of his life. This report counted decisively in his favour when, during the winter of 1838–39, the British government, after reflecting on the alarming prospect of a continuing, unchecked inflow of immigrants into New Zealand, came to accept that it had an obligation to supervise the affairs of that country.[8] Hobson, conveniently in England at the time and available therefore for interview, seemed to be just the man that Lord Glenelg, the secretary of state for colonies, had in mind when he spoke of the government's intention 'to appoint an officer who will be vested with the powers, and will assume the character of British Consul in New Zealand'.[9] After Hobson, having been sounded out on such an appointment, had agreed to serve 'in the character of British Consul' and of prospective lieutenant-governor, he was directed, on 1 July 1839, to sail to New Zealand.[10] During August 1839 his appointments were officially confirmed.

On 25 August Hobson left England for Australia on HMS *Druid*, with his wife Eliza – to whom he was devoted – his young family,[11] and Lieutenant Willoughby Shortland, a naval officer later to be described by enemies of Hobson as 'his old shipmate'. Hobson carried with him lengthy instructions from his secretary of state, Lord Normanby, which enjoined, above all else, fair dealings with the Maori, from whose chiefs he must seek, where possible, a cession of sovereignty.[12] The *Druid* arrived in Sydney on 24 December 1839. Before setting out for New Zealand, Hobson spent much time during the next twenty-five days closeted with his superior, Governor Gipps. Gipps reiterated the responsibilities of consul, as they had been outlined in Normanby's instructions and helped Hobson in his further responsibility of selecting his officials for the new colony. Those appointed were George Cooper, collector of customs; Willoughby Shortland, police magistrate; Felton Mathew, acting surveyor-general, James S. Freeman, private secretary; and Simon E. Grimstone, clerk.[13] It is significant that no colonial secretary

*Caricature of Felton
Mathew, 1832, taken from
Mrs Mathew's Scrapbook.*
MATHEW PAPERS,
AUCKLAND CITY
LIBRARIES

was appointed, simply because no one of sufficient ability had
been on offer in Sydney.[14] It is significant also that, as Shortland
alone was personally known to him, Hobson was seemingly
obliged to accept on trust, as his other public servants, those
candidates whom Gipps recommended. Here we have the origins of the scandalous story endlessly repeated by early Auckland
settlers that Gipps had seized the chance to foist on Hobson
those second-rate officials whom he felt he could happily do
without;[15] 'a strange lot of cast-off old Sydney officials', the settlement's first baker called them.[16]

In the years ahead, Auckland and Wellington colonists were to
denounce Hobson and his successors, Shortland and FitzRoy, for
conducting administrations damned by these critics as extravagant
and incompetent. It is true that within four years George Cooper
was exposed as an embezzler of public and private funds and
obliged to resign his post.[17] Nor has the record of these early
officials for outbreaks of intrigue, and for speculation in town
lands, recommended them to posterity. Even before he reached
New Zealand, Felton Mathew seemed to reveal a cloven hoof
when he admitted to his wife: 'I have made up my mind to buy
as much land as I can possibly find money for, and if that do not

prove a fortune to me in four or five years I am much mistaken.'[18] In practice, the officials proved neither so incompetent as embittered white settlers of Auckland and Wellington painted them, nor so self-seeking as this unbridled declaration by Felton Mathew suggests. And the undoubted deficiencies of the first official group were to be offset in time either by appointments which Hobson subsequently made (George Clarke, W. C. Symonds, David Rough and Edward Shortland come to mind), or by imaginative appointments from England, such as Dr John Johnson (surgeon-general) in 1840, and William Swainson (attorney-general) and William Martin (chief justice) in 1841, the latter two being men with marked legal abilities.

But in the last resort, much of the responsibility for the shortcomings of the administration in New Zealand were to arise, not through the failings of the governor's men, but through the policies of the home government mediated through the Colonial Office. When the decision was made to send a consul to New Zealand, the British Treasury instructed Governor Gipps that he was 'to make all necessary arrangements on the most moderate scale', and 'on the express condition that the expense will be defrayed entirely from revenue to be raised in New Zealand'.[19] The under-secretary of the Colonial Office, James Stephen, embodied these frugalities in the immensely detailed, so-called Normanby Instructions, which the Colonial Office laid down for Hobson to follow once he arrived in the Antipodes.[20] Two of the financial principles enunciated in those instructions deserve to be singled out. First, the level of immigration would have to depend on land revenue, which in effect meant the profits that were expected to accrue to the Crown from the sale of land bought cheaply from Maori.[21] Second, 'the proper rate' of emolument of officials, to be appointed by Gipps and Hobson in concert, 'must be fixed with the most anxious regard to frugality in the expenditure of the public resources'.[22] In this second instruction, folly masqueraded as frugality. Constrained by the low level of salaries set, Gipps found that he was unable, on Hobson's behalf, to induce qualified people in Sydney to join the new lieutenant-governor's staff. The upshot – within seven weeks of his arrival in New Zealand, a chastened Hobson was to be found writing to Normanby complaining that he was hamstrung by his lack of skilled administrators and legal advisers.[23]

These two instructions enunciated by the Colonial Office draw attention to a source of great mischief that our historians have tended to overlook; namely that governors in early New Zealand, regardless of the party in power in Britain, had to cope with skinflint metropolitan governments. This was a time when retrenchment and financial prudence were regarded in the mother country as the greatest of fiscal virtues. Consequently, the British were bent on establishing an administration on the cheap in New Zealand; one that would provide all requisite services and works and build up an immigration fund with a minimum of grants-in-aid from Home. And in practice the local administration could achieve these economies only by buying Maori lands at a fraction of the price at which it would later resell them to settlers at Crown auctions. These financial constraints also help to explain why the early governors failed to act as protectors of the Maori people (as the Colonial Office genuinely hoped they would), why they failed both to guarantee the tribes in the possession of their lands, forests and fisheries (as they were bound by the Treaty of Waitangi to do) and to provide safeguards for Maori against the demands of new settlers who brought in their wake an increasingly disruptive way of life.[24]

II

On 18 January 1840, Hobson and his official party of six officials, three servants, and four troopers of the New South Wales mounted police left Port Jackson in a 20-gun frigate, HMS *Herald*, which was under the command of Captain Nias.[25] The crossing of the Tasman was uneventful save for the stormy quarrels which blew up between Hobson and Nias, two officers who were revealed to be as jealous and prickly about questions of status as they were violent of temper.[26]

On landing at the Bay of Islands on 30 January, Hobson quickly made himself and his intentions known to senior CMS missionaries there, and to Busby the British Resident. With their help he sent out circular letters calling together Maori chiefs for a conference at Waitangi on 5 February.[27] Despite the short notice, chiefs in the immediate region – almost entirely Nga Puhi – attended in good numbers, as did an unexpectedly large gathering of interested European spectators.[28] Hobson began the discussion (korero) by outlining through his translator, Rev. Henry Williams, the terms of the proposed cession of sovereignty that he wanted Maori to make. Six hours of animated debate followed, some Maori chiefs speaking for, some against.[29] At an indecisive stage, the meeting was adjourned until the following day.

Colenso, the printer-missionary, who fifty years later gave a firsthand account of the Waitangi gathering, recalled a curiously prophetic episode that took place at the conclusion of the first meeting after he and Hobson had walked back together to the beach, deep in conversation. Colenso said that just before the governor reached the launch that was to take him back to the *Herald*, an elderly native chief rushed up to the official party and, after intently scrutinising Hobson's face (in Colenso's words), 'exclaimed in a shrill, loud, and mournful voice, "Aue! he koroheke! E kore e roa kua mate".'[30] At Hobson's insistence, a reluctant Colenso translated in these words, 'Alas! An old man. He will soon be dead.' Onlookers were mystified. Hobson was only forty-seven; he was scarcely an old man. Yet before a month was out, the governor's suite had reason to look back on this outburst not as the maundering of a demented chief but as a prophecy that lay beyond the reach of western understanding.

On the following morning, at the request of a number of the chiefs, the meeting resumed a day earlier than had been planned. Food was running low among the three or four hundred Maori who had remained at Waitangi. It was also apparent that some of the chiefs who had been undecided on the previous day had meanwhile made up their minds, and were ready to sign the treaty that had, by chance, been prepared overnight on parchment ready for signing.[31] Before the day was out, forty-three chiefs, principally from the Bay of Islands region though many, admittedly, not of first rank, had signed.[32] Why this sudden change of heart? It has been said that the material benefits of collaboration and the influence of the Protestant missionaries overcame the initial Maori misgivings.[33] Even so, for most Maori it was a treaty taken on trust. Colenso maintained that, even while the chiefs were in the act of signing the treaty on 6 February, he had deliberately warned Hobson that they did not 'fully . . . comprehend' the document they were signing, and that they 'had no idea whatever as to [its] purport'.[34] Hobson brushed aside this warning. But there is little doubt that the implications of the treaty were imperfectly understood, not least of all because sophisticated western legal concepts – sovereignty, Crown pre-emption[35] and the like – were rendered in what was, in the last resort, no more than a makeshift Maori translation. The last word should be left with Hone Heke (later to rebel against the Crown), who during the first day of the Waitangi discussions is reported to have remarked: 'The Native mind could not comprehend these things: they must trust to the advice of their missionaries.'[36] Most Maori attending the gathering did. Not all missionaries were happy that this should have been so. Four years later a committee of the British Parliament reported that since 'the natives were incapable of comprehending the real force and meaning' of the treaty of Waitangi, it had therefore amounted to little more than 'a legal fiction'.[37]

At the Kohimarama conference of Maori tribes, which Governor Gore Browne convened in 1860 to check the deteriorating relations between Maori and European, Paora Tuhaere, a leader of Ngati Whatua o Tamaki, emerged as a latter-day critic of the treaty. He maintained that it had not, in practice, guaranteed to Maori, as it had promised, 'the full, exclusive and undisturbed possession of their lands and estates, &c.'[38] He seemed inclined to blame the haste of Nga Puhi leaders in signing an agreement that they did not fully understand.

> I am the man who found fault with the Treaty of Waitangi [earlier at the conference]. I formed my own judgment upon it and seeing it to be wrong I condemned it. I find fault with it because the Ngapuhi foolishly signed their names to it without due consideration. . . . They did not send for all the Chiefs of this Island to come to enter into that Treaty of Waitangi.[39]

Aware that this cession of sovereignty by Nga Puhi, however precipitate, had made him a lieutenant-governor in fact as well as in name, Hobson appreciated nevertheless that his jurisdiction was over no more than a limited area in the vicinity of the Bay of Islands. He arranged a further campaign, therefore, to gain the signatures of chiefs of the region who had not attended the Waitangi meeting.[40] His first venture was to form a signature-gathering party under himself, which was made up of officials and Captain Nias, with two missionaries acting as guides and interpreters. They set out from Paihia on 10 February and crossed the narrow part of Northland between the Bay of Islands and the Hokianga harbour, where the group then linked up with Wesleyan missionaries.[41] On 12 February, 3000 Maori, of whom four to five hundred were said to be chiefs, attended a great meeting at the Wesleyan mission station at Mangungu and discussed whether they should sign the treaty. After some early opposition, fifty-six chiefs decided to sign. If one takes into account the signatures of eight important chiefs which the party collected at the Waimate CMS mission station while en route to Hokianga, the total number of chiefs who had signed the treaty by 12 February had risen, by Colenso's reckoning, to 'about one hundred and twenty'.[42]

Installed back in his cabin on the *Herald* at the Bay of Islands after this excursion, Hobson wrote to Governor Gipps reporting on his success.[43] Then in more sombre mood, he wrote to his secretary of state in London, stressing his need for a larger military force if he, as lieutenant-governor, was to make British sovereignty in New Zealand effective and real.[44] These despatches written, he began preparing for an extended journey to the south on board the *Herald*, initially with three objects in view:

- to collect further signatures of chiefs on the treaty;
- (most germane to this present book) to visit 'the Thames',[45] in effect the shores of the Waitemata, so that he might determine whether that locality could provide a suitable site for the main government settlement; and
- 'to visit . . . as early as possible' Port Nicholson (where, on 22 January, the *Aurora* had landed the first batch of New Zealand Company settlers), in order to bring that settlement under British jurisdiction.

By the time the journey south came to be made, however, stores taken aboard the *Herald* were sufficient to provision a visit only to the Hauraki gulf and the Firth of Thames. In spite of earlier protestations that a visit to the Cook Strait settlement was urgent, that had been now postponed.

One need not doubt, however, that Hobson was anxious to see Tamaki. From his first days in New Zealand, he obviously had had that location rather than Port Nicholson in mind as a possible capital. According to the Rev. Henry Williams:

> On the first day of my seeing Captain Hobson [30 January 1840], he enquired of me my opinion as to the proper site of the seat of Government, – whether I thought the Bay [of Islands] would be a good place for that purpose. I objected to the Bay, as too confined; as being too generally occupied by Europeans and natives, and also situated at the extreme end of the island; but stated that the land about the Tamaki and Waitemata was not occupied by either natives or Europeans, and possessed advantages beyond all other places; commanding convenient access by the river Thames to the interior of the country; the river Kaipara to the North, through extensive kauri forests; also by Manukau to the river Waikato, which takes its rise in Taupo lake, in the centre of the island; that there was a vast extent of fine country without an inhabitant; that the island of Waiheke and other islands formed safe roadsteads, with their numberless small bays, for vessels of all sizes.
>
> This part of New Zealand, with the rivers and bays, had not been visited by any Europeans, except by the Missionaries, who alone possessed correct and general information.[46]

The late Ruth Ross, normally a judicious historian, criticised Henry Williams for giving 'a rather misleading conception of the possibilities of the Waitemata's water connections'.[47] Why she should have written this is hard to understand. E. J. Wakefield, by no means an apologist for early Auckland, spoke of Tamaki's waterways as providing a system of 'great inland water-communication'.[48] Or again, Ernst Dieffenbach, who in 1840 was, like Wakefield, a dutiful servant of the New Zealand Company, nonetheless considered the Tamaki foreshore as 'very judiciously chosen for the site of a town'. Tamaki, he said, provided a 'great facility of communication with the coast and the interior of the northern island', with the added advantage of 'being the central point for the most powerful native tribes'.[49] In the 1840s this was a generally held view, except among the incorrigible partisans of some other settlement. Williams was mistaken, however, in imagining that missionaries alone had recent firsthand knowledge of the isthmus. By this time, W. C. Symonds, agent of the Manukau land company, and for this reason an equally enthusiastic supporter of Tamaki as a venue for European settlement, was as well informed as any missionary on the present condition of that locality. But Williams could scarcely have known that Symonds was exploring the Tamaki isthmus at the very time that he first met Hobson on the *Herald*.

Back to February 1840. Captain Symonds put in an appearance at the Bay of Islands a few days earlier than 14 February – we cannot be any more precise than that – that is, the date that Hobson returned from signature-collecting at Hokianga.[50] Symonds's arrival coincided with that of a Maori embassy composed of seven chiefs, mostly Ngati Whatua o Tamaki, but with one or two Waikatos.[51] This group, led (according to the Maori record) by Te Kawau's tamaiti (nephew), Reweti, had been deputed by the hui at Orakei mentioned in the last chapter, to give effect to the vision unfolded to it by Titai the matakite, by inviting the governor to settle in their midst. When they came north, these emissaries offered a gift of Tamaki land to Hobson as an inducement for him to come to live there.[52] At the Orakei land court hearing held many years later, J. C. McCormick, the lawyer, asked his client Te Kawau whether he had been one of 'the people who sold Auckland to the Europeans'.[53] Doubtless recalling this offer of Tamaki land that he had instructed his emissaries to make to the governor many years before when they had reached the Bay of Islands, the aged Te Kawau replied: 'I did not sell it. I gave it to them.' Gifting this land would have been no great sacrifice to make, either for Ngati Whatua as a tribe, or for Te Kawau as its chief. For any tribe to have a resident Pakeha living in its midst raised its status and increased its ability to get western goods.[54] And for Te Kawau to have the most powerful European in Aotearoa living on *his* land, as (so to speak) *his* Pakeha Maori, would not only have immeasurably strengthened his mana, but also have protected him from the attacks of powerful and aggressive neighbours who had, for so long, made Tamaki-makau-rau a desert place.

Apihai Te Kawau's anxiety to have the governor living in Tamaki makes greatest sense when we appreciate how vulnerable Te Kawau's people still were. Charles Terry described Ngati Whatua in 1840 as a numerically weak tribe – able to survive against old enemies such as the Nga Puhi and Hauraki iwi only if in alliance with a powerful tribe.[55] Ngati Whatua of Tamaki, he wrote, 'were always subject, from their position, to surprise and attack from others . . . and thus, from being formerly a numerous and powerful, influential people the whole tribe does not [now] exceed two hundred and fifty fighting men'.[56] It was fortunate, he added, that 'the Ngati Whatuas are connected by marriage, with the Waikato Natives, who are now the most numerous and powerful tribe in the North Island'.[57] Ernst Dieffenbach, who traversed the isthmus in early 1841, spoke in similar vein. He referred to Ngati Whatua as 'this unfortunate tribe, pressed by Nga-pui from the northward, the Nga-te-paoa from Hauraki, and the Waikato from the southward, who have dwindled down to almost nothing, and their whole number in the neighbourhood does not amount at present to more than 200'.[58] There are no documentary records to tell us to what extent (if at all) Apihai's invitation to the governor to come and live at Tamaki on gifted land influenced Hobson's later decision to establish a settlement there. But it is hardly unreasonable to assume that this offer would still have been much on Hobson's mind when he came to the Waitemata a fortnight later.

Although not formally part of this embassy of chiefs, Symonds arrived at the Bay in their company.[59] We lack conclusive evidence, however, which confirms what has sometimes been inferred, that he set out with the chiefs from Tamaki itself.[60] The chiefs presumably came north by an 'overland' route, which took in the upper Kaipara and the valley of the Mangakahia, a tributary of the Wairoa river.[61] It is most likely, therefore, that Symonds linked up with their party as they passed through that part of Northern Wairoa to which he had quite recently returned.[62] One issue is not in doubt; namely that, as the chief agent of the Manukau Company, Symonds had every bit as strong a motive as his Maori companions to persuade the governor to take up residence in Tamaki. But whether he openly added his voice to the pleas of Te Kawau's emissaries at this time, we do not know.

No sooner had Hobson returned from Hokianga, than he began to assemble a party that would set out on the *Herald* to collect signatures of southern chiefs for the treaty, and to inspect Tamaki as the site for a government settlement. The official party accompanying Hobson was made up of Cooper, Mathew and Freeman, and of course Captain Nias and his officers.

Hobson also invited Rev. Henry Williams, whom he valued for his skill as translator and for his mana among Maori. The other apologist for Tamaki, W. C. Symonds, was also on the *Herald* but not, as has sometimes been assumed, on the initiative of Hobson who, in fact, had no previous knowledge of that man, though he knew and admired his brother. Felton Mathew explained the addition of Symonds to the party in these terms:

> We are joined . . . by Captain Symonds, a son of Sir William
> Symonds, who is a settler in New Zealand, and whom captain Nias
> has invited to accompany us to the Thames. He is a very fine young
> man and a decided acquisition. . . . As he has travelled in the Island,
> his testimony has much weight.[63]

At this stage, it was imagined that after the governor's party had made its appraisal of Tamaki, Symonds's usefulness would have come to an end, and that he would leave the official party.[64] (As things fell out, during the visit to Tamaki Symonds impressed Hobson in such short order that the governor recruited him as a temporary official.) The Tamaki chiefs who had come north with Symonds also returned to the Waitemata as passengers on the *Herald.*

On 21 February, the *Herald* sailed to 'the Thames', arriving on the following morning in the inner waters of the Hauraki gulf. After sheltering overnight on 23 February in the northern bay that lies between Rangitoto and Motutapu,[65] the ship cautiously made its way into the Waitemata harbour. It anchored 'in the stream', in the relatively deep water which lay opposite the promontory which Maori called Te Rerenga-ora-iti, and which Europeans later named Point Britomart[66] after a Royal Navy brig of that name which surveyed the Waitemata in late 1840. Already the quarrelling between Hobson and Nias that had marred the Tasman crossing had erupted once again. (Commenting on a subsequent 'explosion . . . between the two Captains', Felton Mathew characterised the pair as 'obstinate, wrong-headed fellows, and as fit to act together as fire and tow [flaxen fibre]'.)[67] Matters came to a head when the governor spoke of the part that he expected the *Herald* to play in the collection of signatures and the survey of the harbour and its adjoining coastline. Nias bristled, became obstructive, refusing to allow the *Herald* to enter waters which he deemed to be too shallow, or to put ship's boats willy-nilly at the disposal of the governor's party.[68] But Hobson was determined to appraise the broad upper harbour, shallow in parts though it might be. So he took steps to make himself independent of his nemesis Nias, by hiring a 30-ton schooner, the *Trent* (Captain Bateman), that happened to be temporarily in Waitemata waters.[69] This vessel was inconveniently encumbered, however, by what Mathew called 'a deck cargo of divers pigs',[70] and having these animals as companions probably made the daylong excursion over the upper harbour on 24 February an unpleasant and trying experience. As on the first day in Waitemata waters, so over the remainder of this week, the party followed the practice of dividing into small groups that explored separately, as weather allowed, by boat or by foot, various parts of the harbour and isthmus. Over-night these parties returned to the *Herald*, which was anchored off a bay not named in the ship's log, but which was probably Waiariki, immediately to the east of Point Britomart.[71] There is no reference in the records to Hobson's party encountering significant numbers of Ngati Whatua. Logan Campbell, who, as a member of a small group of Pakeha land speculators, visited Te Waitemata a few weeks later, found the two main Ngati Whatua villages at Okahu and Rangitoto-iti deserted. On the isthmus, 'Nature reigned supreme'.[72] Campbell's group discovered that the Ngati Whatua inhabitants of Orakei were over on the Manukau preparing stores of winter food.[73] That is where Hobson's party, no doubt, would have found them had its explorations taken in a crossing of the isthmus.

That part of Tamaki which Hobson did have the opportunity to visit quickly impressed him as a fine site for European settle-ment. The Rev. Williams recalled that 'His Excellency was not long in pointing out the spot, the present site of Auckland, seeing immediately its various advantages'.[74] But Williams's recollection was faulty here. For although Hobson was quickly impressed by Tamaki in general, he was far from having decided at the time of this first visit exactly where he wanted his settlement to be. As he later made clear to his minister in London, his object of 'selecting a site for a township . . . was not accomplished'.[75] More explor-ation would be necessary to decide that. This explains why – after the first day's exploration of the upper harbour – Felton Mathew remarked in his journal, echoing his master's voice no doubt: 'The general appearance of the country is certainly favourable; and I am inclined to think that this will be the seat of our future Government. At all events, there is no doubt that Symonds and I shall be left here to explore it.'[76] Four days later, this surmise seemed confirmed, when Hobson arranged for Mathew and Symonds to be left behind so that they could explore the whole region more thoroughly before any final decision was made. (No doubt the garnering of signatures of the Ngati Whatua chiefs on a copy of the Waitangi treaty was a further reason to include Symonds in this new commission.) The surveyor-general wrote to his wife that:

> I am going, accompanied by Captain Symonds, to explore the
> country between this and Manukou, from thence trace the rivers
> Waikat[o] and Waipa as far up as time will allow into the interior. . .
> . Almost the whole of the journey will be performed in a boat or in
> canoes, and I intend returning here by the 18th March. I think with
> such a companion as Symonds I shall find it pleasant. . . .[77]

This journal entry was made on Friday 28 February. Symonds had already left the official party two days before to go to Coromandel where he had been authorised by Hobson to charter a boat which he and Mathew could use for their exploratory journey. But a crisis hit the official party that not only put an end to this plan but to Hobson's visit to Tamaki as well.

On Saturday 29 February, the party was confined to the *Herald* by a violent north-easterly storm. Felton Mathew wrote that after 'blowing great guns' during daylight hours, the weather deteriorated still further at nightfall, to become 'a perfect hurricane'.[78] Mathew, admittedly a landsman, spoke of the barometer falling 'with a rapidity I never before witnessed'.[79] The ship, with extra anchors out, weathered the storm that blew itself out by Sunday midday.

But meanwhile catastrophe struck. While in his cabin on the Sunday morning, Hobson suffered a stroke, which paralysed his right side and seriously impaired his speech. That some weakness in his physical constitution had predisposed Hobson to this attack is obvious. But recent events played their part, too. Scholefield emphasised how 'Hobson was fatigued by the worry and the exertions of the past week and irritated by the endless disputes [with Captain Nias]. It seemed as if obstacles were being put in Hobson's way which he was powerless to overcome. These worries affected his health as much as the constant exposure and physical fatigue.'[80] A modern neurologist would be inclined to agree. Overwhelmed at first by his sudden affliction, Hobson surmised that (in Mathew's words) 'his fitness for his office is at one blow destroyed'.[81] When, later in the same day, Mathew went to the governor's cabin, Hobson told him that 'he had at once made up his mind that he was unfit for the cares of office, and must resign and return to Sydney'.[82] When a session of cupping and blistering on the following day served only to enfeeble Hobson, the ship's surgeon, Dr Alexander Lane, felt constrained to urge on the governor an 'immediate return to Sydney', a course of action that Hobson himself had already decided in his own mind he must take.

For almost three days after Hobson's stroke, however, the *Herald* remained anchored in the Waitemata awaiting the return of Henry Williams. The missionary later recorded the circumstances of his absence. Williams said that, a day or so before the stroke that felled Hobson, he had been despatched by the governor to Fairburn's mission station at Maraetai. His assignment was 'to communicate with and collect the natives of the Thames, and around' who were prepared to sign a copy of the Treaty of Waitangi.[83] He had some success. On the evening of Wednesday 3 March, Williams sent a message back to the ship arranging for officials to rendezvous with him on the following day, when he and Fairburn promised to bring a group of Maori chiefs willing to sign the treaty. Hobson being ill, Captain Nias acted as head of the official party that responded to Williams's request, sailing in a ship's boat to the prearranged spot where the ceremony of signing took place. Exactly where they met is unknown; the copy of the treaty simply records that the ceremony was held at 'Waitemata'. (A likely meeting place would have been at one of the headlands of the Tamaki river, which was almost halfway between the Maraetai mission station and the bay where the *Herald* was anchored.) The seventeen chiefs who came with Williams and Fairburn were Marutuahu, mainly Ngati Paoa and Ngati Maru.[84] Theirs were the only signatures gathered during Hobson's first visit to Tamaki.

When Nias met up with Williams, he told him of the calamitous stroke suffered by Captain Hobson, informing him that the governor 'had been disabled by an attack of paralysis, and considered that he was not able to hold his office, and had determined to sail for Sydney'.[85] After the official party returned to the *Herald* in mid-afternoon, however, orders were given to weigh anchor not for Sydney, but for the Bay of Islands.[86] Hobson had decided at the last moment not to resign his post but to convalesce instead at the Bay of Islands. In his 'Early Recollections', Henry Williams maintained that it was he who was responsible for changing the governor's mind, when he came back to the ship:

> On my seeing Captain Hobson, I suggested his not determining so immediately to relinquish his office as Governor in New Zealand; that I would guarantee quarters on shore, either at Paihia or Waimate, but recommending Waimate as being more quiet.[87] The 'Herald' returned to the Bay, and Captain Hobson was conveyed to good quarters at Mr. Davis' house, where every attention was paid to him, having the presence of his own Surgeon and Secretary.[88]

On 6 March the *Herald* dropped anchor at Kororareka. Probably in response to medical advice, Hobson remained on shipboard for three days, gathering strength. Shortland then conducted him to Waimate, with the governor being borne on a litter through the bush over the last stages of the journey.[89] Quitting the ship must have been a relief to Hobson. At Kororareka he and Nias had quarrelled violently yet again over an official report that had to be submitted to Governor Gipps.[90] After leaving the governor at Waimate in the care of the missionary couple, Rev. Richard Davis and Mrs Davis, Shortland – promoted by Hobson to the position of temporary colonial secretary – returned to Kororareka to act as head of government during his chief's convalescence.

But Shortland had not been granted extensive discretionary powers. Although physically disabled, the governor, whose mental faculties (in the opinion of the *Herald*'s surgeon) 'had not been in the most remote degree affected or impaired',[91] had laid down precisely the main lines of policy that his deputy must follow.[92] The governor had told Shortland that his most urgent task was to ensure that further signatures to the Treaty of Waitangi were gathered.[93] As Hobson later explained to Lord John Russell, in order to ensure 'that the public service did not suffer [because of his paralytic stroke], I commissioned Captain Symonds of the British army, and the following gentlemen of the Church Missionary Society, namely the Rev. Mr. Henry Williams, the Rev. Mr. [A. N.] Brown, the Rev. Mr. Maunsell, and the Rev. Mr. William Williams to secure the adherence of the chiefs of their respective districts to the treaty of Waitangi.'[94] Each of these agents equipped with a copy of the treaty was authorised to 'treat with the principal native chiefs, in the southern parts of these islands'.[95] Hobson gave specific instructions to these agents that while they should strive to secure the 'adhesion' of the 'high chiefs' to the treaty, they should do so only after 'first explaining to them its principle and object, which they must clearly understand before you permit them to sign'. (With the wish, no doubt, father to the thought, Hobson mistakenly continued to assume that Maori could quickly understand the clauses of this ambiguous treaty and the benefits that must accrue to them from signing, provided that those things were patiently explained to them.) In the next two months, further people were engaged in this activity of signature-gathering: additional missionaries including those of the Wesleyan persuasion, officials such as Shortland and Dr Johnson, and navy and army officers who were transported on the *Herald* to remote coastal areas scattered through the three islands of New Zealand. It is revealing that the first emissary whom Hobson commissioned was Captain Symonds.[96]

III

On 12 March, Captain Nias set out from Kororareka for Sydney, in order to reprovision his ship for the lengthy cruise around New Zealand, which was expected to bring in sufficient signatures to complete the cession of sovereignty to the Crown.[97] When the *Herald* arrived in Port Jackson a fortnight later, Governor Gipps was alarmed by the most recent intelligence it brought from New Zealand. 'He had expected to hear', wrote Scholefield, 'that the sovereignty had been completed, and that Hobson had selected a site for his capital. Instead, he was told that the main work was only begun, that no town site had been fixed upon, and that the Lieutenant-Governor was dying.'[98] Nor was Gipps reassured to find that, at this time of crisis, Hobson had entrusted the administration of the infant colony to Shortland. Gipps regarded Shortland as an inexperienced official, and one in whom he had very little confidence. He was certainly not prepared to leave the affairs of New Zealand in Shortland's hands should the stricken lieutenant-governor die.[99]

Gipps extricated himself from this impasse with some ingenuity. Some three months before, Lord John Russell had undertaken 'to send a force of 100 men to New Zealand' as soon as news had come through of the 'grant or cession of territory from the New Zealand chiefs in the Northern Island'.[100] Three weeks' experience of New Zealand conditions quickly convinced Hobson, however, that any delay in sending troops was fraught with danger. He was apprehensive that disputes would break out between the two races which military force alone could put down. He informed his secretary of state that he 'greatly feared' that a 'mania for land-jobbing' and 'conflicting claims for land… will create a violent ferment through every class of society, both native and European'. After explaining how the musket wars had thrown traditional Maori land ownership into extraordinary confusion, he continued:

> My present object . . . is to show your Lordship how many sources of disagreement exist between natives and Europeans, and how requisite it is that the executive government should have a force at command that will enable it to act with vigour; not I hope by the hostile employment of troops, but by the moral effect their presence will produce.[101]

Gipps took up this idea of promptly despatching a substantial number of troops to New Zealand, but for a reason quite different from the one that Hobson had offered. Aware that a detachment of sixty men and a captain from the 80th Regiment were, at that time, being held in readiness to embark for New Zealand,[102] Gipps persuaded General O'Connell, commanding officer of the military forces at Sydney, to increase the number to be despatched to 100. Gipps's thinking was that the detachment thus enlarged would be in excess of company strength, and would therefore qualify for a commanding officer of field rank.[103] Gipps was well aware that a civil appointment could then be attached to the charge of an officer of this seniority, enabling him to act, in this instance, as a provisional lieutenant-governor should the present incumbent die or be forced by illness to relinquish his post. It was a stroke of good fortune for Gipps that such a senior officer was at hand. This was Major Thomas Bunbury, a well-regarded and resolute officer of the 80th Regiment. Bunbury was temporarily without a charge, having just finished a tour of duty commanding the garrison at the penal settlement at Norfolk Island.

In his memoirs, Bunbury wrote of the unusual circumstances attached to his posting to New Zealand. He recalled that Gipps unexpectedly summoned him to his office at Government House, Sydney. There the governor asked him bluntly whether, if he were sent as the commanding officer of the detachment of the 80th Regiment about to be stationed in New Zealand, he would also be prepared to take up additional administrative duties in the event of an emergency. Gipps explained that the intelligence from New Zealand was 'very bad': according to 'the last accounts', the lieutenant-governor there was 'in a dying state from an attack of paralysis'. Gipps confessed that this alarming news had placed him in something of a quandary, for (as he confided in Bunbury) he had little confidence in Hobson's subordinates.[104] Bunbury's memoirs continued:

Major Thomas Bunbury in old age. From G. H. Scholefield, Captain William Hobson.

> Under these circumstances he wished me to go to New Zealand and assume the charge of the government; should I find the Governor dead or incapable of performing personally the duties, I was to receive £1000 per annum, and he had little doubt that my appointment would be confirmed by the Home Government. . . . He further informed me that the 'Herald', sloop of war, should follow for the Bay of Islands in a few days, for it was absolutely necessary that the tribes on the coast to the southward should be visited to obtain their adhesion to the treaty.[105]

After mulling over this unusual proposal. Bunbury agreed, undertaking, in Gipps's words, 'to provide for the administration of the government, in the possible event of the relinquishment of it by Captain Hobson'.[106]

On 16 April 1840, accompanied by Mrs Hobson and her family, Bunbury arrived on the store-ship HMS *Buffalo* at the Bay of Islands, with a party of troops that was to join a somewhat larger detachment of the 80th, which had arrived a few days earlier. The strength of the unit at this time was 'one field-officer, one captain, two subalterns, four sergeants, two drummers and eighty rank and file'.[107] Later in the year, the unit was further strengthened by 'the addition of two subalterns and fifteen men from the regiment at Sydney. They were principally artificers, an assistant-surgeon, an officer of Engineers [Lieutenant Lugard] and a master of the works.'[108] Some weeks after the foundation of Auckland in September 1840, this detachment of the 80th Regiment was sent to Tamaki to build Fort Britomart, in which, on completion, its members were to live as the garrison of the new capital. Some of those associated with the regiment, such as Bunbury, Ensign Best and Mr George Graham, were to win a degree of prominence and a place in our historical annals. The rank and file of this garrison, however, come down to us today as anonymous, without a voice, unsung. Yet theirs is the honour of being among Auckland's 'first shippers'.

It so happened that on the day that Bunbury arrived at the Bay of Islands, Hobson had moved from Waimate to Paihia. Bunbury, having his own vested interest in the state of Hobson's health, lost no time in visiting the governor and ascertaining for himself how fit was Hobson to resume duties. He reported to Gipps that he found the governor much better than he had been led to expect; for while he was still not able to write, he could at least 'affix his signature' to official documents.[109] Yet Bunbury could see that although Hobson was improving physically day by day and was in full possession of his mental faculties, his nervous state remained fragile. As Bunbury wrote in his reminiscences:

> [Hobson] was in great dread of having again to embark in the 'Herald', which was daily expected from Sydney.[110] Her commander [Nias], according to his statement, was anything but a gentleman, and now that he was in such a fair way of recovery it would retard his cure if not kill him. He begged most earnestly that I would take that duty for him, saying that the captain would behave quite differently towards me, if it were only to recover credit and show the world that he, Captain Hobson, was in the wrong. It was a grievous sacrifice for me to make, the troops not having yet landed or arrangements been made for their accommodation, but I could not prevail upon myself to refuse him.[111]

Thus it was that on 28 April, two days after the *Herald* arrived back at Kororareka, she set out once again, this time bearing not the lieutenant-governor, but Bunbury. According to the ship's log, Bunbury was 'charged with a diplomatic mission',[112] in effect securing the Crown's sovereignty and authority over New Zealand. The cruise of the *Herald* over the next nine weeks included calls on tribes living in the Thames, the Bay of Plenty, the eastern and southern coasts of the South Island, Stewart Island, and the Cook Strait region including Port Nicholson.

On 21 May 1840, long before the return of the *Herald* to the Bay, Hobson made two proclamations vesting in Queen Victoria full sovereignty over the whole country. The first proclamation claimed the North Island on the ground of cession by chiefs; the second claimed the Middle (South) and Stewart Islands on the ground of discovery.[113] Paul Moon argues in his recent study of the governorship of Captain Hobson that what he calls these 'precipitate' and 'unilateral' proclamations owed less to Bunbury's progress reports from the *Herald* or to the signed copies of the Treaty of Waitangi returned by the governor's emissaries, than they did to (in Moon's view) Hobson's somewhat ridiculous suspicion that the provisional administration set up by the New Zealand Company settlers at Port Nicholson was bent on challenging British sovereignty.[114]

IV

Bunbury, Nias and his fellow officers on the *Herald* gathered signatures for the treaty from far-flung places. But the main work of persuading Maori chiefs, the overwhelming majority of whom lived in the North Island, to sign the treaty was carried out by agents appointed by the governor who were in the field even before the *Herald* began her cruise. 'Missionaries of the Church of England and the Wesleyan Church', wrote Scholefield, 'were in the southern parts of the island; Shortland and Dr. Johnson [Colonel Surgeon] had gone to the extreme north; [Henry] Williams in the schooner *Ariel* was treating with the chiefs on both sides of Cook Strait.'[115]

The first in the field, however, were the emissaries authorised to carry copies of the treaty to the chiefs of Tamaki and Manukau, and into the extensive region of the west coast, running from the southern heads of the Manukau harbour as far south as the Mokau river. This was the group of treaty advocates to which Captain Symonds belonged. During his visit to the Waitemata, Hobson had recognised how well equipped was Symonds to be ambassador to Maori in this particular region. Some parts of it Symonds already knew at first hand, having recently traversed the isthmus and the north Manukau lands. Moreover, he seemed to be well regarded by the Maori people, whose language he was fast acquiring.[116] Symonds was recruited to be (in Buick's phrase) 'the ambassador to the west'[117] in the following way. On returning to Tamaki from the Thames in early March, Symonds found that Hobson's stroke had aborted the inspection visit of Tamaki and its adjoining lands that he and Mathew had been commissioned to make. It seems that he reverted therefore to his previous role of agent, making preparations to receive the first Manukau Land Company settlers, and that he moved into Mitchell's house at Karangahape, which became his base and place of residence, off and on, over the next few months.[118] Shortly after arriving there, however, he received a letter dated 13 March from Shortland, the new acting colonial secretary, telling of a complete change in the governor's plans, but one in which Symonds had an important part to play. It was the governor's wish (wrote Shortland) that Symonds should co-operate with missionaries of the western area of the greater Tamaki region in the business of procuring signatures for the Treaty of Waitangi.[119] In the same month Hobson made Symonds a police magistrate,[120] but whether Shortland notified Symonds of this in the same letter, probable though that seems, is not known.

Symonds acted immediately on the governor's instructions. He later reported that he 'assembled as many of the Manukau chiefs as could be collected at short notice, and with the assistance of Mr. Hamlin, a catechist in the Church mission, explained to them the views of Her Majesty's Government, and solicited their signatures to the treaty'.[121] On 20 March a second meeting followed, this one more fully attended, and to which newcomers came: from Waikato, from the western littoral of the Firth of Thames, and from Tauranga. Some signatures were harvested for the treaty at this meeting, including, predictably enough, those of the three main chiefs of Ngati Whatua o

Tamaki, Te Kawau, Tinana and Te Reweti,[122] who were anxious to persuade the governor to settle in Tamaki. (Paora Tuhaere, Te Kawau's successor, recalled, years later, that his uncle had signed the treaty on 20 March 1840 after 'some conversation' with Symonds.[123] Given the vested interest of both Ngati Whatua and Symonds in attracting the governor to Tamaki, it is not unlikely that the first informal overtures over the sale of Waitemata land also took place then.)[124]

On 3 April, Symonds left Manukau for the Rev. Robert Maunsell's mission station at Maraetai near the south Waikato heads. On arrival he was gratified to find that Maunsell, who had already been supplied with a copy of the treaty, had used a gathering of chiefs for a missionary meeting which he had recently held as an opportunity for obtaining 'many signatures'.[125] Maunsell and his fellow missionary, the Rev. B. Y. Ashwell, had collected signatures from thirty-two chiefs representative of seventeen different tribes, names which, the missionaries claimed, 'embrace, as we conceive, with the exception of two, the names of the principal men of Waikato'.[126] Symonds wrote in his report that, after examining these signatures, 'I found that, with the exception of very few, all the leading men of the country as far south as M[o]kau, had acknowledged the sovereignty of Her Majesty'.[127] Discovering that 'these few' were confined to chiefs living in the neighbourhood of the west coast harbours of Aotea and Kawhia, which constituted the mission field of the Wesleyan minister the Rev. John Whiteley, Symonds despatched a copy of the treaty to that particular missionary as well. He proposed that Whiteley take over the task of obtaining 'the cession of sovereign rights from as many of the chiefs as you may deem sufficient, stretching as far to the southward as possible among the Maniapoto'.[128] Confident that Whiteley would shoulder this duty, Symonds concluded that he himself need go no further. (His confidence was justified; Whiteley and his fellow missionary James Wallis were able in the weeks ahead to persuade ten important chiefs in Kawhia and thereabouts to sign.)[129] On 18 April, Symonds returned to what he vaguely termed 'Manukau' where, a week later, he obtained the adherence of a further seven chiefs to the treaty.[130] But Te Wherowhero and several others present refused to sign although, as Symonds conceded, 'they manifested no ill-will to the Government'. Indeed, in the years to come, Te

The Rev. John Whitely, 1806–69, Wesleyan missionary. AUCKLAND CITY LIBRARIES

Wherowhero acted as a protector of the settlement of Auckland in its first, somewhat defenceless, years.

It is at this point that we must return to what Tuhaere asserted at the Kohimarama conference in 1860: that Maori chiefs were persuaded to sign a treaty in 1840 which they did not understand, and they were often induced to do so because of the prospect of a material reward. Using the famously successful signature-collecting journey of Henry Williams to illustrate his point, he maintained that in visiting the tribes:

> Blankets were brought by Mr. Williams [Te Wiremu]. Those I call the bait and the hook was within; he [the chief] took the bait and was caught; the chief did not know there was a hook within; he took the bait and was caught. Mr. Williams's bait was a blanket; the hook was the Queen's Sovereignty. When he came to a Chief he presented his hook and forthwith drew out a subject for the Queen.[131]

This had not been Hobson's original intention. Before despatching his signature-collecting emissaries, the governor had expressly given a formula for negotiation with Maori that generally kept to the letter and spirit of Normanby's instructions. Cession of sovereignty, he said, must be entered into 'fair[ly]' and 'intelligently'.[132] No chief should be permitted to sign the copy of the treaty unless its terms were clearly understood.[133]

However, it was Hobson himself (presumably acting on the well-intentioned advice of missionaries) who first associated treaty-signing with festivities and gifts. On 13 February 1840, the day after the signing of the treaty at Mangungu, a lavish celebration was held beside the Hokianga at nearby Horeke, which was marked by a huge feast, and the distribution of blankets for chiefs and tobacco for men.[134] And the reports of the signature-collectors over the next few months leave no doubt that it had become customary to reward each chief of rank who signed with a blanket.[135] Indeed, when in early April, the Rev. Maunsell failed to reward chiefs after they had signed a copy of the treaty at a meeting near the Waikato heads, 'great excitement prevailed among the natives'. Symonds admitted that his arrival at the mission station at that very time was 'most opportune'. He found that local Maori, because of a 'report which had reached them of presents having been given by the Government to all to the northward who had subscribed to the treaty . . . were in the act of remonstrating very angrily with Mr. Maunsell on his having kept them in the dark on the subject'. They demanded that he return the treaty, which they had signed, so that they could destroy it. Only when Symonds 'distributed a few presents' and promised that all who had signed would be treated likewise, were the signatories mollified and 'excitement allayed'.[136]

Hobson's view seems to have been that giving blankets was an act of bounty unrelated to the chiefs' signing of the treaty. If distinguishing between an act of bounty and the inducement of a bribe proves difficult for us today, how much more so would it have been for Maori in 1840.

V

In the last days of April, Symonds returned to the Bay of Islands, bearing his signed copies of the treaty.[137] He reported to Hobson, who was then temporarily in residence at Paihia but preparing to shift to a recently acquired base for the government at Okiato (which the lieutenant-governor subsequently renamed Russell in honour of his secretary of state, Lord John Russell). Yet Hobson looked on this new government establishment at Okiato as no more than makeshift.[138] According to Ruth Ross, 'Hobson's illness had not weakened his determination to fix his capital on the shores of the Waitemata'.[139] Nevertheless, it would appear that at this stage Hobson's mind was somewhat more open than Ross imagined it to be. In fact he had just sent (18 April) his surveyor-general, Mathew, on a southern cruise in the general direction of the Thames to investigate a series of likely sites for the seat of government. But when, on his return, Mathew pronounced that 'the "Tehmaki" is the most desirable spot that can be selected',[140] this would have simply served to confirm Hobson's early preference for a location on the Waitemata shoreline. But the governor still had an open mind on precisely where that should be. Of one thing we can be sure. Hobson's interest in the Tamaki served to increase the standing of Symonds with the governor. No other person in Hobson's circle had his firsthand knowledge of the isthmus, no other was so familiar with its adjoining harbours. Herein lies the explanation of why Hobson, at this juncture, made

REWI   TAWHANA   TAONUI   WETERE TE RERENGA
TE RANGITUATAKA   TE NAUNAU

the surprising choice of appointing Symonds as the deputy of his surveyor-general.

Hobson's continued use of Symonds as a government official and, it was further suspected, as his secret adviser, stirred up among contemporaries a debate that continues still among modern historians. The author of the most recent study of Hobson maintains that the invitation to Symonds to become an official was an 'ill-advised' appointment by 'a negligent and inept Governor'.[141] Certainly the appointment of Symonds angered the New Zealand Company, who saw an obvious conflict of interest for a government official who was also the chief agent of a land company whose interests (as Sherrin and Wallace expressed it) 'were manifestly concerned in securing the location of the official capital on their property, or in its vicinity. . . .'[142] The New Zealand Company could claim, reasonably enough, that Symonds was prone to use his privileged position, and indeed had done so while Hobson had been ill, to decry the strong claims of Port Nicholson to become the capital, while championing those of Tamaki.[143] True or not, it was inevitable that Symonds was forced to play an ambivalent role. The competing claims on his loyalties had their outward and visible sign in the divided life he led over the next year; sometimes operating out of Russell or Auckland as a government official, sometimes acting as a company agent resident on the Manukau shore. Certainly the prospectus which the New Zealand and Manakau Land Company published in September 1840, unabashedly made much of the influence which it implied Symonds was able to exert on the government. Clause 4 read:

> As neither the Bay of Islands, nor any of the harbours to the northward, were considered by the Governor, as eligible for the capital or future seat of government, the Company authorized Captain Symonds, who accompanied Captain Hobson to the Waitemata, to offer His Excellency every facility which their property[144] will afford for the selection of a capital, as well as to adopt such plans in the distribution of the sections of land as will harmonise with the views of Government. . . .

Unfortunately, the documentary record of Symonds's life between the months of May and August 1840 is very thin; consequently, the charge that he used his official position opportunistically can be neither proved nor disproved. But this much can be said in his defence. New Zealand Company critics apart, all spoke well of Symonds. At the time of his death he was praised as 'public-spirited and independent to the highest degree'.[145] And one can understand why Hobson turned to such a man during his first months as governor. Hobson became all too aware of the conspicuous lack of talent among his first officials, and of their penchant for petty intrigue.[146] During the visit to the Waitemata in February 1840, he recognised that he had in Symonds a man who was resourceful, knew the country thereabouts well and had sufficient skill in the language to deal with local chiefs as few of Hobson's first officials could. As Nancy Taylor put it: 'But if Symonds's interests needed Hobson's favour, Hobson needed Symonds'.[147] And continued to need him. Looking ahead, we can note that after Symonds, in the role of temporary deputy governor, had organised the first wave of settlement of Auckland, Hobson was anxious not to let him go. Writing to Gipps, he sought permission to retain Symonds as a magistrate in New Zealand, testifying that already 'he [Hobson] had derived great assistance from Captain Symonds's intelligence, activity, and intimate knowledge of the country'.[148]

Symonds was a valuable man.

CHAPTER X

Hobson's Choice

I

In Captain William Hobson there was much to admire. He was brave, conscientious, and diligent in his public duties. His private life was beyond reproach; he was a loving husband and a devoted family man. Yet of all the governors of the Crown Colony years he was the least popular and the most calumniated. In Hobson's last months of office, leaders in the colony's two main settlements, Wellington and Auckland, petitioned for his recall in language deliberately calculated to humiliate and wound him. Settlers in Auckland wanted him removed on the grounds that he had 'reduced . . . the country to bankruptcy';[1] those in the New Zealand Company settlement demanded his recall 'because of his systematic neglect of our welfare'.[2] In Auckland, the settlement he created, in which one might have expected a measure of goodwill towards him, relentless opponents known as 'the Clique' so detested him that they were accused of having hounded him to his death and, that done, of 'exulting over his grave'.[3] Two circumstances contributed mainly to Hobson's sheer fall from grace. First, there was the complicated racial situation in the colony arising out of the land hunger of the settlers that quickly laid bare the governor's incapacity to fill a position quite beyond the reach of his limited abilities and experience. Second, there was the intractable conflict between

*The governor's wife,
Mrs Eliza Hobson.
Sketch, 1840?,
by John Johnson MD.*
AUCKLAND CITY
LIBRARIES

the policies of the Colonial Office – mindful of its obligations to the native people and of the need for fiscal prudence – and the extravagant expectations of the white settler community.

In his pioneering history of early New Zealand, A. S. Thomson maintained that the governor's naval background deprived him of the resilience and adroitness that his new post demanded. 'A man who had spent thirty years of his life at sea', wrote Thomson, 'was ill suited to lay the foundations of a colony in the midst of natives.'[4] Nor did his personality help. Though loyal to those whom he trusted, he could be obstinate and unforgiving towards those whom he did not. His shortcomings were aggravated, continued Thomson, when '[i]t accidentally became known that, like most officers of the royal navy, Captain Hobson was keenly alive to newspaper criticism, and after this discovery he never had a day's peace. Newspapers unknown beyond the place where they were printed kept him in a perpetual fever.'[5] Yet when Hobson took office, it would have required a governor of most subtle and discerning mind and of considerable diplomatic suavity to have hushed settler protest, given that his appointment coincided with the time when the feud between the Wakefield company and the Colonial Office was at its height.[6] Hobson had a nigh impossible task. This tyro governor inherited, wrote Beaglehole, not only the

Evangelical policies of Dandeson Coates of the Church Missionary Society, and of like-minded James Stephen – the grey eminence, so to speak, at the Colonial Office – but was also subject to the humanitarian imperatives of two successive Whig secretaries of state, Lords Glenelg and Normanby. None of these powerful figures could see any virtue in the principles of the New Zealand Company. And so Hobson, who himself had 'no capacity for intrigue', had through a spin of the wheel of fortune become the heir to the legacy of years of intrigue between Evangelical Christians and 'systematic' colonists.[7] 'From the circumstances of his appointment, and his previous knowledge of the country', wrote Beaglehole, 'it is inconceivable that he should not have been strongly biased.'

Within weeks of his arrival in New Zealand, Hobson was at loggerheads with the New Zealand Company. This dissension had its origins in the steady flow of settlers into Port Nicholson where, by the end of 1840, the white population had built up to over 1750.[8] Shortly after the first batch of settlers arrived in the *Aurora*, on 22 January 1840, the need to maintain law and order in the young settlement led the leaders of that community to set up a provisional council and to appoint temporary magistrates. When Hobson learned of these arrangements he reacted melodramatically. First, he issued a proclamation demanding that this 'illegal association' should immediately submit to his authority, and then he sent a detachment of thirty soldiers under Shortland to ensure that this was done. In truth, the confrontation that Hobson conjured up was very much a storm in a teacup. On Shortland's arrival, the Wellington leaders submitted without a breath of complaint. Shortly after (1 July), a public meeting was held at which the Cook Strait settlers confirmed this submission by adopting a loyal and dutiful address to the lieutenant-governor. But the company's representatives on this particular occasion also made it clear they were not to be regarded as mere ciphers. And they declared that they would look on Hobson's readiness to accept Port Nicholson as the capital and to live among them, as the touchstone of his goodwill. (This for Wellingtonians was no small matter. They believed that for Hobson to locate his capital in the north would both damage Wellington's prestige, and create a rival magnet drawing in future colonists.)[9] Thus it came about that, in his speech moving

the adoption of the address, Dr Samuel Evans blended his sentiments of respectful loyalty to the Queen with a blunt indication
that the settlers expected the governor to shift his capital from
the Bay of Islands to Port Nicholson.

> He [Evans] was satisfied with the harbour; it was the true geographical
> centre of the islands, and surrounded by a large agricultural district,
> and he was sure that the Government must ultimately be brought
> there, containing as it did by far the greatest European population in
> the islands. . . . We might add, that in planning the surveys of our
> future town, we had, as far as possible, anticipated the wants of
> Government, and set apart the most valuable sections of land for the
> convenience of the public offices, and the personal accommodation of
> your Excellency, feeling assured, as we do, that sooner or later this
> must necessarily become the seat of government for these islands.[10]

Hobson replied to this address in a letter replete with viceregal
punctilio. But he left no doubt in the minds of the company's
leaders that, in turning down their invitation to set up his capital
in Port Nicholson, he had made a decision that was unalterable.

> In declining the offer, I can assure you the Association and settlers
> generally that I am not insensible to the great sacrifice I make of my
> own ease; but it is a sacrifice which is due to the public service, from a
> conviction of the advantages of fixing the seat of Government in a more
> central position, and one better adapted for internal communication.[11]

This rebuff to the Port Nicholson settlers would probably have
been bearable, just, had not New Zealand Company directors in
London and settlers in New Zealand later learned of the despatch
which Hobson wrote to his secretary of state giving his version of
the confrontation with the Wellington settlers. In an attempt to
justify his intemperate reaction to the setting up of a provisional
government at Port Nicholson, Hobson expressed an opinion that
the company's proceedings had amounted to 'high treason'.[12] This
offensive piece of sophistry – for so Hobson's statement was
regarded by the company – was further compounded in a later
despatch in which Hobson – who had no personal knowledge of
Port Nicholson, never having visited it – compared its harbour
and other amenities unfavourably with those of the Waitemata.

In justifying his preference, the governor cited a tendentiously unfavourable report that Shortland had made on the basis of his brief visit to Port Nicholson. While Shortland had been pointedly muted in praising the port's advantages, he had dwelt emphatically on its supposed 'principal defects'. He spoke of such matters as the severe winter cold, and 'the violent winds, which always blow in and out of the harbour, and with such force as to prevent merchant ships from either entering or going out'.[13]

Yet even had Hobson disregarded Shortland's report and accepted without demur the trumpeted merits of the Cook Strait settlement, there is no doubt that he never seriously considered setting up his capital there. On that issue the policies of the governor and the New Zealand Company were irreconcilable. The company directors in London and its settlers in the Cook Strait could see no alternative to placing the seat of government in the centre of European settlement, where the governor would be, of course, subject to the company's influence, perhaps even become (as James Stephen feared) 'their servant'.[14] The Colonial Office and Hobson, on the other hand, insisted that the capital should be in the centre of Maori population. And the governor was also mindful of the fact that if he must, so to speak, sup with the company devil, he would best do so with a long spoon. But until the issue was decided once for all, the despatches of Colonel Wakefield and Captain Hobson to their respective superiors in London, each puffing the settlement of his own choice, have been likened, not inappropriately, to the advertisements of 'rival storekeepers'.[15] Ultimately Hobson had his way; his preference for Tamaki prevailed. But he was not to be forgiven. Joseph Somes, governor of the company in London, denounced Hobson's choice of the Waitemata for the site of his 'artificial capital' as dictated by the 'hostile view' he invariably adopted towards the 'enterprising inhabitants' of Port Nicholson.[16] This quarrel over the siting of the capital envenomed the relationship between the company and the government for years to come.[17]

II

Deciding where the capital should be became a pressing issue shortly after Hobson's paralytic seizure.[18] The arrival at the Bay of

Islands of the first government immigrants on the *Westminster* on 16 March 1840, and of troops of the 80th Regiment from Sydney in the month following, made setting up permanent headquarters for the government in the Bay a matter of particular urgency. In the middle of March, Hobson detailed Felton Mathew, the surveyor-general, to examine possible sites. After an inspection of Kororareka, Mathew declared that this, the main Pakeha settlement in the Bay, was unsuitable chiefly on the grounds that it lacked an adequate harbour for shipping and sufficient land for settlement. After investigating other sites including Waitangi, he recommended Okiato, a small bay used as a whaling station, a few kilometres further up the Bay from Kororareka. He argued that not only was it able to provide a good anchorage for a number of vessels at any given time, but it also had existing buildings, which could serve, with little modification, as a house for the governor and as offices for his senior officials. Mathew was so confident that his recommendation would be accepted that he negotiated a provisional sale with the owner, J. R. Clendon, without the governor's full knowledge. (He was later censured by Gipps for having recommended an unwise purchase.) On 23 April, Hobson agreed to buy Okiato for £15,000. On 1 May he formally took possession, renaming it Russell, in honour of his new secretary of state, Lord John Russell.

But Hobson never envisaged Russell as his permanent capital. Its location in the Bay of Islands made it remote from the bulk of the population, present and future – an irremediable defect. Hobson's eyes were already turned firmly south. As early as 6 April he instructed Felton Mathew to prepare for an expedition whose 'principal object', as the surveyor-general expressed it, 'was to select an eligible spot for the Chief settlement and seat of Government of the[se] Islands'. Mathew correctly represented his governor's wishes when he added a further note that 'a speedy determination of this most important question was the great desideratum'. [19] Twelve days later, accompanied by his wife Sarah (who had arrived on the *Westminster* shortly before), Mathew embarked at Kororareka on the *Ranger*, a revenue cutter which, with its master Captain Carkeek[20] and crew, was temporarily on loan from the New South Wales government. Thus began a two-month exploratory cruise taking in the coastline from Whangarei to the Thames including both sides of the Firth. But, on Hobson's instructions, the harbours at Whangarei,[21] Mahurangi[22] and Waitemata – including the Tamaki isthmus[23] – and the Tamaki river,[24] were the particular places that the governor wished to be subjected to the most comprehensive examination. Much is known about this voyage, partly because of the detailed, if somewhat pompous report which Felton Mathew compiled for the governor, and partly because of the entertaining and ebullient journal that his wife Sarah kept during the cruise.[25]

After inspecting the Whangarei and Mahurangi harbours, Mathew rejected them as unsuited to the governor's requirements, mainly because they were 'too far north and too near the Bay of Islands'.[26] When the *Ranger* reached the Waitemata, Mathew's investigation began in earnest. 'I now applied myself', he assured Hobson, 'to a careful and deliberate examination of that harbour and of the spot which I once on a previous occasion visited in company with his Excellency, and which at first sight, appeared to present some advantages which were likely to render it available for the purpose I had in view.'[27] During the visit that Hobson himself had made in February, he had been impressed by the upper harbour that lay to the west of the islet then called 'The Sentinel' but now known as 'Watchman's' (though the beach on the shore nearby is still called Sentinel Beach).[28] Mathew felt himself obliged, therefore, to explore this region extensively. Travelling mainly by rowboat, he surveyed the harbour almost as far as Riverhead, mapping harbour channels, shoals and foreshores, noting, where he could, water depths. Portions of the scrub-covered inland he covered on foot. He was unimpressed. 'I am compelled to arrive at the conclusion', he reported to Hobson, that the upper harbour 'is totally unfit for the seite [*sic*] of the principal Settlement, and indeed ill adapted for a settlement at all.'[29] Among the disadvantages that he listed were: the shortage of timber and of freshwater streams, the restricted opportunities for access by land to the Manukau harbour, and the problems posed for shipping by the numerous shoals and by the straitened nature of the few deep-water channels.[30]

The *Ranger* then worked eastwards along the southern shoreline, moving swiftly towards Orakei. While she lay off Waitaramoa (Hobson Bay), she was visited by a group of four Pakeha men. In *Poenamo*, Sir John Logan Campbell – one of the quartet who made the visit – records that these four adventurers had come to

Captain James Reddy Clendon, 1801–72, trader and US Consul in New Zealand. AUCKLAND CITY LIBRARIES

241

the Waitemata from Coromandel to make a speculative purchase of Ngati Whatua land in anticipation of the capital being established on the Tamaki isthmus. Led by 'Bully' (William) Webster, 'Te Wepiha', the almost mythical Pakeha-Maori entrepreneur living at Waiau, this party included three Scots, two of whom (William Brown and Campbell himself) were to be the founders of Auckland's first merchant firm and to become in time very wealthy men. But at this stage they were unshaven, full-bearded – pioneer style – probably dressed in what Campbell called their usual 'appropriate' if 'free and easy fashion', a long, blue-flannel workman's shirt, not tucked in, but worn as an overall or jacket, 'confined around the waist with a common leather strap'.[31] Their pioneer garb and demeanour gave no premonition of that later eminence, at least in Sarah Mathew's scornful eyes. In her journal entry for 1 May she wrote that:

> In the afternoon a new and interesting object was descried in the Bay, a large boat filled with people bearing down towards us. . . . As it came alongside we perceived that it contained several white men and a number of natives.[32] One of the former came upon deck and asked for the 'Surveyor General', who, of course, made his appearance. The object of these gentlemen seemed to be to find out where the new settlement was to be, but as nothing is as yet decided they did not obtain the information they sought. They were a strange set of beings, settlers from the Thames and Coromandel Harbour – and such specimens of settlers; many degrees below those of New South Wales in apparent respectability: truly the early settlers in a new colony do become most extraordinary beings, somewhat, I imagine, of the Kentucky style, 'half horse, half alligator, with a touch of the earthquake': they were not welcomed with much cordiality, so they soon pushed off again, and we saw the smoke from their camping place some few miles off.[33]

Surprisingly, Mathew's inspection of the southern coastline directly east of The Sentinel, where two kilometres or more of modern Auckland's port facilities are now densely concentrated, seems to have been little more than perfunctory. Nor did the Orakei-Kohimarama shoreline hold much interest for him. But not so 'Tehmaki', as he called the valley of the Tamaki river. He spent a week there, exploring it thoroughly.[34] He was alert enough to recognise that the chief drawback to 'Tehmaki' (even if he underestimated it) – was the inadequacy of the river as a modern means of communication. The obvious problem was a cluster of hazards at the mouth of the river: a submarine volcanic reef stretching from Motukorea (Brown's Island), and various sandbars and shoals where the river joined the harbour.[35] This defect, he considered, could be easily overcome once the entrance had been surveyed and 'accurately buoyed'.[36] And vessels drawing up to twelve feet of water, after having negotiated the entrance, could at all tides (as he pointed out) use the main river channel to penetrate inland for several miles.[37] In his opinion, this was most fortunate, because five miles in, the vessels would be able to reach a deep-water anchorage at the very spot Mathew thought most suited to become the government settlement. He had in mind, here, the land bounded by Wai-Mokoia (Panmure basin), Maungarei (Mount Wellington) and the western bank of the Tamaki river. This was the fertile area which twenty years before had been thickly occupied by Te Hinaki's branch of the Ngati Paoa and which is now the site of modern Panmure. Mathew's report was rhapsodic. It spoke of level well-drained land, volcanic soils 'of the finest description', an 'abundance of fresh water', access to the Otahuhu portage, and above all conti-guity with the 'immensely important' Tamaki isthmus.[38] This isthmus, 'the connecting link between the East and West coasts', Mathew believed to be 'the very key to the whole Island, North and South, the centre through which every line of communica-tion must unavoidably pass', making it 'most peculiarly adapted [to be] the seite of the Metropolis'.[39] In proposing 'Tehmaki' (Panmure) as a possible capital, Mathew tried to forestall Hobson's anticipated objection that it lacked an anchorage for steamers and larger ships. This shortcoming, he said, could easily be overcome by creating a 'small settlement' on the southern shore of the Waitemata that would serve as a port from which cargoes could be transhipped by lighters, or similar ves-sels, to and from 'Tehmaki' itself.[40]

We can confidently assume that Hobson was gratified with the general thrust of the Mathew report. The conclusion that of all the bays surveyed from Whangarei to the southern extent of the 'Frith of Thames', none had the advantages of the Waitemata, chimed in sweetly with the governor's own preference. (Mrs Hobson confided to a friend shortly after this that her husband was 'quite determined that the Seat of Government will be at the Thames'.)[41] But Hobson, having already had his fingers burnt by Mathew's advocacy of Okiato, was unimpressed by this new idiosyncratic proposal that the capital be placed not on the Waitemata harbour itself, but on the riverbank of a tidal estuary running inland from it. Though still 'in a weak state of health',[42] Hobson decided, therefore, to take advantage of having the *Ranger* still at his disposal, and go himself to Tamaki where he could subject Mathew's recommendations to a closer scrutiny. The official party which accompanied Hobson on the *Ranger* on this voyage was Dr John Johnson (colonial surgeon), George Clarke (a former CMS catechist recently appointed protector of the aborigines), David Rough, a young sea captain whom the governor had just recruited to his staff,[43] and George Graham, the newly arrived military clerk of works. To provide a measure of pomp and circumstance Hobson took four mounted police as well. We know much about the detail of this inspection visit, which began when the *Ranger* set out from the Bay of Islands in the last week of June 1840, mainly because, fifty-six years later, Rough gave a full and factual account of it, seemingly unblurred by the passage of time.

Captain David Rough.
AUCKLAND CITY LIBRARIES

After arriving in the inner gulf, the group stayed over the weekend at a bay in Waiheke island. On the Monday, Hobson went without delay to the Tamaki river to check on the site Mathew had recommended for the capital. Rough recorded that the governor became so frustrated by the 'intricate channel' which the *Ranger* had to follow in order to reach Wai Mokoia, that he promptly 'gave up all idea of selecting that part as the site of an important settlement'.[44] However, as Rough recalled the occasion, the time spent on the excursion to the Tamaki river had been by no means wasted.

> The Chiefs from the neighbouring tribes from Manukau and Waikato having been invited to meet the Governor, a tent was pitched on the beach of the first bay on the west side of the Tamaki [Karaka Bay?]; the Union Jack was hoisted and the treaty of Waitangi was spread out for signature on a table at which stood His Excellency, and behind him, mounted police in their showy uniform. Mr Fairburn [CMS missionary from Maraetai] interpreted and the rest of us attended as witnesses.

The sun shone brightly, and the gathering of natives, clad in their mats, the canoes drawn up on the white sandy beach, the cutter at anchor and the small group of Europeans beside the flag, in front of the fine trees on the slope of the hills behind, formed a very picturesque and striking scene of an event in the early history of the Colony.[45]

The signatories to the treaty were said to be 'Thames natives from Wharekawa',[46] almost certainly Ngati Paoa.

This treaty signing completed, the *Ranger* sailed westwards into the Waitemata harbour proper, to anchor overnight in the lee of The Sentinel. All was in readiness for Hobson to investigate the upper harbour, which he still favoured as the site of his settlement. That evening, while the cutter rode at anchor, Johnson the surgeon and David Rough spoke out in a way that introduced elements of the contingent and unforeseen into this exploration, elements that were completely to reshape the future. Rough recalled the exact occasion when, for the first time, Hobson's attention was drawn away from the upper harbour in the general direction of the site that the governor later decided to choose.

Dr Johnson, an accomplished artist, was the first to draw attention to the inviting appearance lower down [towards Freeman's Bay], and I offered to leave the cutter and remain behind to take soundings and examine the shore at low water before daylight the next morning.

Just as the sun rose, I climbed up the cliffs to where 'Ponsonby' now is, and beheld a vast expanse of undulating country, mostly covered with fern and Manuka shrub; several volcanic hills in sight, and, near the shore, valleys and ravines in which many species of native trees were growing, whilst the projecting cliffs and headlands were crowned with pohutukawa trees (Metrosideros Tomentosa). . . . But there was not a sign of cultivation nor of human habitation, the nearest native village being out of sight. The cutter had sailed up the harbour, and not even a canoe was to be seen on the spacious surface of the Waitemata.[47]

As author, I have no difficulty in visualising that part of the shoreline depicted by Rough, as he recalled his investigations of the Waitemata coastline to the east of today's Curran Street. In the later 1930s, I was one of a group of boys who, during the summer would dive off the small wooden jetty at St Mary's Bay for a dip.

Sometimes we would swim west to Shelly Beach, sometimes east to the Victoria Boating Club beside the gasworks, at that time the furthest point westward that the Harbour Board's reclamation had reached. As we swam past small launches and yachts, we could see at the water's edge, frittering cliffs of Waitemata sandstone fringed by pohutukawa trees much as Rough described them. Today, all has been transformed. Widespread reclamation, highways to the Harbour Bridge, piers and marinas, have filled almost the whole bay and erased the physical record of the past. Younger readers must use their historical imagination, therefore, to picture this area as Rough found it.

When the cutter returned later in the day to pick him up, Hobson had lost his enthusiasm for the upper harbour. Like Mathew before him, he had become 'dissatisfied with the narrowness of the channel' and the general appearance of the land.[48] According to Rough:

> He was therefore pleased at the report I was able to give of the anchorage and depth of water near the shore where I had taken soundings.
>
> In the afternoon, His Excellency, accompanied by Dr Johnson, Mr Clarke, and myself, landed and walked along the shore to what is now called Freeman's Bay. All we saw appeared favourable for the site of a settlement. Captain Hobson was much pleased, and without fixing on a particular spot for a site, we returned to the Bay of Islands.[49]

III

It is anomalous that the story of the settlement of Auckland in 1840 has customarily been written almost entirely from western records, and consequently from the perspective of the colonising power alone. Little is said of the tangata whenua of Tamaki, of those who had most to win and to lose from the takeover of the isthmus. Yet Maori were active participants in the settlement of Auckland, and their story must also be told. By recourse to the evidence recorded in the Native Land Court Minutebooks for the Orakei claim, 1866–68, it is possible to reconstruct many of the activities of Apihai Te Kawau's people as they resettled Tamaki in anticipation of the coming of the governor.

As we saw earlier, progressive resettlement of 'this side' — as Maori witnesses usually referred to Te Waitemata's shore — began as early as 1838. In spite of continuing feuds with Nga Puhi and Ngati Paoa, Ngati Whatua were sufficiently emboldened by the missionary-induced peace and the protective presence of Potatau Te Wherowhero to return to that shore. 'We were afraid to come here [Orakei] to reside permanently', Paora Tuhaere admitted, 'but not afraid to cultivate. We did not all come. We came in parties of about ten.'[50] Some whare were built beside the gardens and clearings, but only as temporary habitations. Until 1839 Ngati Whatua continued to have their main gardens beside the Manukau. That is where they also had their permanent settlements: in the Mangere area (particularly at Whakarongo pa), and at Onehunga, which they shared with Potatau and his Ngati Mahuta followers, who divided their time between that place and the Awhitu peninsula. By the time that Hobson came on the *Herald* in February 1840, Ngati Whatua had established gardens at Horotiu, Rangitoto-iti (lower Upland Road), Pourewa (land to the north of today's Purewa estuary), Okahu, and Whakatakataka (in the region of today's Paritai Drive).[51] But these recently developed gardens, as Paora Tuhaere conceded, 'were not extensive'.[52] The Horotiu lands, having been worked for three years, were about to be abandoned as they 'had been worn out'.[53] Workers had moved over the ridge to Waiariki — which modern readers may identify as the seaward-facing slopes to the east of Anzac Avenue. There they cleared the scrub to grow seed potatoes for use in the new gardens of Orakei, where many Ngati Whatua had moved to take up permanent residence in the spring of 1839. (Judge Fenton remarked that they also planted peach trees on the place where the Auckland Provincial Council chambers stood at the time of the court hearing.)[54] The recollections of Paora Tuhaere place the move to Waiariki in an exact time context.

We prepared a clearing at Waiariki when a man-o-war [*Herald*] came, the first vessel I saw here. Thirty of Te Taou were staying here at that time. The sailors came to get water; the old men turned them away and said they should not have water without paying. The sailors went on board, got swords and guns and took the water. . . . When the potatoes were in bloom that we had planted, the first emigrant ship came [*Anna Watson*, on 15 September 1840].[55]

Te Taou did not in fact use this crop grown at Waiariki as seed potatoes for their new gardens at Orakei as they had originally intended. Instead, when harvested, the potatoes were sold as provisions to the new government settlers.[56] This incident provides an interesting comment on the obvious readiness of the tribe to trade with the first immigrants.

During the half-year between the arrival of the *Herald* and the coming of the government party on the *Anna Watson*, Te Kawau felt sufficiently confident that the governor would establish his headquarters on the Waitemata, that he moved the bulk of his followers, except for some of Te Uringutu, there.[57] As Te Kawau worded it, 'I left . . . my other places, namely Mangere and Onehunga, when I came here to reside permanently where I was found by the Europeans'.[58] Upon making Okahu his main residence, he immediately set about fortifying it – 'in fear of Nga Puhi and Ngati Paoa', his nephew explained.[59] Shortly after, Tinana settled permanently at nearby Rangitoto-iti, where he also set up a pa.[60] Around both of these pa there were extensive cultivations. This return of Te Taou, Ngaoho and Te Uringutu to their old Waitemata lands was a measure of the growing confidence of their chiefs that the governor intended to settle in their midst. The series of government visits to the Waitemata harbour, and the appointment in June of Captain Symonds as deputy surveyor, a settler with a close knowledge of Tamaki and its people,[61] clearly foreshadowed what the administration intended to do. It seems likely, too, that during the winter of 1840, most of which Symonds probably spent on the Manukau, he would have revealed the governor's present intention to settle on Tamaki. There was no need for secrecy. Such a disclosure would have been a positive advantage for Hobson, for it would have prepared the way for Crown agents to begin to negotiate the purchase of the Tamaki lands.

IV

On 11 August, Hobson returned to the Bay of Islands on the *Ranger* to find, anchored in the bay at Kororareka, HM Brig *Britomart*, master Captain Owen Stanley – a talented officer and the brother of the even more gifted ecclesiastic, the Rev. A. P.

Stanley.[62] The *Britomart* had come from Port Jackson a week before to relieve the *Herald*, which had just returned from her lengthy signature-gathering cruise to the south.[63] The immediate business that Hobson had to turn to inevitably involved the *Britomart*, namely forestalling French designs, real or imagined, on Akaroa in the South Island.[64] But once Hobson had cleared up this 'threat' of French intervention, and the even more fanciful threat of a rival administration coming into being at Port Nicholson, he was able to turn his attention once more to the question that lay heavy on his mind. Where should he relocate his government headquarters? His second visit to the Waitemata had, at least, cleared up two vital issues. First, he no longer doubted that his settlement should be on the Tamaki isthmus. Second, although he obviously had not yet decided on a precise site, he had made up his mind that it would no longer be in the upper harbour, but somewhere on the southern shoreline of the Waitemata west of The Sentinel.

Rough recalled that 'Soon after our return, orders were given to make preparations for sending officers, workmen, and stores to the Waitemata. I was offered, and willingly accepted, the appointment of Harbour Master there.'[65] Stores were assembled, and workmen recruited both being brought in mainly from Sydney. John Stacpoole, the biographer of William Mason (newly appointed superintendent of public works) tells us that Mason 'evidently had a house prefabricated for himself and had timbers prepared for the store which was the first building to be erected in the new capital'.[66] The government set in train its own building programme, too; it contracted Henry Tucker, a Bay of Islands carpenter, to construct a number of frame houses for transhipment to the Waitemata. It also chartered the recently built (1838) 310-ton barque *Anna Watson*,[67] to move people and provisions to the new settlement. Rutherford records how 'Felton Mathew and George Cooper got in early with a request that they might be allowed to select lots in advance of the first sale, so that they could build their houses at once, before the winter'.[68] The governor agreed to concede this privilege to all officials, provided that, after the first auction of town lands, they paid the average price realised for similar lots at the sale.[69] In practice this concession was to enable even minor officials to buy some of the choicest sections in the new town at below the ruling rate. This right extended to officials was subsequently to arouse great resentment among the first non-government settlers in Auckland.[70]

Sarah Louise Mathew, 1805–90, writer of lively pioneer journals. AUCKLAND CITY LIBRARIES

Rough wrote that during August materials and provisions were loaded under his supervision onto the *Anna Watson*, whose captain, Thomas Stewart, Sarah Mathew tartly characterised as 'our John Bull Skipper . . . a little round fat oily man, very good natured, but not I think overwise'.[71] Some notion of the thoroughness of the preparations can be gathered from the inventory of what the superintendent of works placed on the barque: '33,000 shingles, 12,607 feet of scantling running measure, 4,700 superficial feet of planking, 8 tons of coal, 8 tons of bricks and 1 ton of iron. In addition', continues Stacpoole, 'there were 83 tons of luggage, tents, and tarpaulins and sundry goods which could not be measured.'[72]

When the *Anna Watson* departed the Bay on 13 September, it had as its cabin passengers seven officials, Mrs Mathew, and five private travellers. According to Rutherford's reconstruction of the passenger list, it also carried 'in steerage, 32 mechanics with their wives and children – 15 women and 28 children, of whom 19 were under 10 years of age'.[73] The great weight of responsibility for the enterprise, of course, fell on the officials. These were: Felton Mathew, surveyor-general; Dr John Johnson, colonial surgeon and health officer; Captain W. C. Symonds, police magistrate; David Rough, harbour-master; William Mason, superintendent of works; and Edward Marsh Williams (eldest son of Henry Williams), interpreter. (The list reminds us that New Zealand was a land of opportunity for young European men. Five of the seven officials were aged thirty or less; each of these younger men, save Symonds, who died young, lived on to the end of the century or beyond, winning eminence in his chosen calling.)[74] Sets of instructions that had been issued to each officer on 11 September made it clear that more was expected of them than their official title might have suggested. Williams, the least of the officers at the new settlement, was required to act, not only as interpreter, but as sub-protector of aborigines, postmaster, and clerk of the Bench as well. Clearly, the duties of those commissioned were to be multifarious.

That was no problem. It was only what officials in any colonial outpost expected in the course of duty. What was not, however, was a further set of instructions issued to Captain Symonds.

For not only was he directed to take possession of a portion of Tamaki land 'the same having been presented to Her Majesty by the Native Chiefs who owned it', but he was also empowered to act as referee should any dispute arise between departments.[75] This ruling galled the senior officials, who conscious as ever of seniority and status, immediately recognised that this power of arbitration granted to Symonds made him virtual leader of the expedition. The more senior of them were incensed that they had been passed over for an outsider who held no more than a temporary appointment and was, as they saw it, an officer junior to them in rank and status. Felton Mathew's response was to write to the governor asking that 'immediate steps' be taken to relieve him [Mathew] of his duties. 'I decline recognising that gentleman as an Official Referee or acknowledging him directly or indirectly, in any other capacity than as Police Magistrate.'[76] Dr Johnson tendered his resignation in similar terms. Both resignations were leaked to the press at Kororareka.[77] Hobson wrote to each officer telling him not to be a fool and to withdraw his resignation. He followed this up with the threat that, if this were not done, the governor would set about getting immediate replacements.[78] Both officials discreetly backed down. But Sarah Mathew's entry in her journal, for the day that the official party embarked, betrays the feelings of injured pride that lingered on.

> Our expedition is a great and important one and it is much to be regretted that, from the injudicious measures of our Governor, the various members of it are not so harmonious as could be wished. There are people who are so unfortunately injudicious as to contrive to damp the ardor and neutralise the exertions of their most efficient officers at the moment when the utmost exertion and the greatest enthusiasm would seem to be required.[79]

The following day she was rather more explicit though indicating that she was perhaps more reconciled to the leadership of Symonds than was her husband.

> Captain Symonds is considered in some light as the head of the expedition much to the disgust of the older and superior officers; he holds nominally the rank of Police Magistrate: he is a fine gentlemanly young man, who but for the mistrust and jealousy thrown around him

by his equivocal position, would be an agreeable companion, barring his attachment to cigars.[80]

Some historians have castigated Hobson for appointing Symonds as leader of the expedition.[81] On the contrary, his choice had much to commend it. As one who was outside the governor's suite, Symonds was well suited to arbitrate fairly on any quarrel between status-proud officials (whose rivalry had become notorious) over the demarcation of duties or the allocation of supplies. More importantly, the success of the expedition depended entirely on the readiness of Ngati Whatua to sell the site at Tamaki that the government wanted. Who better to ensure that than Symonds? He had been the main collector of signatures for the Treaty of Waitangi in the region, and his knowledge of, and standing with, Te Kawau's people was unequalled by any other European. Leadership of the party could only add to Symonds's mana, and encourage Ngati Whatua to sell.

Anticipating somewhat, we can see how in the weeks ahead Symonds was to justify Hobson's confidence in him. During the first weeks of the settlement at Auckland, a bizarre rumour surfaced that a Maori war-party was about to invade, sending (Logan Campbell observed ironically) 'a thrill of terrible excitement through the settlement'.[82] Symonds, continued Campbell, knew the rumour was ridiculous. 'He had been in the colony for some time, had been thrown a great deal amongst the Maoris and understood their language and had arrived at a pretty accurate estimate of their character.' He was aware that 'at the time... the one desire of the Maoris was to get the Pakehas to come and settle amongst them', not to harass them.[83] But aware of the alarm of his less experienced 'official colleagues', after a 'hearty laugh' in private, Symonds mounted nightly pickets to allay their fears. An unnecessary precaution. As he had predicted, there was no invasion. More will be said about this ' invasion crisis' in the next chapter.

About noon on Tuesday 15 September the *Anna Watson* dropped anchor off Freeman's Bay to find that there was another ship moored close to the North Shore that had been awaiting her arrival.[84] This was the 303-ton barque *Platina*[85] which had arrived in the Waitemata three days before, reputedly the first English merchant vessel ever to do so.[86] The *Platina*, which had been chartered by the New Zealand Company in February 1840 to carry provisions to Port Nicholson, had also carried, at the request of the British government, prefabricated materials and furniture for Governor Hobson's house. According to Sherrin and Wallace, the company directors had written to Colonel Wakefield, directing him 'to have the house carefully forwarded to any place Governor Hobson might indicate, although the directors plainly intimated that they expected Wellington to be chosen as the seat of government'.[87] When the *Platina* called at Hobart en route to New Zealand, however, the ship's master, Captain Michael Wycherley, collected revised instructions telling him, that after dropping the company's passengers at Port Nicholson, he was to carry on to the Waitemata to deliver the governor's house.[88] It is hardly to be wondered at that when the Port Nicholson settlers were told that the governor's house was to be erected elsewhere, they were 'bitterly disappointed' and chagrined.[89] Mrs Mathew's journal has its own smug observation that 'the Platina has brought several people from Port Nicholson who have resolved to settle here, being disgusted with that place'.[90]

On the following morning, wrote Rough, 'the Surveyor general and I examined the shore, and finding the deepest water near Point Britomart (afterwards so called) the *Anna Watson* was moved from Freeman's Bay, where we had first anchored, and moored abreast of what is now called Commercial Bay [close to the site of today's Ferry Buildings] selected by Mr Mathew as the best place on which to erect a building to hold the Government Stores.'[91] On such a minor consideration did the location of the centre of the new settlement, and therefore of modern Auckland, turn. Upon the arrival of the ship at its new anchorage, a party of Maori came by canoe from Orakei to see, as Rough expressed it, 'what we were about'.[92] Protracted bargaining over the sale of the selected Waitemata site then took place between Symonds assisted by E. M. Williams and Ngati Whatua chiefs led by Te Reweti. It appears that negotiations spread over two days (16–17 September) before agreement was reached on the provisional sale of a roughly wedge-shaped parcel of land, running from Opou (Cox's Creek) to the western side of the bay called Waitaramoa, and having the summit of Maungawhau as its apex.[93] By this agreement Ngati Whatua made a provisional cession of land to the government, who paid 'six pounds sterling, in earnest', until its final 'purchase may be effected' at a later date, when boundaries and consideration (money and goods) would be more precisely defined.[94]

By Friday 18 September all was ready for the formal establishment of the settlement. Two days before, Mason had rowed 'up the river' with sawyers to a point on the shore opposite to what he called 'the Ranger Rock'.[95] There he felled two young kauris to be used as flagstaffs.[96] (The extra spar was intended for Motu Korea where, Hobson had been informed, two Pakeha squatters – William Brown and Logan Campbell – would need to be dispossessed by a declaration of Crown ownership.) Mason towed these spars back to Commercial Bay, where mechanics on board the *Anna Watson* 'barked and prepared' them as flagstaffs.[97] On the Thursday, officers selected a spot in the vicinity of Commercial Bay where the royal flag would fly. They chose the headland at the east of the bay (soon to be called Point Britomart), 'a bold promontory', commented the Kororareka press, 'commanding a view of the entire harbour'.[98] Hobson had made it known to the party before it left Russell that he intended to honour his benefactor and patron, Lord Auckland, by calling this new government town Auckland. That is how it came about that the words 'Auckland' and '18th September 1840' were carved on the base of the staff on which the proclamation flag was to be flown. Sarah Mathew, the sole European woman to attend the ceremony, noted that on that memorable Friday, 'a beautiful morning seemed to smile on the auspicious circumstance of taking formal possession of . . . the land'.[99] At half-past noon the whole party, officials and a handful of sailors, came ashore and climbed the slope to the high point where the flagstaff had been raised in readiness. 'The Officers of the Government present on the occasion', reported the *New Zealand Advertiser*, 'consisted of the Police-Magistrate – the Colonial Surgeon – the Harbour-Master – the Superintendent of Works – the Sub-Protector of the Aborigines – and the Surveyor General and his Lady.'[100]

The ceremony began at one o'clock when Captain Symonds, attended by his interpreter Williams, read, in the presence of a group of Ngati Whatua chiefs, the agreement that had been arrived at on the previous day. A minor contretemps then ensued. 'At this stage of the business', wrote Mrs Mathew, the principal chief[101] stepped forward and in a long vehement harangue seemed to be making very strong objections to admitting the Pakehas at all among them; though on the previous day all had been arranged to his satisfaction. He said that a Pakeha who had resided long among them told him that the Queen of England would take all their land from them, and that they should then have none to live on. In reply he was told through the interpreter that this was false and that he should not believe what was said by bad white men who were only deceiving them for their own purposes; but that the governor would come to see that neither Pakeha nor Mauris [*sic*] were wronged and that all he or his Officers promised them should be strictly performed. After some further discussion about the boundaries, it was at length decided, and the three principal chiefs signed the agreement or 'puka-puka', as they call all writings,[102] which was also signed by the Police Magistrate and one or two other Government officers.[103]

Local historians have tended to regard this eleventh-hour protest made by the chiefs as some sort of amusing 'native' charade, deserving mention only to entertain readers but certainly not warranting serious explanation.[104] Yet that leaves us with a version of events which becomes almost a caricature. For this 'long vehement harangue' really signified a great deal to the Maori negotiators. Not that the Ngati Whatua contemplated reneging on their former promise to give land to the governor to encourage him to live among them. The trade and protection that the governor would bring to Tamaki remained as alluring as ever to the tribe. But new misgivings had arisen. One only was mentioned by Mrs Mathew: the alarm stirred up by some unnamed Pakeha 'that the Queen of England would take *all* [italics mine] their land from them'. We need not doubt that Ngati Whatua were genuinely alarmed. For on one principle the tribe was immovable, both then, and in the years to come – that the land sloping northwards down to the sea from the ridge along which today's Remuera Road runs, must remain untouchable, inalienable. In his reminiscences Logan Campbell gave an account of how he had tried, four months earlier, to buy some of the 'Remuera slopes stretching down to Orakei Bay'. To this request the Ngati Whatua chiefs had 'unhesitatingly given . . . a very decided and prompt "Kahore" (No)'.[105] This territory was re-garded as part of the ancestral Orakei land which the tribe was determined to hold on to, not only for its established cultivations, but as a perpetual trust, a nest egg to be kept for the generations to come.[106] This show of dissent by Maori at Point Britomart over the terms of a land sale that Symonds had imagined had been quite settled the day before had a further significance. The Waitangi Tribunal asserted in 1997 that 'impassioned declamation' was a 'standard oratorical tool' of the traditional Maori to solicit 'a clear position on a point in issue. . . . The Maori way is to clear the air' by raising what is (to them) an unacceptable point of view, 'in order to compel a forthright denial'.[107] It was also, I believe, intended to be a warning shot across the bows of the Crown party, an intimation that this transaction was not to be misconstrued. A willingness to sell was not to be regarded as the acquiscence of a subordinate party. Rather was it a token of goodwill as Maori entered a relationship conferring benefits and obligations on both races. It has recently been persuasively argued that, for some Maori groups in the 1840s, deeds of sale were often an extension of (and possibly were regarded in some cases as being more important than) their signing of the Treaty of Waitangi itself.[108] It is significant that the two sets of negotiators, both for the treaty signing at Manukau on 20 March and for the land sale at Point Britomart on 18 September, were identical: Symonds for the Crown; and Te Reweti, Te Kawau and Tinana for Ngati Whatua. That those two occasions should have been conjoined in the minds of both parties was inevitable. In his abrasive speech made before agreeing to the provisional sale of Auckland, was not Reweti recalling to the minds of those present the notion of a compact expected to benefit both parties that Ngati Whatua leaders believed they had entered into with Symonds when signing the treaty seven months before?

Once the Ngati Whatua chiefs had signed the provisional deed of sale on 18 September, the 'ceremony of taking formal possession in the name of Her Majesty was duly performed' at Point Britomart.[109] Captain Rough ran up the flag of St George amidst the cheers of bystanders. This was immediately followed, first by a royal salute of twenty-one guns from the *Anna Watson*, and then a salute of fifteen guns from the *Platina*. At this juncture, according to the proudly patriotic Sarah Mathew, 'Her Majesty's health was . . . most rapturously drunk' by those at the foot of the flagstaff, the toast being acclaimed by three-times-three hearty cheers.[110] To these cheers, the crew aboard the *Anna Watson* gave reply (according to the Kororareka Correspondent of the *New Zealand Advertiser*) by firing a salute of seven guns 'in honour of His Excellency the Lieutenant Governor Hobson'. This was responded to by 'three hearty cheers and one cheer more from those on shore'.[111] These 'cheers long and loud repeated from the ships', wrote Mrs Mathew, were to 'the very evident delight of the Natives of whom nearly 100 had assembled round us. A few of the Rangatiras or chiefs were given wine to drink the Queen's health.'[112] When the prolonged cheering came to an end, the official party returned to the *Anna Watson* for a celebratory luncheon.

The afternoon's celebrations took the form of a regatta. 'The gentlemen', wrote Mrs Mathew, 'got up a boat race among themselves, another for the sailors, and a canoe race for the natives, which all came off with great éclat.'[113] The surveyor general's five-oared gig raced against the six-oared captain's gig from the *Anna Watson*, 'both pulled in excellent style by amateurs', it was reported. There was also a contest for a purse of £5 between the whaleboats of the captain and the harbour master. Rough's team won the purse. There seems to have been no prize for the winner of the race between the two large canoes paddled by Maori. But according to Mrs Mathew: 'the Natives were each given half a pound of Tobacco, with which they seemed much delighted.' She closed her journal entry for the day with the observation that 'In the evening Captain Rough gave us a few songs to the accompaniment of his guitar, but he had shouted himself somewhat hoarse, in honour of her Majesty in the morning.'[114]

V

A month passed before Hobson was free to come to the Waitemata to see the early development of the settlement that he had done so much to bring into being. There was much afoot at the time in the Bay of Islands. He had to await the arrival on 16 September of HM Corvette *Favorite*, which was due to replace the *Britomart* as the Royal Navy vessel plying New Zealand waters. Then there was a further week to wait for the *Britomart* itself, which returned from a southern cruise bearing reassuring reports of the dutiful submission to Her Majesty of the French settlers at Akaroa and of the New Zealand Company settlers at Port Nicholson.[115] The way was then clear for Hobson to come to Auckland to formalise his purchase of land from Ngati Whatua and to inspect the new government settlement. On 15 October he left the Bay on the *Favorite*, following upon the *Britomart*, which had left some four days before bearing the colonial secretary, Shortland, and George Clarke, protector of the aborigines. On the eve of his departure, the governor sent a despatch to his secretary of state in London giving his reasons for having decided to make Auckland on the Waitemata the future capital of the colony. There was a measure of special pleading in the case he made, a significant enclosure in the despatch being Shortland's report on Port Nicholson which, as we have seen, had been noticeably faint in its praise of that settlement. Hobson wrote:

> I . . . further do myself the honour to acquaint your Lordship, that, after mature consideration, I have decided upon forming the seat of government, on the south shore of the Waitemata, in the district of the Thames.
>
> In the choice I have thus made, I have been influenced by a combination of circumstances: 1st, by its central position; 2ndly, by the great facility of internal water communication by the Kaipara and its branches to the northward, and the Manakou and Waikato to the southward; 3rdly, from the facility and safety of its port, and the proximity of several smaller ports abounding with the most valuable timber; and finally, by the fertility of the soil, which is stated by people capable of appreciating it, to be available for every agricultural purpose; the richest and most valuable land in the northern island being concentrated within a radius of 50 miles.
>
> The purchase of this district has not yet been completed, but the chief protector of aborigines is at present engaged in making preliminary arrangements for that purpose, & I intend visiting the Waitemata in a few days, when I hope to obtain the possession of the whole tract of country around[116]

It would appear that George Clarke had already been sent on ahead in the *Britomart* for the precise purpose of confirming the provisional purchase of Ngati Whatua land that Symonds had made a month before. It should be noted that Clarke, since midyear, had combined in his person the seemingly antagonistic posts of chief land purchase officer for the Crown, and protector of the aborigines. He had been aware of a potential conflict of interest from the outset. How, he asked himself and others, was a single person to balance his obligation to purchase land cheaply for the Crown against his bounden duty to safeguard Maori from exploitation?[117] Completing the purchase of land in Auckland, however, did not seem to have troubled his conscience unduly. He and Symonds were able to settle that matter with the Ngati Whatua chiefs by the time Hobson arrived in Auckland.

Mrs Mathew's journal for Saturday 17 October has this to say about the coming of the governor: 'Today arrived the *Favorite* with His Excellency the Governor on board. . . . The Frigate[118] looked beautiful at anchor off the Flag Staff Point and with H.M. Brig *Britomart*, which has been here for some days, and a few small craft the Harbour looked quite respectable.'[119] On the following afternoon Hobson made a leisurely inspection of the settlement of tents and raupo whare which provided temporary housing for officials and workmen, expressed his satisfaction with the locality which the surveyor general had chosen,[120] and indeed with all the work that had been done up to date.[121]

On Tuesday 20 October, the deed of sale for the purchase of Auckland was executed. Proceedings began with the governor leading the official party up the foot-track that had been cleared through the fern from the tidal shoreline of Store Bay to the whare occupied by Captain Symonds. Symonds (according to an early visitor) 'had perched himself on a cliff point, which commanded a view of the whole harbour',[122] having chosen to separate himself from the other officials who decided to live in Waiariki, or Official Bay, as it was becoming known. The only other occupant of Symonds's house, which served as the magistrate's office by day and as a home by night, was the interpreter, Edward Meurant.[123] George Clarke wrote of the final transaction, which took place in the whare, in these terms:

> On the 20th the Chiefs Te Kawau, Tinana, and others, met at the house of Captain Symonds, where, to the satisfaction of all parties, we finally adjusted the considerations for the land, the deed of conveyance being read to the chiefs in the presence of His Excellency the Governor, the officers of the "Favorite", and of several of the Civil Department.[124]

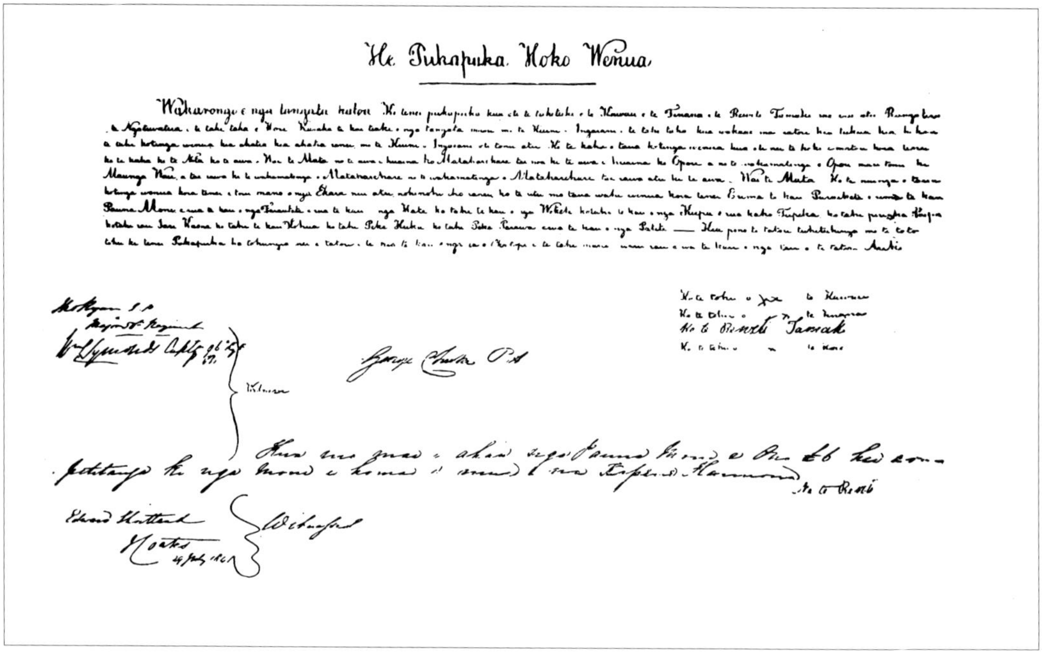
He Pukapuka Hoko Wenua

Facsimile of the original Deed of Purchase of the site of the City of Auckland. English translation opposite.

Because the land conveyed on this occasion has since developed into today's Auckland's Central Business District and its adjoining densely settled inner suburbs, incontestably the most valuable single block of real estate in New Zealand, the terms of the deed of sale deserve to be recited in full.

The shape of the land thus sold could be likened to a wedge of pie with a serrated edge, or to a triangle whose base was the irregular southern coastline of the Waitemata harbour with Maungawhau (Mount Eden) forming the apex. The eastern boundary of the block was Mataharehare. In this deed Mataharehare is called a stream.[126] But in most records that name is given to the place where the stream – more properly called Te Rua-reo-reo (which can still be seen today flowing through a council reserve) – met the beach on the western end of the bay called Waitaramoa. It seems that the extremity (waka matenga) of Te Rua-reo-reo from which the survey line ran to Maungawhau would have been located near today's Newmarket railway station. The location of Mataharehare is relatively easy to identify. Close to the original spot would be the modern roundabout which stands at the intersection of Brighton Road, Ayr Street and Shore

---

TRANSLATION

Listen all people to this Book written by Kawau, Tinana, Reweti Tamaki and other Chiefs of the (tribe) Ngatiwhatua on the one side by George Clarke Protector of the Aborigines for the Queen of England on the other side they have consented to give up to sell a portion of land to the Queen of England for ever and ever (for whatever purposes Her Majesty may deem right). The Boundary of the said piece of land we have now sold is this—The Boundary to the North is the River of the Waitemata from the River named Mataharehare¹ reaching the River called Opou² and from the extremity of Opou² in a straight line to Maunga Wau³ up to the rise or extremity of Mataharehare¹ and from the extremity of Mataharehare¹ up to the River of Waitemata the extent of this piece of land is this Three Thousand acres more or less. The payment for the said Land is this Fifty Blankets Fifty Pounds of Money Twenty trousers Twenty shirts Ten waistcoats Ten caps Four Casks of Tobacco One box of pipes One hundred yards of gown pieces Ten iron pots One bag of sugar One bag of Flour Twenty Hatchets. This writing with our signatures in this book is true signed by us on the Twentieth day of October in the Year One Thousand Eight Hundred and Forty of our Lord.

(Signed) *G. Clarke, P.A.*

(Signed *The Mark of* ✕ *Kawau*   *Ko Te Reweti Tamaki*
         The Mark of ✕ *Tinana*   *The Mark of* ✕ *Horo*

Witnesses:—

   Thomas Ryan, J.P., Major, 50th Regt.
   Wm. C. Symonds, P.M., Capt., 96th Regt.

I have received Six Pounds in Money (£6) in addition to the money (named above) from Captain Symonds.

(Signed) *Na Te Reweti*

Witnesses:—.

   Edward Shortland
   J. Coates

29th July, 1841

¹Mataharehare, Bay at the foot of Brighton Road, Hobson Bay.
²Opou, Cox's Creek. ³Maunga Wau, Mount Eden.

Road. The western extremity of the block, a few kilometres up the harbour, is the mouth of the stream, which the deed refers to as Opou, but which is more commonly referred to nowadays as Cox's Creek. The western boundary of the block moved inland from that point up the irregular course of the Opou stream for about a kilometre. The point of confluence where a number of small tributaries run into Opou stream in today's Grey Lynn Park is presumably 'the extremity' mentioned in the deed at which the western boundary became the surveyed line to Maungawhau.

Two points about this deed are worthy of note. First, the Maori vendors obviously could not have envisaged that the northern boundary of the block, the shoreline which ran roughly east to west from Mataharehare to Opou, would be transformed to a revolutionary extent by future reclamation. For them that boundary of the land which they sold was the shoreline *as it then existed*. Nor had Maori at the time of the sale any intention of alienating any portion of the harbour floor. The Crown has implicitly recognised this Maori understanding of the transaction, by awarding compensation in the 1990s to Ngati Whatua consequent upon its sale of reclaimed land surrounding the Auckland railway station.

Secondly, some comment should be made on the construction which the Waitangi Tribunal put upon this transaction of 20 October 1840. The Tribunal suggested in its 1987 Orakei Report (*Wai* 9) that the transaction should not be regarded as a 'simple conveyance'. Rather was it, in the Tribunal's view, like a number of land sales of that period, 'a treaty of cession of tribal lands', in which 'the intent' of Ngati Whatua was to share the land, not completely to alienate it. The Tribunal attempted to justify this view by basing it on 'the oral tradition recording a people's understanding' of such agreements.[127] It is surely evident that however appropriate this Tribunal interpretation may have been when applied to many deeds of conveyance, it cannot be applied to this sale of central Auckland. First, it flies in the face of the great weight of evidence presented at the Native Land Court hearing for Orakei in 1868. The point was repeatedly made that the tribe was prepared to sacrifice ownership of this particular piece of land if that would serve to induce the governor to settle beside the Waitemata.[128] Second, as I have shown, such was the numerical and military weakness of the tribe after the musket wars, that surrendering 3000 acres of land, which they neither used nor needed, seemed to Ngati Whatua at that time a small price to pay for the solid benefits of security and trade.

Indeed, during the signing of the deed of sale in Symonds's whare, the chiefs promised, in Clarke's words, 'to sell a still larger tract of country when the Governor should finally reside among them'.[129] Hobson was so taken by this readiness to sell that, before the day was out, he wrote an official letter to Clarke, in which he commissioned him 'to treat with the Ngatiwhatua tribe, on behalf of Her Majesty the Queen, for the possession of the largest portions of their territory, if possible in a continuous section.'[130] After reminding Clarke of the need to make ample provision for Native reserves, Hobson authorised him to pay, in money or in goods, an amount that was 'equitable both for the Government and the Natives'. To enable Clarke to go ahead with these purchases, Hobson arranged for him to remain in Auckland, and asked him to 'submit to me as soon as possible an account of your proceedings'.[131]

During his remaining days in Auckland Hobson made a crossing of the isthmus to the Manukau by which, according to Mrs Mathew, he 'seemed much fatigued'.[132] He also chose where he wished the prefabricated Goverrnment House to be erected within an enclosure of fifteen acres. He urged that the building of the governor's house should proceed 'with all speed'.[133] He also indicated that he hoped to come down permanently, early in the new year, just as soon as the house was sufficiently close to completion as to accommodate him and his family in comfort. On 28 October he returned to Russell on the *Ranger*.

A week or so later Clarke reported to the governor on his land-buying activities in Waitemata and Manukau. 'I have lost no favorable opportunity', he wrote, 'of getting the outlines of the country proposed as an addition to that already paid for, which I am happy to say is so far adjusted as to fully warrant the survey commencing immediately. I have not been able to make purchases to the extent desired in His Excellency's instructions, but am in treaty for a considerable extent of land beyond that already purchased.'[134] Heartened by this report and elated by his recent satisfactory visit to Waitemata, Hobson thought the time was ripe to report on what had been achieved to his Minister of State. 'I have lately returned from a visit to the Waitemata', he wrote,

> where I found the officers of Government, and the mechanics and labourers under their orders, proceeding with the necessary works for establishing the town which I contemplate being the future seat of government, and which I purpose distinguishing by the name of 'Auckland'.
>
> I beg leave to call your Lordship's attention to the necessity for directing emigration to the proposed capital. The country around it is, as I have already reported, decidedly the best in New Zealand; and although from the deficiency of surveyors I am not in a condition to sell land at the moment, yet having already purchased from the natives a tract of land computed at 30,000 acres, and having engaged nearly as much more, I shall be enabled to do so within six months to an extent sufficient to meet any demand that is likely to arise from immigration.[135]

When the facts and opinions expressed in this despatch became known to the principals of the New Zealand Company in London and to the settlers of Port Nicholson, both groups were incensed. Once again Hobson had cited Shortland's tenden-tious report disparaging Wellington, speaking of 'the tremendous violence of the prevailing winds', using such 'extraordinary misrepresentations', wrote E. J. Wakefield, in order to highlight the specious advantages of this new 'proclamation capital' of Auckland.[136] But even more objectionable had been Hobson's request that the Colonial Office use its influence to divert emigrants – the lifeblood of any new settlement – to Auckland where there was a great dearth of workmen. This opened an old wound. Already, once it became known that the capital was to be established on the Waitemata, some New Zealand Company settlers with an eye to the main chance had begun to shift north to Auckland, capitalists to invest in town land, artisans to secure work. E. J. Wakefield recounted in detail how this new quarrel with the governor broke out. On 5 November 1840, after spending eleven days in Auckland, the *Favorite* arrived at Port Nicholson. It did not bear Hobson to make his long overdue and long-promised visit to Wellington, for he 'with his suite and hangers-on', remarked Wakefield sourly, had remained in 'his metropolis'. But it did bring a magistrate bearing a notice from the official Gazette, which he placed that same day, in the local paper, the *New Zealand Gazette and Britannia Spectator.*[137]

GOVERNMENT NOTICE

Police Office, Port Nicholson,

November 5, 1840.

The undermentioned Mechanics will be engaged for the service of the Government at Auckland, at the terms stated, viz.:–Four carpenters, first rate, 9s. per diem; six carpenters, second rate, 8s. per diem; six pairs of sawyers, 8s.6d. per diem; three bricklayers, 7s.6d. per diem,; two stone masons 7s.6d. per diem. Sixpence per day extra if they find themselves with provisions. The mechanics will be allowed one quarter of an acre of land to reside on whilst in the service of Government, at a peppercorn rent. Provisions will be supplied at cost price; the wages to commence on arrival at Auckland; the engagement to be for six or twelve months, at the option of the Lieutenant-Governor.

Michael Murphy,

Chief Police Magistrate.[138]

This was the last straw. The attempt by the governor to entice to his 'nominal metropolis',[139] labour brought out by the

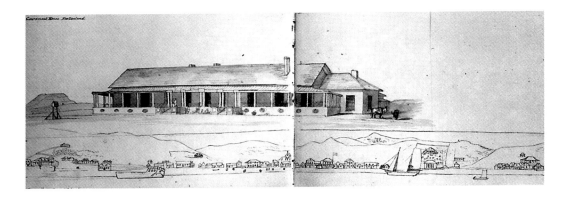

New Zealand Company to Port Nicholson at great expense, served only to inflame, as Bell, secretary of the company, expressed it, the already existing 'evil tendencies' towards rivalry, between the 'proclamation town [Auckland] and the towns formed by emigration [those of the New Zealand Company]'.[140] Nor were the company settlers mollified by Hobson's defence that he had advertised for workmen throughout the whole colony without any special reference to Port Nicholson.[141] They remained unconvinced. He was no better than an unprincipled sea captain who, deficient of crew, sought to lure sailors from other vessels with extravagant promises. They nicknamed him 'Captain Crimp'.[142] The name stuck till the day Hobson died.

First Government House, Auckland, 1844? Pencil and sepia wash by Edward Ashworth. Below this is a rough sketch of 'Korarika'. ALEXANDER TURNBULL LIBRARY

A Chronicle of Events

1840

September:

13   *Anna Watson* leaves Russell with official party; *Platina* arrives in Waitemata.
15   Arrival in Waitemata of *Anna Watson*. Mathew and Rough select Store Bay (later called Commercial Bay) as landing place of settlement.
17   Negotiations take place with Ngati Whatua chiefs for the provisional purchase of the 3000-acre block of land that is to become 'Auckland', referred to on the final deed of sale as 'Mataharehare, Opou, and W[h]au'.
18   Proclamation of Crown settlement of Auckland.
19   Erection of government store begins.
21   Flagpole put up on Motukorea (Brown's Island).
24   Government store completed.
25   *Platina* and *Anna Watson* begin to discharge their cases of cargo.

October:

3   Prefabricated parts of Government House, and its furniture now landed.
9   Commissioners appointed in Sydney to investigate pre-Treaty land purchases in New Zealand: 'The Old Land Claims'.
13   HM Brig *Britomart* arrives with Shortland (colonial secretary) on board.
17   Hobson arrives on HM Corvette *Favorite* for a twelve-day inspection visit of Auckland, during which he sanctions choice of sites of government offices and military barracks that Mathew has provisionally selected.
20   Signing by Ngati Whatua chiefs of final deed of sale for Auckland.
28   Hobson departs for Bay of Islands on the *Ranger*.

November:

14   Mathew completes the survey of Auckland and submits to Hobson his plan of the town, part of which is to be put up for auction.

27   Arrival of the *Diana* with soldiers of 80th Regiment who are to build a fort and barracks on Point Britomart.

December:

?   Arrival of *Chelydra*, under its master Captain David Smale.
21   Arrival of Logan Campbell in Auckland.

1841

January:

6   Panic in Auckland over the false rumour of a threatened Ngati Paoa invasion of the settlement.
c.12   Hobson begins a three-week inspection visit of Auckland.

February:

3   Hobson returns to Bay of Islands.
16   Hobson writes to governor of NSW announcing the removal of the seat of government to Auckland.
26   Arrival in Waitemata of *Chelydra* (chartered by Hobson), bearing 30 troops and 21 mechanics from Port Nicholson.

March:

5   Postponement announced of the Crown auction of Auckland town sections previously advertised for 12 March.
13   Lt-Gov. Hobson makes his official landing in Auckland.

April:

9   Crown auction of town allotments takes place.

May:

3   New Zealand proclaimed a full colony independent of NSW with Hobson appointed as a full governor.

CHAPTER XI

The Founding of Auckland

I

Hobson had charged the advance party sent to the Waitemata in mid-September 1840 with three main tasks. The most important of these he entrusted to his new 'Deputy Governor' Symonds: he asked him to secure from Ngati Whatua an indefeasible title to the land on which the government settlement was to stand. Second, the surveyor-general, Felton Mathew, was responsible for selecting a part of the shoreline, behind which this government settlement would be placed.[1] Finally, Mathew (again) was instructed to make haste in surveying the site of a town in readiness for settlers, so that Auckland could become a capital in fact as well as in name.

As we have seen, the first objective was achieved, although only after some unexpected last-minute hesitation, when Ngati Whatua agreed to sell a substantial block of land on the northern shore of the isthmus near the harbour entrance. This enabled Mathew to nominate, with all speed, the bay at the mouth of the Horotiu as his port. He was much influenced in this choice by soundings carried out by harbour master Rough; these indicated that some of the deepest water in the harbour lay off the point of land at the eastern side of the bay (Point Britomart). Realising the third objective, however, namely a prompt survey of the town area in order to enable private settlers to purchase allotments was to prove a much taller order.

The 'three thousand acres more or less' that Ngati Whatua sold to the Crown in 1840 was part of a desolate and deserted landscape providing few resources to assist in the development of a town. And little material help could be expected from a parsimonious home government. Consider this despatch which Lord John Russell sent to Hobson just at the time that the infant capital was beginning to take its first steps. He warned that:

> Frugality is one of the indispensable bases of all good government. . . . The governor of an infant colony should aim at nothing beyond the decencies of a private and moderate establishment. . . . At the commencement, and for some years afterwards, we must be content with what is useful, plain, and solid, remitting to a future day what is merely ornamental. On this principle every work should be undertaken, the charge of which is defrayed from the public revenue; and even so, the utmost possible parsimony will still be inadequate to secure the means of attaining many objects highly conducive to the general good.[2]

These principles the Colonial Office reiterated in the following year, having wearied of Hobson's appeals for more soldiers, more officials, and more survey staff. 'I take this opportunity', wrote Lord John Russell in reply,[3] 'of impressing upon you the necessity of observing a strict economy in the expenditure of your Government; and of informing you that unless the expenditure is kept within moderate bounds, it will not receive the sanction of Her Majesty's Government.' Obviously Auckland's development was to be financed on a shoestring.[4]

II

European Auckland had its beginnings in the bay chosen by Mathew, which lay at the mouth of the Horotiu. On the day following the hoisting of the flag on Point Britomart, workers set about erecting the government store near the shoreline of this bay, which they called Store Bay. When the surveyor-general came to draw up the town plan, however, he gave it the loftier name of Commercial Bay. Appropriately so, for here he envisaged that the port and the mercantile area would be permanently located. And time was to prove him right.

The Horotiu itself was a freshwater stream fed by a collection of small tributaries flowing down steep gullies most of which merged in that relatively low-lying area which modern Aucklanders associate with the civic buildings and Aotea Square. From this point of confluence, the Horotiu flowed seawards down the west side of today's Queen Street, connecting with the shoreline, which was then approximately where Swanson Street is now. In 1840, the tidal beach ran from there in an easterly direction more or less along the line of modern Fort Street – known in pioneer days as Fore Street, an abbreviation of Foreshore Street – before connecting with the base of Point Britomart. In its lower reaches the Horotiu became transformed into what Logan Campbell described, in old age, as 'an unpassable flax swamp',[5] which, fringed by toi-toi and the occasional pohutukawa, discharged oozily into Commercial Bay.[6]

Store (later Commercial) Bay in December 1840; government store in foreground, tents and breakwind huts behind.
CAMPBELL PAPERS,
AUCKLAND MUSEUM
LIBRARY

Up from the Horotiu valley, the ridges and the land beyond lay before the official party as a wilderness of dun-green fern, manuka scrub and tupakihi. (In this mild moist climate, even where cleared cultivations had once been, fern and scrub were known to grow rampantly within three or four years to a height of six feet or more.)[7] Campbell recalled that, when he first landed on the tidal beach at Commercial Bay in December 1840, there was 'a sea of fern stretching as far as the eye could reach'.[8] Sarah Mathew, who, soon after settling at Official Bay, took 'a long and beautiful walk . . . [along] a native path' as far as Maungakiekie, spoke of the vegetation of the isthmus which she encountered as akin to a 'jungle'. She referred to valleys and glens 'almost impenetrable from the luxuriant vegetation, dwarf trees or shrubs and tangled fern with interlaced vines and creepers'.[9] Yet despite all this growth, there was no usable building timber within easy reach of the town. That, and firewood in quantity, had to be obtained from more distant parts.[10]

The ubiquitous scrub, which proved such an obstacle to Mrs Mathew during her excursion, was an even greater nuisance to the party led by her husband as he worked day by day surveying the block bought from Ngati Whatua. He told the governor that 'the dense covering of Fern and Underwood, and in many cases the impenetrable jungle with which the country is clothed' meant that 'every section line must be cleared before it can be measured'.[11] Obviously, 'burning off' was the quickest way to get rid of the scrub. But to do this was risky. George Graham, the clerk of works attached to the army, recounted how, early in October 1840, manuka fired for that purpose by Mathew's assistants near Mount Eden quickly raged out of hand and swept towards the harbour, finally racing down the valley of the Horotiu.[12] Mrs Mathew, who at that time was still living aboard the *Anna Watson* described the scrub fire as she viewed it from the ship's deck:

> Large columns of smoke obscured the shore, and I could make out nothing till the return of the [survey] party to the ship in the evening when I found that the fires on the hills to clear away the Fern and Scrub for the Survey had, from the change of wind, taken the direction towards the bay, and rushed down the little valley with such rapidity, that no efforts could arrest its progress, and it was with the greatest difficulty that the Store with its valuable contents was saved.[13]

The government store in Commercial Bay spoken of here was the first wooden building to be built by Europeans in Auckland. On 24 September 1840, the day following its completion, workmen began filling it with cases of cargo ferried ashore from the two barques. That done, the building of Auckland itself could begin. Not the provision of housing for officials and the government workmen; they, for the foreseeable future, regardless of rank, were to be accommodated in tents. Priority was given to the construction of government offices.

Felton Mathew sited these offices up on the ridge to the east of Horotiu, roughly in the area of today's lower Princes Street. This encouraged the officials to choose as their place of residence nearby Waiariki, which as a result became known as Official Bay. It was a picturesque spot. 'Our tents were pitched . . . in a beautiful wooded bay', recalled Captain Rough, 'amongst the rich evergreen trees then growing on the slopes, and at that spring season adorned with beautiful white clematis. A terrace, now Jermyn Street [near where modern Anzac Avenue runs today] was formed in front of the tents, commanding a charming view of the harbour and picturesque islands beyond.'[14] Sarah Mathew was equally enthusiastic: 'The landscape is really a gem', she wrote.[15] Officials had the exclusive right to live in this most favoured of locations. In contrast, private settlers who arrived before the inaugural Crown auction were compelled to squat in tents or shanties at Commercial Bay, or in the lower part of today's Shortland Street.[16] In retaliation for not being allowed to settle themselves temporarily at Waiariki, these newcomers gave to Official Bay the derisory nickname of 'Exclusion Bay'.

Princes Street, c. 1843.
Pen and wash drawing by
Edward Ashworth.
AUCKLAND CITY ART
GALLERY

271

The government mechanics, most of whom had been recruited in Sydney before coming to Auckland, were directed to pitch their tents in the much less salubrious bay that adjoined Waiariki.[17] This spot, which Mathew envisaged as the permanent settlement for government artisans, quickly acquired the workaday name of Mechanics' Bay.[18] The mechanics – carpenters, pit-sawyers, masons, and the like – pitched their tents there in a low-lying area near the beach, which soon became littered with bricks, logs and other materials of trade. Nearby were a sawpit and a brickyard. In defiance of their mean surroundings, or perhaps in an old-world quest for privacy, some of the mechanics enclosed their tiny allotments with small wooden fences.[19]

Within a day or two of the mechanics and officials having pitched their tents, Ngati Whatua came on a visit from Orakei, offering to put up native whare in exchange for cheap items of trade, such as blankets, calico goods and tobacco.[20] Both mechanics and officials eagerly agreed, and were soon using these Maori houses either to replace their tents, or to provide additional accommodation. The autobiography of Mrs Mathew leaves us in no doubt that her whare added much to her comfort and convenience in these early months.

> [A]fter a time we got Natives to build us a regular Native house of two rooms, with a roof of Palm leaves and Rapoo, or reed thatch over it; this was really a much more comfortable habitation than the tent, especially in wet or windy weather.[21] The doors and window frames, we bought from an enterprising carpenter who made these things for sale, and for glass we had oiled calico, which kept out the rain and gave us light enough within, tho' of course no view.[22]

These heavily thatched double-lined huts were not only more comfortable than tents; but, as Stacpoole reminds us, were also 'far warmer than the unlined weatherboard houses which were to follow'.[23] Mrs Mathew was so satisfied with her whare that she continued to occupy it well into 1842 in spite of European-style housing having become available in the meantime.[24]

William Mason, as superintendent of public works, oversaw the construction of the government offices. Some of his building supplies had been prefabricated in the Bay of Islands, while the superstructure of the Government House itself had been pre-

Mechanics' Bay, Auckland,
1843? Pencil sketch by
Edward Ashworth.
ALEXANDER TURNBULL
LIBRARY

fabricated in London. But for his remaining material Mason had to rely on the local region. He reported that his first job on arrival was to discover supplies of suitable sand, seashells for lime, clay for bricks, and timber for building.[25] By the end of the month, he was able to reassure the governor that he had abundant supplies of sand and lime, and had also been successful in selecting 'a site for a Brick yard combining all the advantages that could possibly be expected in one spot'.[26] Further, he had succeeded in getting logs that were already being pit-sawn on the foreshores of Mechanics' Bay and Freeman's Bay.[27] (Freeman's Bay became popularly known in Hobson's time, so Logan Campbell told his children many years later, as 'Waipiro Bay'. 'For there', Campbell explained, 'the sawyers lived and caroused and got periodically drunk with such regularity that Waipiro Bay was too appropriate a name for it not to go by – I must translate Waipiro for you – literally stinking water, but the word [was] used by the Natives to designate spirits.')[28]

In spite of the ingenuity shown by Mason in obtaining local building materials, construction of public buildings was to be subject to discouraging delay. The building of the governor's house comes particularly to mind. Hobson insisted that, as with all government offices, construction must not begin until he had come to Auckland and personally approved of the site which

273

Mathew had chosen – in this case where Old Government House stands today. And usually there was much preparatory clearing to be done. Valuable time, writes Stacpoole, was also taken up by 'the employment of men . . . in cutting a road to Government House and clearing the ridges for the Surveyor General'.[29]

III

It is fitting that we should now turn to the construction carried out by the military, since the most considerable public buildings in Auckland in the twenty-four years that it was the capital[30] were the military barracks which, at their greatest extent, provided accommodation for nearly a thousand men.[31]

Hobson deliberately delayed sending the military to the Waitemata. His policy was to keep troops of the 80th Regiment stationed beside him at the Bay of Islands as long as possible, enabling him to send quickly to any trouble spot a detachment of soldiers under a junior officer. Further, as with the civil administration so with the military, the regiment was not to be allowed to set up its new headquarters in Tamaki until Hobson himself had selected the spot where the troops were to be stationed.[32] (Even when the regiment came to Auckland, placement of individual buildings within the fort was deputed, in Hobson's absence, not to the commanding officer but to the surgeon-general, a member of the governor's suite.) Major Bunbury, as commander of the regiment in New Zealand, resented on principle these 'wayward proposals of the Local Government'.[33] But he could do little to frustrate them. And he fretted at the delay in getting his men, who had lived in tents ever since they had come from Sydney, settled in permanent quarters in Auckland. However, after despatching the government advance party to Auckland, Hobson seems to have relented, for he asked Bunbury to meet with him in order to 'discuss the disposition of the military'.[34] Upon calling on the lieutenant-governor, Bunbury found Hobson in a 'favourable mood' of which he was able to take full advantage. 'I urged the necessity' (he recalled) 'of his allowing me to proceed with the detachment to the new seat of government at the Thames, in order to prepare a barrack for the accommodation of the men, as I dreaded in the dilapidated condition that our tents were, that the men should have to remain in that boisterous climate, another winter without cover.'[35]

Hobson fell in with Bunbury's proposal that the 80th should now make ready to shift to Tamaki. But (predictably) he ruled that they could do so only after he personally had revisited Auckland and approved of the exact site for the barracks. In the meantime Bunbury, almost as though fearing that the governor might change his mind, made decisive preparations. He dismantled his unit's only permanent structure in the Bay of Islands, a prefabricated wooden barrack that the regiment had brought with them from Sydney. (During the regiment's first months in Auckland this relocated barrack was converted into a hospital, and a temporary store for the commissariat.)[36] In addition, he took steps to charter the brig *Diana* from Sydney as a troop transport. This was the vessel which ultimately, on 27 November,[37] was to arrive in Commercial Bay with about fifty soldiers (a number of whom were artificers), constituting the bulk of the forces of the 80th Regiment then serving in New Zealand.

The unit encamped on the five-acre site at the head of Point Britomart on which Hobson's approval had fallen. This was not, in fact, where Bunbury wanted the barracks to be. He preferred the somewhat more elevated spot about a quarter-mile inland, which Maori named Rangipuke, a very gently sloping extinct volcano (almost a miniature plateau), roughly the high area where Albert Park and some of the university buildings are to be found today.[38] (Bunbury *did* ultimately get that prime spot for the barracks, but only when Governor FitzRoy came three years later. And the first occupants were to be not Bunbury's men, who had departed in the meantime for their next place of duty in India,[39] but soldiers of the famed 58th Regiment, 'the Black Cuffs', under Colonel R. H. Wynyard.)[40]

Back to November 1840. Since the outstanding feature of the Auckland garrison's duty in the first two years was the construction of Fort Britomart, something must be said about the engineering staff who were responsible. The nominal head of construction during the 1840s was the regimental engineering officer stationed in Auckland, successively Lieutenant Lugard and Captain W. B. Marlow. But their specialty in each case was military engineering, not barrack and fortress construction. The significant engineer in practice was the clerk of works, George

Graham (1812–1901).[41] Graham, who was born at Windsor, near London, received at the age of nineteen an appointment as a clerk of works in the Board of Ordnance, a body reconstituted later in the century as the Royal Engineers. Graham began his career with an extended tour of duty in Ireland, where in spite of his youth he is said to have distinguished himself. (Certainly much of his building, during Auckland's first decade, seems to have duplicated on a miniature scale the kind of fortress construction to be found in Ireland, in places such as Charles Fort, at Kinsale, County Cork.)[42]

Graham came to New Zealand in 1840 after service in China and Australia. He supervised during the 1840s first, the construction of Fort Britomart, and then the stone buildings of the Albert Barracks, including the massive defensive stone wall surrounding the twenty-three acres on which those barracks stood.[43] All these buildings have since been demolished, save for a small portion of the ten-to-twelve-foot high defensive wall, loop-holed and with flanking angles, which was constructed after Heke's northern war.[44] This remnant of the wall has been preserved in perpetuity in the university grounds. Truth to tell, the disappearance of these military buildings was regarded as no great loss by earlier generations, even among people anxious to preserve Auckland's historical heritage. Pioneer accounts agree that the fort buildings, like the still-surviving old Mount Eden prison which they closely resembled, were grim and forbidding. Perhaps both sets of structures were made deliberately so. Graham said that when Fort Britomart was first constructed, 'We believed that the intention of the Government was to send convicts [to Auckland]'.[45] But the remnant of the Albert Barracks wall, equipped with its embrasures for musket fire, and constructed out of intractable honeycomb basalt rock (superbly shaped nevertheless by Maori stonemasons), stands in a different case. It is justly admired today, and remains a showpiece of the University of Auckland campus.

For the construction of Fort Britomart, Graham had to rely substantially on soldiers of the 80th Regiment. On their arrival in Auckland, Bunbury divided them up into work parties, which he placed under Graham's direction. Graham recorded in his journal: 'We commenced building a Barrack with Scoria & brick, making bricks of the Clay on the Spot and Sawing timber &c, near the whole of the work being done by soldiers of the 80th Regt,

Major Bunbury having the Command of the Troops'.[46] Bunbury later recorded the fruits of their labours:

> The barrack formed two sides of a square, one side, containing two stories, was loop-holed, and was capable of containing two hundred men. The building was of stone, built on a tongue of land separated from the main-land by a broad, deep ditch and parapet. It had evidently at some time or other been a fort of the natives.[47] The entrance was across the ditch, a part of the parapet having been thrown down to fill it up for that purpose. On one side of the interior was built an octagonal loop-holed guardroom, and on the other side it was proposed to build a similar one for cells, also loop-holed. . . . The area in which the buildings and hospital stood was not large, and in a few hours had we deemed it necessary, it might have been made inaccessible, excepting at the usual place of entrance. The finishing of the building, doors, windows, &c., really did great credit to the soldiers who executed them, and the officers got the natives to build them huts round the enclosure.
>
> Handy men, employed as artificers, received one shilling and eight pence per diem, labourers ten pence; but it was with the greatest

Fort and barracks at Point Britomart, viewed from the south. Lithograph by P. Gauci, c.1841, in Terry's New Zealand.

difficulty we could keep the former, particularly the carpenters, to their work. They were constantly enticed away and secreted by the [non-government] inhabitants to assist in putting up their wooden houses, labour being at that time so scarce that even the Governor's architects were tempted, in spite of my contrary orders, to employ them.[48]

Bunbury's work force was enlarged when, in late February 1841, thirty men under Lieutenant A. D. W. Best rejoined the regiment after a nine-month tour of duty at Port Nicholson, where they had been relieved by a detachment of the 96th Regiment from Van Diemen's Land (Tasmania).[49] As Best resentfully noted in his journal, the members of his platoon were immediately 'converted into workmen' just as the earlier arrivals had been.[50] A traditional officer to the core, Best was unimpressed by the preoccupation of the unit with unsoldierly duties. His journal entry for 1 March recorded:

> As there was only one other Officer at the Camp I took my Tour of weekly duty which confined me to the Camp during the remainder of the week. This is very nasty soldiering no parades drills or anything that is consonant with a military life but instead of these a party of dirty fellows dragging carts of great stones for building foundations &c others working as Carpenters others again as Blacksmiths and all the Barrack lumbered up with stones, lime,[51] handcarts and other filth. The Major [Bunbury] building mad and our doctor with the disinterested feeling usual to Scotchmen always grumbling because the Mess house did not get on quicker that being in fact the only building in any state of forwardness while the men were all in Tents and he living in a comfortable Rapoo Hut.[52]

Bunbury, on the other hand, became caught up in the enterprise. He was well pleased with his soldiers-cum-builders; maintained that 'the whole were kept in constant readiness to throw down the implements of their craft, and resume the musket and the bayonet'.[53] On 2 August 1841, he wrote proudly to his regimental commander in Sydney:

> The detachment of the 80th regiment in this colony has proved effective as a body of artificers, when employed under officers of the

Ordnance in erecting the barracks at Auckland, and I am of opinion that it would not be found difficult to teach any detachment of troops which may hereafter follow them, under similar instruction, the use of the rocket, or any other missile with which it may be deemed advisable to supply them to aid their efficiency.[54]

IV

Hobson appreciated that Auckland would progress from being a 'proclamation capital' to a genuine town only when it drew in immigrant settlers as well as government employees and soldiers. Yet seven months were to go by after Auckland's founding before private capitalists were able to buy allotments. For this delay the surveyor general can not bear the sole blame. Admittedly, he had obvious weaknesses. He did not impress James George, Auckland's first baker, who originally met Mathew in Hobson's company in January 1841 when they came walking up from Commercial Bay. 'I was surprised at his pomposity,' wrote George. 'I thought he made himself greater than His Excelency [*sic*]!'[55] To be sure, Mathew could be unappealing. He was self-important, and inclined to show the insolence of office. But he was not lazy.

James George, Auckland's first baker, from his carte de visite, *1867*. AUCKLAND CITY LIBRARIES

The 3000-acre block, which came into Crown hands on 18 September 1840, was completely unsurveyed. Mathew, who had wailed from the outset that he was in 'utter want' of 'a numerous and efficient Survey force' of assistant surveyors and draftsmen,[56] was expected, single-handed, to make haste in wresting a town plan from this scrub-covered block. Little wonder the surveyor general had misgivings. Before he left Russell he warned his governor not to look for miracles. '[I]t is not to be expected that the labours of a solitary individual, however well directed his efforts, or however strenuous his exertions, can be attended with very important results.'[57] For months he continued to harp on this string; justifiably so it would seem. Late in 1840 he complained that 'I find the business of my Department daily increasing, a variety of duties pressing on my time and attention – and not even a Clerk or Draftsman provided, to render me the slightest assistance.'[58] Having to submit 'to the drudgery of my profession' was (he characteristically remarked) 'a concession which could not be expected from an officer of my standing'.

There were other delays, and these, too, were by no means of Mathew's making. The survey of the town of Auckland was effectively held up for a month waiting for Hobson to come to Tamaki in person to approve of the sites which Mathew had provisionally set aside for the port, the government offices and the town's commercial centre. Once Hobson sanctioned these, Mathew set to work, driven, he said, 'by my anxiety not to lose a moment in prosecuting the all important object of the Survey of the Town'.[59] By 14 November he had surveyed sufficiently to draw up a plan of the town, though this did not include a survey of the individual allotments. After endorsing this plan, Hobson transmitted it to Sydney for the final approval of the Governor-in-Council there, an essential step at this juncture, as the colony of New Zealand was still a dependency of New South Wales.

Confident that Governor Gipps's approval would be no more than a routine matter, Hobson publicly announced during December in the Kororareka newspaper, that the sale of the Auckland town allotments would take place on 12 March 1841.[60] This eagerly awaited intelligence spread like wildfire through New Zealand, New South Wales and Van Diemen's Land, leading in the weeks before the sale to a steady influx into Auckland of land buyers – some genuine settlers, but many others mere speculators anxious only to make a killing. However, a week before the advertised sale was due to take place, it was put off until 19 April. This postponement was constitutionally unavoidable. When he precipitately set the date of the first auction, Hobson had overlooked an enactment of the New South Wales Council that laid it down that no sale of Crown land could take place until three months had elapsed since the publication of the original notice in the Sydney Government Gazette.[61] But coming on top of earlier delays and saturation advertising, this postponement had the effect of intensifying interest far and wide. The numbers able to bid at the Crown auction, personally or through agents, increased greatly. The result was grossly inflated prices that were to impoverish many genuine settlers.

In the minds of many early settlers, the surveyor general became the scapegoat for the shortcomings of the first auction of town allotments. They pilloried Mathew's survey plan unmercifully. Dr S. M. D. Martin, the most strident critic of this plan, was particularly scathing about its concentric character, which earned for its designer the derisory nickname of 'Cobweb Mathew'.[62] Martin ascribed to the surveyor's English background this 'strange and unaccountable blunder in laying out the town', which turned its back on the principle of rectangularity of street and section that had become traditional in Australian town plans. According to Martin, Mathew, as a 'native of Bath' had decided to take 'the plan of that town, and after improving it to his own taste, [to apply] it to Auckland'. Mathew's folly, according to Martin, first took root on the summit of Rangipuke, the squat volcanic hill on which, as we have seen, the Albert Barracks were later located. It was there that

> [t]he Surveyor planted a pole, and from that pole, as a centre, he
> described a number of circles, to which he gave the names of
> quadrants, circuses and crescents. . . . With the exception of the spot
> on the top of the ridge, there was not an inch of level ground occupied
> by those circles, or cobwebs, as they were properly termed. . . . The
> worthy Surveyor-general had such a horrid dislike to nature, that he
> determined, in every possible manner, to oppose it. Instead of paying
> some slight attention to the lay of the land, and availing himself of the
> level of ranges and hollows for the formation of straight lines, he
> invariably cut them up with curves and circles.[63]

Martin also went on to deride the generous allowance Mathew made for the future reclamation of the foreshore of Commercial Bay.

> A very large portion of the town has been laid out on a mud flat in
> front of the beach, which is all under the sea at high water. . . . Why
> the town should be laid out on these mud flats, while there is an
> abundance of dry land in the vicinity, is more than any person but
> Mr. Felton Mathew can tell. Where he intends to get money to fill in
> the sea-covered part of the town, I know not.[64]

When he first submitted his concentric plan to the governor, Mathew justified his unusual disposition of streets with this argument:

> I have consulted the peculiar character and formation of the ground, a
> factor which I conceive to be indispensable in the arrangement of New

Towns, as a means . . . of avoiding the enormous expense entailed on the community, by the necessity which subsequently arises for cutting down hills and filling up hollows, where the streets are laid out in parallel lines, and at right angles, without any reference to the form of the ground. Guided by these principles, I have in several instances, adopted the crescent form, as one to which the ground is peculiarly adapted.[65]

Critics of the plan were unconvinced. Thereafter, according to James George, 'Mathew was forever known among the Old Identities of Auckland as "Cobweb".'[66]

Mathew defended his inclusion of future harbour reclamations with equal spirit.

The portion of the Bay immediately in front of the town, included between the two Points named (with His Excellency's approval) Point Stanley and Point Britomart, is dry at low water, and a ledge of Rock extends from either point, which will be found to facilitate the erection of a Pier or Jetty. . . . The formation of a Quay from Point to Point will be the means of securing a large extent of very valuable land, the sale of which will far more than counterbalance the expense of executing these works. . . . I anticipate that at a very early period, the Government will find it desirable to carry these investments into effect, and with this view, I have shown them on my Plan.[67]

The case that Mathew made for these ambitious and unusual features of his plan is by no means a trifling one. The spider-web design was far from the ridiculous arrangement contemporary critics made it out to be. True, it created problems, most notably those connected with drainage. But in practice these proved easy enough to solve. Nor was the plan carried out in its entirety; impractical and extravagant features were pragmatically dropped. Further, his proposals for the reclamation of the tidal foreshore were neither grandiose in conception, nor potentially a costly burden on the community, as contemporaries maintained. Within fifty years, much valuable land, which was reclaimed more or less in the way that Mathew had originally envisaged, came into the hands of local authorities, for whom it created an enduring source of leasehold income. Reclaiming land also tended to be a self-financing process in yet another way. During

Auckland's first fifty years, reclamation land provided security for overseas lenders whose advances enabled the Harbour Board to finance extensive facilities and docks far beyond Mathew's original imaginings.[68] But, as we shall later see, it is not easy to exonerate Mathew from the charge that, by leaving the city allotments so large, he made it easy for land jobbers to subdivide their purchases in pursuit of quick speculative profits.

V

At the end of 1840 there were few Auckland settlers who were not government employees. George Graham's recollection was that at the time he came with the army detachment to the early settlement there were 'only about twelve free inhabitants'.[69] This is probably an underestimate; but not by much. Once the settlement was founded in September 1840 a trickle of private settlers began. Rough wrote that some came from the Bay of Islands in 'small coasting vessels'.[70] And then there were the occasional adventurers, coming and going, people like James George and Thomas Hellyer, who arrived from Waiheke island or from other parts of the Hauraki gulf.[71] But pioneer recollections and contemporary drawings leave little doubt that even four months after its foundation Auckland had few private settlers. A drawing of 'Auckland in 1840' by 'WY',[72] depicts no more than a smattering of private settlers squatting in tents or in native-built huts either at Commercial Bay or beside the track leading from it (roughly today's Shortland Street) to the ridge where the government offices were being built.

Logan Campbell recalled that, when he first settled in late December, Auckland was merely 'a handful of houses and a handful of people only, all peeping out at each other from amongst the scrub and six-feet-high fern all around'.[73] For Campbell, 21 December 1840 had been the great turning point in his life. On that day he left his island home of Motukorea in the inner gulf 'to proceed to swell the as yet easily counted inhabitants of Auckland and launch the Firm of Brown and Campbell'.[74] On his arrival at Commercial Bay he reported to the governor's brig,[75] which was anchored in the harbour at the time. An unnamed official gave him permission to pitch his eight-by-six-foot tent in Store Bay; 'a

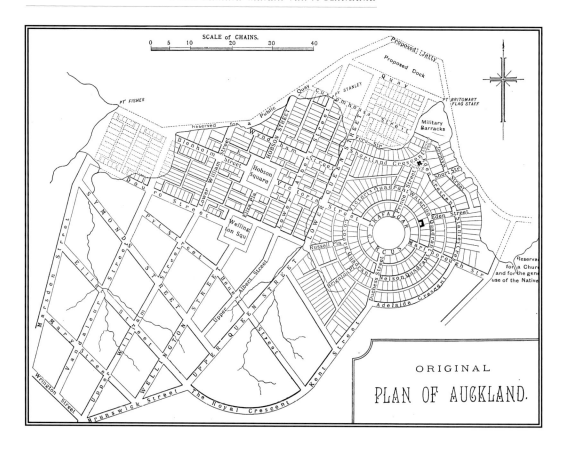

SCALE of CHAINS.

ORIGINAL

PLAN OF AUCKLAND.

Felton Mathew's 'cobweb' plan. British Parliamentary Papers

stone's throw from the beach where stood the Government Store ... surrounded by nothing but a few tents and breakwind huts'.[76] 'The capital at this juncture', he wrote, 'was represented by great fields of fern. . . . The street lines of the town were just beginning to be cut by the surveyors.'[77]

Like the officials before him, Campbell lost no time in arranging for Maori to construct a raupo whare beside his tent. He paid for this hut 'by so many yards of print and calico', as he paid in the months ahead for his staple diet – pork and potatoes – 'canoe borne by our native providers'.[78] Te Kawau, from whom he had recently bought a herd of pigs to graze on the fernland of Motukorea, had informed him that, in these very early days, Maori preferred to be paid by goods not gold: 'Heaha te pai te moni?' he said to Campbell. 'What is the good of money? I can't put it on my back and wear it, or in my pipe and smoke it.'[79] So Campbell paid up in goods. Anyway, Campbell's immediate purpose in coming to Auckland was not to trade, although that was his long-term goal. (Whilst he, a former doctor, and Brown, a former solicitor, had been on Motukorea, they had foresworn their respective professions to enter the small world of commerce in the new capital.) But in the meantime he held a watching brief for spying out a desirable site to buy for his firm at the first Crown auction. Many years later, he told his family that in order to kill time, 'I used to stroll about and watch the Government House and Offices being built and how the survey of the town lots was getting on, the one object in the future being the sale of these, as nothing of a permanent character could be undertaken until one knew which was the spot that was to become one's own.'[80] His private journal has this unusual entry for 30 December: 'Went to see how government house progressed – saw joists of large room laid – outhouse erections also going on. Had a korero with some Waikato Maoris who offered to supply me with a fair lady!'[81] Campbell declined this customary gesture of Maori hospitality.

Campbell settled in Auckland at just about the time that the small trickle of settlers was turning into a stream. Charles Terry wrote that 'As soon as it became publicly known, that the seat of Government for the Colony of New Zealand was fixed on the Waitemata, numerous persons from various parts of the Islands, as well as from Sydney, Van Diemen's Land and South Australia, congregated at Auckland, the name of the embryo capital, awaiting anxiously . . . the first sale of town allotments.'[82] After a visit to Auckland in February 1841, Hobson reported to Governor Gipps that 'a large number of persons have collected on the spot for the purpose of buying allotments'.[83] They continued to come. Typical of these was the Scottish gentleman-adventurer, Dudley Sinclair, not long since prominent in the affairs of Port Nicholson.[84] He arrived from there on the *Chelydra* on 26 February, a fellow passenger of the thirty soldiers of the 80th Regiment under Lieutenant Best, and the twenty-one mechanics whom Hobson (alias 'Captain Crimp') had recruited.[85] The *Chelydra*, under its owner Captain David Smale, appears to have been the ship most active in bringing newcomers to the infant Auckland settlement. In the last months of 1840 and during 1841, the *Chelydra* made a number of trans-Tasman trips, on one of which, according to its midshipman

Mr Williams, it found at anchor in the harbour 'two or three other ships arrived from Sydney, including the *Minerva* and the *Goshawk*'.[86] Williams also wrote of an earlier voyage when the passengers had been mainly labourers.

> The *Chelydra* brought altogether about forty immigrants, some of whom settled at Russell, whilst others went on to Auckland. They were for the most part mechanics, there being, so far as I can remember, not a single farmer in the lot. They brought nothing in the vessel excepting a small quantity of blue-gum timber, mortised and all ready set up for houses. Until this was got out and erected, however, the settlers had to be content with whares built of ti-tree, in the construction of which the Maoris lent valuable assistance. The settlers brought no furniture with them, and had for some time to content themselves with fern for bedding, and rough timber for many other articles.[87]

The postponement of the auction of the town allotments until 19 April enabled even more people to attend the sale. Interest was further intensified, when about a week before the sale, the rumour, well founded in the event, gained currency that New Zealand was about to be declared a dependency of New South Wales no longer but a full and independent colony in its own right.[88]

VI

Historians have been inclined to overlook the fact that at the time that Auckland's Pakeha population first began to appear, Maori were already resettling Waitemata's shores. Twenty-first-century Auckland is a city of considerable cultural diversity. It is well to remember that although Auckland, as we know it, was a European creation, it had from its very beginning a mixture of peoples.

Ngati Whatua motives for inviting the governor to come and live at Tamaki, as we have seen, were complex. But within that complexity we can discern certain firm objectives: the search for security, the hunger for the white man's goods, and the desire to gain access to literacy and western technology, although this last incentive, while never to be underestimated, is less easy to document. Regardless of motive, when European settlement began in Tamaki, Maori returned as well. And not just Ngati Whatua alone. It was earlier noted that in December 1840 Campbell encountered Waikato labourers helping to assemble the prefabricated Government House.[89] A little later Ngati Paoa from Waiheke came to the same site to supply both timber and labour for the erection of the picket fence enclosing the Government House grounds.[90] Some incomers (unlike these Waikato and Ngati Paoa workers) came to settle. Most did not; they were usually visitors coming merely to trade. But the goodwill of Maori of the region – whether they were Ngati Whatua residents or merely transients bent on trade – did much to ensure Auckland's survival. A European settler of the 1840s hailed the Maori people 'our very life blood, the vital fluid'.[91] This was not hyperbole. Maori were Auckland's original provisioners, a ready labour force to hand, and a source of constant profit to its first merchants. Not a few successful early Auckland businessmen acquired the start-up capital on which their later fortunes were based from land bought cheaply from Maori or from the steady profits accumulated from the native trade. Above all, it should be remembered that during Auckland's first six years, in a region where Maori were numerous and well armed and white settlers few and relatively defenceless,[92] friendly Maori rather than redcoats were the protectors of the young capital.

Periodically, rumours of a Maori invasion, generally unfounded, swept through the Pakeha community during its first dozen years or so. As was seen earlier, the first such alarm occurred early in January 1841, when a Pakeha Maori living on Waiheke came to Auckland to report to Symonds that a Ngati Paoa war-party was gathering on that island to make an attack on Auckland.[93] Captain Symonds was convinced that there was no danger, as was the recently arrived Logan Campbell, whom he consulted on the matter. But Symonds diplomatically fell in with the wishes of his rather more alarmed colleagues. He enrolled all adult males as militia, arranged for nightly pickets to patrol the bays, and converted Barrack Point into a refuge to which all could fly should the attack eventuate. By the time that Hobson came to Auckland a week later (13 January), the governor found that 'all the ferment' created by this 'most absurd and unfounded report' had subsided'. [94] He notified Gipps that 'soon after my arrival, a deputation from the suspected tribe waited on me, and denying any intention of molesting us, only seemed solicitous to recommend themselves to my favourable consideration'. As well they might. Like Ngati Whatua, Ngati Paoa wanted trade not war.

The staple fare of the first white settlers was pork and potatoes.[95] Because pork was the only fresh meat they could get, said Mrs Mathew, 'we used to dress it in a variety of ways, with seasoning to make it resemble beef, mutton, or veal'.[96] This must have been some culinary feat, for the flesh of the free-running, fern-fed 'Captain Cookers', as these local pigs later became known,[97] was lean, dark coloured, and with a highly distinctive flavour. She added that 'the natives would perhaps bring some fish, if I bribed them with a present of tobacco or flour or sugar.'[98] It is interesting to note that, as Campbell had already discovered during the first months of the settlement, Maori continued to prefer western commodities as payment for their goods, or for services provided in the building of huts and the like.

The old saying that the Maori people victualled Auckland during the summer of 1841 with the 'three Ps' – Pork, Potatoes and Peaches – though memorable, understates the range of food increasingly supplied. A favoured seashore location soon appeared for the sale of produce. This was the sandstone platform on which Auckland's first jetty was later built, projecting out into Commercial Bay from that part of the beach now lying somewhere below the spot where Queen's Arcade meets Queen Street.[99] Having beached their canoes at this or some nearby bay, Maori sellers would bear their goods in flax baskets to this favoured market place, and there lay them out for sale: potatoes, pumpkins, kumara, maize, watermelon, onions, peaches, pork and fish.[100] (They learned in time the usefulness of dealing with coin of the realm; a soldier who came in 1845 remarked that although prices at these markets were still reasonable, 'the natives, especially the women, were keen higglers in exacting the last farthing'.)[101] Maori also supplied the pioneer European community with bulky commodities. 'We had at that time [1840–41] plenty of wood', reminisced Mrs Mathew; 'the natives used to bring in huge loads on their backs.'[102] Rough recalled that, before long, 'the Natives from neighbouring villages' were bringing in 'horse provender' as well.[103]

By July 1841, however, provisions in Auckland had become 'scarce and very dear',[104] and this in spite of the industrious efforts of local Maori – Te Kawau's people at Okahu had forty acres already in cultivation and were clearing scrub to make fresh gardens.[105] But the problem proved short-lived. The lure of white men's goods, once sampled, was irresistible. From ever more distant places Maori came in canoes and sailing craft with supplies of food and firewood to sell so that they might buy blankets and clothing, tobacco and pipes, guns, saws or axes, sugar and biscuits, and a variety of other consumer goods.[106] Among the travellers, the practice grew up of calling in at the Ngati Whatua settlement at Orakei, 'that they might be supplied with food before coming to town'.[107] Some faraway travellers came from the Kaipara, some across the age-old portage at Otahuhu from the Manukau harbour and the lower Waikato, others from the distant islands of the gulf and from the furthest reaches of the Firth of Thames. Bays close to the European settlement became the site of the encampments of these traders from afar: Mechanics' Bay (Te Toanga Roa),[108] St George's Bay (Wai-a-Taikehu), Judge's Bay (Taurarua) are a selection only of the places where they beached their canoes and put up makeshift breakwind tents. Mary Ann Martin, wife of the colony's first chief justice, and author, forty years later, of a charming set of memoirs entitled *Our Maoris*, recollected that by the time of her arrival in May 1842:

Lady Martin, wife of Chief Justice William Martin and author of Our Maoris.
AUCKLAND CITY
LIBRARIES

> The valley below our house [in Taurarua], through which ran a little
> stream, was a favourite camping-place for Maoris who came from the
> neighbouring islands and mainland to trade in Auckland. Early on
> every fine morning we used to watch the little fleet of canoes skim
> across the harbour with their sails set. Sometimes a red blanket did
> duty for a sail. When the wind was contrary, ten to twenty men
> paddled each canoe, which was heavily laden with produce. . . . Many
> of these crews returned in the evening to their own villages, but those
> who came from a distance could not get back in one day, and preferred
> our quiet bay to the neighbourhood of the town. We used to go down
> when the first hubbub of the landing was over. In a short time, the
> canoes were drawn up high and dry, their triangular sails set up as
> tents. The men would be busy cutting fern from the hill for their
> beds, while the women and girls scraped potatoes for the evening
> meal, or waded with bare legs into the mud at low water to find their

favourite shellfish. Soon a fire was blazing, and the pot put on, gipsy fashion.[109]

Canoes trading with Auckland were to become an integral part of pioneer Auckland's famed 'mosquito fleet'. In 1853, William Swainson wrote of one of its most colourful manifestations:

> The Waitemata is well adapted for boat-sailing. Canoes from all parts of the Gulf are continually arriving and departing; and with nearly 100 vessels from distant ports, upwards of 600 coasters, and nearly 2,000 canoes yearly entering the port, its sheltered waters present a lively, business-like appearance. But never, perhaps, is it seen to so great an advantage as when once or twice a year the native chief Taraia and his tribe [Tama-Te-Ra], from the eastern boundary of the Gulf, pay Auckland a visit in their fleet of forty sail of well-manned war canoes. Drawing them up in a line upon the beach, and with their masts and sails pitching a long line of various figured tents, they encamp themselves for several days. The neighbourhood of their camping ground presents the appearance of a fair: pigs and potatoes, wheat, maize, melons, grapes, pumpkins, onions, flax, turkeys, geese, ducks, fowls and firewood, are exposed for sale in great abundance, and meet with a ready market. But the money they receive in payment does not leave the town: for several days the shops and stores are frequented by careful and keen-eyed customers. Their 'shopping' ended, they take their departure with the first fair wind, laden with spades, blankets, ironware, and clothing of various kinds; their fleet departing, homeward bound, in a body as it came, the canoes extending over the surface of the harbour, with their many-shaped sails of mat and canvass wide-spread to catch the western breeze.[110]

Back in 1840–41, however, there were resident Maori who were able to benefit from the European presence without having to come by canoe to trade. This of course was true of Ngati Whatua, who as tangata whenua, had unchallenged possession of the isthmus, apart from that land on the western bank of the Tamaki river which they had gifted to Ngati Paoa half a century before. Although Te Kawau maintained his kainga on the Manukau, namely at Whakarongo (Mangere) and at Onehunga, he was able to resettle the bulk of the constituent tribes of Ngati Whatua o Tamaki (Te Taou, Te Uringutu and Nga Oho) beside

the Waitemata. There lay that portion of the Ngati Whatua ancestral lands which the tribe was determined to keep intact — the territory lying between the south shore of the Waitemata rising up as far as the ridge along which the native track ran to Tamaki. (In the 1840s this became the cart road to St John's College; today it roughly follows the route of Remuera and St John's Roads.)

To the inviolability of this region Te Kawau made one exception. In 1841, he gave to Kati Te Wherowhero, the Ngati Mahuta chief and brother of Potatau, the block known as Pukapuka, which ran northward from the aforesaid ridge to the Orakei basin. This block he gifted to be Kati's 'place of abode'.[111] When Kati's wife Matire Toha was asked, years after, why the gift was made, she replied simply: 'love of Kawau to Kati'.[112] But there was more to Te Kawau's gift than that, just as there was more to the gift of Omahu in Remuera made to Potatau at the same time.[113] (Or for that matter to the gift of Onehunga land near Te Tatua, that he had made two years earlier.) It must not be forgotten, as Paora Te Iwi of Ngati Tamaoho reminded the Orakei Court, 'that Waikato

Taurarua (Judge's Bay), watercolour by Thomas Biddulph Hutton. The house shown is that of the attorney-general, not that of Justice Martin which gave to the bay its European name.
AUCKLAND CITY ART GALLERY

291

brought the tribes back' to Tamaki, and that 'they had no chief [with the requisite power] but the Waikato chief who brought them, Te Wherowhero'.[114] And as Rev. Robert Maunsell also reminded the same court in 1868, 'Ngati Whatua were a very small body' willing to give isthmus land to Te Wherowhero, 'because they wanted protection against the Hauraki natives'.[115] Maunsell could equally have included Nga Puhi as a feared enemy. Ngati Whatua appreciated that giving Waikato a landed stake in Tamaki would be conducive towards ensuring the protective presence there of that great tribe.

As a consequence of his becoming the protector of Ngati Whatua, Te Wherowhero effectively became the protector of the government settlement of Auckland as well. We need only to go forward to the famous Remuera feast (paremata) which Waikato hosted in 1844 to see a spectacular demonstration to Maori and Pakeha alike of the extent of Te Wherowhero's rangatiratanga (commanding influence and status) in this centre of European government. At the vice regal reception, which followed upon the Remuera feast, Governor FitzRoy tacitly recognised the unique mana of Te Wherowhero, when he placed that ariki in a special position of honour. In a subsequent despatch, FitzRoy justified to his secretary of state this respectful treatment of Te Wherowhero. Waikato had become, he wrote, 'one of the most powerful as well as numerous tribes in New Zealand', and its leader Te Wherowhero, through the extent of his influence and alliances, was 'probably the greatest chief' in the colony. In the 1840s Potatau Te Wherowhero was almost the arbiter of peace and war in northern New Zealand.[116]

If Te Wherowhero of Ngati Mahuta was persuaded to settle on Tamaki land because Te Kawau valued his protection, other tribes were anxious to come there because they wanted to trade. Reference has already been made to the fact that as an inducement to sell the Kohimarama Block George Clarke offered to Ngati Paoa the right to settle on part of St George's Bay, so that they might be close to the centre of trade.[117] Paora Tuhaere, a chief of Ngati Whatua, spoke of 'people of strange tribes' – Te Arawa, Nga Puhi, Ngai Te Rangi, Waikato, Ngati Paoa, and others – living, during the early years of the colony, in the Orakei district, with the acquiescence of his people, 'each tribe with its own cultivation'.[118] Asked by the Orakei Court why these strangers were there, Paora simply replied: 'they came to our place . . . that they might be near the pakehas'.[119]

Rather different from these isolated stopping places was the more substantial block of land granted by Ngati Whatua in 1842–43 to the people of Waikato lineage, Ngati Tamaoho and Ngati Te Ata, whose traditional rohe were on the southern Manukau and on the Awhitu peninsula. The land which Te Kawau granted was located in an area where modern Remuera merges into Epsom. It has been aptly defined as having 'the shape of a triangle bounded by Manukau Rd to the West, Remuera Rd to the North and a straight line between the approximate location of the Planetarium in One Tree Hill Domain and the corner of Market Rd and Remuera Rd'.[120] There are a number of reasons why Te Kawau was prepared to bestow so generously large a piece of land on these two tribes. Relations between Ngati Whatua and their Manukau neighbours were good. Te Hira, son of Te Kawau, was married to a Ngati Te Ata woman.[121] This was by no means uncommon. Over the years a considerable amount of inter-marriage between the Tamaki and Manukau peoples had resulted in a shared ancestry, which made for friendly dealings.[122] As an instance of this we may note that over many years, Ngati Te Ata and Ngati Tamaoho had amicably crossed Ngati Whatua territory, to establish temporary stations on the Waitemata from which they exercised fishing rights. A grant inland for more prolonged occu-pation could be regarded as an extension of this. Further, when Ngati Tamaoho and Ngati Te Ata were involved in one of the last tribal wars in the early 1840s, Te Kawau, in his words, 'called them to come hither' that they might have a place of refuge.[123] Perhaps most influential of all the reasons why Te Kawau was prepared to place the Manukau tribes within reach of Auckland and its trade was the obligation to render utu or payback for the asylum that the lower Waikato peoples gave to Ngati Whatua during its years of wandering at the time of the musket wars. Judge Fenton believed this to be a powerful consideration. In his 1869 Judgment he wrote that

> There is no doubt that Ngatiteata, with the other Waikato tribes who returned with Potatau, had rendered considerable services to Apihai and his people. These services were requited by the gift of a piece of land near Onehunga to Potatau, of Pukapuka to Te Kati his brother,

and of Remuera to Wetere Te Kauae [of Ngati Tamaoho]. The above
remarks apply equally to Paora Te Iwi [of Ngati Te Ata].[124]

However, these grants of land to the south Waikato tribes were
to prove, during the early 1840s, in spite of best intentions associated with the original gifts, a source of friction between the
newcomers and Ngati Whatua, who continued to claim mana
whenua over the isthmus. For Ngati Whatua never intended
these grants to be regarded as outright gifts allowing the occupiers to sell the land at some future date. As Apihai Te Kawau
saw things, the occupiers had simply been given what lawyers
would call a right of usufructary possession. Such an occupancy,
or usufruct, conferred a temporary right to reside on and to cultivate the land, but only on the sufferance of the tribe in whose
chief the mana of the land still remained vested.[125] When no
longer occupied in this way, complete control of the land was
supposed to revert to the original tribe. In Governor FitzRoy's
time, however, chiefs of Ngati Te Ata and Ngati Tamaoho chose
to treat the land, which they had only occasionally used, as their
own and they set about selling it to private European buyers. Te
Kawau and his fellow chiefs were furious.[126] But the Waikato
occupiers went ahead and sold just the same.[127]

On balance, however, had Ngati Whatua reason to be pleased
with the initial outcome of the decision to invite the governor to
come and reside among them? Probably yes. When Warena
Hengia, chief of the Nga Oho hapu of the Tamaki tribe, was
asked this question at the Orakei court, he seemed in no doubt.
He replied: 'when the governor came we were enriched. That is
the end to the matter.'[128]

At the Kohimarama Conference of Maori chiefs convened by
Governor Gore Brown in 1860, Ngati Whatua o Orakei expressed
the same sentiments. In a reply to an address given by the
governor, in which he expressed alarm at growing disaffection
among tribes in Taranaki and Waikato, Paora Tuhaere, Te Keene
and seventeen other chiefs wrote:

> Listen to us, whilst we speak to you and explain our views and
> sentiments. They are the same as in times past, even from Governor
> Hobson's time down to our own – the present. We have always firmly
> adhered to you and to the Queen's sovereignty. Do not suppose we are

holding on to the New Zealand customs. It is not so; for it was we [Ngati Whatua] who called you as a great and powerful people to establish yourselves on our lands on the shores of the Waitemata, that you might be a parent to us, and that we might be your child.[129]

Has the Crown shown a corresponding sense of parental trustee-ship? This is an issue that modern New Zealanders might well ponder.

VII

Hobson had been unwilling to shift himself and the capital from Russell to Auckland until adequate public buildings had been built to make it an effective seat of government. Believing that such a point had been reached by February 1841, he informed Governor Gipps that he intended to begin progressively moving his senior officials on the government brig *Victoria* to Auckland in readiness for his own shift there.[130] On 13 February his colonial secretary, Shortland was despatched. The colonial treasurer George Cooper followed a fortnight later. On 12 March the *Victoria* dropped anchor in the Waitemata with the governor himself and his family aboard. He came ashore on the following day to be received, according to Rough, by 'a guard of honour, and by all the officers of government as well as the European settlers and many natives'.[131] What Rough recalled as a rather grand and memorable occasion seemed otherwise to another spectator on that occasion, Logan Campbell.[132]

> It was at this date [13 February 1841] that our first Governor Capt. Hobson publicly landed at Auckland – he, his wife and a small band of officials landed on the reef in Commercial Bay and walked up [the] still fern clad Shortland Street with a grand band of one fife and one drum playing I suppose the Hobson march, and Auckland's first Government House – a wooden structure sent out from home and built on the same site as the existing house – was taken possession of.[133]

Campbell elsewhere records that while this 'triumphal march' was taking place, the *Chelydra*, which was berthed in the harbour, fired a vice regal salute.[134]

Campbell's sour retrospective comment on the arrival of the governor reflected the resentment of the first settlers of Auckland at the postponement of the sale of the town allotments that had already been long delayed. Campbell related to his family that 'on the 5th March Auckland gave forth its first growl against the Government, for on that day it declared the sale postponed to the 19th of April'.[135] A further five weeks would surely increase the number of bidders for this limited number of sections. Two groups of competitors, Campbell recalled, were particularly aggrieved:

> The Sydney land sharks who had come down to speculate in town lots waxed furious, because it gave time for as many more sharks to arrive and compete at [the] forthcoming sale and make lots cost so much more. But the fiat had gone forth so it availed not for them to gnash their teeth with vexation of spirit. It was a blow to us bona fide settlers too, for we would be run up for our lots, which we were not going to buy in speculation but for legitimate occupation.[136]

These forebodings were to be realised only too well. By the date of the auction, buyers or their agents, thronged the new capital. It had been anticipated that bidding would be keen, especially on the part of Australian investors. For the Australian experience had taught that, when sections in newly formed towns were put up for auction, rich prizes were won by those who were first in the field. Moreover, a week before the auction, the spirit of competition was further inflamed by the receipt of intelligence that New Zealand was no longer to be an appendage of New South Wales, but was about to be made an independent colony.[137] Nevertheless, competition in Auckland exceeded all expectations. Bidding became so feverish that prices were driven to extraordinary levels which (according to one observer) 'at the time seemed to paralyse with astonishment the majority of persons assembled'.[138]

A combination of circumstances, for some of which the local government must bear responsibility, had conspired to ignite this speculative spirit among the crowd. First, the supply of sections was inadequate to meet the demand. It has been estimated that only 116 sections, a third of those surveyed and marked on the plan, were to be submitted to public competition.[139] Yet, according to one account, there were 800 applicants competing for this limited offering.[140] Second, these sections were unusually large for what was to be the centre of a nineteenth-century colonial town: 'the town allotments mostly exceeded a quarter of an acre in area, many were three-eighths, and ten above half an acre'.[141] Such large sections could become highly profitable. Speculators, aware of a big unsatisfied demand, could confidently buy a section with a 10 per cent deposit, then elect to split it into small allotments for immediate resale.[142] (George Graham took time off from fortress building to do just that. He noted in his diary for 19 April: 'I purchased No.8 Allotment Section 4 for £270 and sold half the same day for £180 to a Mr Stone.')[143]

It is no surprise therefore that dominating the bidding was, in Terry's words, 'the phalanx of land jobbers, attracted by the hopes, from the limited number of allotments, and the greater number in proportion, of settlers, that by the power of their purses they should reap a golden harvest'.[144] In the event, the speculators, fly-by-night land-jobbers, and adventurers, spoken of by Terry, had a field day.[145] They competed furiously with bona fide settlers, who were committed, come what may, to stay in Auckland. And the speculators generally prevailed. One analysis of the auction indicates that speculators rather than actual occupants bought just on 60 per cent of the allotments that fell to the hammer.[146]

Hobson reported back proudly to his secretary of state that the auction had been a resounding financial success: '119 allotments, containing 44 acres, sold for the gross sum of . . . £24,275 17s. 9d., being at the average of £555 per acre.'[147] Before the auction he had authorised an upset price of £100,[148] a figure which some considered far too ambitious. How wrong they were. The sale reached an average figure of almost £600 an acre which was a figure without precedent in the annals of the British Empire. Yet back in London the hard-headed permanent colonial undersecretary, James Stephen, had misgivings about this demonstration of land mania:

> I confess that I cannot partake of the pleasure which the governor feels
> in the high prices obtained for these Town Allotments. It is surely
> quite preposterous that Land should fetch so high a price in Auckland
> as in the immediate vicinity of London or Liverpool. This must be one
> of the bubbles which burst as surely as they are blown.[149]

Back in Auckland, however, Hobson and his officials were
elated. Rough recalled how the high yields of the auction were
regarded as 'a welcome replenishment to the nearly exhausted
funds of the New Zealand treasury'.[150] But Rough was also
honest enough to concede that in the long run the auction damaged the settlement. Because the real beneficiaries were, in his
view, the 'speculators, . . . little real progress in substantial
buildings, or improvement of the lands and streets was made
until some years later on'.[151] Even more damaging were the false
conclusions which the officials drew from the inflated prices
realised at this auction and its successor for suburban and
country allotments held in September of the same year. They
were persuaded that these high prices would hold and that the
government could go on indefinitely deriving an adequate
income from the resale of land bought cheaply from Maori.[152]
Stagnant land prices at Crown auctions held in 1842 soon
showed the fallacy of this reasoning.

One can well understand why the settlers were infuriated by
the intrusion of speculators into the sale of town allotments (as
they were when on 1 September 1841 suburban and country lots
were auctioned). The furious bidding of speculators forced the
price of some sections to exceptional levels. The allotment at the
corner of Queen Street and Shortland Crescent, 'then actually a
swamp' observed Logan Campbell, sold at the rate of £1200 an
acre.[153] All too often the speculators outbid the real settlers, then
subdivided their holdings into smaller lots which they promptly
resold at great profit. Genuine settlers who were committed to
staying in Auckland come what may, having established their
little stores and businesses and even built dwellings on allotments of their choice, were forced to bid beyond their means,
and were often stripped of their spare capital.[154] Campbell and
his partner Brown were defeated by the competition. 'We had
hoped to purchase the lot on which we had meanwhile squatted',
wrote Campbell, 'but the land sharks ran the price beyond what
the maiden firm's small purse could stand, and so we had to be
content to get one higher up the street.'[155]

The auction marked the real beginning of the estrangement of
the settler community and the official-military establishment. The
government was blamed, illogically one would say, for the delayed
auction, rather more justly, for the limited number of sections that

were put to the auctioneer's hammer, and for the over-large sections ready-made for subdivision that were put on offer. For each of these factors in varying degrees had led to exorbitant land prices. But it is difficult to find an excuse for the participation of the officials in the public auction itself. Settlers were galled to notice that among those bidding for scarce allotments and forcing prices up to exorbitant levels were Willoughby Shortland, Felton Mathew, George Cooper, and other officials. This was considered intolerable, given that thirteen of the officials had, before the auction, availed themselves of the privilege of buying at moderate prices, sections in Official Bay reputed to be among the choicest in the whole settlement. In the months ahead, the settlers bitterly branded the officials 'the Auckland Official Land-Jobbing Association'.[156] These flaws in the selling of Auckland disrupted the fragile social unity of the new community and quickly turned many of the early settlers into enemies of the governor and his officials.[157]

Yet 19 April 1841, the day when first allotments were sold, must be regarded as a red-letter day in the story of Auckland. It was then that the settlement really came into being. Thereafter the tide of European immigration set in strongly. When the first official census was taken in 1858 Auckland was easily the largest settlement in the colony of New Zealand. It remains so today. So many European immigrants came in colony's first twenty-five years that it was feared that in Auckland, and in the colony as a whole, Maori would go under, that the white flood would submerge the brown rock. A century and a half has shown these fears to be unfounded; and especially in Auckland, the city with the largest Polynesian population in the Pacific. Auckland flourishes, but Tamaki-makau-rau remains.

THE SALE OF TAMAKI LAND 1840–1844

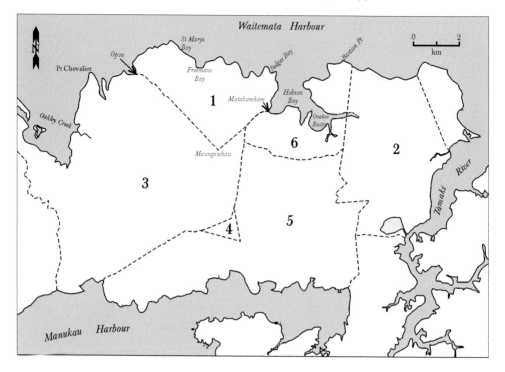

Key:

1. Mataharehare, Opou and [Maunga] Whau Block, September 1840, 3000 acres.

2. Kohimarama Block, 28 May 1841, c. 6000 acres; southern boundary ill-defined.

3. Waitemata to Manukau Block, 29 June 1841, c. 12,000 acres.

4. Manukau Road Purchase, 14 September 1842, 200 acres.

5. Corridor of land – between Blocks 2 and 3 and south of Remuera Road, bought by Europeans during 1844 when Governor FitzRoy waived Crown Pre-emption.

6. Remuera – Orakei lands which Ngati Whatua wished to preserve.

Note: This map does not indicate small purchases and Old Land Claims eg. of Fairburn, Hamlin and Dalziel.

Map based on the calculations of Maurice Alemann and maps of sales provided in 1992 by the Department of Survey and Land Information.

AFTERWORD

I chose to bring this book on earliest Auckland to its formal close with the Crown sale of the first town allotments on 19 April 1841. I did not intend to imply, however, that this particular date marked a disjunction in the story of Auckland, and that, with the steady inflow of European settlers over the next decade, the settlement entered upon a completely new phase of development. Books with beginning and ending dates that claim to enclose distinct periods, more often than not, represent the convenience of historians rather than the actualities of history. The adage that history is a continuum, even if trite, is nevertheless true. Never more so than for Auckland after 1840. Hence this afterword, which attempts to bring to some finality three issues which were left dangling in the previous pages:

- the fate of the Waitemata and Manukau Company;
- the continuing European purchase of the Tamaki isthmus; and
- the extent to which Maori expectations of the benefits Europeans would bring were realised in the years ahead.

I

The early numbers of Auckland's first newspaper, the *New Zealand Herald and Auckland Gazette,* which began publication in July 1841, leave little doubt that settlers in the new capital generally expected that the Manukau Land Company (as the Scottish company was by then popularly called) would establish, under the leadership of Captain Symonds, a settlement of some consequence on the northern shore of the Manukau harbour. In September 1840, the directors of the company in Britain had called for applications for 220 land orders. Each land order (or 'section') was made up of 100 acres of so-called 'country land' and one town allotment.[1] Out of this particular issue, 80 sections were sold to buyers. Scottish labourers of attested character were also recruited as 'assisted passengers' to provide a work force for the new settlement.

On 31 December 1840, the first group of colonists left the Clyde on the barque *Brilliant* to act as an advance party to prepare the settlement. This vessel, dogged by problems of seaworthiness and of a complex itinerary – it made calls at Sierra Leone, Cape Town and Australian ports including Hobart – did not reach Puponga Point on the Manukau until 29 October 1841. The small party of twenty-seven first shippers (twenty-three adults and four children) received, on that day, a dispiriting introduction to colonial life. Captain Symonds, the company's agent in New Zealand, welcomed them with the crushing news that they could not take official possession of any of the land on which they had landed. No Crown grant could be made until Crown land commissioners had determined the legality of the original purchase made by Mitchell in 1836. The governor's council had ruled that, while awaiting this determination of title, the immigrants would be 'permitted to squat, for a period not exceeding two years, upon lands . . . on the Manukao river, to be pointed out by the surveyor-general'.[2] Admittedly, the land on which the new arrivals had been given 'permissive occupancy' was at Karangahape, just as Symonds had hoped it would be. But he had done little to prepare for their coming, other than to arrange for the erection on the beachfront of a few native-built whare in which they were to be temporarily housed.[3] The land survey, which he had carried out before their arrival, was little more than rudimentary.

Why Symonds had devoted so little time to preparing for the coming of the settlers is nowhere recorded. There are two possible explanations which, taken in conjunction, seem plausible. Obviously he had been influenced by uncertainty over how much land would be granted, and, more importantly, just where that inevitably reduced grant would be located. It is very likely, too, that the delay could have arisen out of the multifarious activities lying outside his company responsibilities that Symonds had allowed himself to be caught up in. In a matter of twenty months, apart from his responsibilities as the company agent, he had variously served as an emissary collecting signatures to the Treaty

of Waitangi, assistant-surveyor to Felton Mathew, police magistrate, deputy governor during the foundation of Auckland, and explorer of the Waipa valley region and of the Hot Lakes district, while attached to a party led by Ernst Dieffenbach.

Felton Mathew's inspection report on the settlement, which he made as surveyor-general two months after the arrival of the *Brilliant*, would have made depressing reading for the governor to whom it was presented. Mathew wrote that there was still no town plan in existence, 'a few stakes only having been placed to indicate the intersection of the intended streets'.[4] He reported that he had made

Point Britomart viewed from Commercial Bay, c. 1842. P. Gauci lithograph after J. J. Merrett in Terry's New Zealand.

> A very careful inspection of the ground, which I certainly cannot consider by any means well adapted for the seite [*sic*] of a Town, on account of its limited extent, no less than its rugged and impracticable character. The utmost extent of the land which can be considered in any way suitable for building purposes, does not in my estimation exceed 40 acres. . . .
>
> In addition to the rugged and mountainous character of the surrounding country the soil is of the poorest and most sterile description, and the greater part of it densely wooded.

Cornwallis, as the new settlement had come to be called, had (in Mathew's opinion) no future as an agricultural settlement. He forecast, oddly enough, that it might survive as a port for the Manukau, 'as an Emporium for the supply of the shipping frequenting the harbour'.[5]

What sealed the fate of the Manukau Company settlement, however, was the death of Symonds a bare month after the arrival of the *Brilliant*.[6] On 26 November 1841, a messenger came across the harbour from the mission station at Orua Bay near the south Manukau head, appealing for a surgeon to come and attend to the missionary wife, Mrs James Hamlin, who had fallen seriously ill. As none was available at Cornwallis, Symonds offered to go instead and to do what he could. He went to the *Brilliant*, which still lay offshore, and gathered together some medical supplies. According to a contemporary account, 'by the advice of the Captain [of that ship], in consequence of the day being gusty, and there being at the time a considerable sea, Symonds took the ship's long boat instead of his own'.[7] With a crew of five, made up of Symonds, two sailors, Mr Adam ('a gentleman') and a Maori, the longboat set out. The *New Zealand Herald and Auckland Gazette* reported that

> Shortly after leaving the [*Brilliant*], a violent and sudden squall struck the boat, which was observed to go down head-foremost, about a mile from the ship. . . . Owing to the dangerous sea running, it was found impracticable to proceed to the unfortunate men, and those on the ship were compelled to witness their unhappy fate. The two seamen disappeared almost immediately. Mr Adam swam for a long time, in company with Captain Symonds, but at length sank. Captain Symonds, who was an expert and powerful swimmer, was observed to make the most extraordinary exertions. He swam more than an hour and twenty minutes, encumbered with a particularly heavy kind of nailed boots, and two thick pea coats, (which latter he was seen attempting to take off) when he disappeared.

Before he went under, Symonds shouted to his Maori companion, who had been trying to help him take off his clothing, 'Ka mate ahau' ('I'm going to drown'), and urged him to swim to the shore and save his own life. The Maori was the sole survivor. He lived on to old age.[8]

Hobson predicted that the loss of Symonds as an officer would be 'long felt as a public calamity' for the colony.[9] For the Cornwallis settlers, however, the loss was irreparable. He alone had the powers of leadership and knowledge of the conditions of the colony that would have given the struggling settlement any chance of survival.[10] During the ensuing months, the settlers combined a miserable subsistence existence with clearing bush from their land and laying out the company's paper town. The arrival of the next ship, the *Osprey*, gave a glimmer of hope for the Cornwallis community. It carried machinery for a steam sawmill where the men could work under the management of a young entrepreneur, Theophilus Heale.[11] But though a quantity of timber milled at Cornwallis was sold in both New Zealand and Australia, the operation failed within a year, and the partnership between Heale and the Scottish company dissolved. The settlers lost heart, and drifted away to Onehunga and Auckland, where there was at least the prospect of some employment and of a modicum of comfort for their families. Seven settlers who had purchased land orders from the company are said to have exchanged these for government scrip to the value of £4,844, which could be used to buy land in the settlement of Auckland.

Auckland, c.1842, looking westwards from Point Britomart. P. Gauci lithograph after J. J. Merrett in Terry's New Zealand.

In 1846 the lands claims commissioners finally awarded the Manukau Company 1927 acres in the Puponga-Cornwallis district. But by this time Cornwallis was virtually deserted, a ghost town. The settlement, of which so much was expected, is today a small holiday resort and a minor dormitory suburb for city commuters.

II

It will be recalled that shortly after Ngati Whatua chiefs sold to the Crown the first block of Tamaki land (called 'Mataharehare, Opou Wau'),[12] George Clarke, the land purchase officer, told Hobson that the tribe was ready to sell more. He reported that once the governor settled in Auckland, the chiefs had undertaken to sell 'a still larger tract of country'. Hobson, much encouraged, urged Clarke to continue to negotiate.[13]

But the first purchase that Clarke clinched after Hobson arrived was in fact with Ngati Paoa. On 28 May 1841, twenty-four Hauraki chiefs, predominantly Ngati Paoa, sold the Kohimarama Block of about 6000 acres on the west bank of the Tamaki river. (See map, p.300.) This large sale took in most of what are today regarded as Auckland's affluent eastern suburbs. Why Ngati Paoa were so ready to sell is no mystery. They had, by this time, virtually abandoned Tauoma, which, it will be remembered, became deeply tapu after the slaughterous battles of Mauinaina and Mokoia twenty years before. The remnant of Tauoma people had now resettled among other members of their iwi mainly on Waiheke and other inner gulf islands, and on the western littoral of the Firth of Thames. The block which Ngati Paoa sold to Clarke extended from near the western headland of the Tamaki river at least as far south as Mokoia (Panmure).[14] How far beyond that point the southern boundary legally lay was uncertain, as it abutted Hamlin's pre-1840 purchase, yet to be adjudicated upon.[15] Likewise, the western boundary of the block was ambiguous, apart from the fact that it went no further than Lake Waiatarua. (Ngati Whatua subsequently objected that the block encroached on their land, especially on its Waitemata frontage.) Maurice Alemann, a land consultant, has explained this continuing uncertainty: according to him, many

West view of Commercial
Bay, *pen and wash by
Edward Ashworth.*
AUCKLAND CITY ART
GALLERY

of the block's boundary markers, which were designated in the
deed by their now-forgotten Maori names, have been lost.
Moreover, the western boundary line 'was not explicitly surveyed. In the end it was marked on [the twentieth century]
Cadastral Maps as a result of a survey of the land West of the line
resulting from various Crown and Pre-emption Waiver
Purchases from Ngati Whatua.'[16]

Payment for the block was spelt out in the deed as:

Two Horses – One large Boat and all its sails – One hundred pounds
in Money – Two hundred Blankets – Twenty Cloaks – Ten Frock
Coats – one hundred pairs Trousers – one hundred shirts – Ten pieces
print – Forty Shawls – Three Casks Tobacco – Two Pails – Three Tents
– Twenty Caps – Ten pairs Boots – Six bags Flour – Two bags Sugar –
Two cross cut saws –Two pit-saws – Two Saddles – and Two Bridles.[17]

An even more spectacular sale, known as the 'Waitemata to
Manukau Purchase', followed shortly after. (See map, p.300.) On
29 June 1841, five Ngati Whatua chiefs, headed by Te Kawau,

sold this block of about 8000 acres for £200, four horses, thirty
blankets, ten cloaks, one tent and a desk.[18] The eastern boundary
line ran from Orakei through to the summit of One Tree Hill –
within months, however, this line was shifted westwards to
Manukau Road – thence in a more or less direct line to Lynfield
Cove on the Manukau, and from there along the coastline to the
end of the Whau portage in Green Bay. The western boundary
was the Whau portage itself, while the northern boundary was
the Waitemata coastline between the Whau mouth and Opou.
This block included not only some of the more important suburbs of today's central isthmus such as Mount Eden, the western
portions of Epsom and Three Kings, but the whole of the pre-
World War II western suburbs beyond Cox's Creek as well.[19]
After disposing of the Waitemata to Manukau Block, Ngati
Whatua chiefs made only one further sale before the waiver of
Crown pre-emption in 1844. In September 1842 they sold for
£40 a triangular wedge of land of 200 acres lying between Royal
Oak, Maungakiekie and Three Kings (see map, p.300.).

While conceding that these, and later sales to the Crown, by
Ngati Whatua for ridiculously low sums could seem to indicate
a spirit of 'continued recklessness' on the part of their chiefs,[20]
what is noteworthy is the land the tribe chose *not* to sell. Not
available to Pakeha, and this included those direct sales made to
settlers during the waiver of Crown pre-emption (1844–45),
were those lands which lay behind the shoreline between the
western boundary of the Kohimarama block and the western
side of today's Hobson Bay extending back to Tamaki (Remuera)
Road.[21] The purchases that European buyers were able to make
of Epsom, Maungakiekie and Onehunga lands during 1844–45
show that Ngati Whatua had decided to confine their landhold-
ings to Remuera-Orakei and to Mangere. This explains the
annoyance of Te Kawau when, on 27 March 1844, 'Epiha Putini
. . . of the Ngatitemaoho Tribe' sold to the Crown fifty acres of
land 'situated on the North side of the road leading to Tamaki'.[22]
Ngati Whatua looked on this land as not Putini's to sell. The
tribe's view was that it had been provisionally and temporarily
gifted to the Waikato people, and was in no way available for
them to dispose of. By selling this land they had alienated part
of the Ngati Whatua nest-egg land, a grievous loss in itself, and
a dangerous precedent that could be (and was) exploited by

Waikato hapu holding land by just such a usufructary tenure in
the months to come.

III

There is not enough space here to discuss at any length the complex issue of the direct sale of Tamaki land by Maori to Pakeha
during 1844–45.[23] But some reference must be made to this
important episode. For it was by this means that the fertile volcanic lands lying between the Kohimarama block, and the
Waitemata to Manukau block, together with much of the coastal
area of the inner Manukau harbour between Hillsborough and
Te Papapa, came into European hands.

The representative of the Crown to whom Epiha had sold the
fifty-acre block of Remuera land just spoken of was Governor
FitzRoy. In the last week of 1843, Robert FitzRoy had taken
over the control of the colony from Shortland, who had been
administering it since Hobson's death in September 1842.
FitzRoy entered upon a desperate situation. The colony was
almost bankrupt. The expectation, aroused by the first Crown
auctions in Auckland, that the administration could be financed
by high profits coming from the resale of land bought at nominal prices from Maori, proved a delusion. Crown auctions in
1842–43 revealed a dearth of buyers and a collapse of property
values. This downturn manifested itself in a drastically reduced
income for the Crown and economic stagnation for the settler
community.[24] At this juncture, settlers in Auckland began to
look on cheap abundant land as a panacea for all the economic
ills currently afflicting them. For their part, some local Maori,
stirred up by Pakeha malcontents, agitated for the ending of pre-
emption which, they maintained, denied them the right to sell
their land directly to Europeans at higher figures than Crown
agents were prepared to offer.

Assailed by dissatisfied parties on all sides upon his arrival,
FitzRoy, by early 1844, was persuaded to capitulate on a number
of key points of government policy. Most significant for Pakeha
and Maori living in Auckland was his issue of a proclamation on
26 March 1844, waiving Crown pre-emption over Maori land,
provided that a tax of ten shillings was paid for each acre of land

bought. Anticipating this change in the regulations, unscrupulous settlers, in order to steal a march on rivals, had entered into clandestine negotiations with Maori willing to sell long before the proclamation. In the forefront of the would-be sellers were Ngati Tamaoho and Ngati Te Ata to whom Ngati Whatua had given Epsom land south of Tamaki Road (today's Remuera Road) – in effect payback land that had been granted so that these Waikato hapu might have easy access to trade with Pakeha in Auckland. When Ngati Whatua found out that the Waikato hapu were proposing to sell this land, they were furious, considering that since their 'guests' no longer intended to occupy it, they should return it to Ngati Whatua, the rightful owners according to Maori customary law. Ngati Whatua opposition to these threatened sales was fanned by the fear that should lands south of Remuera Road be sold, pressure could build within their own tribe to sell parts of the Remuera-Orakei land lying *north* of that road. The chiefs regarded that ancestral land as sacrosanct, as held in trust for generations to come. Hence the great significance of the sale of Remuera land which Epiha Putini made to the governor on the day following the proclamation ending Crown pre-emption. By this purchase FitzRoy seemed to be giving viceregal sanction to the claim of the Waikato tribes to sell the land that they had briefly occupied.[25]

FitzRoy's proclamation allowing private land deals has been likened to the opening of floodgates.[26] There was a torrent of purchases, including the formalising of a number of those deals already conducted by stealth. The tribes who were first to sell were Ngati Tamaoho and Ngati Te Ata. They quickly unloaded most of the 1500 acres of land they held in the Mt Hobson (Remuera)-Mt St John area. Ngati Whatua initially held back, partly on principle, partly because they disputed the eastern boundary of the lands that the Waikato tribes wanted to sell.[27] Then they too joined in, alienating virtually all of their isthmus land south of the Remuera Road up to the point where it met the Kohimarama Block. (See map, p.300.)

On 10 October 1844, a further proclamation reduced the tax on land purchased by direct sales to one penny an acre. But as virtually all the valuable land of the central isthmus had already been snapped up in sixty-four purchases made under ten-shilling-an-acre waiver,[28] this tax change need not detain us here. Precisely

1. *Corner Queen and Shortland Streets*
2. *Shortland Street*
3. *Cowey, Solicitor*
4. *Broadbent's Store*
5. *Cornack, Watchmaker*
6. *Nathan & Joseph*
7. *High Street*
8. *Commercial Hotel*
9. *Commons' Store*
10. *Mackenzie, Druggist*

11. *O'Connell Street*
12. *Gibson and Mitchell (first brick building, and the only one at this date except St. Paul's)*
13. *Brown and Campbell.—The firm of Brown and Campbell moved from their range where to new wooden building 2nd June, 1844 ; originally only one storey, the street was filled in eight feet in front, when a second story was built.*
14. *Theatre*
15. *Langford and Gardner*
16. *Scott's Grocery Shop*

17. *Exchange Hotel (site now occupied by Bycroft and Co.)*
18. *New Zealand Banking Co.*
19. *Royal Hotel (now Northern Club)*
20. *Porter's Lodge, Government House Gate*
21. *St. Paul's (opened by Bishop Selwyn, May 7, 1843)*
22. *Captain Tucker's House*
23. *Captain Porter's Store and House*
24. *W. S. Grahame's House and Store*
25. *Victoria Hotel*

26. *Williamson and Crummer's Store*
27. *The Old Government Store (first wooden building erected in Auckland—now the Market)*
28. *Acacia Cottage—Brown and Campbell's House (now occupied by the firm's storeman) the oldest wooden house now extant, erected June, 1843)*
29. *Mechanics' Institute*
30. *Wesleyan Chapel (opened 2nd July, 1843)*
31. *Post Office—Custom House*
32. *New Building, Queen Street (empty)*
33. *Rich's Store*

Gilbert Bros., Printers, 56 High Street, Auckland

Published by W. J. Weir, 84 Victoria St. W.

how much central Auckland land was bought with ten-shilling certificates is not easy to determine. The boundaries listed on deeds are often vaguely defined. But Alemann made an attempt to estimate the total. After aggregating individual purchases from the deed records, he arrived at a figure in excess of 12,000 acres.[29] We should note that of this total, a substantial area ultimately came into the hands of the Crown. One estimate of the land that so reverted is 2500 acres.[30] There were two reasons for the Crown becoming such a beneficiary. First, the proclamation had laid down that of the land bought, 'one-tenth part, of fair average value, as to position and quality' was to be 'conveyed to Her Majesty for public purposes, especially the future benefit of the aborigines'. Second, land disallowed by Commissioner Major Matson when, in 1847, he investigated purchases made under the FitzRoy proclamations, did not automatically revert to the sellers but was generally retained by the Crown.

How much was actually paid to Maori vendors is hard to establish. Much of the consideration was in the form of goods.

Auckland in 1844, lithograph based on sketch of J. Adam published by W. J. Weir.

Alemann's estimate, which combined cash and goods paid to Ngati Whatua for the 6979 acres that they sold, was approximately £1,894, that is, an average price of five shillings an acre.[31] But this figure must be regarded as provisional. And we should also note that no historian has as yet aggregated what the Waikato tribes realised on the many small sales by which they disposed of their 1500 acres. But an examination of the individual deeds of transfer indicates that their Epsom land commanded high prices. The land they had briefly occupied was generally flat or gently sloping, of fine volcanic texture, and close to the three main access routes to town, Remuera, Manukau and Great South Roads. A former study of the land purchases which James Dilworth made in this area would suggest Waikato asked a minimum figure of one pound an acre.[32] But looking at the ten-shilling acre sales over the whole isthmus, it is obvious that prices varied widely. Small parcels of high-quality land in inner Epsom changed hands at thirty shillings to two pounds an acre. Elsewhere in the volcanic corridor, prices generally ranged from three or four shillings to fifteen shillings an acre. The reason for the variation can be mysterious to the modern observer. But not in every instance. One can easily understand why some land went for a few pence an acre. The rock-littered land in the upper Manukau at Southdown changed hands at nominal figures; rocky and inaccessible Puketutu island (479 acres) was sold for ten blankets and five pounds cash.[33]

I shall not debate here whether Ngati Whatua, holders of the mana whenua over Tamaki-makau-rau, and main vendors, first to the Crown, and then to private buyers under the FitzRoy land proclamations, acted improvidently during the early 1840s in alienating the great bulk of their isthmus lands. But this much should be said: it is unreasonable to expect them to have had foreknowledge of the consequences of landlessness. The position in which they found themselves was quite beyond the scope of their former experience. Perhaps they were over-confident that the Crown in the future would respect their wish to hold on to their Orakei lands. But equally it is not unreasonable to have expected officers of the Crown, as part of their fiduciary responsibility, to ensure that a modicum of land remained in Maori hands.[34] For it was commonplace knowledge among colonisers, including governors and officials, that with the growth of settlement, the value of city and suburban land in Australasian settlements increased at an extraordinary rate. Auckland's subsequent history dramatically bore this out. Land commissioner F. Dillon Bell reported in 1862 that allotments in the city of Auckland increased in value by 'at least ten times' between 1844 and 1862.[35] This must be regarded as a conservative estimate. Certainly those settlers who bought city or suburban land in the early days of the settlement and held on to it had become, by the 1860s, wealthy people.[36] Exemplars of this phenomenon were William Brown, Logan Campbell, the Taylor family, James Williamson, James Dilworth, Edward Costley and Hugh Coolahan. There were lesser men who, by the same means and by this time, had acquired a modest competence as well.

It is significant that large city and suburban estates bought in Auckland during this early period were greatly enriched when the city expanded to convert farmland into highly priced metropolitan land. Where those estates, some of which came into the hands of church and philanthropic trusts, were kept intact into the twentieth century, their owners, enjoyed a double economic advantage. For they

- were provided with venture capital if they chose to sell off small parcels of their large estate, or alternatively to use this land as security for bank loans, and
- were enabled to become major leaseholders, thereby ensuring a constant income.

This development highlights how Maori were disadvantaged by the early loss of their Tamaki land.

IV

The decimation of native Americans from the time of Columbus, and of the aboriginal populations of the Pacific, was not mainly the result of wars or the breaking of treaties. It was primarily the impact of European diseases on previously unexposed populations; and then the corrosive effects of international commerce on the societies and economies of indigenous inhabitants. From the viewpoint of the people afflicted, the different ways in which this demoralisation, decline or extinction occurred seem besides the point.

Gareth Stedman Jones, *Independent*, London, 3 July 1995.

The Waitangi Tribunal, after investigating the Orakei claim in 1987, reported that when the Auckland settlement was established, Maori and European who began living together on the isthmus for the first time entered upon 'a mutually beneficial relationship'.[37] For a short while this state of affairs remained undisturbed. Through the relationship both communities enjoyed security. Ngati Whatua and neighbouring tribes also benefited from 'a rapidly expanding market for their produce'.[38] Settlers likewise profited from their dealings with Maori, obtaining plentiful provisions and cheap and efficient labour. Maori acquired European skills, conducted trade in western-designed sailing boats, grew exotic cereals such as wheat, and built flourmills.

But the relationship soured. As white settlement in Auckland accelerated, reaching 8096 by 1849, a figure that included a substantial and growing military component,[39] so did the need for Maori protection decline. And as we have seen, as early as 1843, settler demand for land became more insistent. By the 1850s, some Maori tribes, particularly Waikato to the south of Auckland, became most reluctant to sell.

Could the 'mutually beneficial relationship' have continued? Most historians are cautious about such questions, seeking to avoid discussing the 'ifs' of history. They tend to believe that speculation is not their metier, for it may tempt them to neglect unpredictable variables and to stumble into the quicksands of judgmentalism. And, after all, few of us feel that we live in a Manichaean world of light and darkness, heroes and villains, oppressors and victims. Yet the question must be asked, because some revisionists write as though the course of colonisation could have been checked at a point where Maori could have continued to remain in a relationship with Europeans of equality and mutual respect.

The French have the political concept of 'cohabitation', which they use to denote how ideologically unsympathetic, even antithetic groups, can work (and have worked) together for the common weal. Could cohabitation have worked in pioneer Auckland, between, on the one hand, the Maori society, communal in ownership, socially and economically organised according to kinship, and on the other, a European settler community, individualistic in its economy, technologically advanced, and incorrigibly convinced of the superiority of western ways? In the modern world there are few if any instances of an enduring cohabitation, within the one polity, of a primitive and an advanced economy. The reality is that laissez-faire capitalism tolerates no rivals, and that western consumer goods are a potent wedge breaking apart the resolve of pre-industrial communities to preserve their traditional social order.

In the story of Auckland, and of New Zealand, as in that of the rest of the modern world, impersonal forces of change, not the folly or villainy of the rulers and the ruled, are the usual determinants of change.

> I am going to Auckland tomorrow,
> The abode of the Pakeha,
> The place tobacco and blankets are sold;
> Where the governor and the soldiers live,
> Where the prison stands,
> Where the large ships lie,
> The fire boats are seen,
> Where men are hung;
> Tomorrow I shall go to Auckland.
>
> *Maori song of the 1850s*

NOTES

1 TAMAKI-MAKAU-RAU AND ITS PEOPLES

1 Taimoana Turoa, 'The Hauraki Iwi', Thames, 1995, p.48.
2 Paul Monin, 'Commissioned Report for [Hauraki] claim, Wai 406, for Waitangi Tribunal', Dec. 1996, p.9.
3 For physical geography of Tamaki, Paul Williams & G. Ross Cochrane, 'Auckland's Physical Environment', ch.1 in *Auckland and the Central North Island,* eds Warren Moran & J. Taylor, Auckland, 1979.
4 The logs were probably felled karaka trunks.
5 F. L. Phillips, *Landmarks of Tainui,* vol.1, Otorohanga, 1989, pp.6-12.
6 Walter Brodie in 'Minutes of Evidence given to Select Com. on NZ', no. 13, p.25, 1844 Sess., *BPP, Cols, NZ.*
7 J. Logan Campbell, *Poenamo: Sketches of Early Days in New Zealand,* London, 1881, p.107.
8 Monin, 'Report . . . for Wai 406', p.8.
9 George S. Graham, 'The History of Kauri Point', M15, in MS120, Graham Papers, the George S. Graham Papers in the Auckland War Memorial and Institute Library, (AML). Unless otherwise indicated, all references hereafter to work by Graham will relate to this specific collection.
10 Janet M. Davidson, 'Auckland Prehistory: A Review', *Rec. Auckland Inst. & Mus.,* no. 15, Dec. 1978, pp.4, 10.
11 This paragraph on early settlement is particularly based on: Janet Davidson, 'Auckland' in *The First Thousand Years: Regional Perspectives in New Zealand Archaeology,* ed. Nigel Prickett, Palmerston North, 1982, pp.29-30; and Davidson in *OHNZ,* 2nd ed., 1992, p.7. Susan Bulmer was tireless in assisting me in my work on ch.1. Agnes Sullivan gave much helpful advice after she had read my first draft of

this and two successive chapters.
12 Davidson, 'Auckland Prehistory', 1978, pp.4, 11; Davidson, 'Auckland' in Prickett, 1982, pp.34-35. Janet Davidson's pioneering work in Auckland archaeology and prehistory has proved indispensable for this chapter.
13 L. O. Kermode, inform. See also Susan Bulmer, 'Nga Mara – Traditional Maori Gardens' in *A History of the Garden in NZ,* Auckland, 1995, *passim.*
14 Davidson, *OHNZ,* 1992, p.21.
15 Susan Bulmer, 'Settlement Patterns in Tamaki-makau-rau', in *Oceanic Culture History,* Dunedin, 1996, p.643.
16 D. R. Simmons, inform.
17 Davidson, 'Auckland' in Prickett, 1982, p.44.
18 Anne Salmond, *Two Worlds: First Meetings between Maori and European, 1642–1772,* Auckland, 1991, p.31.
19 Puni Reweti, 'The Natives and the Governor', *NZH,* 23 Jul. 1904, Graham Papers, N1, AML.
20 G. S. Graham, 'The Tamaki Isthmus before the Pakeha', *NZH,* 13 Jan. 1925.
21 G. S. Graham, 'Maori History of the Isthmus' in John Barr, *The City of Auckland,* Auckland, 1922, p.20. See also Graham, 'Maori Place Names', p.11, M6, of MS120, AML.
22 Graham in Barr, p.10.
23 *Important Judgments Delivered in the Compensation Court and the Native Land Court, 1866–79,* Wellington, 1879; Fenton's 'Orakei Judgment' (FOJ), p.57.
24 Salmond, *Two Worlds,* p.39.
25 Monin, 'Report . . . for Wai 406', 1996, citing W. J. England, p.9.
26 Davidson, 'Auckland Prehistory', 1978, p.6.
27 Ibid., pp.10-11.
28 Bulmer, 'Settlement Patterns in Tamaki-makau-rau', p.645.
29 Davidson, *OHNZ,* 1992, p.19.
30 Turoa, p.49.

31 *An Encyclopaedia of New Zealand,* vol. 2, Wellington, 1966, p.88.
32 D. R. Simmons, 'A New Zealand Myth: Kupe, Toi and the "Fleet"', *NZJH,* vol. 3, no. 1, pp.14-31.
33 For a brief critique of Smith and the old ethnographic school, see James Belich, *Making Peoples,* Auckland, 1996, pp.24-25.
34 Davidson in *OHNZ,* 1992, p.6.
35 Davidson, 'Auckland Prehistory', 1978, pp.1, 9.
36 FOJ, p.57.
37 In Barr, 1922, pp.1-32.
38 S. Percy Smith, *The Peopling of the North: Notes on the Ancient History of the Northern Peninsula,* Wellington, 1898, Introduction, p.1 and p.33.
39 See B. G. Biggs, *Encyclopaedia of NZ,* vol. 2, p.454 for an explanation of the historical value of Maori legends in building up a 'factual record of the past'.
40 There is little doubt, however, that *Tainui* and *Arawa* arrived more or less simultaneously.
41 See, e.g., the case for so regarding Maori tradition and genealogy, made by Bruce Biggs in his introduction (p.7), in P. T. H. Jones and Bruce Biggs, *Nga Iwi O Tainui,* Auckland, 1995.
42 John Waititi, 'An Outline of Auckland's Maori History', *J. of Ak. His. Soc.,* Oct. 1963, p.9.
43 Sources for Tainui visit to Tamaki: Phillips, *Landmarks of Tainui,* vol. 1, pp.6-9; Te-Warena Taua, 'Tamaki-makau-rau: The People', typescript, Auckland Museum Lib., 1987; Biggs in *Encyclopaedia of NZ,* vol. 2, pp.451-3; Elizabeth T. Jackson, *Delving into the Past of Auckland's Eastern Suburbs,* Auckland, 1976, vol. 1, pp.7-8; David Simmons, *Maori Auckland,* Auckland, 1987, pp.27-28; Graham in Barr, 1922, pp.6-8; Turoa, pp.38-40.
44 Phillips, vol. 1, p.8.
45 Simmons, *Maori Auckland,* pp.27-28.
46 Phillips, vol. 1, p.8.
47 Taua, 1987, p.3.

48 Sources for this para: Waititi, p.8; E. T. Jackson, vol. 1, p.8; Turoa, p.9.
49 *Encyclopaedia of NZ*, vol. 2, p.88.
50 FOJ, p.61; Barr, *City of Auckland*, pp.8-9.
51 For *Aotea*: Jackson, *Delving in the Past of Auckland's Eastern Suburbs*, vol. 1, p.9; Simmons, *Maori Auckland*, pp.24-26; Graham in Barr, *City of Auckland*, p.10.
52 Margaret Orbell, *The Illustrated Encyclopedia of Maori Myth and Legend*, Christchurch, 1995, pp.109-10; Biggs in *Encyclopaedia of NZ*, vol. 2, p.453.
53 Smith, *Peopling of the North*, pp.38-47.
54 G. S. Graham, 'A History of Te Korekore', typescript, dated 17 Apr. 1914, M14, MS120, AML.
55 See also Simmons, *Maori Auckland*, p.23; Waititi, p.9; Graham in Barr, p.10.
56 Smith, *Peopling of the North*, pp.81-82; George Graham, 'Romance of One Tree Hill', *NZ Centennial News*, 25 Oct. 1938, pp.17-18; *North Shore News*, 15 Dec. 1938; M. H. Wynyard, *The History of One Tree Hill . . . known . . . as Maungakiekie*, 2nd ed., 1958; Taua, 1987, p.2; Simmons, inform. Wynyard and Graham are not always reliable in their account of this episode. See also Te Rangi Hiroa, *The Coming of the Maori*, Wellington, 1950, pp.351-2.
57 One account speaks of Korokino's mother as being of Waiohua stock.
58 See, e.g., Orbell, 1995, pp.34-35, 63-64; Salmond, *Two Worlds*, p.44.
59 Graham, 'Romance of One Tree Hill', p.17.
60 J. L. Campbell, *Poenamo: Sketches of the Early Days in NZ*, London, 1881, p.105. Campbell's claim to have coined the name is open to question.
61 Dieffenbach, *Travels in New Zealand*, London, 1843, vol. 1, p.291.
62 F. von Hochstetter, *Geology of New Zealand*, Wellington, 1959, p.194. (Reprint of Stuttgart, 1863 edition, translation C. A. Fleming.)
63 *Daily Southern Cross*, 14 Aug. 1875.
64 Ibid.
65 J. Davidson in Prickett, 1982,

pp.34-5. The term 'Archaic' has fallen into disfavour, and especially in the case of Tamaki, inasmuch as it suggests a periodisation which implicitly conceals the essential continuity characteristic of the garden-based economy in the region.
66 Susan Bulmer, *Sources for the Archaeology of the Maori Settlement of the Taamaki Volcanic District*, Wellington, 1994, p.45.
67 FOJ, pp.53-96. How the hearings and judgment of the court dragged on from November 1866 to late 1869, and why, are explained in the *Orakei Report of the Waitangi Tribunal (Wai 9)*, Wellington, 1987, pp.36-37.
68 FOJ, p.59.
69 Ibid., p.57.
70 Ibid., p.58.
71 Orakei Native Land Court Minutebook (hereinafter OMB), vol. 2, p.187 (Te Waka Tuaea).
72 Ibid., vol. 1, p.191 (Paora Te Iwi); vol. 1, p.139 (Tamati Otatu Tangiteruru); Graham, MS120, M44, p.5, AML. Note that each account varies in certain detail.
73 Simmons, *Maori Auckland*, p.23.
74 FOJ, p.61; G. S. Graham, 'Nga Matura', M44, Graham Papers, AML.
75 Susan Bulmer in unpub. paper 'City without a State', citing Agnes Sullivan.
76 Agnes Sullivan, 'Maori Occupation of the Otaahuhu District up to 1840', p.13.
77 FOJ, p.62.
78 Sources for Te Kawerau: George Graham, 'History of the Kawerau Tribe of Waitakere', *JPS*, vol. 34, New Plymouth, 1925, pp.19-33; Graeme Murdoch, 'Nga Tohu o Waitakere', in *West Auckland Remembers*, ed. James Northcote-Bade, Auckland, 1990, pp.9-32.
79 Murdoch, p.12.
80 Smith, *Peopling of the North*, pp.67-68; Graham, 'History of Kawerau Tribe', pp.21-22; Murdoch, 'Nga Tohu o Waitakere', p.14.
81 For more on Te Kawerau, see Murdoch, p.19, and Smith, *Peopling of the North*, p.76.
82 Chief sources for Ngai Tai: Te Warena Taua, 'A History of the Maori People', in *The History of*

Howick and Pakuranga, ed. Alan La Roche, Auckland, 1991, pp.27-43; Turoa, 'The Hauraki Iwi', pp.38-41.
83 Monin, 'Report . . . for Wai 406', pp.8, 14.
84 Taua, 1991, pp.28-29.
85 Sources for Ngati Paoa: Turoa, pp.34-37; Bronwyn Kayes, 'Ancestors of Ngati Paoa', n.d., AML.
86 Monin, p.17. Fenton unabashedly did so. In his famous judgment he admitted that he 'used the name as meaning *all* the Thames tribes, unless some other tribe is indicated'. (FOJ, p.84; italics mine.)
87 Report of James Mackay, 27 Jul. 1869, *AJHR*, 1869, A-17, p.17.
88 Turoa, oral inform.
89 Turoa, 'The Hauraki Iwi', p.36.
90 R. C. J. Stone, *Young Logan Campbell*, Auckland, 1982, p.64.
91 Sullivan, 'Maori Occupation of the Otaahuhu District', pp.1-28.
92 Ibid., p.12.
93 Ibid., pp.6-7, 13-14.
94 FOJ, p.59.
95 Monin, p.16.
96 Orbell, *Maori Myth and Legend*, 1995, p.238; Graham in Barr, p.17.
97 Turoa, p.27.
98 Sources for the killing of Kahurautao: Waititi, 'Auckland's Maori History', 1963, p.9; Jackson, 'Auckland's Eastern Suburbs', vol. 1, pp.12-13; Graham in Barr, pp.17-18; Turoa, p.27.
99 G. S. Graham, 'Lecture on Mangere Mountain', Graham Papers, M33; E. C. Franklin, *Mt Eden's First Hundred Years*, Auckland, 1956, p.15.
100 Ibid., 'Maungawhau', N14.
101 Stone, *James Dilworth*, Auckland, 1995, p.24.
102 Dumont d'Urville, *New Zealand 1826–1827*, trans. Olive Wright, Wellington, 1950, pp.154-5.
103 In Fenton's Orakei Judgment he is called Tarakumikumi.
104 For Kapetaua episode: FOJ, pp.61-62; Waititi, p.9; Jackson, vol. 1, pp.13-14; Monin, 'Report . . . for Wai 406', pp.16-17; Turoa, pp.18-19. Kapetaua has alternative spelling of Kapetawa in some accounts.

105 Turoa, p.4.
106 FOJ, p.62.

2 FROM WAIOHUA TO NGATI
  WHATUA-O-TAMAKI,
  C.1600–1800

1 Paora Tuhaere, 'Chronological
  Table of Ngati Whatua,
  1530–1822', Grey Collection,
  MSGG725, APL.
2 Graham in Barr, p.20.
3 Ibid.
4 Percy Smith discusses this
  problem in his Introduction to
  Peopling of the North. Historians
  have been obliged to rely heavily
  on Native Land Court records,
  where most witnesses were
  interested parties trying to
  establish claims and selective
  (understandably) in the evidence
  that they provided.
5 OMB, vol. 1, p.225 (Warena
  Hengia); Paora Tuhaere, 'A
  Historical Narrative concerning
  the Conquest of Kaipara and
  Tamaki by Ngati-Whatua', *JPS*,
  1923, p.230.
6 Buck, 1950, p.83.
7 Ibid., p.311.
8 Ibid., p.187.
9 Anne Salmond, *Two Worlds*, 1991,
  p.281.
10 Buck, 1950, p.298, was in no
  doubt, believing experimentation
  to have taken place, at first, on
  'inanimate wood rather than
  sensitive skin'.
11 Angela Ballara, *Iwi*, Wellington,
  1998, p.33 discusses diffusion of
  cultural traits and artefacts. Cook
  was astonished by the speed with
  which intelligence passed from
  district to district in Aotearoa.
12 Buck, 1950, p.135; R. A. Cruise,
  *Journal of Ten Months' Residence in
  New Zealand*, p.25.
13 Salmond, *Two Worlds*, p.39.
14 Smith, *Peopling of the North*, p.80.
15 Graham in Barr, p.13.
16 L. G. Kermode, oral inform.
17 Smith, *Peopling of the North*, p.64.
18 Ibid.
19 It was a back-up food to kumara,
  of course, even in times of peace.
20 Waititi, p.8.
21 Graham in Barr, p.20.
22 Usually with intra-hapu strife that

remained unresolved, one party
(often the weaker) would relocate
itself elsewhere, sometimes with a
tribe to which it was related. This
was a well-developed custom for
avoiding armed conflict.
23 FOJ, pp.61-62.
24 See, e.g., OMB, vol. 1, p.21
  (Paora Te Iwi); vol. 1, pp.10,
  215-6. Monin, 'Report . . . for
  Wai 406', pp.8-9, demonstrates
  that on the Gulf islands, rights
  were shared, but in a different
  manner.
25 OMB, vol. 1, p.39. The division of
  land he was referring to was the
  title system under British law.
26 Salmond, *Two Worlds*, p.44.
27 Rahui is the term for a ritual
  prohibition, sometimes to prevent
  trespass, sometimes to preserve a
  resource, whose visible form could
  be a post, hank of hair, stone or
  some such object.
28 A.W. Reed, *Illustrated Encyclopedia
  of Maori Life*, Wellington, 1963,
  pp.107, 177.
29 Buck, p.367.
30 Graham in Barr, pp.19-20.
31 OMB, vol. 1, p.192 (Paora Te Iwi).
32 Smith, *Peopling of the North*, p.77.
33 Stone, 'Historical Report on
  Maungakiekie and One Tree Hill',
  Cornwall Park Trust Board,
  Auckland, 1995.
34 Aileen Fox, *Pa of the Auckland
  Isthmus. An Archaeological Analysis*,
  Auckland, 1977, p.12.
35 For Tainui traditions of attacks on
  Maungakiekie, see Jones and
  Biggs, *Nga Iwi o Tainui*, pp.322,
  332.
36 For further information, Bulmer,
  *Sources for . . . Tamaki Volcanic
  District*, 1994, p.43.
37 Aileen Fox, *Maungakiekie: The
  Maori Pa on One Tree Hill*,
  Auckland, 1978, (unpaginated).
38 Smith, *Peopling of the North*, pp.78-
  79.
39 The citadel on Maungakiekie has
  interesting similarities to that on
  the Hill of Tara in Co. Meath,
  Ireland, where Celtic high kings
  dwelt in the pre-Christian era; see
  Catharina Day, *Guide to Ireland*,
  London, 1986, pp.413-4.
40 For information on the pahu see
  Buck, pp.253-4, and Reed,
  Encyclopedia, p.80.

41 The Orakei NLC judge asked
  Warena Hengia: 'Have you ever
  heard of Whakarewatahuna?' He
  replied 'Yes. [It was] a slab of
  unpolished stone. . . . [Kiwi] hung
  it up as a sounding bell or gong
  for him.' (OMB, vol. 2, p.5). This
  stone has sometimes been confused
  with the ritual kumara stone
  called 'Te Toki i tawhio' (the stone
  which travels around), which
  originated at Te Arai, but was later
  relocated at various parts of
  Tamaki until removed to Cornwall
  Park where it remains; *Cornwall
  Park; A Handbook*, Auckland,
  1985, p.13. See also Elizabeth
  T. Jackson, 'Auckland's Eastern
  Suburbs', vol. 1, pp.11-12.
42 Whether the wooden slab was
  hollowed in some way to help it to
  reverberate, oral records nowhere
  make clear.
43 Smith, *Peopling of the North*, pp.79,
  87.
44 For Ngati Whatua origins see
  Orakei Report Wai 9, 1987, p.12.
45 Graeme Murdoch, 'Nga Tohu o
  Waitakere', 1990, p.14.
46 Smith, *Peopling of the North*, pp.68-
  69.
47 *Orakei Report Wai* 9, p.12.
48 Smith, *Peopling of the North*, p.83.
49 Exogamous marriages, by
  facilitating military alliances,
  sometimes worked to provoke war.
  But equally they could serve to
  avert hostilities. (Te Rangi Hiroa,
  p.367).
50 An uhunga may also be a solemn
  ceremony preparatory to the burial
  of a chief's bones.
51 Estimates range from 30 to 200.
  See, e.g., Paora Tuhaere, OMB,
  vol. 2, p.78.
52 Smith says that Kiwi threatened to
  suspend Waha-akiaki's bone from
  the branches of the totara on
  Maungakiekie.
53 Tuhaere, 'The Conquest of Kaipara
  and Tamaki...', *JPS*, 1923,
  pp.231-2; see also Tuhaere in
  OMB, vol. 2, p.79. George
  Graham believed that what sealed
  the fate of Kiwi and Waiohua was
  the curse Kiwi levelled at Waha-
  akiaki before they parted. Kiwi, he
  said, threatened to form the
  breastbones and ribs of the
  Kaipara chief into a cage for his

pet tui to be hung on the branches of Te Totara-i-ahua on the summit of Maungakiekie. ('Romance of One Tree Hill', *NZ Centennial News*, 25 Oct. 1938.)

54 FOJ, p.63; Smith, *Peopling of the North*, p.84.

55 Smith, *Peopling of the North*, p.86.

56 The pukaea was a wooden trumpet for sounding the alarm.

57 Smith, *Peopling of the North*, p.87.

58 G. S. Graham, 'Maori Chieftainship' in *NZH*, 26 Jun. 928; see also Graham Papers, N35.

59 Paul D'Arcy, *NZJH*, vol. 34, no.1 (Apr. 2000), p.121. It will be recalled that during the earlier exchange of curses at Kaipara, Kiwi prophesied that he would not die until Rehu, the atua or god who dwelt within him, decided that his time had come.

60 Paora Tuhaere, 'History of the Ngati Whatua Tribe with their Genealogy', Grey Collection, APL, p.9.

61 Ibid.

62 Smith, *Peopling of the North*, p.87.

63 The number killed varies greatly in accounts. Warena Hengia claimed to have heard from Te Taou relatives, who fought in the battle, that the number of Waiohua killed was 200. This is a credible figure.

64 Paora Tuhaere, OMB, vol. 2, p.80.

65 Graham in Barr, p.22.

66 It was reputed to be a lizard, the physical form favoured by 'virulent deities'. See J. S. Polack, *Manners and Customs of the New Zealanders*, London, 1840, vol. 1, pp.241, 244. Another account has two large stones found in Kiwi's body.

67 OMB, vol. 2, p.80.

68 FOJ, p.63; Warena Hengia, OMB, vol. 1, p.224.

69 FOJ, p.63.

70 Smith, *Peopling of the North*, p.88.

71 Graham, 'Mangere Mountain', Graham Papers, M33, p.7.

72 Smith, *Peopling of the North*, pp.88-89.

73 OMB, vol. 2, p.82 (Paora Tuhaere).

74 Ibid., pp.178-9 (Te Waka Tuaea of Ngati Whatua o Kaipara).

75 'The Bastion' was then a very

small sugar-loaf island that had become 'detached' from the mainland by sea erosion. It disappeared with road construction and reclamation on Tamaki Drive in the early twentieth century.

76 Smith, *Peopling of the North*, pp.89-90; Elizabeth T. Jackson, vol. 1, pp.15-16.

77 OMB, vol. 1, pp.224-5. FOJ, p.63, and Smith, p.89, both imply that there was the final takeover within a year.

78 Tuhaere, 'Chronological Table', APL. Yet at the Orakei NLC hearing in Oct. 1868 he testified that the Waitemata pa fell *before* Mangere. (OMB, vol. 2, p.81.)

79 OMB, vol. 1, pp.224-5; Smith, *Peopling of the North*, pp.89-90.

80 FOJ, p.63.

81 See, e.g., Ballara, *Iwi*, pp.82, 89, 90.

82 OMB, vol. 1, p.190.

83 Fenton uses 'extinct' on p.64 of his judgment. This term is repeated by Smith in *Peopling of the North*, p.90.

84 Jones and Biggs, p.228, tells of this family relationship.

85 Norman Smith, *Native Custom and Law Affecting Native Land*, Wellington, 1942, pp.62-68; cf. Ballara, *Iwi*, p.139.

86 FOJ, p.82.

87 See, e.g., Stone, *James Dilworth*, Auckland, p.57.

88 Maurice Alemann, 'Early Land Transactions in the Ngati Whatua Tribal Area', MA thesis, University of Auckland, 1992, p.153, Appendix 2.

89 OMB, vol. 1, pp.224-5; Smith, *Peopling of the North*, pp.89-90.

90 OMB, vol. 1, p.214; see also p.10.

91 FOJ, p.59. Te Kawau had Waiohua blood on the maternal side.

92 Ibid., p.65.

93 Smith, *Peopling of the North*, p.91.

94 OMB, vol. 1, p.213 (Apihai Te Kawau).

95 FOJ, pp.65-66.

96 OMB, vol. 1, p.225 (Warena Hengia).

97 Ibid., vol. 1, p.218 (Te Kawau).

98 See, e.g., Graham in Barr, pp.25, 26; Waititi, p.10.

99 OMB, vol. 1, p.56 (Hori Tauroa).

100 OMB, vol. 1, p.34 (Paora Te Iwi).

101 Monin, 1996, pp.16-20. Their rights to Waiheke were shared with other hapu.

102 Turoa, p.35.

103 Fenton's estimate was 'about 1780' (FOJ, p.66). Te Kawau testified to the Orakei court in 1868 that the gift (koha) of Tauoma was made when he was (signalling with his hand) 2 feet 6 inches tall, i.e. an infant. As he took part in the Battle of Hingakaka c.1807 as a warrior-chief, this would seem to place the gift in the 1780s.

104 FOJ, p.66.

105 OMB, vol. 1, pp.226-7.

106 Not to be confused with the Te Tahuri who had been Kiwi Tamaki's mother.

107 Kehu, described as a 'teina', could have been a sibling; but cousin seems the more likely relationship.

108 Warena Hengia, OMB, vol. 1, p.226.

109 FOJ, p.66. Lake Waiatarua is today a wetland park of the Auckland City Council. For a precise description of the original boundaries of the gifted land, see OMB, vol. 1, p.208.

110 K. M. Holloway, *Maungarei*, Auckland, 1962, p.39.

111 OMB, vol. 1, p.226 (Warena Hengia).

112 For Maori use of tupakihi, see Murdoch Riley, *Maori Healing and Herbal*, Paraparaumu, 1994, pp.484-8.

113 Fenton's term.

114 FOJ, p.66.

115 Versions from the opposing tribal viewpoints are provided in the 1868 OMB, vol. 1, Te Kawau of Ngati Whatua, p.218 and Tamati Otatu of the Ngati Hura hapu of Ngati Paoa, pp.134-6.

116 Paora Tuhaere in 'Chronological Table', APL.

117 G. S. Graham, 'Maori Proverbs', M38, Graham Papers, AML.

118 The exact site of this bloody battle is not made clear in the Native Land Court records. Fenton, not always reliable as to dates and places, states in his judgment (p.67) that the fight took place 'at Rangimatariki near the Whau'.

119 FOJ, p.67.

120 Ibid.

121 Ibid.
122 For this section, Jones and Biggs, pp.328-9.
123 Turoa, p.36.
124 Leslie G. Kelly, *Tainui*, Wellington, 1949, p.278.
125 Ibid.
126 Ibid., pp.278-9.
127 Ibid., pp.199-200.
128 Ibid., p.200.
129 Jones and Biggs, pp.228, 248, 322.
130 Kelly, p.279.
131 Holloway, p.41.

3 PEACE AND WAR, C.1800–21

1 S. Percy Smith, *Maori Wars of the Nineteenth Century*, 2nd ed., Christchurch, 1910, p.219; A. S. Thomson, *The Story of New Zealand: Past and Present – Savage and Civilised*, London, 1859, vol. 1, pp.128, 140-1; G. S. Graham, 'Primitive Weapons of the Maori', and 'Maori Projectile Weapons', M58 and M59, Graham Papers, AML.
2 Buck, 1950, p.367.
3 A. S. Thomson, *The Story of New Zealand*, vol. 1, 1859, pp.122-3. Agnes Sullivan does not agree, believing that instances of large-scale, long-range warfare occur 'over the whole time range of Maori historical tradition', and that it was only the 'frequency and intensity' of 19th-century wars that were new. (Letter to author, 4 Jan. 1999.)
4 Ballara, *Iwi*, p.237.
5 Belich, *Making Peoples*, p.159.
6 J. C. Beaglehole, *The Discovery of New Zealand*, London, 1961, pp.62-85.
7 R. A.Cruise, *Journal of a Ten Months' Residence in New Zealand*, 2nd ed., London, 1824, p.52.
8 Ibid., p.20.
9 Ian Pool, *Te Iwi Maori*, Auckland, 1991, pp.53-54.
10 The best brief historiographical treatment of this issue is in Belich, *Making Peoples*, pp.173-8.
11 Pool, p.63.
12 Ibid., p.46.
13 Pool, pp.41-42, persuasively relates fecundability (fertility) of Maori to a settled gardening economy.

14 Material on Marsden is based on: J. R. Elder (ed.), *The Letters and Journals of Samuel Marsden, 1765–1838*, Dunedin, 1932; A.T. Yarwood, *Samuel Marsden*, Melbourne, 1968; G. S. Parsonson, *DNZB*, vol. 1, 1990, pp.271-3.
15 Elder, p.143.
16 Ibid., pp.318-9.
17 *Earliest New Zealand: The Journals and Correspondence of the Rev. John Butler*, comp. by R. J. Barton, Masterton, 1927.
18 A launch or longboat (usually flat-bottomed) was, in that period, the largest boat attached to a man-of-war.
19 The best background for this section of the chapter is provided by James Belich, *Making Peoples*, Auckland, 1996, and J. M. R. Owens, 'New Zealand Before Annexation', in *OHNZ*, 2nd ed., Auckland, 1992, Ch. 2.
20 Elder, p.283.
21 *Earliest New Zealand*, p.100.
22 Cruise, p.270.
23 See Angela Ballara, in *DNZB*, vol. 1, pp.450-2 (Biog. of Te Horeta), and D. R. Simmons, 'Cyclical Aspects of Early Maori Agriculture', *Records of the Auckland Institute and Museum*, Dec. 1975, p.84.
24 Elder, pp.268, 282-3, 289.
25 Ibid., p.279.
26 *Earliest New Zealand*, p.97.
27 Ibid., pp.97-98.
28 Ibid.
29 Cruise, pp.52, 66-67.
30 Thomson, vol. 1, pp.315-6, discusses the 'worldly motives' of Maori who 'begged' to have a missionary reside with them.
31 Kumara gardens or stores were often the target of 'hit and run' raids.
32 Cruise, p.204.
33 F. E. Maning, *Old New Zealand: A Tale of the Good Old Times*, Auckland, 1863, p.17.
34 See, e.g., Cruise, pp.205-6.
35 Cruise, p.44, suggests that this was much the preferred pattern of settlement.
36 This para. is based on the evidence in the OMB, vol. 1, pp.215-6 (Te Kawau), and vol. 2, pp.7-8, and vol. 1, pp.222-3 (Warena Hengia).

37 Ibid., vol. 2, p.11 (Te Kawau).
38 Ibid., pp.211, 216 (Te Kawau); Norman Smith, *Native Custom and Law Affecting Native Land*, Wellington, 1942, pp.48, 57, 58, 68.
39 Elder, p.279.
40 *Earliest New Zealand*, p.98.
41 Cruise, p.216.
42 Ibid.
43 Agnes Sullivan, 'Maori Occupation of the Otaahuhu District up to 1840', Maori Studies Department, VUW, 1981, passim.
44 OMB, vol. 2, pp.15-16 (Warena Hengia).
45 Ibid., vol. 1, pp.38-39 (Horia Tauroa).
46 Ibid., p.216 (Te Kawau).
47 FOJ, p.68.
48 OMB, vol. 1, pp.215-8 (Te Kawau).
49 See Ch. II.
50 Graham in Barr, pp.25, 27.
51 Terry, *New Zealand*, London, 1842, p.56.
52 Simmons, 1975, pp.85, 87.
53 Elder, p.280.
54 Terry, *New Zealand*, p.37.
55 Ibid., p.56.
56 Ibid., pp.56-57.
57 For a more detailed statement on developments, in the first half of the nineteenth century, affecting Maori husbandry and foods, see Thomson, 1859, vol. 1, pp.152-61.
58 Cit. Simmons, 1975, p.87.
59 Cruise, p.270.
60 Elder, p.313.
61 Terry, p.55.
62 Stone, *Young Logan Campbell*, p.47.
63 John Logan Campbell, *Poenamo: Sketches of Early Days in New Zealand*, London, 1881, pp.297-9. For the pig farm on Puketutu, see OMB, vol. 2, pp.86, 142-3.
64 Stone, *Young Logan Campbell*, pp.82-83, 96.
65 Campbell, *Poenamo*, pp.336-8.
66 Cruise, p.270.
67 Ngati Paoa of Tamaki, like Ngaitai, also had fishing stations on the inner gulf islands, which they shared with other Hauraki hapu.
68 Those not concerned with the production of food, would have been engaged in other activities:

domestic crafts e.g. canoe- or house-construction, stone tool making, arts e.g. weaving, net-making, or activities of a religious or educational character, etc.

69 OMB, vol. 1, p.215 (Te Kawau).

70 A. S. Thomson, vol. 1, pp.152-3 lists the main fish eaten by Maori, but mistakenly omits shark. J. Polack, *Manners and Customs of New Zealanders*, London, 1840, vol. 1, pp.191-203 is also helpful.

71 The main stands of bush available for the Tamaki people were on the margins of the region, in the Waitakere ranges to the north-west and in the Hunua ranges to the south-west.

72 A. S. Thomson, vol. 1, p.30.

73 Ibid., pp.189-90; Cruise, p.106.

74 D. R. Simmons, oral inform.

75 Simmons, 1975, pp.85-86. Simmons has also pointed out verbally that the extent of secondary regrowth on former garden sites was carefully noted by Maori gardeners, when they were assessing the readiness of former garden sites for re-use.

76 Graham, 'The Maori Mere Pounamu', N9; 'Primitive Weapons of the Maori', M58; both Graham Papers, AML.

77 Buck, pp.402-3. Elsdon Best, *The Maori*, Wellington, 1941, vol. 2, p.300, fully explains the concept, and how it had its origin in the actual physical construction of a small sliding greenstone door, that was intended to actualise the forging of a lasting peace between the two hitherto estranged tribes. An exchange of greenstone mere, often mana-filled family heirlooms, could also impart solemnity and sincerity to a peace-making. For more, see G. S. Graham, 'Primitive Weapons of the Maori', in the Graham Papers, MS120, M58, p.18

77 Elder, p.279.

78 Ibid.

79 Ibid., pp.254-5.

80 Taimoana Turoa, 'The Hauraki Iwi', p.32.

81 Ana Pihema et al., 'Apihai Te Kawau', *DNZB*, vol. 1, pp.459-60.

82 Elder, p.284. See also *DNZB*, vol. 1, pp.304-5 (Angela Ballara).

83 For the battle of Hingakaka, see Jones and Biggs, *Nga Iwi O Tainui*, pp.348-57, Leslie G. Kelly, *Tainui*, pp.287-96, and Phillips, *Landmarks of Tainui*, vol. 1, pp.115-22.

84 Phillips, vol. 1, p.121.

85 Bruce Biggs considered, on linguistic grounds, that 'hingakaka' is more likely to mean 'fishing by nets' (*Nga Iwi O Tainui*, p.356.). Both translations of the name given here, however, imply, metaphorically, a heavy loss of life.

86 Smith, *Maori Wars of the Nineteenth Century*, pp.31-49. This important battle will be discussed in the next chapter.

87 This account of Te Amiowhenua is based on Kelly, *Tainui*, pp.331-50, Smith, *Maori Wars of the Nineteenth Century*, pp.208-24; The Minutes and Judgment of the Native Land Court hearings for the Orakei block, conducted by Chief Judge F. D. Fenton (1868), and for the investigation of the Manukatutahi titles conducted by Judge E. W. Puckey (1884); the biographies of Te Kawau, Te Rauparaha and Te Wherowhero in *DNZB*, vol. 1, 1990; Malcolm McKinnon (ed.), *New Zealand Historical Atlas*, Auckland, 1997.

88 OMB, vol. 2, p.16 (Warena Hengia).

89 Smith, *Maori Wars of the Nineteenth Century*, p.223.

90 Ibid.

91 Puckey in the Manukatuitahi Judgment speaks of elements in this taua periodically dropping off, en route, in order to return home.

92 Steven Oliver in *DNZB*, vol. 1, pp.526-8.

93 Kelly, *Tainui*, pp.341-50, has the best coverage of the battle of Okoki.

94 OMB, vol. 2, p.188 (Te Waka Tuae).

95 Ibid., vol. 2, p.17 (Warena Hengia).

4 WAR FROM THE NORTH, 1821–26

1 Keith Sinclair, *A History of New Zealand*, rev. ed., Auckland, 1991, p.24.

2 Polack, vol. 2, p.1.

3 G. S. Graham, 'Primitive Weapons of the Maori', M58, Graham Papers.

4 A. S. Thomson, *The Story of New Zealand*, vol. 1, p.124.

5 OMB, vol. 2, p.52 (Matire Toha). The proverb referred to was 'The marriage of a woman is an act of binding [which makes] the peacemaking unbreakable'.

6 Polack, vol. 1, p.103.

7 Turoa, 'The Hauraki Iwi', p.36.

8 Ballara, *Iwi*, p.236.

9 *New Zealand Historical Atlas*, pp.28-29.

10 Ballara, in *DNZB*, vol. 1, pp.201-2.

11 'Moremonui, a fragmentary memoir of Tiatora of Kaihu', trans. G. S. Graham, 8 Jan. 1921, M8, Graham Papers. But cf. Smith, *Maori Wars of the Nineteenth Century*, pp.31-40, where a different cause of the battle is given.

12 Smith, *Maori Wars of the Nineteenth Century*, pp.44-48, has the most detailed account of the battle.

13 Their intention was probably to reach Mangawhare (near Dargaville) by turning inland at Bailey's Beach, or by passing through the Mahuta gap.

14 A Historic Places plaque at the site of the battle commemorates this fact.

15 Smith, *Maori Wars of the Nineteenth Century*, p.48.

16 Inform. supplied by John Stacpoole. These two plantations are in the neighbourhood of Ohaewai.

17 *DNZB*, vol. 1, pp.450-2 (Angela Ballara).

18 This version of the meeting and the threat made there is based on Anaru Makuihara of Ngai-tai, 'The Fall of Mokoia and Mauinaina', p.1, M7, Graham Papers. Smith in *Maori Wars of the Nineteenth Century*, pp.183-4, states that the threat was made in the Bay of Islands *after* the three had sailed back together there from Port Jackson; but the balance of evidence is against Smith's account.

19 Turoa, p.36.

20 Ibid.

21 This was a humiliating defeat,

which a joint Marutuahu war-party inflicted on Nga Puhi in the Bay of Islands during the 1790s.

22 The battle of Moremonui, 'The seagulls' feast'.

23 Smith, *Maori Wars of the Nineteenth Century*, pp.183-4.

24 Sources used for this section on the conquest of Mokoia and Mauinaina are: Orakei NLC Minutebooks; Fenton's Orakei Judgment; Graham Papers, AML; Smith, *Maori Wars of the Nineteenth Century*, pp.177-90; Kelly, *Tainui*, pp.350-2; Holloway, *Maungarei*; Jackson, *Auckland's Eastern Suburbs*, vol. 1.

25 Mokoia had been the first of the two pa built, under the super-vision of Tangiteruru, Kahukoti, and Te Putu; OMB, vol. 1, p.114.

26 Smith, *Maori Wars of the Nineteenth Century*, pp.177-8, citing the Rev. T. Buddle.

27 OMB, vol. 1, p.209.

28 Ibid., vol. 1, p.210 (Apihai Te Kawau).

29 Ibid., vol. 2, p.15 (Warena Hengia). The hapu were Ngaoho, Uringutu, and Akitai.

30 Ibid., vol. 1, p.210.

31 Ibid., vol. 2, p.8 (Warena Hengia).

32 Ibid., p.16.

33 Smith, *Maori Wars of the Nineteenth Century*, p.180.

34 Ibid.

35 Anaru Makiwhara, of Ngai Tai, Maraetai, 'The Fall of Mokoia and Mauinaina and the Death of Kaea', M7, Graham Papers.

36 OMB, vol. 1, p.215 (Apihai Te Kawau).

37 G. S. Graham, 'The Maori Mere Pounamu', p.2, N9, Graham Papers.

38 He was mortally wounded when a musket ball penetrated his chest in an action at Whangaroa in 1827, though he lingered some months before dying.

39 Kelly, *Tainui*, p.352.

40 Ibid., pp.351-2.

41 Smith, *Maori Wars of the Nineteenth Century*, p.188. Hongi later provided the Rev. Samuel Marsden with a sanitised account of the battle.

42 For example, Kelly, *Tainui*, p.351.

43 Anaru Makiwhara, 'The fall of Mokoia ...', p.1.

44 Ibid., p.2.

45 Ibid. From Mokoia to Tuakau would have been a distance of 45 kilometres.

46 FOJ, p.69.

47 The chief source of this paragraph is Anaru Makiwhara, 'The Fall of Mokoia ...'.

48 *Missionary Register*, 1823, cit. *Earliest New Zealand*, pp.216, 252.

49 Kelly, p.352. Kelly does not differentiate between Mauinaina and Mokoia.

50 Waititi, 'An Outline of Auckland's Maori History', p.10.

51 Smith, *Maori Wars of the Nineteenth Century*, p.190.

52 Cruise, pp.204-5.

53 OMB, vol. 1, p.75 (Hetaraka Takapuna).

54 Charles Terry, *New Zealand*, London, 1842, p.37.

55 FOJ, p.73.

56 Smith, *Maori Wars of the Nineteenth Century*, p.191.

57 Ibid., pp.190-9.

58 Ibid., pp.192-6.

59 G. S. Graham, 'The Maori Mere Pounamu', N9, Graham Papers.

60 *Early Journals of Henry Williams*, Christchurch, 1961, p.344 (11 Nov. 1833).

61 William Williams Journals, vol. 3, p.348 (2 Jan. 1834).

62 'The Aroha Judgment', in *Important Judgments*, Wellington, 1879, p.110.

63 Ibid., pp.110-11.

64 Barton, *Earliest New Zealand*, p.216.

65 Smith, *Maori Wars of the Nineteenth Century*, pp.226-7, estimated that the taua numbered as many as 3000 fighting men.

66 Barton, pp.216-7.

67 The main settlements of Ngati Whanaunga were at Manaia, on the coast just south of the modern township of Coromandel, but the iwi had pockets of settlement elsewhere.

68 Ngati Tama-Te-Ra were widely spread through the Coromandel peninsula and the islands of the Hauraki gulf.

69 The homelands of Ngati Hei were in the Whitianga area.

70 Turoa, p.28.

71 OMB, vol. 1, p.22 (Paora Te Iwi).

72 Horotiu was the name given by Maori to that section of the Waikato river valley lying between Cambridge and Ngaruawahia.

73 FOJ, pp.69-70.

74 Barton, *Earliest New Zealand*, pp.173-4 (statement by Rewa).

75 OMB, vol. 2, pp.111-2 (Paora Tuhaere).

76 Murdoch in *West Auckland Remembers*, 1990, p.18.

77 OMB, vol. 1, p.210.

78 Ibid., p.211.

79 The main sources for this war are: Kelly, *Tainui*, pp.356-67; Smith, *Maori Wars of the Nineteenth Century*, pp.224-41; OMB, *passim*; FOJ, pp.69-70 – but his dates are once again unreliable.

80 Phillips, *Tainui*, vol. 1, pp.176-8 has physical description.

81 Cit. Kelly, p.359.

82 Ibid., p.360. An initial affray fought with traditional weapons at the south-eastern side of the pa had seen the defenders 'draw first blood'. Phillips, vol. 1, p.176.

83 Angela Ballara, *DNZB*, vol. 1, pp.526-7 (Potatau Te Wherowhero).

84 Elder, *Letters and Journals of Marsden*, p.341.

85 OMB, vol. 1, p.69.

86 Smith, *Maori Wars of the Nineteenth Century*, pp.233-4.

87 Kelly, *Tainui*, p.363.

88 Smith, *Maori Wars of the Nineteenth Century*, p.233.

89 Kelly, *Tainui*, p.263. Most of the women released were highborn, demonstrating a further sign of goodwill, as a preliminary to peacemaking.

90 OMB, vol. 2, pp.38-39 (Matire Toha).

91 FOJ, p.70; help in identifying locations was provided by D. R. Simmons.

92 Chief sources for this alleged plundering are J. Polack, *Manners and Customs of New Zealanders*, vol. 1, p.44, and Smith, *Maori Wars of the Nineteenth Century*, p.262.

93 Smith, *Maori Wars of the Nineteenth Century*, p.262.

94 FOJ, p.70.

95 OMB, vol. 2, p.29 (Ruka Taurua).

96 FOJ, p.70; see also OMB, vol. 1, p.227 (Warena Hengia).

97 Steven Oliver, *DNZB*, vol. 1, pp.504-7.

98 Ballara in *DNZB*, vol. 1, p.202.

99 Belich (*Making Peoples*, p.157) settles guardedly for an estimate of those killed as 'perhaps about 20,000', and discusses why extravagant estimates must be discounted.

100 Chief sources used for this account are Smith, *Maori Wars of the Nineteenth Century*, pp.329-47; OMB, 1868.

101 OMB, p.128 (Warena Hengia).

102 G. S. Graham, 'Taporapora: Murupaenga's Lament', N31, Graham Papers.

103 Hoera of Nga Puhi, cit. Smith, *Maori Wars of the Nineteenth Century*, p.352.

104 Smith, *Maori Wars of the Nineteenth Century*, p.343.

105 OMB, vol. 1, p.211.

106 Ibid., vol. 2, p.63 (Pairoma Ngutahi, who actually fought in the battle).

107 Smith, *Maori Wars of the Nineteenth Century*, pp.345-6.

108 *Earliest New Zealand*, p.277 (Rev. John Butler).

109 Sources used in this section are: FOJ, p.72; Phillips, *Landmarks of Tainui*, vol. 2, pp.137-9.

110 OMB, vol. 1, p.83 (Hetaraka Takapuna).

111 FOJ, p.72.

112 OMB, vol. 2, pp.18-19 (Warena Hengia); Angela Ballara, *DNZB*, vol. 1, pp.345-6.

113 Ibid.

114 OMB, vol. 1, p.75 (Hetaraka Takapuna).

115 OMB, vol. 1, p.137 (Tamati Otatu).

116 Ibid., vol. 1, p.83 (Takapuna).

117 These range from 70,000 to 200,000.

118 Ian Pool, *Te Iwi Maori*, pp.238-9.

119 Reports and evidence prepared for the Waitangi Tribunal by Barry Rigby, Ann Parsonson, Philippa Wyatt, R. P. Boast, and others too numerous to mention exemplify this salutary trend.

120 *NZ Historical Atlas*, Plate 29.

121 Chief Judge Fenton maintained that events that took place during 'these unsettled times' in a region of about 100 miles radius from Auckland directly affected Tamaki. Such a region almost coincides with what he described as that 'part of New Zealand comprised between lines drawn from Cape Rodney across to the West Coast, and from Waikato to Tauranga' which were roughly the rohe that 'were in the possession of one great tribe, called, ... Ngaoho.' (FOJ, pp.57-58).

122 For more on this see D'Arcy, 'Maori and Muskets', p.122, who draws on, among others, the seminal work of Dorothy Shineberg.

123 K. R. Howe, *Where the Waves Fall*, Sydney, 1984, p.219.

124 Ibid., pp.215-6.

125 For his 1821 raids Hongi organised a force of 2000 men with over 1000 muskets and for his 1822 Waikato campaign a force of 3000. (Ibid., p.216.) CMS missionaries were astonished at the unprecedented size of these taua.

126 See reference notes for each of these pa for sources of estimates of those killed.

127 Dumont d'Urville, *New Zealand 1826–1827*, trans. Olive Wright, Wellington, 1950, p.152.

128 See, e.g., ibid., p.154.

129 Ibid., pp.156, 158-61.

130 FOJ, p.72.

131 Ibid., p.73.

132 Evidence of John Cowell on this matter in OMB, vol. 1, pp.66-67.

133 Ibid., vol. 1, pp.177-8. Charles Marshall was a trader with the Ngati Paoa and Waikato tribes after November 1830.

134 FOJ, p.73.

5 'WANDERING ABOUT THE FACE OF THE EARTH'

1 'Apihai's followers' is a literal translation of the term 'Apihai ma', which is widely used in the Orakei Minutebooks to comprehend Te Taou, Nga Oho and (often) Te Uringutu.

2 OMB, vol. 1, p.228 (Warena Hengia).

3 FOJ, p.72.

4 OMB, vol. 2, p.19 (Warena Hengia).

5 Ibid.

6 Ibid., vol. 1, pp.229-30 (Warena Hengia); FOJ, p.73.

7 *DNZB*, vol. 1, pp.345-6.

8 Dumont d'Urville, *New Zealand, 1826–1827*, Wellington, 1950, p.168.

9 *The Early Journals of Henry Williams*, Christchurch, 1961, p.43 (23 Feb. 1827).

10 OMB, vol. 2, pp.19, 230.

11 Ibid., Te Aroha Minutebook, vol. 2, p.323 (Warena Hengia).

12 'Te Aroha Judgment', in *Important Judgments*, Wellington, 1879, p.111; OMB, vol. 2, p.19 (Warena Hengia). For stylistic reasons, I believe that Maning alone wrote this report and that it was not a collaborative exercise with his fellow judge, H. A. H. Monro.

13 Te Aroha Minutebook, vol. 1, p.151 (Haora Tipa).

14 'Te Aroha Judgment', p.110.

15 Turoa, 'The Hauraki Iwi', p.45.

16 *New Zealand Historical Atlas*, Plate 29; *DNZB*, vol. 1, pp.504-7 (Te Rauparaha), p.571 (Waitohi).

17 'Te Aroha Judgment', p.111.

18 Ibid.

19 Ibid.

20 Ibid.

21 Ibid., Te Aroha Minutebook, vol. 2, p.323 (Warena Hengia).

22 There is no reliable documentary record of the actual date of the attack.

23 C. W. Vennell, pp.163-9, in vol. 2 of Phillips, *Landmarks of Tainui*, has the most detailed, if over-lurid, account of this massacre and its consequential war. See also Te Aroha Minutebook, vol. 1, p.8 (Haora Tipa). No precise date can be given for this massacre because there is a conflict in the evidence given by claimants and witnesses in the Te Aroha NLC hearing.

24 Vennell, p.164.

25 FOJ, pp.74-75.

26 Te Aroha Minutebook, vol. 2, pp.336-7 (James Farrow). J. A. Wilson, in *The Story of Te Waharoa*, Christchurch, 1906, p.214, speaks of the 'fertile plain of Tepiri [near Matamata] abounding in flax'.

27 Hugh Carleton, *The Life of Henry Williams*, Auckland, 1874, vol. 1, p.195.

28 Te Aroha Minutebook, p.338.

29 Vennell in Phillips, *Landmarks of*

Tainui, vol. 1, p.164.

30 Te Aroha Minutebook, vol. 2, pp.309, 318 (Warena Hengia).

31 Ibid., p.309.

32 J. A. Wilson, *The Story of Te Waharoa*, p.212.

33 Te Aroha Minutebook, vol. 2, p.319 (Warena Hengia).

34 Ibid. Distances in the Native Land Court evidence were expressed in Maori terms, e.g. the length of the pa was estimated by the witness to be from 'the Albert Barracks to the [Partington's] Windmill'.

35 'The Origins and Meanings of Maori Place Names', M54, Graham Papers.

36 Ibid. The reference to 'many thousands' is a clear exaggeration.

37 This name was not unique. At least one other North Island pa was so named.

38 'Te Aroha Judgment', p.112.

39 Kelly, *Tainui*, p.384.

40 J. A. Wilson, p.210.

41 For the timing of the battle, nowhere precisely stated, see Te Aroha Minutebooks, vol. 1, p.84 (Haora Tipa); vol. 2, p.336 (James Farrow). December 1830 is a likely date.

42 For detailed published accounts of the Battle of Taumatawiwi, see C. W. Vennell in Phillips, *Landmarks of Tainui*, vol. 1, pp.163-9, and Kelly, *Tainui*, pp.384-6, both of which, however, must be used with caution.

43 Part of the steep bank and all the approaches to it were submerged with the damming of the Waikato river to form Lake Karapiro.

44 Te Aroha Minutebook, vol. 2, p.303 (Warena Hengia). Hengia, though a Te Taou and Nga Oho chief, fought with the Ngati Paoa vanguard throughout the day, and is able to provide an invaluable, unbiased, firsthand account of the course of the battle.

45 Ibid., p.304.

46 Ibid., vol. 1, p.81; vol. 2, p.304. Some witnesses at the Te Aroha Court said that, during the retreat to Hao Whenua, some of the musketeers, who had exhausted their metallic shot, made do with firing round river pebbles.

47 Ibid., vol. 2, p.324 (Paramena Te Ruamutu).

48 Ibid., p.329.

49 This figure suggests that the total number of men, women and children of Apihai's tribe with him in the fortress would probably have been between 300 and 350. (See Pool, pp.34-35, for the basis of this calculation.)

49 Ibid., p.305 (Warena Hengia).

50 'Te Aroha Judgment', p.115.

51 G. S. Graham, Graham Papers, M54, p.15.

52 Vennell, in Phillips, *Landmarks of Tainui*, vol. 1, p.168.

53 For estimates of total casualties, including both sides, as being under 100, see Te Aroha Minutebook, vol. 2, pp.323, 328. Since Ngati Whatua chiefs, with no Land Court axe to grind, supplied these figures, they are believable. However, James Farrow who lived among Ngati Haua at that time said that he heard that 'there were a good many dead on both sides' (ibid., p.338).

54 Te Aroha Minutebook, vol. 2, p.323 (Warena Hengia).

55 Ibid., vol. 2, p.111.

56 'Te Aroha Judgment', p.115.

57 See, e.g., the battle of Pukerangiora, 1831 (Kelly, *Tainui*, pp.387-91.)

58 'Te Aroha Judgment', p.115.

59 Te Aroha Minutebook, vol. 2, p.324 (Paramena Te Ruamutu).

60 Ibid.

61 Te Aroha Minutebook, vol. 1, p.82 (Haora Tipa).

62 'Te Aroha Judgment', pp.115, 119.

63 Some accounts speak of peace being made on the second day after the battle.

64 Haora Tipa develops this version fully in the Te Aroha Minutebook, vol. 1, pp.82-83.

65 Te Aroha Minutebook, vol. 2, p.324 (Paramena Te Ruamutu).

66 Te Aroha Minutebook, vol. 2, pp.305-6. Warena Hengia simply repeats what Taharoku recalled of Te Waharoa's speech, which was highly metaphorical.

67 Ibid., vol. 2, p.327 (Paramena Te Ruamutu).

68 'Te Aroha Judgment', p.119.

69 Ibid. The wording used here is the author's.

70 Te Aroha Minutebook, vol. 2, p.328.

71 Te Aroha Minutebook, vol. 2, p.306 (Warena Hengia).

72 One group left in the first week; the last is said to have taken three months preparing for their journey, but a number of witnesses cast serious doubt on whether the delay was as long as that.

73 Te Aroha Minutebook, vol. 1, p.84.

74 'Te Aroha Judgment', p.121.

75 Te Aroha Minutebook, vol. 2, p.324 (Warena Hengia).

76 Ibid., p.307 (Warena Hengia).

77 'Te Aroha Judgment', p.121.

78 Ibid., p.120; see also Kelly, *Tainui*, p.386, where the jibe is ascribed to Remi Kukutai.

79 See, e.g., OMB, vol. 1, p.70 (John Cowell).

80 'Te Aroha Judgment', p.120.

81 Ibid., p.121.

82 T. W. Gudgeon, *The History and Doings of the Maori*, Auckland, 1885, p.89. See also D'Arcy, 'Maori and Muskets', p.121, who discusses the traditional importance in Polynesian warfare of the 'drawing of first blood'.

83 Campbell, *Poenamo*, p.218.

84 Gudgeon, p.90; 'Te Aroha Judgment', pp.127, 132.

85 'Te Aroha Judgment', p.119.

86 Ballara, *DNZB*, vol. 1, p.427.

87 The main source of information used in this section is the Te Aroha NLC Minutebook of 1871, with particular reference to the evidence of Warena Hengia, Haora Tipa, Paramena Te Ruamutu and Te Keene Tangaroa.

88 Te Aroha Minutebook, vol. 2, p.323 (Warena Hengia).

89 There is no documentary reference to slaves after the shift from Tamaki.

90 See Pool, pp.34-35.

91 If the travellers were able to count on gathering fern-root or wild berries en route, they would have been able to survive on a smaller quantity of stored food.

92 Te Aroha Minutebook, vol. 2, p.325 (Paramena Te Ruamutu).

93 Ibid., vol. 2, p.307 (Warena Hengia). It is likely that when Apihai's flotilla left, it included a number of smaller dugout canoes

(tiwai), which, according to evidence heard in court, Ngati Whatua had brought with them to Horotiu for crossing the Waikato river.

94 Ibid., p.317. It is interesting that no reference was made to kumara, perhaps because this was not ready to be harvested.

95 Ibid., p.325 (Paramena).

96 FOJ, p.74.

6 YEARS OF EXILE, 1831–36

1 OMB, vol. 1, p.70 (John Cowell).

2 Fairburn Journal, p.13 (3 Feb. 1832).

3 OMB, vol. 2, p.321 (Warena Hengia).

4 Ibid., vol. 1, p.71 (John Cowell).

5 William Williams Journals, vol. 3, p.382 (22 Aug. 1834).

6 OMB, vol. 2, p.152 (William White).

7 For more on this expedition, see Smith, *Maori Wars of the Nineteenth Century*, pp.441-2, and Kelly, *Tainui*, pp.396-9.

8 Fairburn Journal, p.98 (23 Jun. 1837).

9 OMB, vol. 1, p.180 (Charles Marshall).

10 Ibid., vol. 1, p.68 (John Cowell).

11 He probably had Waiheke island in mind.

12 Fairburn Journal, p.13 (27 Jan. 1832).

13 Members of the party were Williams, Fairburn, and Revs A. N. Brown and John Morgan.

14 *Early Journals of Henry Williams*, p.339 (31 Oct. 1833), (punctuation altered). See also ibid., p.417 (27 Feb. 1835).

15 Fairburn Journal, pp.36-37 (31 Oct. 1833).

16 *Early Journals of Henry Williams*, pp.411-2 (17 Feb. 1835).

17 Ibid., pp.202-3 (12 Nov. 1831); see also Carleton, vol. 1, pp.93-94. The cutter *Karere* was built in Paihia by Gilbert Mair, and launched in February 1831.

18 Ibid., p.340 (5 Nov. 1833).

19 See chap. 3.

20 Thomson, vol. 1, p.258.

21 Ibid.

22 Owens, in *OHNZ*, 1992 ed., p.34.

23 Thomson, vol. 1, p.258.

24 William Williams Journal, vol. 2, p.231 (7 Jan.1831).

25 Ibid., vol. 3, p.399 (8 Oct. 1834).

26 Campbell, *Poenamo*, p.80.

27 Owens in *OHNZ*, 1992, p.34, citing the Wesleyan missionary, Rev. Nathaniel Turner. (Tense changed.)

28 Thomson, vol. 1, p.259.

29 Ibid. In the pre-1840 purchases of land around Auckland by Europeans, including missionaries ('The Old Land Claims'), tobacco and blankets were the commodities most commonly used as consideration.

30 William Williams Journal, vol. 3, p.362 (15 Jan. 1834).

31 T. W. Gudgeon, *The History and Doings of the Maoris*, Auckland, 1885, p.89.

32 Ibid., p.90.

33 Smith, *Maori Wars of the Nineteenth Century*, pp.445-6.

34 Owens, in *OHNZ*, p.45.

35 Steven Oliver in *DNZB*, vol. 1, p.506.

36 Potatau means 'impatient'. Te Wherowhero is said to have adopted the name to commemorate the unusual sexual appetite of John Rodolphus Kent, the Pakeha-Maori, who married Amohia, the chief's daughter: Kelly, *Tainui*, p.424. For Kent, see Neil Begg, in *DNZB*, vol. 1, pp.225-6.

37 Kelly, *Tainui*, p.387.

38 Ibid., p.390.

39 Ibid., pp.399-401.

40 Ibid., pp.402-4.

41 Ibid., pp.404-6.

42 Ibid., p.406. See also William Williams Journals, vol. 3, p.400 (11 Oct.1834).

43 William Williams Journals, vol. 3, p.381 (19 Aug. 1834); p.400 (11 Oct. 1834).

44 *Missionary Record*, cited in Smith, *Maori Wars of the Nineteenth Century*, p.457.

45 William Williams Journals, vol. 3, p.356 (10 Jan.1834).

46 Ibid., vol. 2, p.152 (25 Aug. 1828).

47 Elder, *Marsden*, pp.456ff., *Early Journals of Henry Williams*, p.259 (18 Sept. 1832). A typical instance of missionary mediation is the 'Girls' War', Smith, *Maori Wars of*

the Nineteenth Century, pp.155-60.

48 Cit. Smith, ibid., pp.447-8.

49 Kelly, *Tainui*, pp.396-9.

50 The war-party set out in spite of the strenuous attempts of local missionaries to dissuade them. See William Williams Journal, vol. 2, pp.259-61 (24 Nov., 21 Dec. 1831).

51 Smith (p.426) states that 200 members of Ngati Kuri, who also joined the expedition, had old grievances against the Bay of Plenty people that they wanted to square.

52 For more on the struggle between Nga Puhi and Ngai Te Rangi, see Smith, *Maori Wars of the Nineteenth Century*, pp.426-60.

53 William Williams Journal, vol. 2, p.270 (18 Mar. 1832).

54 Ibid., vol. 2, p.273 (11 Apr. 1832). William Williams was here repeating the opinion of his brother Henry, and of H. W. Kemp and W. T. Fairburn, all of whom had been present on the field of battle.

55 Fairburn Journal, p.23 (4 Apr. 1832).

56 Ibid., p.23.

57 Ibid.

58 *Early Journals of Henry Williams*, pp.250-1 (20–21 July 1832).

59 Fairburn Journal, p.30 (7 Apr. 1833).

60 Judith Binney, 'Christianity and the Maoris to 1840: A Comment', vol. 3, no. 2 (Oct. 1969), *NZJH*, pp.148-51.

61 See William Williams Journal, vol. 2, pp.259-61 (24 Nov., 21 Dec. 1831).

62 Rogers, *Te Wiremu*, p.93.

63 *Early Journals of Henry Williams*, p.226 (25 Feb. 1832). See also Carleton, 1874, vol. 1, p.105; the 'servants of Satan' comment was made, however, by his brother; see William Williams Journals, vol. 1, p.88 (18 Mar. 1827).

64 Published authorities used in this section include: Judith Binney, 'Christianity and the Maoris', pp.143-65; Hugh Carleton, *The Life of Henry Williams*, Auckland, 1874; Allan Davidson, *Christianity in Aotearoa*, Wellington, 1991; *The Early Journals of Henry Williams*, Christchurch, 1961; J. R. Elder,

Letters and Journals of Samuel Marsden, Dunedin, 1932; Robin Fisher, 'Henry Williams's Leadership of the CMS Mission to New Zealand', *NZJH,* vol. 9, no. 2, pp.142-53; J. M. R. Owens, 'Christianity and the Maori to 1840', *NZJH,* vol. 2, no.1, pp18-40; *Prophets in the Wilderness,* Auckland, 1974; L. M. Rogers, *Te Wiremu,* Christchurch, 1973; H. M. Wright, *New Zealand 1769–1840: The Early Years of Western Contact,* Cambridge (Mass.), 1959.

65 A Roman Catholic mission under Bishop Pompallier did not begin until 1838 in the Hokianga.

66 Rogers, *Te Wiremu,* p.118; see also *Early Journals of Henry Williams,* pp.424-8.

67 OMB, vol. 1, p.71 (John Cowell).

68 William Williams Journals, vol. 3, p.347.

69 OMB, vol. 2, pp.54-55 (Matire Toha).

70 FOJ, pp.75-76.

71 This episode and its upshot are treated in: Fairburn Journal, pp.49-50 (24 Jun. 1834); Carleton, vol. 1, p.165; Te Aroha Minutebook, vol. 1, p.86 (Haora Tipa).

72 Fairburn Journal, p.50.

73 Polack, vol. 1, p.115, maintained that ravaging the cemetery of one's enemy was the gravest of insults.

74 Te Ironui recruited his group in order to avenge the death at Kauehitiki of Kumete, a lower Waikato chief.

75 The numbers given in NLC Minutebooks vary from 400 to 600. But the important fact, given the nature of this book, is that a sizeable number were of south Manukau or Tamaki origin, an involvement that later exposed them to Ngati Paoa retribution.

76 Te Aroha Minutebook, vol. 2, p.321 (Warena Hengia); OMB, vol. 1, p.137 (Tamati Tangiteruru); p.31 (Paora Te Iwi); vol. 2, p.182 (Te Waka Tuaea).

77 Te Aroha Minutebook, vol. 2, p.333 (Te Keene Tangaroa).

78 Te Aroha Minutebook, vol. 2, p.321 (Warena Hengia).

79 Ibid., p.333 (Te Keene Tangaroa).

80 The higher figure was provided by Fairburn (p.62), the lower by Te Keene.

81 FOJ, p.76.

82 Te Aroha Minutebook, vol. 2, pp.333-6 (Te Keene Tangaroa).

83 William Williams Journal, vol. 3, p.380 (16 Aug. 1834).

84 Ibid., p.377 (6 Aug. 1834).

85 Te Aroha Minutebook, vol. 1, p.86 (Haora Tipa).

86 Fairburn Journal, p.68 (8 Aug. 1834).

87 The chief documentary sources for this episode are the missionary journals of Henry Williams, William Williams, and W. T. Fairburn, who invariably translated *muru* as 'stripping'. Muru was the custom by which a raiding party obtained extra utu by plundering the goods of offending persons – or of their kin – with the people who were thus robbed invariably standing passively by.

88 The best single source for this episode is William Williams Journals, vol. 3, pp.373-9.

89 Kati and Matire had been living at Kotikoti in the Waipa valley over the previous five years. (OMB, vol. 2, p 41 (Matire Toha).)

90 William Williams Journals, vol. 3, p.375 (29 Jul. 1834).

91 Te Aroha Minutebook, vol. 1, p.86 (Haora Tipa of Ngati Paoa).

92 Kelly, *Tainui,* pp.405-22.

93 *Early Journals of Henry Williams,* p.418 (3 Mar. 1835).

94 Ibid., p.427 (22 Mar. 1835).

95 Ibid., p.428.

96 Ibid., pp.430-1.

97 OMB, vol. 1, p.178 (Charles Marshall).

98 Ibid., p.231 (Warena Hengia).

99 Ibid.

100 Ibid., and vol. 2, pp.86-87 (Paora Tuhaere).

101 Ibid.,vol. 2, p.112 (Paora Tuhaere).

7 THE SEARCH FOR PEACE, 1836–38

1 It is notable that the testimony of Maori witnesses, even where they were contending parties, tended to agree wherever matters touching on whakapapa or traditional lore were raised.

2 OMB, vol. 1, p.71 (John Cowell). This figure probably included refugees from Kaipara.

3 Ibid., vol. 2, pp.112-3 (Paora Tuhaere).

4 Ibid.

5 FOJ, p.75. See also OMB, vol. 2, pp.54-55 (Matire Toha).

6 Pehiakura was a main kainga there. OMB, vol. 2, p.113.

7 OMB, vol. 2, p.36 (Matire Toha).

8 FOJ, p.75; OMB, vol. 1, p.179 (Charles Marshall). Ngati Paoa had recovered by this time, to become a powerful force; James Mackay claimed they could now muster 2000 men.

9 OMB, vol. 2, p.85 (Paora Tuhaere).

10 Ibid., vol. 1, p.23 (Paora Te Iwi); see also John T. Diamond, *Once the Wilderness,* Auckland, 1966, p.55.

11 Ibid., vol. 1, p.14.

12 Ibid., vol. 2, pp.87-88, 113, 143 (Paora Tuhaere).

13 *Early Journals of Henry Williams,* p.438.

14 Margaret Hargreaves, 'Early Manukau 1820–65', MA thesis, University of Auckland, 1943, p.7. Maunsell was joined a month later by James Hamlin. In 1838, Maunsell shifted to Maraetai near Port Waikato, leaving Hamlin in charge of Orua Bay.

15 R. A. A. Sherrin and J. H. Wallace, *The Early History of New Zealand,* Auckland, 1890, p.409.

16 *Early Journals of Henry Williams,* p.434, fn.

17 B. T. Smith, 'The Wesleyan Mission in the Waikato, 1831–1841', MA thesis, University of Auckland, 1948, p.36.

18 Ibid., pp.27-28. See also pp.92-108 for the emerging rivalry.

19 *DNZB,* 1990, vol. 1, pp.589-90, biog. by M. B. Gittos.

20 M. B. Gittos, *'Give Us a Pakeha',* Auckland, 1997, p.6.

21 Ibid., p.9.

22 Ibid.

23 Cit. Smith, 'The Wesleyan Mission', p.41.

24 Ibid., pp.27-28.

25 OMB, vol. 2, p.153 (William White); tense changed.

26 Smith, 'The Wesleyan Mission', p.41.

27 Hargreaves, p.4.
28 Gittos, 1997, p.11.
29 Gittos, *Mana in Mangungu*, Auckland, 1982, p.78.
30 *DNZB*, 1990, vol. 1, p.604.
31 Gittos, 1997, pp.14-15.
32 OMB, vol. 2, p.153.
33 See *Early Journals of Henry Williams*, pp.436-7.
34 Ibid., pp.436-9.
35 Sherrin and Wallace, p.537.
36 There were some very minor exclusions.
37 *Early Journals of Henry Williams*, p.438.
38 Ibid.
39 Gittos, 1997, pp.50-51.
40 Whiteley appears to have remained, however, at his Kawhia station for some considerable time. (See *DNZB*, vol. 1, p.590.)
41 W. J. Williams, *Centenary Sketches of NZ Methodism*, Christchurch, 1922, pp.39-42. See also William Morley, *The History of Methodism in New Zealand*, Christchurch, 1900.
42 Gittos, 1997, p.51.
43 OMB, vol. 2, p.153 (White).
44 FOJ, p.76. For Captain Thomas Wing's evidence, see OMB, vol. 2, pp.293-4. Wing's map in which he located Mitchell's half-completed house was tabled and 'proved' before the Court; it is now lodged in the Hocken Library, Dunedin. For Wing's later career as master mariner and harbour-master, see *DNZB*, 1940, vol. 2, p.526, and *DNZB*, 1990, vol. 1, p.604.
45 Sherrin and Wallace, p.537 claimed that, in the month of the purchase, he was 'getting out timber from the creeks discharging into the Manukau harbour', presumably for the house he was building.
46 Gittos, 1997, p.15 provides this very credible explanation.
47 *DSC*, 5 Jun. 1875, Supplement, p.1, col. 7.
48 Ibid.
49 OMB, vol. 2, p.154.
50 Gittos, 1997, p. 14.
51 Trevor Bentley, *Pakeha Maori*, Auckland, 1999, p.27. Bentley was referring to Pakeha Maori as that category is generally defined, but his comment could apply to any European living permanently among Maori at this time.

52 Terry, *New Zealand*, p.36. After his conversion to Christianity, Te Reweti carried the missionary name of William Davis. Terry mistakenly called Te Reweti Apihai's eldest son.
53 OMB, vol. 1, p.15 (Te Kawau).
54 Turton, *Epitome of Official Documents*, Wellington, 1883, p.148 (George Clarke to Colonial Secretary, 4 Nov. 1840).
55 See, e.g., Fairburn Journal, p.71 (5 May 1835).
56 William Williams Journal, vol. 1, pp.87-88.
57 Carleton, vol. 1, p.105.
58 Kelly, *Tainui*, pp.407-22.
59 Carleton, vol. 1, p.107; *Early Journals of Henry Williams*, p.433.
60 *Early Journals of Henry Williams*, p.40, fn.
61 Fairburn Journal, p.87 (5 May 1836).
62 Rogers, *Te Wiremu*, p.123.
63 *Early Journals of Henry Williams*, pp.434-5.
64 Carleton, vol. 1, p.191.
65 Fairburn Journal, p.115 (27 Nov. 1838).
66 Ibid., p.87 (5 May 1836).
67 *Early Journals of Henry Williams*, pp.435-6.
68 FOJ, p.76.
69 OMB, vol. 1, p.23 (Paora Te Iwi). The fact that the deed transferring the land to Fairburn was dated Puneke, 22 Jan. 1836, may have further confused the issue.
70 See *Te Wiremu*, pp.122-5.
71 OMB, vol. 1, p.36.
72 *Early Journals of Henry Williams*, pp.435-7.
73 Fairburn Journal, p.87 (5 May 1836).
74 Carleton, vol. 1, p.191.
75 OMB, vol. 1, pp.23-24 (Paora Te Iwi); p.71 (Cowell); p.178 (Marshall).
76 Patuone was a renowned Nga Puhi chief who, by this time, had married a Ngati Paoa woman and was residing with her tribe. See *DNZB*, vol. 1, 1990, pp.338-40 (Angela Ballara).
77 *Early Journals of Henry Williams*, p.439.
78 OMB, vol. 2, p.332.
79 Fairburn Journal, p.115 (27 Nov. 1838).
80 OMB, vol. 1, p.24.

81 Ibid., vol. 2, p.113 (Paora Tuhaere).
82 Carleton, vol. 1, p.187.
83 The land set apart for the various native tribes was never to be satisfactorily defined. As late as 1854, the surveyor-general C. W. Ligar informed the colonial secretary that he despaired of settling 'the various and complicated claims of the natives on the Block of land known as Mr. Fairburn's Purchase' (OLC 590). See reference note 87 below.
84 Fairburn Journal, p.117 (29 May). The 'stranger' referred to was obviously the new Pakeha missionary owner.
85 Ibid., p.vi of introductory note by Bev Woolley dated Aug. 1991.
86 W. P. Morrell, *The Anglican Church in New Zealand*, pp.17-19.
87 The main source for the Fairburn Purchase are the documents found in the Old Land Claim files at Archives New Zealand, Wellington: OLC 589-90, most conveniently sighted in Repro File 111.
88 A. E. Tonson, *Old Manukau*, Auckland, 1966, pp.50-51, is the most accessible source for the general reader.
89 OLC 589, Doc.5.
90 *Old Land Claims*, Waitangi Tribunal publication, Wellington, 1997, co-authored by D. Moore, B. Rigby, M. Russell, p.79. Russell wrote the pages hereafter cited.
91 OLC 589, Doc.18.
92 Moore et al., *Old Land Claims*, pp.86-87.
93 Ibid., pp.88-89.
94 Ibid., Doc.7.
95 Quotation from document dated March 1992 supplied by Professor Alan Ward.
96 OLC 589, Doc. 7, sworn statement dated 1 Sept. 1841.
97 Ibid., 590, Doc. 97; copy of portion of London minutes of the CMS dated 15 Dec. 1848.
98 Sherrin and Wallace, pp.508-9.
99 M. Russell in *Old Land Claims*, pp.85-86.
100 This passion for economy extended to all branches of government at home and abroad.
101 Ibid., p.93.
102 Ibid., citing Professor Alan Ward.

Professor Ward's initial inquiries into the Fairburn Claim during 1992–3 have informed a great deal of subsequent research.

103 OLC 590, Doc. 133.
104 Ibid., Docs 116-48.
105 See, e.g., Docs 128-9.
106 Ibid., Ligar to Col. Sec., 16 Mar., 1854.
107 OMB, vol. 1, p.41 (Hori Tauroa).
108 Fairburn Journal, p.87 (5 May 1836).
109 Ibid., p.90 (25 Sept. 1836).
110 Ibid., p.95 (23 Jun. 1837).
111 Kelly, *Tainui*, p. 417.
112 FOJ, pp.76-77.
113 OMB, vol. 2, p.2 (?) (Warena Hengia).
114 A branch of Ngati Whanaunga lived just to the north of Whakatiwai, at Waihopuhopu.
115 FOJ, p.78. The 'six years later' is intended by Fenton to date from the Whakatiwai murders.
116 Ibid., p.79.
117 Fenton's chronology seems also to have been upset by his failure to appreciate that there were *two* Otahuhu peace meetings.
118 OMB, vol. 2, pp.294-5.
119 Ibid., p.295.
120 Ibid., vol. 2, p.184 (Te Waka Tuaea).
121 Ibid., vol. 1, p.56 (Hori Tauroa).
122 Ibid., vol. 2, p.118 (Paora Tuhaere).
123 Ibid., vol. 2, p.117. There had obviously been some temporary cultivation at fishing stations the year before.
124 Ibid.
125 Ibid., p.118.
126 Ibid., p.115.
127 Ibid., vol. 2, pp.142-3 (Paora Tuhaere).
128 Ibid., vol. 2, p.333.
129 Ibid., p.6 (Warena Hengia).
130 Ibid., p.88 (Paora Tuhaere).
131 Ibid., vol. 1, p.232 (Warena Hengia).
132 William Williams Journal, vol. 2, p.162 (10 Dec. 1828).
133 See, e.g., ibid., vol. 2, p.163 (10 Dec. 1828).
134 *Early Journals of Henry Williams*, p.166.
135 Ibid., p.268 (18 Dec. 1832).
136 William Williams Journal, vol. 2, p.200.
137 Ibid., vol. 2, p.262; *Early Journals*

of Henry Williams, p.166.
138 *Early Journals of Henry Williams*, p.165.
139 For the 'Girls' War', see Sherrin and Wallace, pp.340-4.
140 *Early Journals of Henry Williams*, p.165.
141 Ibid., p.166.
142 Sherrin and Wallace, p.409.
143 Fairburn Journal, p.103 (30 Apr. 1838).
144 Ibid.
145 OMB, vol. 2, p.113.
146 *Early Journals of Henry Williams*, pp.343, 431.
147 OMB, vol. 2, p.116.
148 Sherrin and Wallace, pp.416-7.
149 Fairburn Journal, p.103 (30 Apr. 1838).
150 OMB, vol. 2, p.114 (Paora Tuhaere).

8 THE RETURN TO TAMAKI

1 For discussion of the grounds of Maori customary title, most of which are relevant to Tamaki, see Norman Smith, *Native Custom and Law Affecting Maori Land*, Wellington, 1942, pp.49-50, 62-68.
2 Elsdon Best, *The Maori Division of Time*, Wellington, 1973, p.10. (Reprint).
3 OMB, vol. 2, p.331.
4 See, e.g., ibid., vol. 2, p.155 (William White).
5 Ibid., vol. 2, pp.63-65 (Pairama Ngutahi of Oruahau).
6 FOJ, p.79.
7 OMB, vol. 2, p.189.
8 Ibid., p.86 (Paora Tuhaere).
9 Ibid., p.181.
10 See, e.g., OMB, vol. 2, p.86 (Paora Tuhaere). Rangitoto-iti lands would be in the vicinity of lower Upland Road and the western side of Orakei Basin in modern Remuera.
11 OMB, vol. 1, p.233.
12 Ibid., vol. 2, p.88.
13 See, e.g., OMB, vol. 2, p.6 (Hengia) and p.119 (Tuhaere).
14 OMB, vol. 2, p.88.
15 Ibid., vol. 1, p.178. As Te Taou was a branch of Ngati Whatua, it is difficult to understand why he regarded them as different.
16 Ibid., vol. 2, p.6 (Hengia). This

Provincial Council building became, in 1883, the site of the first Auckland University College.
17 Ibid., vol. 2, p.89 (Tuhaere).
18 FOJ, p.79.
19 *Poenamo*, pp.98-122.
20 Stone, *Young Logan Campbell* (*YLC*), Auckland, 1982, pp.50-62.
21 Ibid., p.58.
22 *Poenamo*, pp.98-101.
23 Ibid., p.99.
24 Campbell, 'Reminiscences', Campbell PP, pp.98-103.
25 OMB, vol. 1, pp.216-7.
26 Ibid., vol. 2, pp.47-52 (Matire Toha).
27 Smith, *Maori Wars*, p.478.
28 *NZH*, 23 Jul. 1904; article entitled 'The natives and the governor', Maori original by Puna Reweti translated by G. S. Graham. The account given here relies on Puna Reweti's account, unlike the Waitangi Tribunal's Orakei Report which rests heavily on A. W. Reed's *Auckland*, *The City of the Seas*, a questionable authority on some aspects of Auckland's early history.
29 Ibid.
30 For alternative translations, see Sir Hugh Kawharu in *Wai 9*, p.16, and Smith, *Maori Wars*, p.479.
31 Terry, p.36. Te Reweti was a 'mihinare' (missionary) or convert to Christianity, with the alternative baptismal name of William Davis. His was the only Ngati Whatua signature in writing attached to the deed of the sale of Auckland; the other signatories signed with a mark.
32 Puna Reweti maintained that this expedition to the north to persuade Hobson to place his capital at Tamaki took place *after* Apihai Te Kawau had signed the Treaty of Waitangi at Manukau in March 1840. This is wrong, as the following chapter in this book demonstrates.
33 George Clarke to Colonial Secretary, 27 July 1841, Turton's *Epitome*, Section D, p.1.
34 See, e.g., OMB, vol. 1, p.42 (Hori Tauroa of Ngati Te Ata).
35 OMB, vol. 2, pp.2-3 (Hengia).
36 Ibid., p.21 (Hengia).
37 FOJ, p.78.

38 OMB, vol. 2, p.182 (Waka Tuaea).

39 Ibid., vol. 2, p21 (Warena Hengia).

40 Turton's *Deeds*, Wellington, 1877, vol. 1, Deed 207, dated 28 May 1841.

41 Ibid., vol. 1, Deed 192, dated 13 Apr. 1841.

42 The name Mahurangi was usually limited to the peninsula, its harbours and the nearby river valley.

43 Turton, vol. 1, Deed 192, pp.251-2.

44 The goods provided as consideration were '200 blankets, 100 caps, 90 pairs trowsers, 14 coats, 60 cloaks, two horses, two cows'.

45 OMB, vol. 2, p.182 (Waka Tuae).

46 The most detailed investigation of the Mahurangi purchase is by Barry Rigby, in 'The Crown, Maori, and Mahurangi 1840–1841', publication of the Waitangi Tribunal, 1998, especially pp. 20-31, and 139-42.

47 OMB, vol. 2, pp.61-62.

48 Alemann, 'Early Land Transactions in the Ngatiwhatua Tribal Area', pp.64-76. Maurice Alemann's work was seminal in the latter-day revised interpretation of the Mahurangi transaction. See Rigby, pp.12-14.

49 Turton, vol. 1, pp.251-67.

50 OMB, vol. 1, p.138.

51 The account of this peacemaking is based on FOJ, p.80; and the evidence which is recorded in OMB, vol. 2, pp.2-4 (Warena Hengia), and vol. 1, pp.134-43 (Tamati Tangiteruru).

52 See, e.g., OMB, vol. 2, p.3 (Warena Hengia).

53 See, e.g., Isaiah, 43:25. 'I am He that blotteth out thy transgressions for mine own sake and will not remember thy sins.'

54 OMB, vol. 2, p.26.

55 Ibid., p.2; italics mine.

56 Ibid., p.116 (Paora Tuhaere).

57 Steven Oliver in *DNZB*, vol. 1, 1990, p.552, writes that the visit took place in 1844, but textual evidence favours an earlier date.

58 See, e.g., Sir Richard Bourke to Lord Glenelg, 9 Sept. 1837, *BPP, Cols (NZ)*, IUP, vol. 3, pp.22-23; and Enc. pp.23-24.

59 Thomson, vol. 1, p.285.

60 G. H. Scholefield, *Captain William Hobson*, Oxford, 1934, p.194.

61 Ibid. In ancient Cyprus the worship of Aphrodite, goddess of love, was said to have been prevalent. As late as the 19th century, 'Cyprian' was often used as a euphemism for a prostitute.

62 Cit. in Sinclair, *History of New Zealand*, 1991, p.47.

63 Ibid., pp.47-48.

64 Ibid., p.53.

65 Fairburn Journal, p.124 (Apr. 1840).

66 Bourke to Glenelg, 9 Sept. 1837, in *BPP, Cols (NZ)*, IUP, p.22.

67 'Report on the state of New Zealand, 1837', *BPP, Cols (NZ)*, IUP, vol. 3, pp.23-25. Also in G. H. Scholefield, *Captain William Hobson*, Oxford, 1834, p.194.

68 Ibid., p.23.

69 Ibid., p.24.

70 Belich, p.187.

71 In the early years, the promoters of the company used the spelling Manakao, but for convenience the modern spelling is used in this book except in citations.

72 See, e.g., 'Certificates of character of persons receiving a free passage to New Zealand from the New Zealand Manukau and Waitemata Company 1840', NZ/MSS/ 58, APL.

73 *DNZB*, vol. 1, 1990, pp.534-6.

74 Brodie recounted this episode when acting as a witness before the select committee into NZ affairs in 1844; (see IUP reprint of *BPP* on NZ, vol. 2, pp.25-60.) For more on Brodie see Stone, *Young Logan Campbell*, p.92. Brodie was well born, as were certain others of the adventurers in New Zealand who were associated with the Manukau Company; two prominent examples were W. C. Symonds and Dudley Sinclair.

75 Thomson, vol. 2, pp.39-40.

76 *DNZB*, vol. 1, 1990, pp.589-90 (M. B. Gittos).

77 E. J. Wakefield, *Adventure in New Zealand from 1839 to 1844*, vol. 1, p.v.

78 Gittos, *Mana in Mangungu*, 1982, p.105.

79 Sherrin and Wallace, pp.288-91.

80 E. J. Wakefield, vol. 1, pp.163-4.

81 Gittos, *Give us a Pakeha*, 1987, p.22.

82 *Daily Southern Cross*, 5 Jun. 1875, Supp. p.1, col.7.

83 *Dictionary of National Biography*, London, 1909, vol. 19, pp.278-9.

84 *DNZB*, 1940, vol. 2, p.356.

85 T. M. Hocken, *Bibliography of New Zealand Literature*, Wellington, 1909, p.76.

86 *Important Information relative to NZ…*, p.35, in 'Notices of New Zealand', 436.12, Reserve, AML. This information was positively misleading. It was on the treacherous Manukau bar that, on 7 February 1863, the steam corvette HMS *Orpheus* was wrecked with the loss of 189 lives. This shipwreck remains the greatest shipping disaster in New Zealand's history.

87 Ibid., p.36. The primitive Maori gardens referred to here were obviously planted for temporary use.

88 'Regulations of the NZ, Waitemata and Manakou Company', p.37.

89 Report of W. C. Symonds, 7 Feb. 1840, 'Notices of New Zealand'.

90 Peter Adams, *Fatal Necessity*, Auckland, 1977, pp.147-8.

91 E. J. Wakefield, vol. 1, p.163.

92 Gittos, *Give us a Pakeha*, p.24.

93 Ibid.; OMB, vol. 2, p.155 (William White).

94 *Proceedings of the Kohimarama Conference, comprising numbers 13 to 18 of the 'Maori Messenger'*, Auckland, 1860, no.15, p.31.

95 *DNB*, 1909, vol. 19, pp.278-9.

96 *The Journal of Ensign Best*, Wellington, 1966, intro. by Nancy M. Taylor, pp.54-55.

97 Campbell, *Poenamo*, p.305.

98 *The Founding of New Zealand*, pp.56, 61, 188.

99 *Daily Southern Cross*, 7 Jul. 1875, p.3, col.5.

100 W. C. Symonds, 'Notices of New Zealand', AML.

101 Ibid.

102 E. J. Wakefield, *Adventures in NZ*, vol. 1, pp.156-61.

103 Ibid., p.162.

104 Ibid.

105 Sherrin and Wallace, p.478.

106 This was a missionary's name, which the Maori had adopted as an alternative name for himself – a not uncommon practice among

converts to Christianity. 'Dairs' is a typographical error.

107 Sherrin and Wallace, pp.478-9. For the original account see IUP reprint, *BPP, Cols (NZ), Sess.1844,* vol. 2, pp.38-39.

108 W. C. Symonds, 7 Feb. 1840, 'Notices of New Zealand'.

109 Ibid.

110 'Duck' was a strong untwilled material much used at this time for sailor's outer clothing, especially for trousers; 'fustian' was a thick twilled cotton cloth.

111 Symonds's Report, p.32.

112 Scholefield, *Hobson*, pp.102-3.

9 HOBSON, THE TREATY, AND TAMAKI

1 Barr, *City of Auckland*, pp.41-42 makes such a case.

2 Useful secondary sources for Hobson are: G. H. Scholefield, *Captain William Hobson*, Oxford, 1934; Paul Moon, *Hobson, Governor of New Zealand*, Auckland, 1998; T. L. Buick, *The Treaty of Waitangi.* Useful contemporary comment is contained in Charles Terry, *New Zealand...*; William Colenso, *The Authentic and Genuine Signing of the Treaty of Waitangi*, Wellington, 1890; A. S. Thomson, *The Story of New Zealand, Past and Present,* London, 1859, vol. 2; David Rough, 'The Earliest Days of Auckland' typescript, GNZMS 280, APL; Mathew Papers, MSS 78, APL; T. Bunbury, *Reminiscences of a Veteran,* 3 vols, London, 1961.

3 Bunbury, vol. 3, p.55; Bunbury felt that Hobson lacked, however, the capacity for making broad and measured judgements.

4 For George Eden, Earl of Auckland, see *DNB*, Oxford, 1908, vol. 6, pp.357-8.

5 Glyndwr Williams, *Times Literary Supplement,* 11 Feb. 2000, p.27.

6 Scholefield, pp.49-50. Each of these two young officers attained admiral's rank in later years.

7 Ibid., p.186.

8 Lord Glenelg to Governor Sir George Gipps, 1 Dec. 1838, in *BPP, Cols (NZ)*, IUP, vol. 3, p.67.

9 Ibid.

10 Normanby to the Lords Commissioners of the Admiralty, 1 Jul. 1839, in *BPP, Cols (NZ)*, IUP, vol. 3, p.83.

11 There were five children, one boy (also a William), and four girls. The oldest of the children Eliza (called 'Lila') was nine at the time of the *Druid*'s arrival in Australia.

12 Normanby to Hobson, 14 Aug. 1839, *BPP*, 1840/238, p.38.

13 Gipps to Lord John Russell, 9 Feb. 1840, *BPP*, IUP, vol. 3, p.125.

14 Ruth M. Ross, *New Zealand's First Capital*, Wellington, 1946, p.10.

15 S. M. D. Martin, *NZ in a Series of Letters*, London, 1845, p.81.

16 James George, ' A Few Odds and Ends of Remembrances', p.319, NZMS 883, APL. For the vendetta between Auckland settlers and governor's officials see Stone, 'Auckland's Political Opposition in the Crown Colony Period', in *Provincial Perspectives*, Christchurch, 1980, pp.26-27.

17 Ross, 1946, pp.24-25.

18 Felton Mathew to Sarah Mathew, 26 Jan. 1840, First journal letter, p.10, Mathew Papers, MSS 78-89, APL.

19 G. J. Pennington to James Stephen, 22 Jun. 1839, in *BPP, Cols (NZ)*, IUP, vol. 3, p.80-81.

20 Marquis of Normanby to Captain Hobson, 14 Aug. 1839, pp.85-90, ibid., vol. 3, pp.85-90.

21 Ibid., p.89. General revenue, it was expected, would come from import duties on tobacco, spirits, wine and sugar.

22 Ibid.

23 Hobson to Normanby, *BPP, Cols (NZ)*, IUP, vol. 3, p.135.

24 By 1842, Crown land sales had become a minor source of public revenue. Governor Grey, on the other hand was able to operate a solvent administration from 1846 on, partly because of a spectacular increase in revenue from customs duties, and partly from the substantial 'Grants in aid of revenue from HMS Government' (especially in the period 1846–49) that had been denied the early governors. (See *Statistics of New Zealand for the Crown Colony Period, 1840–1852*, AUC publication, Auckland, 1954, Tables 46-47)

25 The most detailed account of the crossing is in Felton Mathew's first journal letter, MS78, APL.

26 Bunbury, vol. 3, p.46 discusses the abrasive personalities of these two men.

27 The most authoritative interpretative account of the treaty-signing meeting at Waitangi happens also, fortunately, to be the most accessible: Claudia Orange, *The Treaty of Waitangi*, Wellington, 1987, pp.32-59.

28 Hobson to Gipps, 5 Feb. 1840, in *BPP, Cols (NZ)*, IUP, vol. 3, p.45.

29 Colenso, *Signing of the Treaty*, 1890, the best eyewitness account of the conference at Waitangi, is also the most complete source for the content of the individual speeches, pp.16-28.

30 Colenso, p.29. (I have used a modern Maori orthography, which differs slightly from that which Colenso used.)

31 Hobson to Gipps, 6 Feb. 1840 in *BPP, Cols (NZ)*, IUP, vol. 3, p.46; Colenso, p.40.

32 *Nga Tohu o Te Tiriti*, Wellington, 1990, pp.2-19.

33 Adams, p.159.

34 Colenso, p.33.

35 On 14 January 1840, before Hobson left for New Zealand, Gipps had proclaimed the Crown's right of pre-emption in the new colony.

36 Colenso, p.33.

37 'Report of the Select Committee on NZ', in *BPP, Cols (NZ), sess. 1844*, IUP, vol. 2, p.5.

38 *Proceedings of Kohimarama Conference*, vol. 7, no. 13, p.41.

39 Ibid., pp.42-43.

40 Hobson to Gipps, 17 Feb. 1840, in *BPP, Cols (NZ)*, IUP, vol. 3, pp.132-4, gives the official version of the Hokianga excursion.

41 The best firsthand account is that of Felton Mathew, in the Mathew Papers, the second journal letter, 9–16 February 1840, pp.1-10, APL. More accessible, however, is the edited version of the Mathew Papers in Rutherford, *The Founding of NZ*, pp.44-45.

42 Colenso, p.36.

43 Hobson to Gipps, 17 Feb. 1840; see above.

44 Hobson to Marquis of Normanby,

20 Feb. 1840, in *BPP, Cols (NZ)*, IUP, vol. 3, p.134. (Forwarded by Gipps to the new secretary of state, Lord John Russell.)

45 In that era, the term 'Thames' took in not only the Firth of Thames, but also the Tamaki strait, the Waitemata harbour, and the Rangitoto channel.

46 Cit. Carleton, *Life of Henry Williams*, vol. 2, pp.17-18; unfortunately, this section of Williams's early journals has been lost, but Carleton had access to them in writing his biography, and so we can confidently rely on this citation.

47 Ross, *New Zealand's First Capital*, 1946, p.16.

48 E. J. Wakefield, *Adventure in New Zealand*, vol. 1, pp.162-3.

49 Ernst Dieffenbach, *Travels in New Zealand*, London, 1843, vol. 1, p.282.

50 Smith, *Maori Wars of the Nineteenth Century*, p.479, speaks of the party from Tamaki having been at the Bay for a fortnight before leaving on 21 Feb., but this is unlikely.

51 *Auckland Star*, 19 October 1933, Letter to Ed., MS120, N29 Graham Papers, AR. Letter written by Graham, presumably based on oral records provided by Ngati Whatua informants.

52 *Wai 9*, p.16, citing A.W. Reed, *Auckland, City of the Seas*, p.40.

53 OMB, vol. 1, p.15.

54 *Wai 9*, p.16.

55 Terry, p.35. The vital alliance, he implies, was with the Waikato people.

56 Ibid., p.35. That estimate suggests a total population of under a thousand.

57 Ibid.

58 Dieffenbach vol. 1, p.291. These figures possibly exclude the people of Orakei and certainly those of Mangere where a significant proportion of the tribe still lived.

59 See, e.g., OMB, vol. 2, p.119 (Paora Tuhaere).

60 Puna Reweti states that this was so in *NZH*, 23 Jul. 1904, but there is no confirmation of this in the minutes of the 1868 Orakei land court hearing.

61 Smith, p.479.

62 See chap. 8.

63 Journal, 18 Feb. 1840, Mathew Papers, Fol. 2, pp.11-12.

64 Symonds seems not to have been in permanent occupation of the Mitchell property in Karangahape until the later part of 1841.

65 Where once a tidal flat separated the two islands, today there is a causeway.

66 Rutherford, *Founding of NZ*, p.61 (footnote), p.159 (map).

67 Mathew Papers, Fol. 3, p.12 (7 Mar. 1840). Mathew misspelt 'tow' as 'toe'.

68 Buick, p.178.

69 Scholefield, p.105.

70 Mathew, Third Journal-letter, in Mathew Papers, Fol. 3, pp.1-3 (23–24 Feb. 1840).

71 Rutherford, *Founding of New Zealand*, pp.60-71. Smith (p.479) states that the *Herald* anchored off Waiariki, but Rutherford who had access to the ship's log does not confirm this. Further, the welcoming meeting which Smith said took place between Apihai and Hobson during this visit, is not recorded by Mathew who was usually reliable with regard to reporting such matters, and the alleged meeting, in consequence, could well have been, as Rutherford puts it, a 'legend' (p.60).

72 Campbell, *Poenamo*, p.99.

73 Stone, *Young Logan Campbell*, pp.57-59.

74 Cit. Carleton, vol. 2, p.18.

75 Hobson to Russell, 25 May 1844, *BPP, Cols (NZ)*, IUP, vol. 3, p.137.

76 Felton Mathew, in Mathew Papers, Fol. 3, p.3 (24 Feb. 1840).

77 Ibid., p.6 (28 Feb. 1840).

78 Ibid., pp.7-8.

79 Ibid. Rutherford, *Founding of NZ*, p.68, cites the captain's log, which gives some idea of the intensity of the gale.

80 Scholefield, p.105. Hobson himself considered that his 'violent illness' had been 'occasioned by harassing duties and by long exposure to wet'. (Hobson to Russell, 25 May 1840, *BPP, Cols (NZ)*, IUP, vol. 3, p.137.)

81 Mathew Papers, Fol. 3, p.8 (1 Mar. 1840).

82 Ibid., p.10.

83 Carleton, vol. 2, p.18.

84 Buick, p.259; *Nga Tohu o te Tiriti*, pp.36-39.

85 Carleton, vol. 2, p.18. These are Carleton's words.

86 Mathew Papers, Fol. 3, p.10 (4 Mar. 1840).

87 Carleton in Scholefield, p.106.

88 Cit. Carleton, vol. 2, p.18.

89 Scholefield, p.105.

90 Mathew, Fol. 3, p.12.

91 Dr Alexander Lane to Governor Gibbs, 28 Mar. 1840, in *BPP, Cols (NZ)*, IUP, vol. 3, p.136.

92 Hobson to Sec. of State for Cols, 25 May 1840, in *BPP, Cols (NZ)*, IUP, vol. 3, p.137.

93 Ibid.

94 Ibid.

95 Ibid., Hobson to Rev. Henry Williams, 23 Mar. 1840, p.139. Hobson enclosed this letter of authorisation to Williams in a despatch to his secretary of state, explaining that it was 'in substance the same as the instructions issued to other gentlemen who were deputed to treat with the native chiefs'.

96 Ibid., 15 Oct. 1840, Enc. 5, p.223.

97 For those who wish to study the treaty-gathering process in context, the best source is Orange, pp.60-91.

98 Scholefield, pp.105-6.

99 Ross, pp.25-26.

100 Lord John Russell to Gipps, 4 Dec. 1839, in *BPP, Cols (NZ)*, IUP, vol. 3, pp.97-98.

101 Hobson to Sec. of St. for Cols, 20 Feb. 1840, ibid., p.135.

102 Bunbury, vol. 3, p.42.

103 Gipps to Russell, 31 Mar. 1840, in *BPP, Cols (NZ)*, IUP, vol. 3, p.136.

104 Bunbury, vol. 3, p.44.

105 Ibid., pp.44-46.

106 Gipps to Russell, 31 Mar. 1840, in *BPP, Cols (NZ)*, IUP, vol. 3, p.136.

107 Bunbury, vol. 3, p.53.

108 Ibid., p.126.

109 Ibid., p.51.

110 The *Herald* dropped anchor at Kororareka on 23 April, exactly a week after the *Buffalo*.

111 Bunbury, vol. 3, p.51.

112 Cit. Scholefield, p.114.

113 Hobson to Russell, 25 May 1840, in *BPP, Cols (NZ)*, IUP, vol. 3, p.138.
114 Moon, p.148. See also Thomson, vol. 2, pp.29-30.
115 Scholefield, pp.113-4.
116 Buick, p.187, maintains in a footnote that, by 1841, Symonds had collected a vocabulary of 3000 Maori words.
117 Buick, p.187.
118 OMB, vol. 2, pp.118, 120 (Paora Tuhaere). Tuhaere said he was there 'a considerable time', but he probably misremembered.
119 Symonds to Shortland, 12 May 1844, encl. in Hobson to Sec. of State, 15 Oct. 1840, in *BPP, Cols (NZ)*, IUP p.223. This report is the main source for the next two paras.
120 Ross, p.54, fn. 143.
121 Symonds to Shortland, 12 May 1840, p.223. 'Manukau chiefs' obviously included Apihai's tribe.
122 Buick, p.262; *Nga Tohu o Te Tiriti*, pp.146-7. Te Reweti's name is often rendered as 'Te Rewiti', but this chief, who could write, always spelt his name with an 'e'.
123 OMB, vol. 2, p.119. Date given supplied by Buick.
124 Sherrin and Wallace (p.537) wrote that Hobson 'authorized Captain Symonds to purchase the site of Auckland, which the latter succeeded in doing by negotiation with the chief Kawau of Orakei. Captain Symonds was *afterwards* appointed Deputy Surveyor-General of New Zealand.' (Italics mine.) This would mean that the purchase of Auckland was set in train *before* June 1840.
125 Symonds to Shortland, 12 May 1840, *BPP, Cols (NZ)*, IUP, vol. 3, p.223.
126 *Nga Tohu o Te Tiriti*, p.125. (Punctuation added.)
127 Symonds to Shortland, 12 May 1840, loc. cit., p.224.
128 Symonds to Whiteley, 8 April 1840, in *BPP, Cols (NZ)*, IUP, vol. 3, p.224. Symonds promised to forward to Whiteley the customary gift of blankets 'to be given to those who subscribe their names, and I request you will distribute them, one to each chief, after signature.'

129 *Nga Tohu o Te Tiriti*, pp.147-9.
130 Ibid., pp.126-7. Three of the chiefs were Ngati Te Ata; the remainder was probably Waikato people living on the south Manukau shore.
131 *Proceedings of the Kohimarama Conference*, no.15, p.43.
132 Orange, pp.77, 86.
133 Ibid., p.69.
134 Ibid., p.65.
135 See, e.g., William Williams to Shortland, 8 May 1840; W. C. Symonds to Rev. John Whiteley, 8 April 1840; in *BPP, Cols (NZ)*, IUP, vol. 3, pp.223-4.
136 Symonds to Shortland, 8 April 1840, ibid.
137 Buick, p.191.
138 Ross, pp.45-51.
139 Ibid., p.51; (tense of extract changed).
140 Mathew Papers, Letterbook no. 5, p.17.
141 Moon, pp.193-4.
142 Sherrin and Wallace, p.537.
143 Corban, p.11; Hargreaves, p.14.
144 In fact the title to 'their property' was anything but secure.
145 *NZ Herald and Auckland Gazette*, 27 Nov. 1841.
146 Ross, p.22.
147 Taylor, *Journal of Ensign Best*, p.55.
148 Ibid., citing Hobson to Gipps, 23 Oct. 1840.

10 Hobson's Choice

1 Thomson, vol. 2, p.57. The phrases cited are Thomson's own.
2 J. Somes to Lord Stanley, 7 Sept. 1841, BPP, 1842/569, p.30.
3 *New-Zealander*, 27 Nov. 1847.
4 Thomson, vol. 2, p.58.
5 Ibid., p.57.
6 McLintock, *Crown Colony Government in NZ*, p.127.
7 J. C. Beaglehole, *Captain Hobson and the NZ Company*, Northampton, Mass., 1927, p.107.
8 *Statistics for NZ in the Crown Colony Period*, Auckland, 1954, Table 20.
9 Swainson, *NZ and its Colonisation*, 1859, p.88; Moon, pp.194-5.
10 Cit. Sherrin and Wallace, p.505. In the latter section of this citation Evans was reading from the text of the loyal address. See also Gipps to

Russell, 12 Sept. 1840, Encl. 2, in BPP, 1841/17, p.80.
11 *NZ Gazette*, 22 Aug. 1840, cit. Beaglehole, p.61.
12 Hobson to Col. Sec., 25 May 1840, *BPP, NZ*, 1841/311, XVII, p.492.
13 Shortland to Hobson, 10 Oct. 1840, BPP, 1841/311, pp.119-20.
14 Cit. Moon, p.195.
15 Sherrin and Wallace, p.532.
16 Somes to Lord John Russell, 29 Jul.1841, BPP, 1841/569, pp.14-15.
17 William Swainson, *NZ and its Colonization*, London, 1859, p.88.
18 For more on Okiato-Russell, see Ross, pp.26-50; Rutherford, pp.112-8; Moon, pp.182-91.
19 Report of Mathew to Hobson, 15 Jun. 1840, p.1, Mathew Reports to Governor, APL, MSS 82.
20 Carkeek later became collector of customs at Wellington.
21 Mathew to Hobson, 15 Jun. 1840, pp.2-5, MSS 82.
22 Ibid., pp.5-9.
23 Ibid., pp.10-16.
24 Ibid., pp.17-24.
25 Sarah Mathew Journal (unpaginated), Fol. No.2, Mathew Papers, APL.
26 Rutherford, p.158. Mathew applied this criticism to Mahurangi, but it was even more applicable to Whangarei.
27 Mathew to Hobson, 15 Jun. 1840, p.10.
28 This tiny island, lying a short distance west of the Auckland Harbour Bridge, has, because its composition of soft Waitemata sandstone, been much eroded and greatly reduced in size since Hobson's time.
29 Mathew to Hobson, 15 Jun. 1840, pp.14-15.
30 Ibid., pp.15-17.
31 Campbell, 'Reminiscences', p.180; *Poenamo*, pp.316-7.
32 The 'natives' were probably made up of Ngati Tama-Te-Ra, who had come with Webster's group, and a few of Apihai's people.
33 Sarah Mathew Journal, 1 May 1840.
34 Ibid., 5-12 May.
35 Report, Mathew to Hobson, 15 Jun. 1840, p.18.
36 Ibid., p.24.

37 Ibid., pp.17-18.
38 Ibid., pp.19-22.
39 Ibid., p.21.
40 Ibid., pp.24-25.
41 Cit. Ross, p.52. 'Thames' in this context clearly means the inner Hauraki gulf.
42 David Rough, 'Notes on the Foundation and earliest days of Auckland', p.4, GNZ, MSS, 280, APL. An edited version of this account appears in *NZH* 11 Jan. 1896.
43 While still convalescing at Paihia, Hobson appointed Rough on the strength of a letter of introduction from a mutual friend (Rough, p.2).
44 Ibid., p.5.
45 Ibid. The prior arrangement of a treaty signing, and the possibility of preliminary negotiations for the purchase of Tamaki land, help to explain why Hobson included Clarke, as an able speaker of Maori and as the recently appointed land purchase officer, in his tour party.
46 Buick, p.260; *Nga Tohu o Te Tiriti*, Wellington, 1990, pp.55-56. The Maori who signed were: Te Ahu [?] Karamu, Kupenga, Ngahuka, Te Rangi, Nga Manu, Raro Manu and Te Hangi. The witnesses were David Rough, George Clarke, and Dr John Johnson.
47 Rough, p.6.
48 Ibid., p.7.
49 Ibid., pp.7-8.
50 OMB, vol. 2, p.118.
51 OMB, vol. 2, pp.1, 6 (Warena Hengia); ibid., vol. 2, p.216 (Te Kawau).
52 Ibid., pp.87-88 (Paora Tuhaere).
53 Ibid., p.89.
54 FOJ, p.79. This building later housed the Auckland University College when it was founded.
55 OMB, vol. 2, p.87.
56 Ibid., p.89.
57 A few people (Uringutu?) were left at Mangere, said Tuhaere, 'to look after the pigs'. (Ibid., p.86.)
58 Ibid., vol. 1, pp.216-7.
59 Ibid., vol. 2, pp.118-20 (Tuhaere); p.51 (Matire Toha). Te Kawau insisted he was living permanently at Okahu *before* the arrival of the *Herald*. This could be open to question.
60 Ibid., p.55 (Toha).

61 Nancy M. Taylor, *Journal of Ensign Best*, p.55.
62 Owen Chadwick, *The Victorian Church*, London, 1970, Part 2, p.507. Dean Stanley of Westminster was later a noted Broad Church reformer.
63 Scholefield, p.125.
64 Ibid., pp.121-36.
65 Rough, p.8.
66 John Stacpoole, *William Mason, The First New Zealand Architect*, Auckland, 1971, p.28.
67 *Lloyd's Register 1840*.
68 Rutherford, p.179, citing Internal Affairs records.
69 Ibid.
70 Stone, 'Auckland's Political Opposition', 1980, p.27.
71 Sarah Mathew Journal, 12 Sept. 1840.
72 Stacpoole, p.28.
73 Rutherford, p.184. Rutherford also supplies the names and occupations of the mechanics in steerage (p.185).
74 The four youthful officers were Symonds (1810-41), Mason (1810-97), Rough (1815-97), and Williams (1818-1909).
75 Rutherford, pp.182-4.
76 Ibid., p.184.
77 *NZ Advertiser and Bay of Islands Gazette (NZA&BOIG)*, 24 Sept. 1840, p.3.
78 Ross, p.54.
79 Sarah Mathew Journal, 11 Sept. 1840.
80 Ibid., 12 Sept. 1840.
81 See, e.g., Moon, pp.206-7.
82 Campbell, 'Reminiscences', p.260.
83 Ibid., p.261.
84 Sources used for the next three paragraphs are mainly: BPP, Rough, the Mathew Papers, and Sherrin and Wallace, pp.544-5.
85 *Lloyd's Register*, 1840, states that this ship was Sunderland-built, that its homeport was London, and that it was owned by Mr R. Brooks.
86 Terry, p.29.
87 Sherrin and Wallace, p.544.
88 *NZH*, 17 Jun. 1879.
89 Rough, p.9.
90 Sarah Matthew Journal, 15 Sept. 1840.
91 Rough, pp.8-9.
92 Ibid., p.10.
93 For a copy of the deed, see Rutherford, p.191.

94 'Agreement relating to Waitemata land', MSPapers 2828, ATL.
95 Mason to Acting Col. Sec., 21 Sept., 1840, cit. Stacpoole, p.30.
96 *Poenamo*, p.305.
97 Stacpoole, p.30.
98 *NZA&BOIG*, 24 Sept. 1840, p.3.
99 Sarah Mathew Journal, 18 Sept. 1840.
100 *NZA&BOIG*, 24 Sept. 1840, p.3.
101 Almost certainly the spokesman was Te Reweti, not the 'principal chief' as Mrs Mathew imagined him to be. This of course would have been Te Kawau. Te Kawau was present and the objections probably emanated from him.
102 Four chiefs in fact signed: Te Reweti, Te Kawau, Te Tinana, and Horo.
103 Sarah Mathew Journal, 18 Sept. 1840. Those who signed the deed on behalf of the Crown were Symonds, Johnson, Mathew and Rough.
104 See, e.g., Una Platts, *The Lively Capital*, Christchurch, 1971, p.15.
105 Campbell, *Poenamo*, p.108.
106 Stone, *James Dilworth*, pp.36-37; *Young Logan Campbell*, p.59.
107 *Muriwhenua Land Report*, p.111; cit Rose Daamen, pp.23-24.
108 Vincent O'Malley, 'Treaty Making in Early Colonial New Zealand', *NZJH*, vol. 33, no. 2 (1999), pp.137-54.
109 *NZA&BOIG*, 24 Sept. 1840, p.3. Sources for eyewitness accounts of the ceremony and of the later celebrations are that paper's 'Special Correspondent', and Sarah Mathew and David Rough.
110 Sarah Mathew Journal, 18 Sept. 1840.
111 *NZA&BOIG*, loc.cit.
112 Sarah Mathew Journal, loc.cit.
113 Sarah Mathew Journal, loc.cit.
114 Ibid.
115 Scholefield, p.151.
116 Hobson to Sec. of St. for Cols, 15 Oct. 1840, *BPP (NZ)*, 1841/311, pp.113-4.
117 Clarke to Col. Sec., 28 Jul. 1840, in H. H. Turton, *An Epitome of Official Documents*, Sec. C, p.147.
118 Its official designation was 'Sloop'; its master at this time was Capt. R. S. W. Dunlop.
119 Sarah Mathew Journal, 17 Oct. 1840.

120 Rough, p.13.
121 Sarah Mathew Journal, 18 Oct. 1840.
122 Campbell, *Poenamo*, p.317. Campbell wrote that at the time of his visit, Symonds was living in what Campbell called a whare.
123 Meurant was a former lay agent of the Wesleyan mission, who was married to a Maori chieftainess of Waikato stock named Kenehuru.
124 Clarke to Col. Sec., 4 Nov. 1840, in Turton, *Epitome*, Sec. C., p.148.
125 Turton, *Maori Deeds of Land Purchases*, Wellington, 1877, vol. 1, Deed No 206, p.268. Two subsequent payments of £8 stg were paid. Punctuation and wording of Turton's publication have been retained in this extract.
126 Mataharehare is the name Maori often gave, however, to the section of the bay (now disappeared because of reclamation) which the colonists renamed St George's Bay.
127 *Wai* 9, pp.20-21.
128 The sole documentary support for this interpretation is contained in Te Kawau's curious response to a question put by his tribe's lawyer, Mr McCormick: 'I did not intend to sell Auckland to the Europeans. I gave it to them'. (OMB, vol. 1, p.15.)
129 Memo of Clarke, 4 Nov. 1840, in Turton, *Epitome*, Sec. C, p.148. H. Hanson Turton himself was responsible for the translation of the deed that he carried out on 4 Sept. 1874.
130 Hobson to Clarke, 20 Oct. 1840, Turton, *Epitome*, p.147.
131 Tense of verb changed.
132 Sarah Mathew Journal, 28 Oct. 1840.
133 Ibid., 28 Oct. 1840; the phrase is Mrs Mathew's. The governor's instruction was presumably given to William Mason; see Stacpoole, pp.31-32.
134 Clarke to Col. Sec., 4 Nov. 1840, Turton, *Epitome*, Sec. C, p.148.
135 Hobson to Sec. of State, 10 Nov. 1840, *BPP*, 1841/311 (NZ), p.31.
136 E. J. Wakefield, *Adventure in New Zealand*, vol. 1, pp.409-10.
137 Ibid., pp.408-9.
138 Cit. Sherrin and Wallace, p.545.
139 J. Somes to Lord Stanley, 7 Sept.

1841, *BPP*, 1842/569, p.28.
140 F. D. Bell to Sec. of State, 3 Apr. 1841, *BPP*, 1841/311, p.131.
141 Hobson to Sec. of State, 10 Nov. 1840, ibid., pp.126-7.
142 Wakefield, vol. 1, p.438.

11 THE FOUNDING OF AUCKLAND

1 Rutherford, p.183. Mathew's instructions read: 'no preparations must however be commenced without my concurrence in the choice of the site having been first expressed'.
2 Russell to Hobson, 9 Dec. 1840, *BPP*, 1841/311, pp.26-27.
3 Ibid., 4 August 1841, *BPP*, 1842/569, p.90. Though this despatch came above Russell's signature it probably emanated from Stephen or some other senior official of the Colonial Office.
4 See Stacpoole, p.29.
5 Campbell, 'Autobiography', p.86.
6 For the physical appearance of central Auckland in 1840, I have referred to the Mathew, Campbell, and George Graham Papers, Rough, Nancy Taylor, Dieffenbach, Sherrin and Wallace, and OMB.
7 OMB, vol. 2, pp.248-9 (George Graham).
8 Campbell, *Poenamo*, p.316.
9 Sarah Mathew Journal, 27 Sept. 1840, Mathew Papers, No.2.
10 Dieffenbach, vol. 1, pp.279, 282.
11 Mathew to Hobson, 16 Dec. 1840, Letterbook No. 5.
12 OMB, vol. 2, p.247. As Graham did not arrive until a month later, he must have been relying on hearsay.
13 Sarah Mathew Journal, 3 Oct. 1840.
14 Rough, p.10.
15 Sarah Mathew Journal, 5 Oct. 1840.
16 Sherrin and Wallace, p.545.
17 Mathew to Col. Sec., 14 Nov. 1840, Mathew Papers, No. 5.
18 Rough, p.10.
19 Ibid.
20 Sherrin and Wallace, p.548. The cost of these whare, expressed in monetary terms, was from about £3 15s. to £10, cost varying mainly according to size and quality. But at this time virtually all

transactions were conducted as barter.
21 Because the surveyor-general's tent served as a drafting office as well as a home, it was unusually large. Mathew occasionally referred to it as a 'marquee'. When Hobson was on his periodic visits to Auckland before the Government House was built, he used Mathew's tent as his working quarters during the day, spending his nights on board the governor's brig.
22 Sarah Mathew's 'Autobiography', cit. Rutherford, p.202.
23 Stacpoole, p.30; see *NZH*, 17 Jun. 1879 for an almost identical comment, made by Logan Campbell.
24 Cit. Rutherford, p.206.
25 Mason to Freeman, 21 Sept. 1840, cit. Stacpoole, pp. 30-31. This brickyard seems to have been on the left upper bank of the Horotiu.
26 Stacpoole, p.31.
27 The bay took its name from one of its earliest European occupants, James Stuart Freeman, the governor's secretary. See Stone, *Young Logan Campbell*, pp.118-9.
28 Campbell, 'Reminiscences', p. 251.
29 Stacpoole, p.31.
30 I shall use the term 'capital' to denote Auckland from 18 September onwards, although Hobson continued to regard Russell as the capital until March 1841 when he came to live in Auckland.
31 W. Swainson, Auckland, *The Capital of NZ*, London, 1853, p.31. *DSC*, 29 Feb. 1864, p.3, gives a description of its buildings at a time of peak demand during the wars of the 1860s.
32 Bunbury, vol. 3, p.128.
33 Ibid., p.129; by 'Local Government' he meant the governor.
34 Ibid., p.130.
35 Ibid., p.131.
36 Ibid., pp.126, 133.
37 FOJ, p.80. George Graham, however, records the date of arrival as 13 Dec. (Graham Diary, MS119, AML.)
38 Forbes Edie Scrapbook, p. 52, APL.
39 Nancy M. Taylor, p.69.

40 Robert Hattaway, *Reminiscences of the Northern War*, Auckland, 1889, pp.1-2.
41 *Cyclopedia of NZ*, vol. 2, p.104; George Graham Diary, MS119, AML.
42 Forts in India and the Antipodes often repeated features of Irish forts.
43 For descriptions of the fort and barracks, see Swainson, *Auckland*, p.31; *DSC*, 31 Mar. 1864; 29 Feb. 1864.
44 For demolition of the fort and military barracks see *DSC*, 1 Mar. 1872; *NZH*, 6 Dec. 1876.
45 OMB, vol. 2, p.239.
46 George Graham Diary, MS119, AML.
47 Bunbury's surmise is correct. The fosse and rampart system he describes here was a characteristic outer defence of a traditional Maori pa. Mr Lesley Kelly names the site of the pa as 'Tangihanga Pukaea'in his map 'Tamaki-makau-rau', Auckland, 1890.
48 Bunbury, pp.133-4.
49 Ibid., p.134.
50 Taylor, *Journal of Ensign Best*, p. 279.
51 For his lime, Graham burnt shells on the North Shore, and he established a brickyard at the site of the first courthouse at the foot of Victoria Street West. For Graham's own account of his work and improvisations, see OMB, vol. 2, pp.243-9.
52 Taylor, p.279 (1 March 1841).
53 Bunbury, p.134.
54 Ibid., p.139.
55 James George, 'Remembrances', p.302. George was a charmingly eccentric speller.
56 Mathew to Col. Sec., 2 Sept. 1840, *BPP*, 1841/311, p.113, encl.
57 Ibid.
58 Mathew to Col. Sec., 16 Dec. 1840, Mathew Papers, LB No.5, p.42.
59 Ibid., 14 Nov. 1840, p.38.
60 Terry, p.130.
61 Ibid., pp.129-30. In this case the three months would not have been up until 28 March 1840.
62 S. M. D. Martin, *NZ in a Series of Letters*, London, 1845, p.132.
63 Ibid., pp.132-3.
64 Ibid., pp.133-4.

65 Mathew to Hobson, 14 Nov. 1840, pp.39-40, Mathew Papers, LB No. 5.
66 George, p.487.
67 Mathew to Hobson, 14 Nov. 1840.
68 John Barr, *Ports of Auckland*, Auckland, 1926, Appendix IX; Sherrin and Wallace, p.555;
69 George Graham Diary, MS119, AML.
70 Rough, p.12.
71 Stone, *Young Logan Campbell*, pp.87-88.
72 Platts, *Lively Capital*, p.18.
73 Campbell, *Poenamo*, p.337.
74 Campbell, 'Reminiscences', p. 247. This paragraph, except where otherwise indicated, is based on 'Reminiscences', or on extracts from Campbell's Journal contained in Folders 5 and 7 of the Campbell Papers.
75 The chartered troopship *Diana* was still anchored at that time in the harbour, too.
76 Campbell, 'Reminiscences', p.249.
77 Campbell, 'Autobiography', p.72.
78 Ibid., pp.250-1.
79 Campbell, *Poenamo*, p.297.
80 Campbell, 'Reminiscences', p.254.
81 Campbell, Journal, Folder 7.
82 Terry, p.129.
83 Hobson to Gipps, 16 Feb. 1841, *BPP*, 1842/569, p.86.
84 Wakefield, vol. 1, pp.436-43.
85 Taylor, pp.52-53, 277-8.
86 Cit. Sherrin and Wallace, p.548.
87 Ibid., p.547.
88 Terry, p.130.
89 Campbell Journal, 30 Dec. 1840, Fol. 5, Campbell PP.
90 *NZH*, 17 Jun. 1879.
91 *New-Zealander*, 13 Feb. 1847.
92 Pool, p. 61, estimates that, in New Zealand, in 1840, Maori 'perhaps' outnumbered European by as much as 40 to 1.
93 Sources used for this episode are Campbell, *Poenamo*, pp.342-58; Campbell, 'Reminiscences', pp. 254-67; Hobson to Gipps, 16 Feb. 1841, *BPP*, 1842/569, p.92.
94 Hobson to Gipps, loc. cit.
95 See, e.g., *Young Logan Campbell*, pp. 90-91.
96 Rutherford, p.201.
97 *The Oxford New Zealand Dictionary*, ed. H. W. Orsman, Auckland, 1997, p.133.

98 Rutherford., pp.200-1.
99 See Charles Heaphy, 'Plan of the Town of Auckland, 1851', APL.
100 For lists of goods sold see Winifred Macdonald, *Auckland, Yesterday and Today,* Auckland, 1957, p.10; Terry, pp.56-57.
101 Robert Hattaway, *Reminiscences of the Northern War*, Auckland, 1889, p.2.
102 Rutherford, p.201.
103 Rough, p.14.
104 Terry, p.60.
105 OMB, vol. 2, p.273 (W. F. Blake).
106 *Young Logan Campbell*, p.112.
107 OMB, vol. 2, p.94 (Tuhaere).
108 A hostel for sojourners built in the early 1840s on the foreshore of the bay, at the foot of what became known in the following decade as Constitution hill, was used by Maori travellers for over a century.
109 Lady Martin, *Our Maoris*, London, 1884, pp.6-7.
110 W. Swainson, *Auckland, the Capital of New Zealand*, London, 1853, pp.33-34.
111 Alemann, pp.126-8.
112 OMB, vol. 2, p.37.
113 Ibid., p.47 (Matire Toha).
114 OMB, vol. 1, p.23.
115 Ibid., vol. 2, p.333.
116 FitzRoy to Stanley, 25 May 1844, *BPP, Cols (NZ)*, IUP, vol. 4, p.227.
117 OMB, vol. I, p.138 (Tamati Tangiteruru).
118 Ibid., vol. 2, pp.93-94.
119 Ibid., pp.91, 94.
120 Alemann, p.119.
121 OMB, vol. 1, p.34 (Paora Te Iwi). Reweti was married to the widow of a great Waikato chief. (Terry, p.36.)
122 FOJ, pp.81-82.
123 OMB, vol. 1, p.217.
124 FOJ, p.83.
125 Smith, *Native Custom Affecting Land,* pp.35-39.
126 Bunbury, vol. 3, p.187.
127 Stone, *James Dilworth*, pp.43-46.
128 OMB, vol. 1, p.1. By the 1850s, however, Ngati Whatua had reason to regret having invited Europeans into their midst, mainly because they feared the loss of their Orakei lands.
129 *Proceedings of Kohimarama Conference*, vol. 7, no. 18, p.23.
130 Hobson to Gipps, 16 Feb. 1841,

BPP, 1841/569, p.92.

131 Rough, p.14.
132 Campbell, 'Reminiscences', p.274.
133 Ibid.
134 Campbell PP, Fol. 7; *NZH,* 17 Jun. 1879.
135 Campbell, 'Reminiscences', p.273.
136 Campbell, pp.273-4.
137 Terry, p.130.
138 Terry, p.139.
139 Terry, p.131.
140 *BPP, Cols (NZ)*, IUP, vol. 4, 1844, p.54.
141 Sherrin and Wallace, p.549.
142 See, e.g., Edwin Hodder, *History of South Australia*, p.117, for a description of this Australasian practice.
143 Graham Diary MS119, AML. The buyer was Captain James Stone.
144 Terry, p.139.
145 Stone, *Young Logan Campbell*, p.94.
146 Terry, p.140.
147 *BPP, Cols (NZ)*, IUP, vol. 3, p.498.
148 Hobson to Gipps, 16 Feb. 1841, *BPP*, 1842/569, p.86.
149 Cit Rutherford, p.199.
150 Rough, p.14.
151 Ibid., pp.14-15.
152 Stone, 'Auckland's Provincial Opposition ...', p.21.
153 Campbell, 'Reminiscences', p.275.
154 Stone, 'Auckland's Political Opposition . . .', p.21.
155 Campbell, 'Reminiscences', p.275.
156 Stone, *Young Logan Campbell*, pp.94-95.
157 Ibid.

AFTERWORD

1 Regulations of NZ Waitemata and Manukau Land Company, AML.
2 Hobson to Russell, 13 November 1841, Enc. No 59, in IUP, pp.526-7.
3 Diamond, *Once the Wilderness*, p.58.
4 Report to Governor Hobson, 27 Dec. 1841, Mathew Letterbook, No.5, pp.56-57, APL.
5 Ibid., p.58.
6 This account of the drowning of Symonds, apart from cited sources, depends on 'GTC', in 'Old Identities', Nos 6 and 9, in *DSC*, 5 Jun. and 7 Jul. 1875.
7 *NZH&AG*, 27 Nov. 1841, cited IUP, vol. 3, p.552.
8 *DSC*, 7 Jul. 1875.
9 Hobson to Russell, 16 Dec. 1841, IUP, vol. 3, p.552.
10 For the subsequent history of Cornwallis, see Diamond, pp.60-65.
11 *DNZB*, 1940, vol. 1, pp.371-2.
12 Turton, *Deeds*, 1877, vol. 1, Deed, No. 206, p.268. The best sources (regrettably unpublished) for Crown purchases of Tamaki land in this period are: Maurice Alemann's MA thesis, 1992; and Alan Ward, 'Supplementary Historical Report on the Central Auckland Lands', Crown Congress Joint Working Party, Wellington, 1992. More accessible, because published, is Stone, *James Dilworth,* ch. 3.
13 Memo, Clarke to Hobson, 4 Nov. 1840, Turton, *Epitome*, Sec. C, p.148.
14 An Old Land Claim arising out of an earlier purchase by a Scot, Alex Dalziel, who claimed land from Achilles Point to the Omaru stream was yet to be resolved by the land commissioners. OLC file 159.
15 OLC file 984.
16 Alemann, p.110 (see below).
17 Turton, Deeds, 1877, vol. 1, p.270. Punctuation as in Turton's printed translation.
18 Ibid., pp.270-1 (Deed 208).
19 Stone, *James Dilworth*, p.36.
20 Alan Ward, 1992, pp.36-37. Ward, however castigates the Crown for allowing this situation to arise in neglect of the Normanby Instructions.
21 Stone, *Dilworth*, p.37.
22 Turton, *Deeds*, No. 209.
23 Recommended sources: for NZ as a whole, Rose Daamen, *The Crown's Right of Pre-emption and FitzRoy's Waiver Purchases*, Wellington, 1998; for Auckland, Stone, *Dilworth*, chap. 3; Daamen, pp.87-118, and Alemann, pp.114-23, have contrasting but complementary approaches to Auckland sales but have excellent material.
24 Stone, *Dilworth*, pp.37-38.
25 Ibid., p.47.
26 Ward, p.30.
27 Ibid., p.32; Stone, *Dilworth*, p.48.
28 Figures based on Turton, 1882.
29 Alemann, pp.115-23. Alemann grouped his purchases under the following headings: Mt Roskill, Onehunga, One Tree Hill (Waikato and Ngati Whatua), Ellerslie, Remuera Road, Otahuhu-Manukau (taking in land on either shore of the Manukau harbour, and Puketutu island).
30 Ward, p.34.
31 Alemann, p.122.
32 Stone, *Dilworth*, pp.53-58.
33 Alemann, pp.122-3.
34 A most cogent case indicting the Crown for its failure to protect Maori interests from settler interests by suspending pre-emption is argued by Daamen, op. cit., pp.177-98.
35 Report in Turton, 1882, p.628.
36 Stone, *Historical Report on the Auckland Metropolitan Area*, Auckland, 1992, p.23.
37 *Wai* 9, p.18.
38 Ibid.
39 The Royal NZ Fencibles in the four garrison towns south of Auckland.

BIBLIOGRAPHY

1. PRIMARY SOURCES

A. MANUSCRIPT

1. Government and Public Archives
Land Information New Zealand: land deeds and historical maps.
Archives New Zealand, Wellington, with special reference to Old Land Claims Files in Repro Section.

2. General Manuscript Sources
Ashworth: Edward Ashworth, Journals 1841–5, ATL, MS 1841–5 P.
Campbell: Sir John Logan Campbell Papers, AML, MS 51.
Fairburn: W. T. Fairburn, Letters and Journals, 1828–49, compiled by Bev. Woolley, APL.
George: George, James, 'A Few Odds and Ends of Remembrances', APL.
Graham: George Graham Diary, AML, MS 119.
Graham: George S. Graham Papers, AML, MS 120; some items also in 'Special Collections', APL.
Manukau Land Company: 'Memorandums of Agreement and Certificates of Character, 1840', APL, NZ/MSS/58.
Mathew: The papers of Felton and Sarah Matthew, APL, NZMS 78–89.
Orakei: Native Land Court 1866–8, Minute Books (3 vols), AUL.
Rough: David Rough, 'Notes on the Foundations and Earliest Days of Auckland as a Settlement', Bournemouth, 1895, APL.
Wharekawa No.5, Native Land Court Judgment, by Judge J. A. Wilson, 1 Dec. 1896, in Hauraki Minutebook No. 42, Dec. 1896, AUL.

B. OFFICIAL PRINTED PAPERS

Appendices to the Journals of the House of Representatives, 1848, G-8, Surplus lands of the Crown: Report of the Royal Commission appointed to Inquire into Claims . . . of the Maori Race.
Great Britain: *British Parliamentary Papers: Colonies: Relating to New Zealand, 1837–45*, either as originally published, or as reprinted by the Irish University Press, vols 1–4, 1968–71.
McLean, Martin, *Auckland 1842–45*, Auckland, 1989. Demographic Study based on the first police censuses of Auckland.
Native Land Court: *Important Judgments Delivered in the Compensation Court and the Native Land Court, 1866–79*, Wellington, 1879.
Statistics of New Zealand for the Crown Colony Period, 1840–52, Department of Economics, Auckland University College, 1954.
Turton, H. Hanson, *Maori Deeds of Land Purchases in the North Island of New Zealand. Vol. 1, Province of Auckland*, Wellington, 1877.
Turton, H. Hanson, *Maori Deeds of Old Private Land Purchases in New Zealand from the year 1815 to 1840, with Pre-emption and Other Claims . . . and the Report of Mr Commissioner F. Dillon Bell*, Wellington, 1882.
Turton, H. Hanson, *An Epitome of Official Documents Relative to Native Affairs and Land Purchases in the North Island of New Zealand*, Wellington, 1883.

C. REPORTS GENERATED BY THE WAITANGI TRIBUNAL AND KINDRED BODIES

Daamen, Rose, *The Crown's Right of Pre-emption and FitzRoy's Waiver Purchases*, Wellington, 1998.
Kayes, Bronwyn, *The Ancestors of Ngati Paoa*, (background paper to *Wai 10*), Wellington, n.d.
Monin, Paul, *Report prepared for Waitangi Tribunal Claim Wai 406* [Hauraki Gulf Islands], Wellington, Dec. 1996.
Moore, D., B. Rigby and M. Russell, *Old Land Claims* (National Theme Report), Wellington, Jul. 1997.
Rigby, Barry, *The Crown, Maori, and Mahurangi*, Wellington, Aug. 1998.
Stone, R. C. J., *Historical Report on the Auckland Metropolitan Area* (commissioned by the Crown/Congress Joint Working Party), Wellington, Apr. 1992.
Wai 9: Report of the Waitangi Tribunal on the Orakei Claim, Wellington, 1987.
Wai 10: Report of the Waitangi Tribunal on the Waiheke Island Claim, Wellington, 1987.
Ward, Alan, *Supplementary Historical Report on Central Auckland Lands* (commissioned by Crown /Congress Joint Secretariat), Wellington, 1992.

D. NEWSPAPERS

Auckland Herald and New Zealand Gazette, Auckland, 1841–42.
{Daily} Southern Cross, Auckland.
New Zealand Herald.

II. SECONDARY SOURCES

A. PUBLISHED BOOKS AND ARTICLES

Adams, Peter, *Fatal Necessity: British Intervention in New Zealand 1830–1847*, Auckland, 1977.
Archey, Gilbert, *Sculpture and Design, an Outline of Maori Art*, Auckland, 1960.
Archey, Gilbert, *Whaowhia: Maori Art and its Artists*, Auckland, 1977.
Ballara, Angela, *Iwi: The Dynamics of Maori Tribal Organisation from c.1769 to c.1945*, Wellington, 1998.
Ballara, Angela, 'Porangahau: the formation of an eighteenth-century community in southern Hawke's Bay', *NZJH*, vol. 29, no. 1,
    April 1995.
Barr, John, *The City of Auckland, New Zealand, 1840–1920*, Auckland, 1922.
Barr, John, *The Ports of Auckland*, Auckland, 1926.
Beaglehole, J. C., *Captain Hobson and the New Zealand Company: A Study in Colonial Administration*, Northampton, Mass., 1927.
Beaglehole J. C., *The Discovery of New Zealand*, (2nd ed.), London, 1961.
Belich, James, *Making Peoples: A History of New Zealanders*, Auckland, 1996.
Bentley, Trevor, *Pakeha Maori: The Extraordinary Story of the Europeans who Lived as Maori in Early New Zealand*, Auckland, 1999.
Best, Elsdon, *The Maori*, 2 vols, Wellington, 1941.
Best, Elsdon, *The Maori Division of Time*, Wellington, 1973. (Reprint of 1922 *JPS* paper.)
Binney, Judith, 'Christianity and the Maoris to 1840: a comment', *NZJH*, vol. 3, no. 2, Oct. 1969.
Brown, William, *New Zealand and its Aborigines*, London, 1845.
Buck, P. H. (Te Rangi Hiroa), *The Coming of the Maori*, Wellington, 1950.
Buick, T. Lindsay, *The Treaty of Waitangi*, (3rd ed.), New Plymouth, 1936.
Bulmer, Susan, 'Settlement Sites in Tamaki-makau-rau Revisited', in *Oceanic Culture History*, eds Janet Davidson et al., Dunedin,
    1996.
Bulmer, Susan, *Sources for the Archaeology of the Maori Settlement of the Tamaki Volcanic District*, Wellington, 1994.
Bunbury, Tomas, *Reminiscences of a Veteran*, 3 vols, London, 1861.
Campbell, J. Logan, *Poenamo: Sketches of Early Days in New Zealand*, London, 1881.
Carleton, Hugh, *The Life of Henry Williams, Archdeacon of Waimate*, 2 vols, Auckland, 1874.
Colenso, William, *The Authentic and Genuine History of the Signing of the Treaty of Waitangi, New Zealand, February 5 and 6 1840*,
    Wellington, 1890.
Crosby, R. D., *The Musket Wars: a History of the Inter-iwi Conflict 1806–45*, Auckland, 1999.
Cruise, R. A., *Journal of a Ten Months' Residence in New Zealand*, (2nd ed.), London, 1824.
Curnow, Jenifer (comp.), *Inventory to the Papers of George Samuel Graham*, Auckland, 1994.
Cyclopedia of New Zealand, vol. 2 (Auckland), Christchurch, 1902.
D'Arcy, Paul, 'Maori and Muskets from a Pan-Polynesian Perspective', *NZJH*, vol. 34, no. 1, April 2000.
Davidson, Allan K., *Christianity in Aotearoa: A History of Church and Society in New Zealand*, Wellington, 1991.
Davidson, Janet M., 'Auckland' in *The First Thousand Years: Regional Perspectives in New Zealand Archaeology*, ed. Nigel Prickett,
    Palmerston North, 1982.
Davidson, Janet M., 'Auckland Prehistory: A Review', *Records of the Auckland Institute and Museum*, 1 Dec. 1978.
Diamond, John T., *Once the Wilderness*, Auckland, 1977.
Dictionary of New Zealand Biography, vol. 1, 1990, ed. W. H. Oliver; vol. 2, 1993, ed. Claudia Orange, Wellington.
Dieffenbach, Ernst, *Travels in New Zealand*, 2 vols, London, 1943.
Earliest New Zealand: The Journals and Correspondence of the Rev. John Butler, comp. by R. J. Barton, Masterton, 1927.
The Early Journals of Henry Williams, 1826–40, comp. L. M. Rogers, Christchurch 1961.
Elder, J. R., *The Letters and Journals of Samuel Marsden, 1765–1838*, Dunedin, 1932.
Elder, J. R., *Marsden's Lieutenants*, Dunedin, 1934.
An Encyclopaedia of New Zealand, 3 vols, ed. A. H. McLintock, Wellington, 1966.
Fisher, Robin, 'Henry Williams's Leadership of the CMS Mission to New Zealand', *NZJH*, vol. 9, no. 2, Oct. 1975.
Fox, Aileen, *Maungakiekie: the Maori Pa on One Tree Hill*, Auckland, 1978.
Fox, Aileen, 'Pa of the Auckland Isthmus: an Archaeological Analysis', *Records of the Auckland Institute and Museum*, vol. 14, 1977.
Gittos, Murray B., *'Give Us a Pakeha': The 1830's Crusade of William White to supply eager Maori tribes on the west of the North Island
    with European settlers*, Auckland, 1997.

Gittos, Murray B., *Mana at Mangungu: A biography of William White, 1794–1875*, Auckland, 1982.
Graham, George, 'History of the Kawerau Tribe of Waitakere', *JPS*, vol. 34, 1925.
Gudgeon, W. T., *History and Doings of the Maori*, Auckland, 1885.
Hattaway, Robert, *Reminiscences of the Northern War*, Auckland, 1889.
Hochstetter, F. von, *The Geology of New Zealand*, (trans. by C. A. Fleming of original publication, Stuttgart, 1863), Wellington, 1959.
Holloway, K. M., *Maungarei: An Outline History of the Mount Wellington, Panmure and Tamaki Districts*, Auckland, 1962.
Howe, K. R., *Where the Waves Fall. A new South Sea Islands history from first settlement to colonial rule*, Sydney, 1984.
Jackson, Elizabeth T., *Delving into the Past of Auckland's Eastern Suburbs*, 8 vols, Auckland, 1876.
Jones, P. T. H. and Bruce Biggs, *Nga Iwi o Tainui: The traditional history of the Tainui people*, Auckland, 1995.
Kalaugher, J. P., *Gleanings from Early New Zealand History*, Auckland, 1950.
Kelly, Leslie, *Tainui: the Story of Hoturoa and his Descendants*, Wellington, 1949.
Lee, J. R., *Hokianga*, Auckland, 1987.
McLintock, A. H., *Crown Colony Government in New Zealand*, Wellington, 1958.
Maning, F. E., *Old New Zealand: A Tale of the Good Old Times*, London, 1863.
Martin, Lady, *Our Maoris*, London, 1884.
Martin, S. M. D., *New Zealand in 1842; or the Effects of a Bad Government on a Good Country*, Auckland, 1842.
Martin, S. M. D., *New Zealand in a Series of Letters Containing an Account of the Colony Before and After its Occupation by the Colonial Government. . .*, London, 1845.
Monin, Paul, 'The Maori Economy of Hauraki 1840–1890', *NZJH*, vol. 29, no. 2 (119).
Moon, Paul, *Hobson: Governor of New Zealand 1840–1842*, Auckland, 1998.
Morley, William, *The History of Methodism in New Zealand*, Christchurch, 1900.
Morrell, W. P., *The Anglican Church in New Zealand: A History*, Dunedin, 1973.
Murdoch, Graeme, 'Nga Tohu o Waitakere', in *West Auckland Remembers*, Auckland, 1990.
New Zealand Historical Atlas, Malcolm McKinnon (ed), Auckland, 1997.
Nga Tohu o Te Tiriti: Making a Mark, comp. Miria Simpson, Wellington, 2000.
O'Malley, Vincent, 'Treaty Making in Early Colonial New Zealand', *NZJH*, vol. 33, no. 2, 1999.
Orange, Claudia, *The Treaty of Waitangi*, Wellington, 1997.
Orbell, Margaret, *Illustrated Encyclopedia of Maori Myth and Legend*, Christchurch, 1995.
Owens, J. M. R., 'Christianity to the Maoris to 1840', *NZJH*, vol. 2, no. 1, 1968.
Owens, J. M. R., *Prophets in the Wilderness, The Wesleyan Mission to New Zealand 1819–27*, Auckland, 1974.
The Oxford History of New Zealand, (2nd ed), ed. Geoffrey Rice, Auckland, 1992.
Phillips, F. L., *Landmarks of Tainui*, 2 vols, Otorohanga, 1989.
Platts, Una, *The Lively Capital, Auckland 1840–1865*, Christchurch, 1971.
Polack, J. S., *Manners and Customs of the New Zealanders*, 2 vols, London, 1840.
Polack, J. S., *New Zealand: Being a Narrative of Travels and Adventures During a Residence in that Country Between the Years 1831 and 1837*, London, 1938.
Pool, Ian, *Te Iwi Maori: A New Zealand Population Past, Present & Projected*, Auckland, 1991.
Proceedings of the Kohimarama Conference (Reprint of nos 13–18 of *Te Karere Maori*), Auckland, 1860.
Reed, A.W., *An Illustrated Encyclopedia of Maori Life*, Wellington, 1963.
Rogers, Lawrence M., *Te Wiremu: a Biography of Henry Williams*, Christchurch, 1973.
Ross, Ruth M., *New Zealand's First Capital*, Wellington, 1946.
Rutherford, J. (ed.), *The Founding of New Zealand. The Journals of Felton Mathew and his Wife, 1840–1847*, Wellington, 1840.
Rutherford, J., *Sir George Grey, KCB, 1812–1898: A Study in Colonial Government*, London, 1961.
Salmond, Anne, *Two Worlds: First Meetings between Maori and Europeans, 1642–1772*, Auckland, 1991.
Scholefield, G. H., *Captain William Hobson: First Governor of New Zealand*, London, 1934.
Scholefield, G. H., *Dictionary of New Zealand Biography*, 2 vols, Wellington, 1940.
Searle, E. J., *Auckland City of Volcanoes*, Auckland, 1964.
Searle, E. J. and Janet Davidson, *A Picture Guide to the Volcanic Cones of Auckland*, Auckland, 1973.
Sherrin, R. A. A. and J. H. Wallace, *Early History of New Zealand*, Auckland, 1890.
Simmons, David, *Maori Auckland*, 1987.
Simmons, D. R. 'Cyclical Aspects of Early Maori Agriculture', *Records of the Auckland Institute and Museum*, vol. 12, Dec. 1975.
Simmons, D. R., 'A New Zealand Myth: Kupe, Toi, and the "Fleet"', *NZJH*, vol. 3, no. 1, 1969.
Sinclair, Keith, *A History of New Zealand*, (revised ed), Auckland, 1991.
Smith, Norman, *Native Custom and Law Affecting Native Land*, Wellington, 1942.
Smith, S. Percy, *Maori Wars of the Nineteenth Century*, (2nd ed.), Christchurch, 1910.
Smith, S. Percy, *The Peopling of the North: Notes on the Ancient History of the Northern Peninsula*, Wellington, 1998.
Sorrenson, M. P. K., 'The Maori People and the City of Auckland', *Te Ao Hou*, Jun. 1959.
Stacpoole, John, *William Mason: The First New Zealand Architect*, Auckland, 1971.

Stone, R. C. J., 'Auckland's Political Opposition in the Crown Colony Period', in *Provincial Perspectives*, eds Len Richardson and W. David McIntyre, Christchurch, 1980.

Stone, R. C. J., *James Dilworth,* Auckland, 1995.

Stone, R. C. J., *Young Logan Campbell*, Auckland, 1982.

Sullivan, Agnes, 'Maori Occupation of the Otaahuhu District up to 1840', Dept of Maori, Victoria University, Wellington, 1981.

Swainson, William, *Auckland, the Capital of New Zealand, and the Country Adjacent*, London, 1853.

Swainson, William, *New Zealand and its Colonization*, London, 1859.

Taua, Te Warena, 'A History of the Maori people', in *The History of Howick and Pakuranga*, ed. Alan La Roche, Auckland, 1991.

Taylor, Nancy M., *Journal of Ensign Best*, Wellington, 1966.

Terry, Charles, *New Zealand, Its Advantages and Prospects as a British Colony*, London, 1842.

Thomson, A. S., *The Story of New Zealand; Past and Present – Savage and Civilized*, 2 vols, London, 1859.

Tuhaere, Paora, 'A Historical Narrative concerning the Conquest of Kaipara and Tamaki by Ngati-Whatua', *JPS*, 1923, pp. 229–37.

Turoa, Taimoana, *The Hauraki Iwi*, Thames, 1995.

Turoa, Taimoana and Te Ahukaramu Charles Royal, *Te Takoto o Te Whenua o Hauraki*, Auckland, 2000.

Waititi, John, 'An Outline of Auckland's Maori History', *Journal of the Auckland Historical Society*, vol. 2, no. 1, Oct. 1963.

Wakefield, E. J., *Adventure in New Zealand from 1839 to 1844*, 2 vols, London, 1845.

Wilson, J. A., *The Story of Te Waharoa*, Christchurch, 1906.

Wright, H. M., *New Zealand: the Early Years of Western Contact*, Cambridge (Mass.), 1959.

B. UNPUBLISHED THESES AND PAPERS

Alemann, Maurice, 'Early Land Transactions in the Ngatiwhatua Tribal Area', MA thesis (Maori Studies), University of Auckland, 1992.

Bulmer, Susan, 'Maori sites in and near Auckland', report to the Auckland City Council, Auckland, 1994.

Corban, B. P. N., 'The Manukau-Waitemata Land Company and the Cornwallis Settlement 1838–60', Assignment in MA History, University of Auckland, 1966.

Hargreaves, Margaret, 'Early Manukau 1820–65', MA thesis (History), Auckland University College, 1943.

Smith, B. T., 'The Wesleyan Mission in the Waikato, 1831–41', MA thesis (History), Auckland University College, 1948.

Stone, R. C. J., 'Historical Report on Maungakiekie and One Tree Hill', Campbell Trust Board, Auckland, 1995.

INDEX